FLOWER

YAMATONADESHIKO SHICHIHENGE

10

Tomoko Hayakawa

Translated and adapted by
David Ury

Lettered by
North Market Street Graphics

Ballantine Books · New York

The Wallflower, volume 10 is a work of fiction. Names, characters, places, and incidents are the products of the author's imagination or are used fictitiously. Any resemblance to actual events, locales, or persons, living or dead, is entirely coincidental.

A Del Rey Trade Paperback Original

Published in the United States by Del Rey, an imprint of The Random House Publishing Group, a division of Random House, Inc., New York.

Del Rey is a registered trademark and the Del Rey colophon is a trademark of Random House, Inc.

Publication rights arranged through Kodansha Ltd.

First published in Japan in 2004 by Kodansha Ltd., Tokyo, as Yamatonadeshiko Schichihenge.

ISBN 978-0-345-48530-4

Printed in the United States of America

www.delreymanga.com

9 8 7 6 5 4

Translator/Adaptor—David Ury
Lettering—North Market Street Graphics

Contents

A Note from the Author

♥ ♥ IT'S BOOK 10! DOUBLE DIGITS! I WAS PLANNING ON DOING ONLY
A SINGLE VOLUME, BUT HERE WE ARE ON BOOK 10! WHAT STARTED
OUT AS FOUR CHAPTERS HAS TURNED INTO OVER FORTY! IT'S ALL
THANKS TO YOU GUYS. THANK YOU SO MUCH! I REALLY MEAN IT!
(TEARY-EYED) HERE'S A PIC OF TEN (WHOM I WROTE ABOUT IN
CHAPTER 39). JUST LOOK HOW BIG HE'S GOTTEN. ♥

—Tomoko Hayakawa

Honorifics

Throughout the Del Rey Manga books, you will find Japanese honorifics left intact in the translations. For those not familiar with how the Japanese use honorifics, and more important, how they differ from American honorifics, we present this brief overview.

Politeness has always been a critical facet of Japanese culture. Ever since the feudal era, when Japan was a highly stratified society, use of honorifics—which can be defined as polite speech that indicates relationship or status—has played an essential role in the Japanese language. When addressing someone in Japanese, an honorific usually takes the form of a suffix attached to one's name (example: "Asuna-san"), or as a title at the end of one's name or in place of the name itself (example: "Negi-sensei," or simply "Sensei!").

Honorifics can be expressions of respect or endearment. In the context of manga and anime, honorifics give insight into the nature of the relationship between characters. Many English translations leave out these important honorifics, and therefore distort the feel of the original Japanese. Because Japanese honorifics contain nuances that English honorifics lack, it is our policy at Del Rey not to translate them. Here, instead, is a guide to some of the honorifics you may encounter in Del Rey Manga.

-san: This is the most common honorific, and is equivalent to Mr., Miss, Ms., or Mrs. It is the all-purpose honorific and can be used in any situation where politeness is required.

-sama: This is one level higher than "-san" and is used to confer great respect.

-dono: This comes from the word "tono," which means "lord." It is an even higher level than "-sama," and confers utmost respect.

-kun: This suffix is used at the end of boys' names to express familiarity or endearment. It is also sometimes used by men among friends, or when addressing someone younger or of a lower station.

-chan: This is used to express endearment, mostly toward girls. It is also used for little boys, pets, and even among lovers. It gives a sense of childish cuteness.

Bozu: This is an informal way to refer to a boy, similar to the English terms "kid" and "squirt."

Sempai/senpai: This title suggests that the addressee is one's senior in a group or organization. It is most often used in a school setting, where underclassmen refer to their upperclassmen as "sempai." It can also be used in the workplace, such as when a newer employee addresses an employee who has seniority in the company.

Kohai: This is the opposite of "sempai," and is used toward underclassmen in school or newcomers in the workplace. It connotes that the addressee is of a lower station.

Sensei: Literally meaning "one who has come before," this title is used for teachers, doctors, or masters of any profession or art.

[blank]:   Usually forgotten in these lists, but perhaps the most significant difference between Japanese and English. The lack of honorific means that the speaker has permission to address the person in a very intimate way. Usually, only family, spouses, or very close friends have this kind of permission. Known as *yobisute*, it can be gratifying when someone who has earned the intimacy starts to call one by one's name without an honorific. But when that intimacy hasn't been earned, it can be very insulting.

THE wallflower
YAMATONADESHIKO SHICHIHENGE
ヤマトナデシコ七変化♡

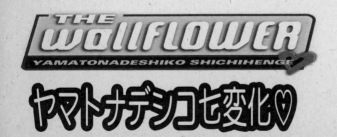

CONTENTS

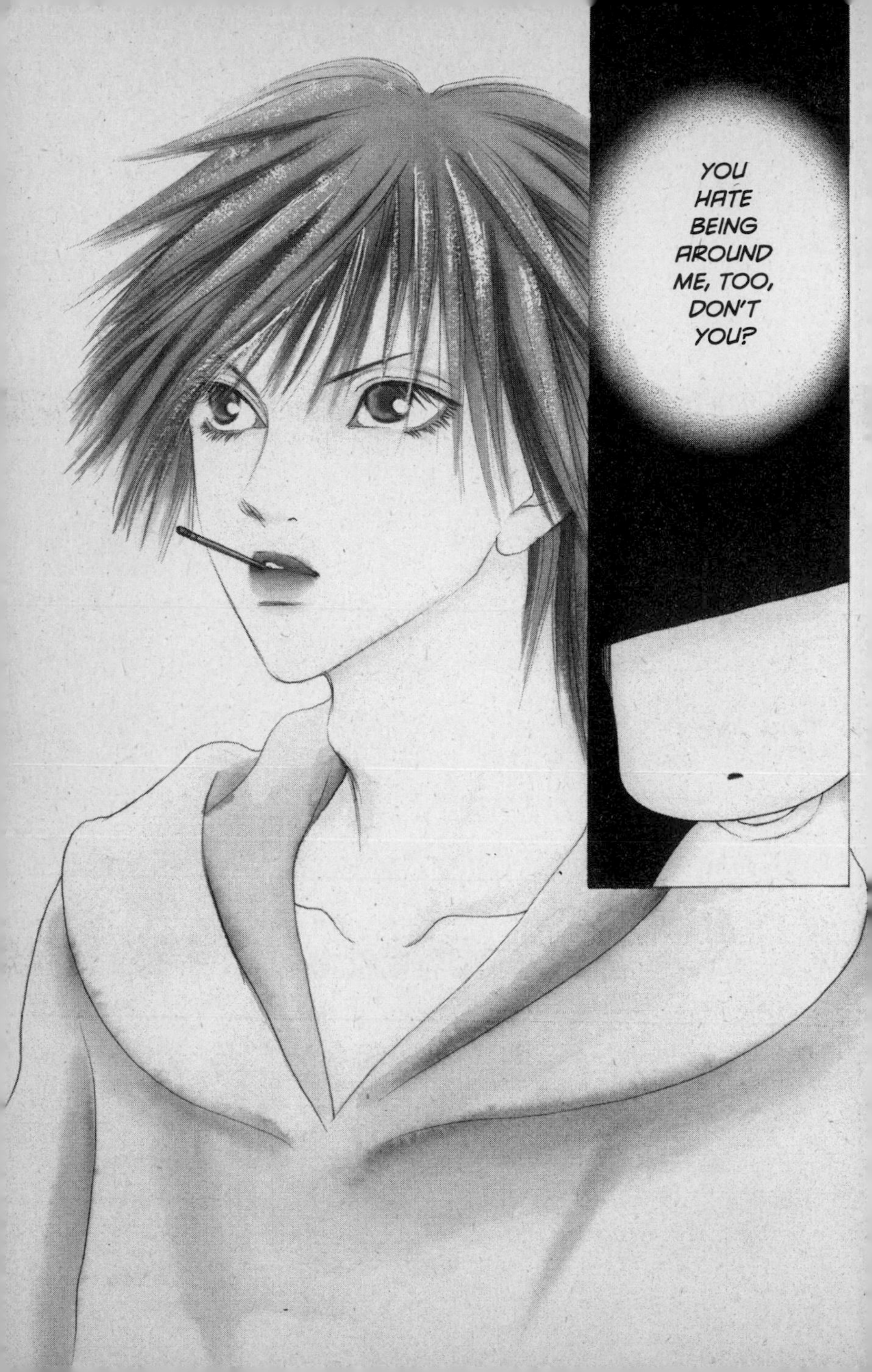
YOU HATE BEING AROUND ME, TOO, DON'T YOU?

CHAPTER 39

LOST iN THE EYE OF THE STORM

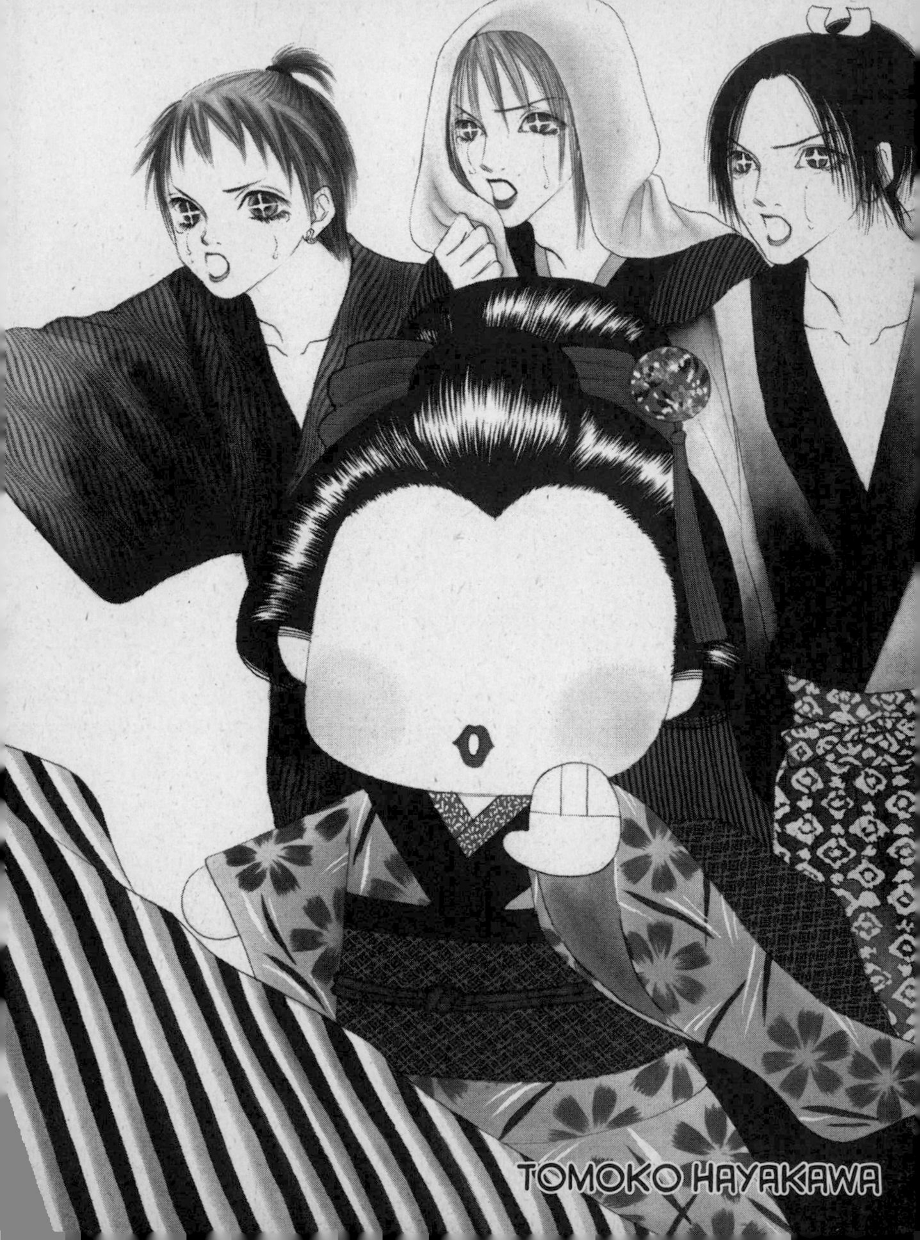

TOMOKO HAYAKAWA

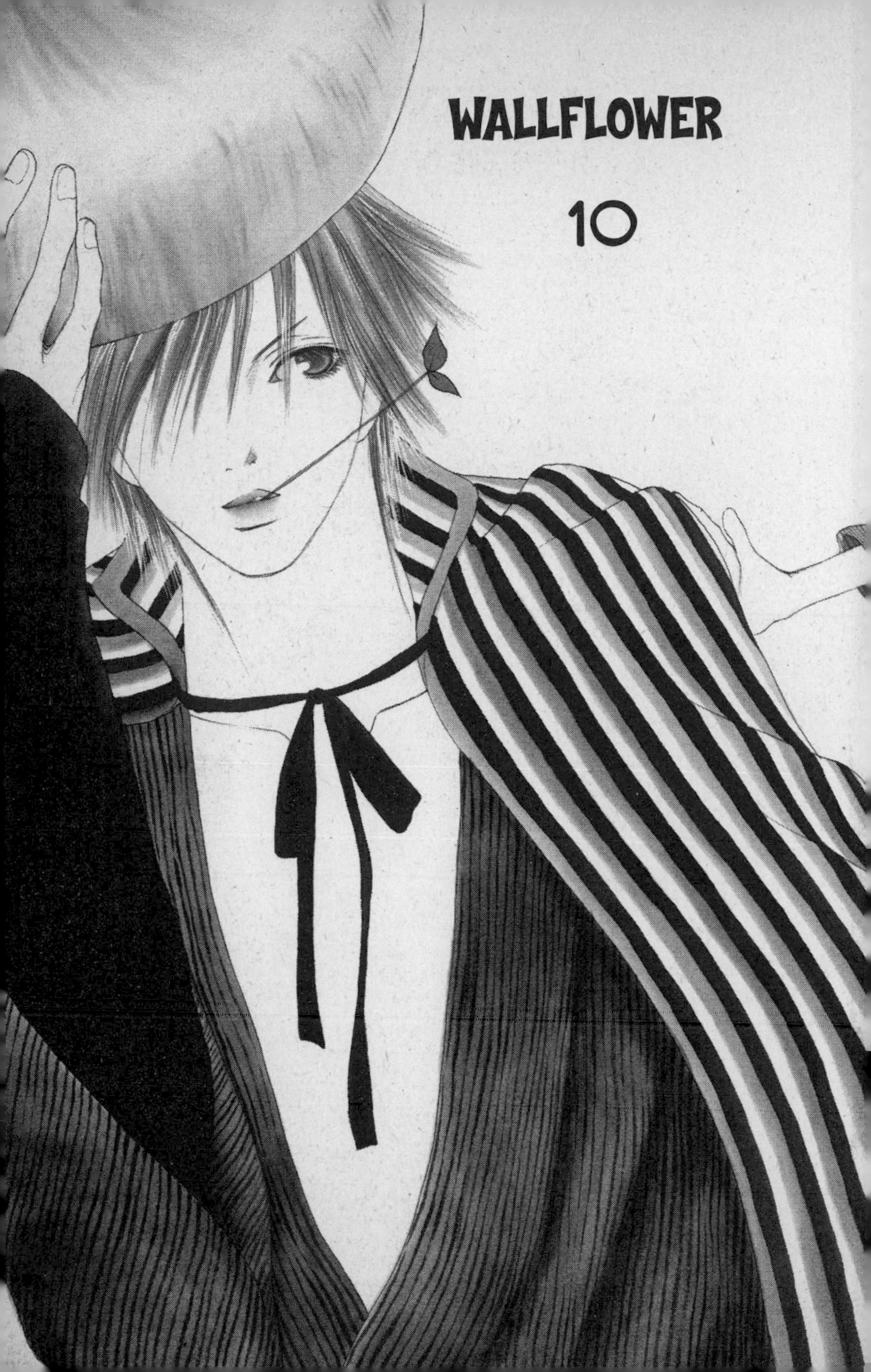
WALLFLOWER
10

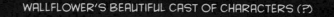

WALLFLOWER'S BEAUTIFUL CAST OF CHARACTERS (?)

SUNAKO IS A DARK LONER WHO LOVES HORROR MOVIES. WHEN HER AUNT, THE LANDLADY OF A BOARDINGHOUSE, LEAVES TOWN WITH HER BOYFRIEND, SUNAKO IS FORCED TO LIVE WITH FOUR HANDSOME GUYS. SUNAKO'S AUNT MAKES A DEAL WITH THE BOYS, WHICH CAUSES NOTHING BUT HEADACHES FOR SUNAKO. "MAKE SUNAKO INTO A LADY, AND YOU CAN LIVE RENT-FREE."

WHEN WE LAST LEFT OUR HEROES, SUNAKO AND KYOHEI WERE STUCK IN THE SAME BEDROOM AT KYOHEI'S PARENTS HOUSE. SUNAKO, BLINDED BY THE CREATURE OF THE LIGHT, TELLS KYOHEI SHE DOESN'T WANT TO BE NEAR HIM. KYOHEI'S STUNNING GOOD LOOKS PROVE TO BE TOO MUCH, EVEN FOR HIS OWN MOTHER. NOW IT SEEMS POOR KYOHEI HAS PLANS TO SET OUT ON HIS OWN.

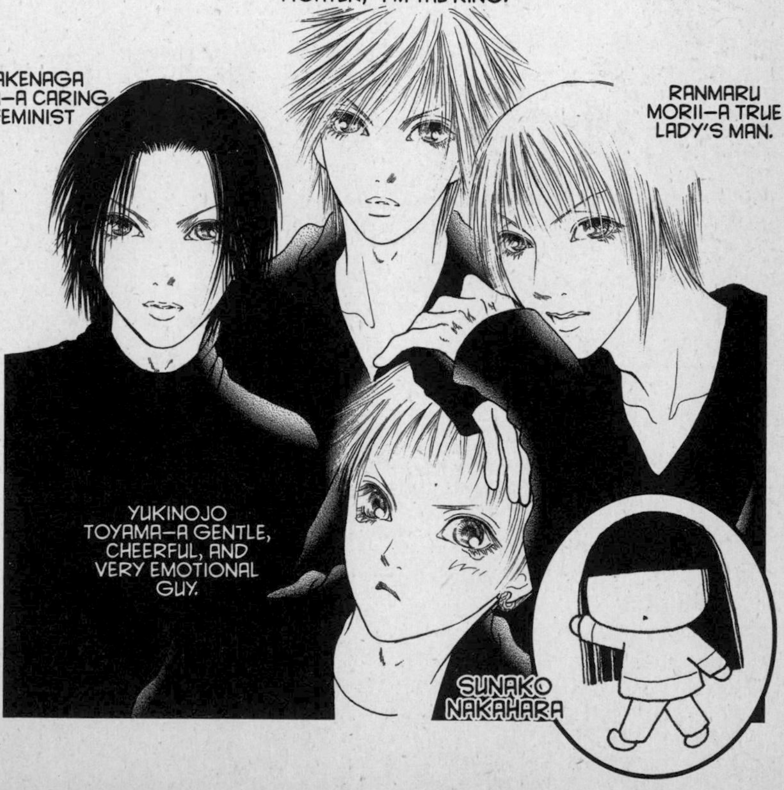

KYOHEI TAKANO—A STRONG FIGHTER, "I'M THE KING."
RANMARU MORII—A TRUE LADY'S MAN.
TAKENAGA ODA—A CARING FEMINIST
YUKINOJO TOYAMA—A GENTLE, CHEERFUL, AND VERY EMOTIONAL GUY.
SUNAKO NAKAHARA

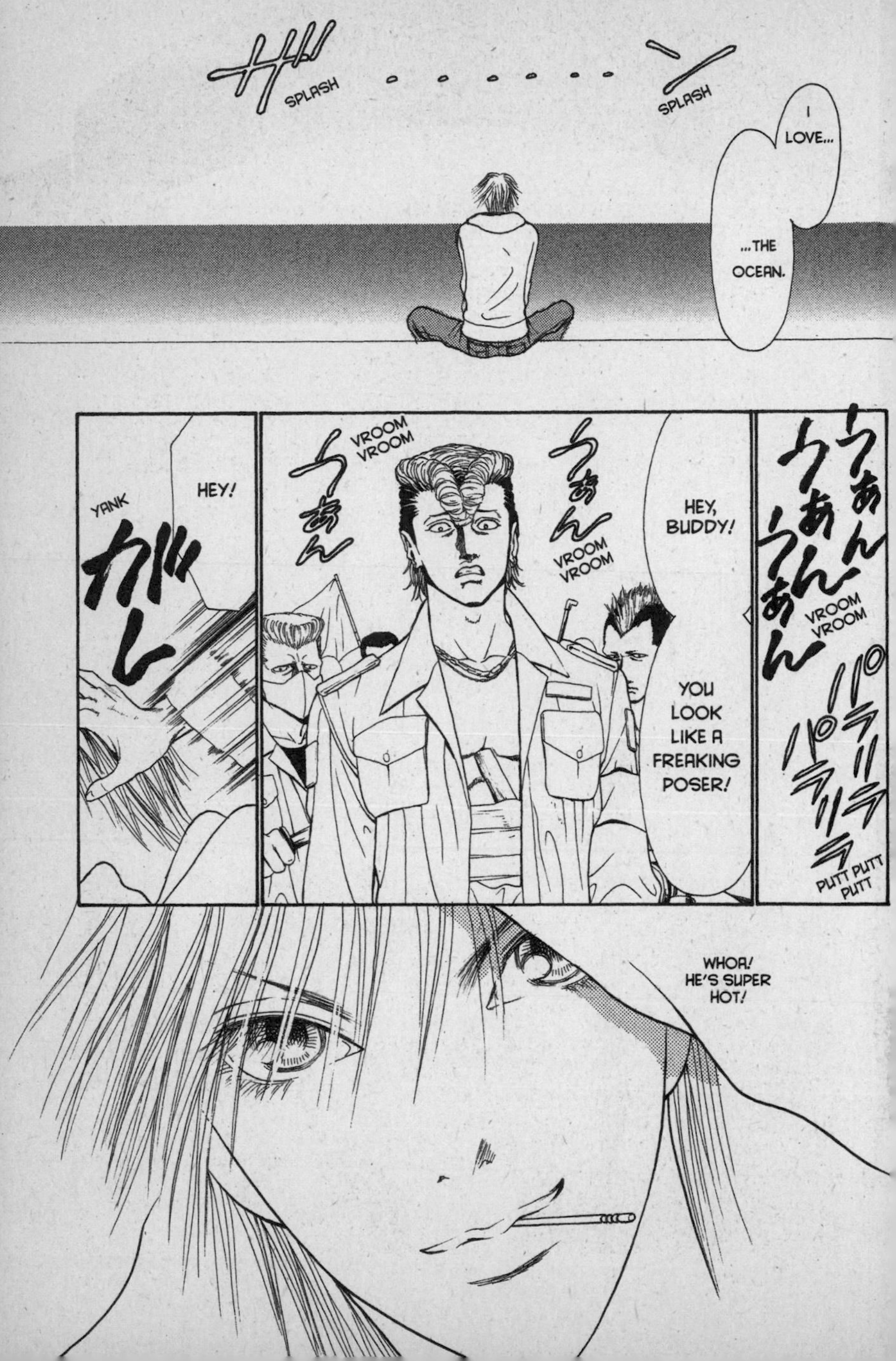
SPLASH
SPLASH
I LOVE...
...THE OCEAN.
VROOM VROOM
PUTT PUTT PUTT
HEY, BUDDY!
YOU LOOK LIKE A FREAKING POSER!
VROOM VROOM
VROOM VROOM
HEY!
YANK
WHOA! HE'S SUPER HOT!

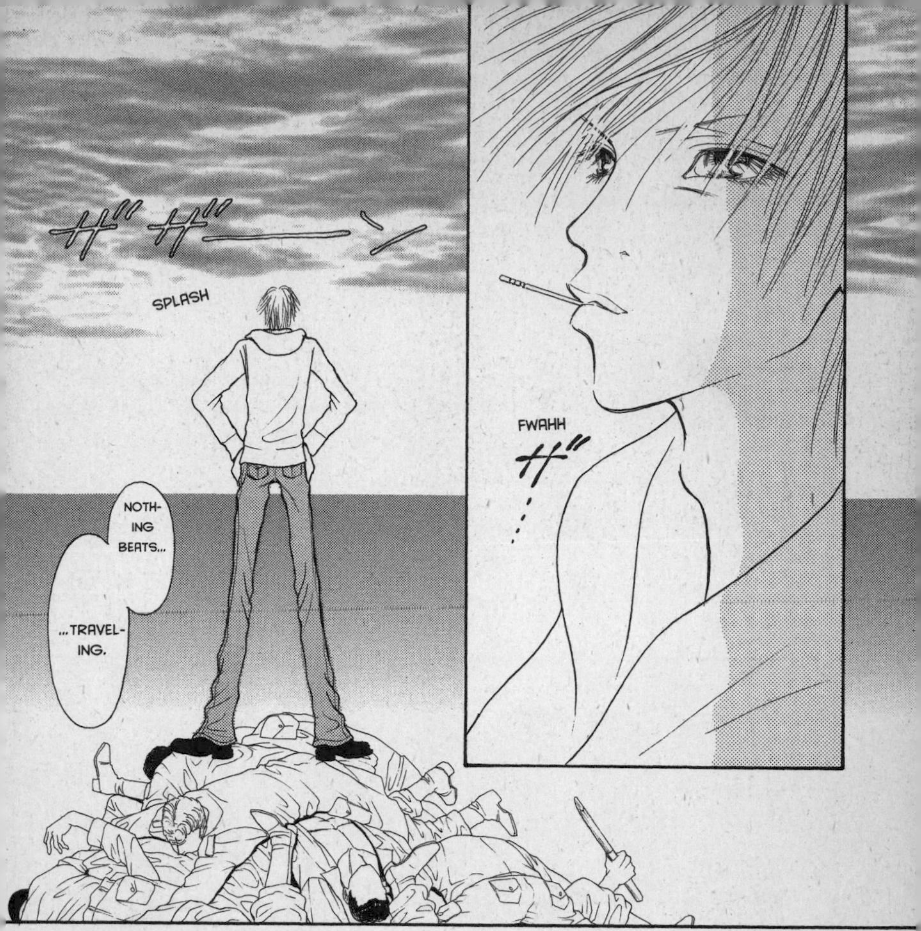
FWAHH
SPLASH
NOTH-ING BEATS...
...TRAVEL-ING.

BEHIND THE SCENES

THE DAY BEFORE THE INTERVIEW, MY EDITOR TOLD ME I HAD TO REWRITE THE WHOLE STORY.

WHILE I WAS WORKING ON THIS STORY, I HAD A LIFE-CHANGING EVENT...TWO OF THEM ACTUALLY. ♥ I KNOW I WROTE ABOUT THIS IN BOOK NINE, BUT...

• I INTERVIEWED KIYOHARU-SAMA (THE HOTTEST GUY IN THE WORLD) FOR A MUSIC MAGAZINE. THAT MADE ME SO HAPPY. I CAN DIE NOW.

• TEN (THE CUTEST LITTLE ANIMAL IN THE WORLD) CAME TO LIVE WITH ME. HE'S SO CUTE, IT'S ALMOST UNBELIEVABLE. WHEN I WAS WRITING THIS STORY, HE WAS THE SIZE OF MY HAND. NOW HE'S SIX TIMES THAT SIZE.

IT WAS A MONTH FULL OF *LOVE...* BUT WORK WAS SO BUSY, I THOUGHT I WAS GONNA DIE.

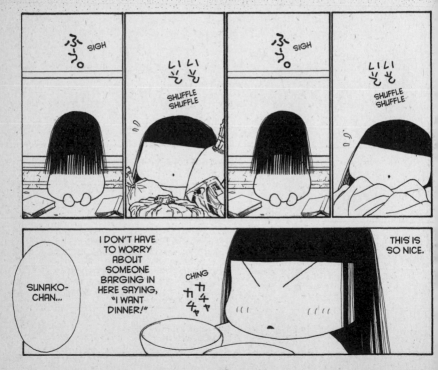

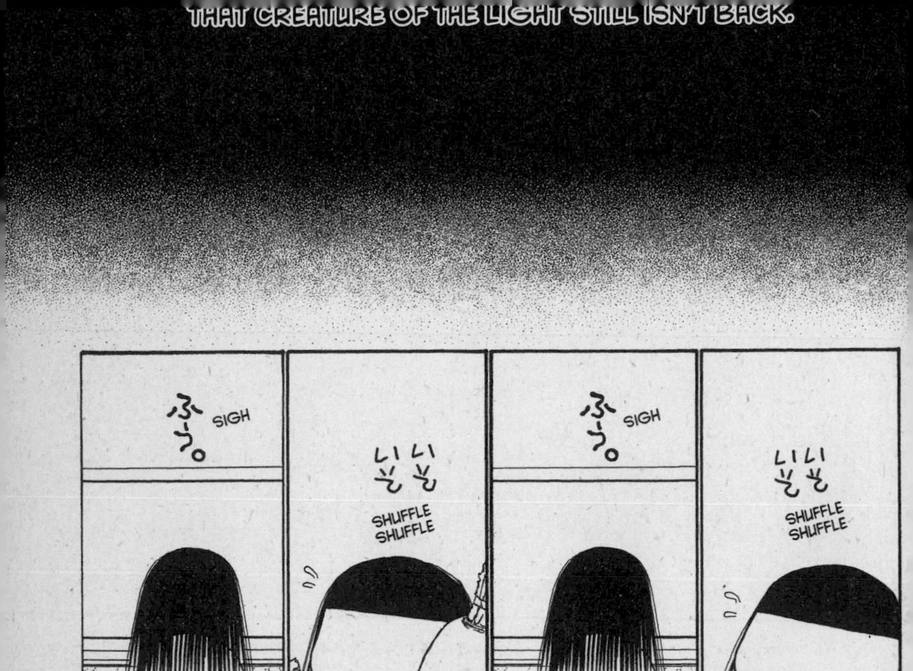
THAT CREATURE OF THE LIGHT STILL ISN'T BACK.
いそいそ
SHUFFLE SHUFFLE
ふぅ。
SIGH
いそいそ
SHUFFLE SHUFFLE
ふぅ。
SIGH
THIS IS SO NICE.
カチャカチャ
CHING
I DON'T HAVE TO WORRY ABOUT SOMEONE BARGING IN HERE SAYING, "I WANT DINNER!"
SUNAKO-CHAN...

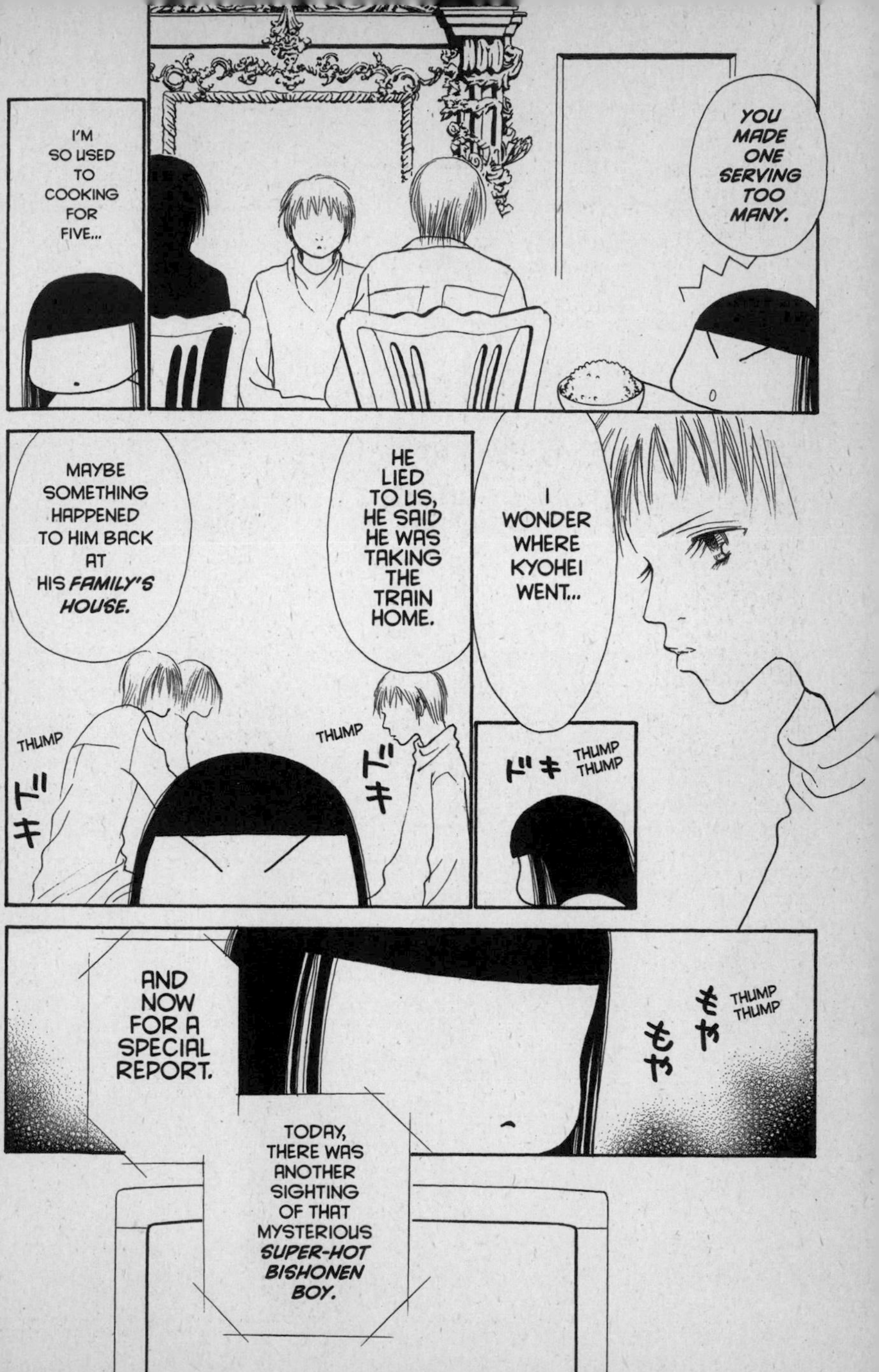
YOU MADE ONE SERVING TOO MANY.
I'M SO USED TO COOKING FOR FIVE...
I WONDER WHERE KYOHEI WENT...
ドキ
THUMP THUMP
HE LIED TO US, HE SAID HE WAS TAKING THE TRAIN HOME.
MAYBE SOMETHING HAPPENED TO HIM BACK AT HIS *FAMILY'S HOUSE.*
ドキ
THUMP
ドキ
THUMP
もやもや
THUMP THUMP
AND NOW FOR A SPECIAL REPORT.
TODAY, THERE WAS ANOTHER SIGHTING OF THAT MYSTERIOUS *SUPER-HOT BISHONEN BOY.*

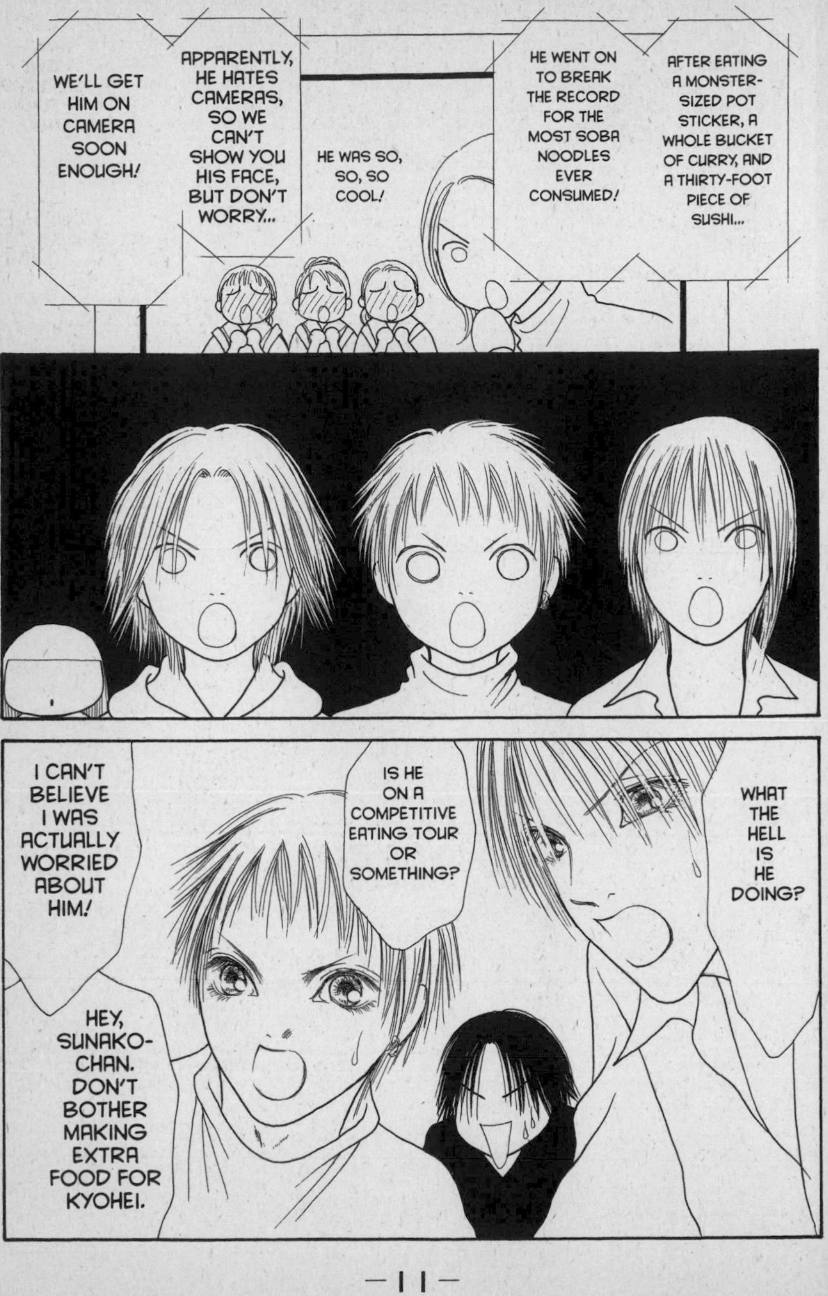
AFTER EATING A MONSTER-SIZED POT STICKER, A WHOLE BUCKET OF CURRY, AND A THIRTY-FOOT PIECE OF SUSHI...
HE WENT ON TO BREAK THE RECORD FOR THE MOST SOBA NOODLES EVER CONSUMED!
HE WAS SO, SO, SO COOL!
APPARENTLY, HE HATES CAMERAS, SO WE CAN'T SHOW YOU HIS FACE, BUT DON'T WORRY...
WE'LL GET HIM ON CAMERA SOON ENOUGH!
WHAT THE HELL IS HE DOING?
IS HE ON A COMPETITIVE EATING TOUR OR SOMETHING?
I CAN'T BELIEVE I WAS ACTUALLY WORRIED ABOUT HIM!
HEY, SUNAKO-CHAN. DON'T BOTHER MAKING EXTRA FOOD FOR KYOHEI.

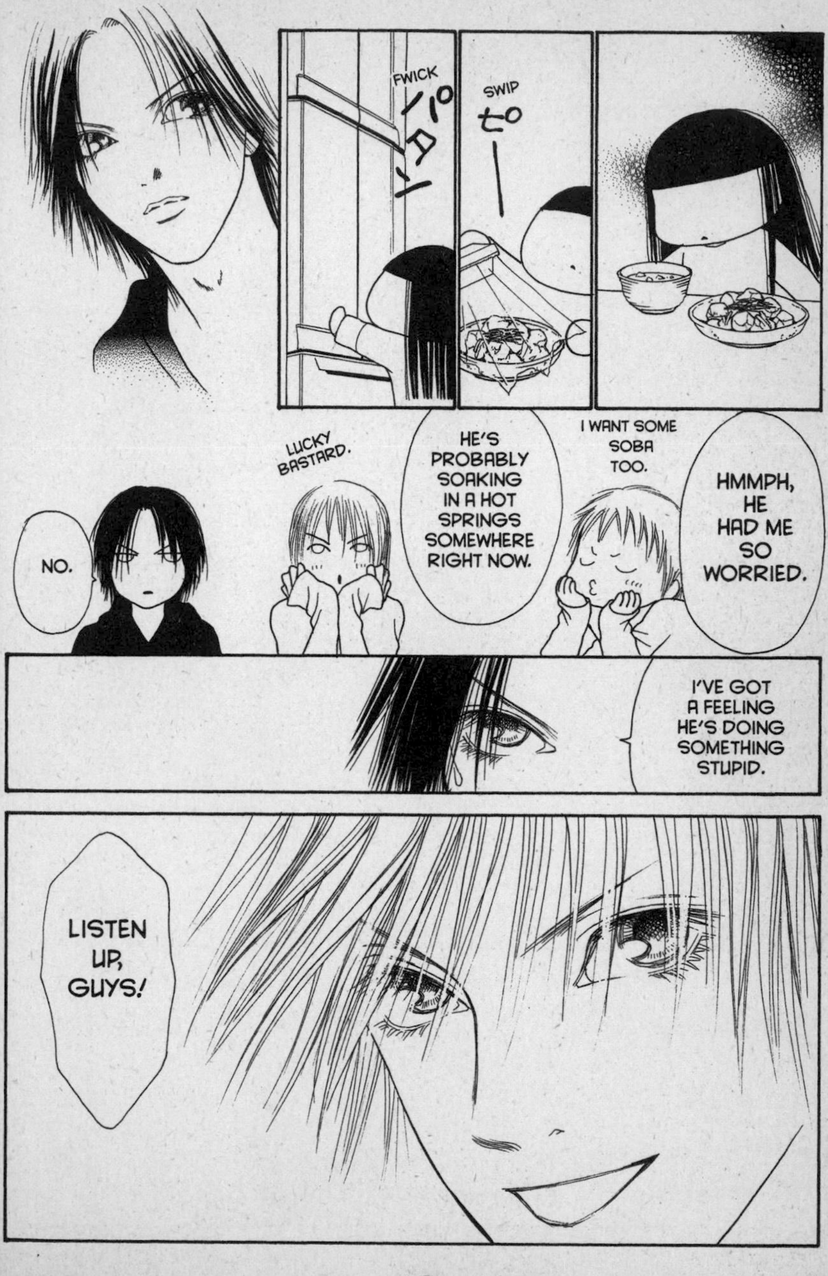
SWIP
ピー
FWICK
パタン
HMMPH, HE HAD ME SO WORRIED.
I WANT SOME SOBA TOO.
HE'S PROBABLY SOAKING IN A HOT SPRINGS SOMEWHERE RIGHT NOW.
LUCKY BASTARD.
NO.
I'VE GOT A FEELING HE'S DOING SOMETHING STUPID.
LISTEN UP, GUYS!

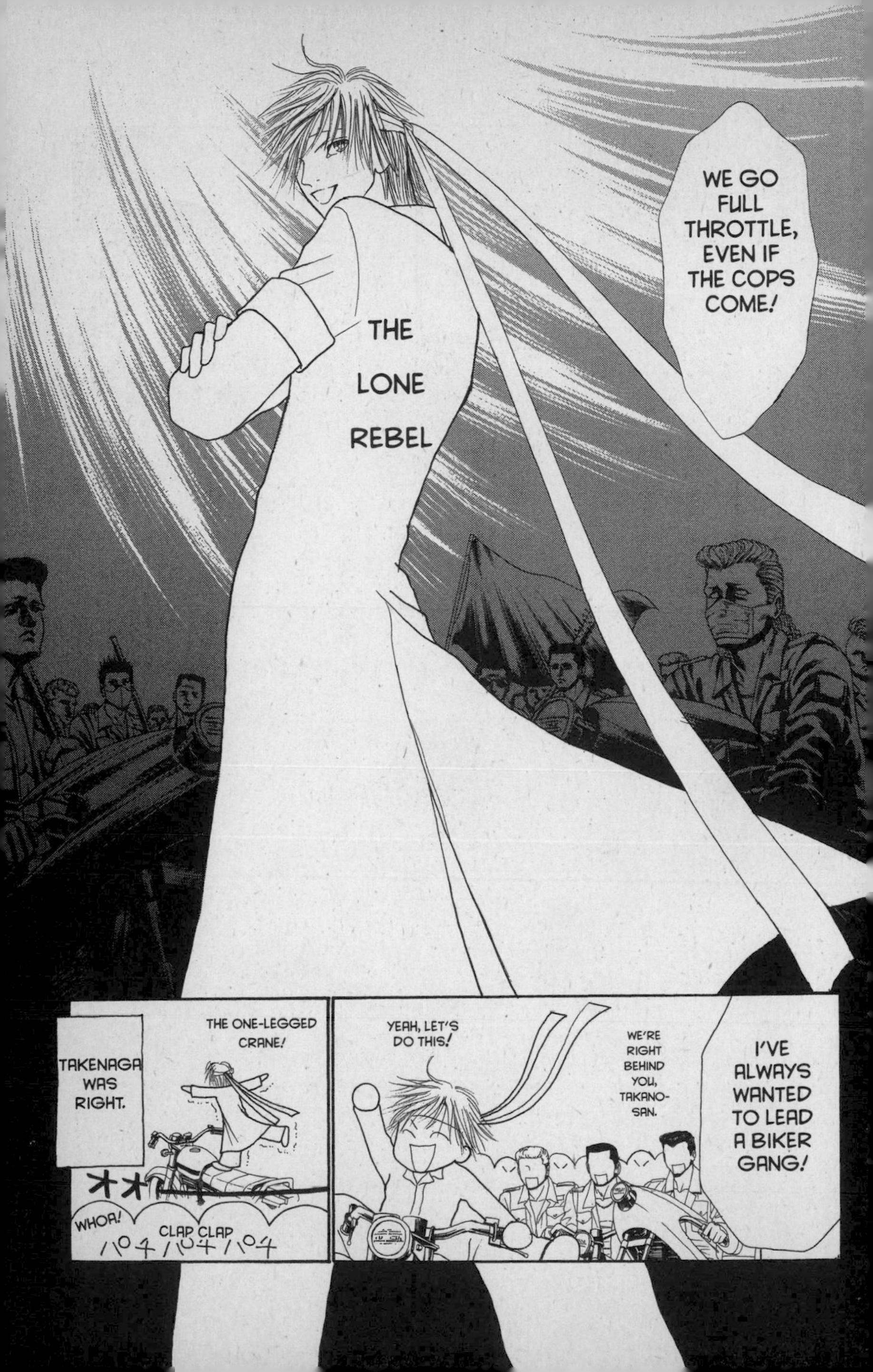
WE GO FULL THROTTLE, EVEN IF THE COPS COME!
THE LONE REBEL
I'VE ALWAYS WANTED TO LEAD A BIKER GANG!
WE'RE RIGHT BEHIND YOU, TAKANO-SAN.
YEAH, LET'S DO THIS!
THE ONE-LEGGED CRANE!
TAKENAGA WAS RIGHT.
オオ
WHOA!
CLAP CLAP
パチパチパチ

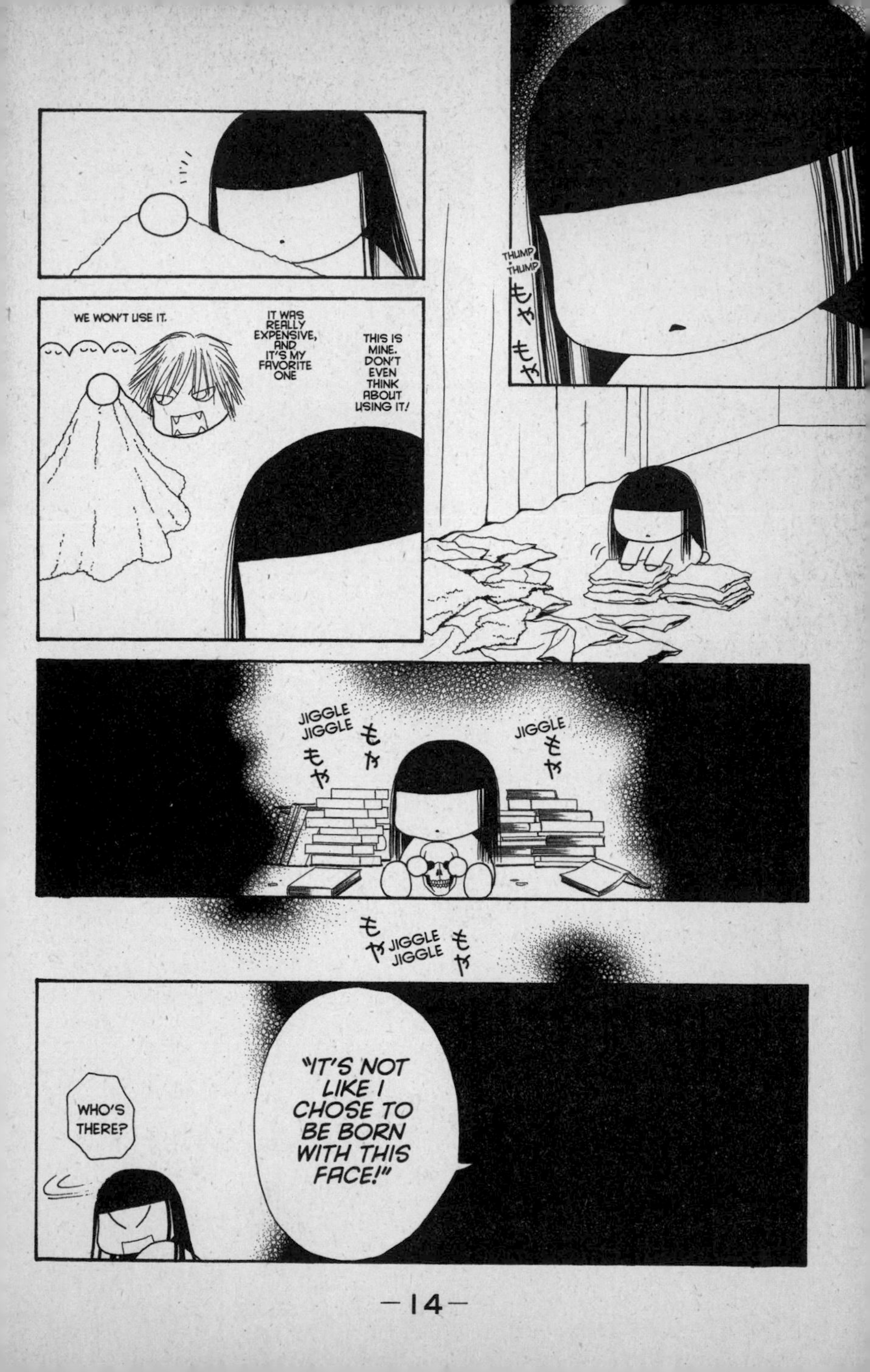
THUMP THUMP
もやもや
THIS IS MINE. DON'T EVEN THINK ABOUT USING IT!
IT WAS REALLY EXPENSIVE, AND IT'S MY FAVORITE ONE
WE WON'T USE IT.
JIGGLE
もや
JIGGLE JIGGLE
もや
もや
もや
JIGGLE JIGGLE
もや
"IT'S NOT LIKE I CHOSE TO BE BORN WITH THIS FACE!"
WHO'S THERE?

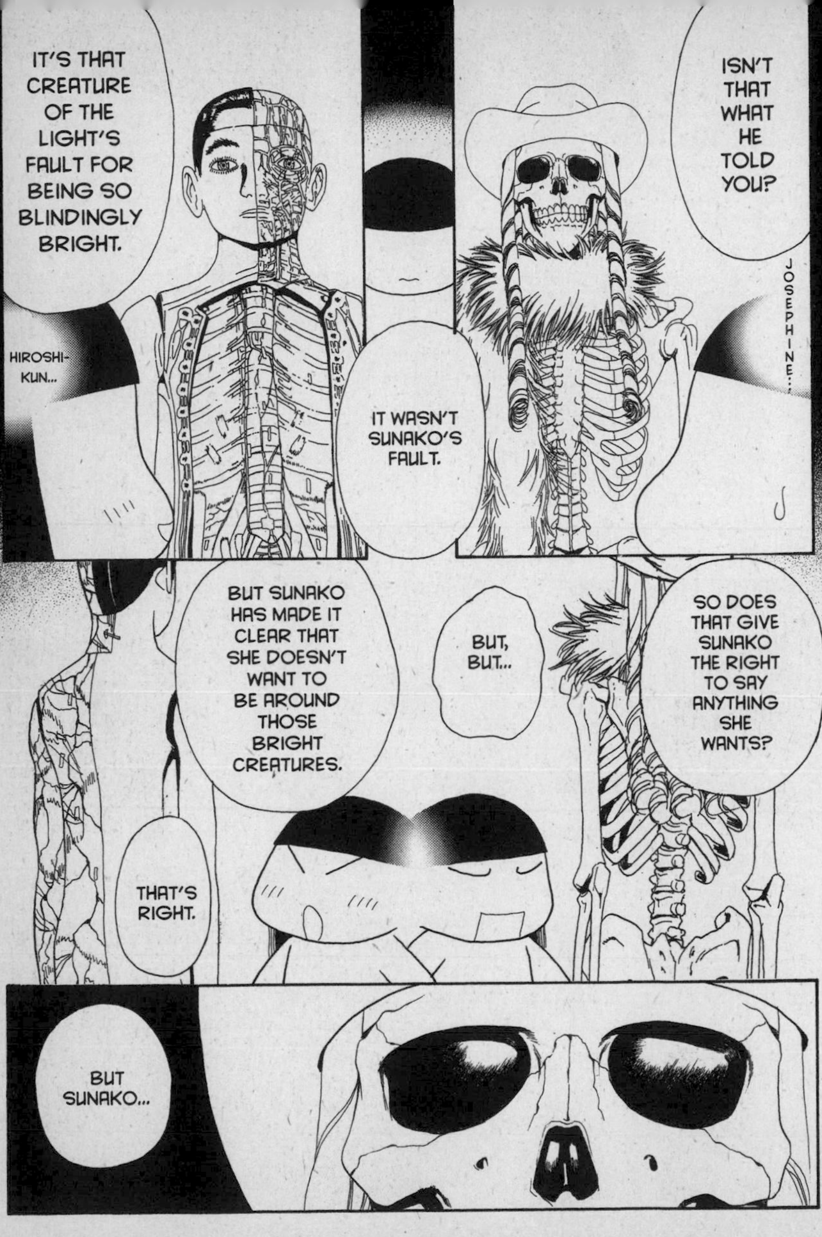
ISN'T THAT WHAT HE TOLD YOU?
JOSEPHINE...
IT WASN'T SUNAKO'S FAULT.
IT'S THAT CREATURE OF THE LIGHT'S FAULT FOR BEING SO BLINDINGLY BRIGHT.
HIROSHI-KUN...
SO DOES THAT GIVE SUNAKO THE RIGHT TO SAY ANYTHING SHE WANTS?
BUT, BUT...
BUT SUNAKO HAS MADE IT CLEAR THAT SHE DOESN'T WANT TO BE AROUND THOSE BRIGHT CREATURES.
THAT'S RIGHT.
BUT SUNAKO...

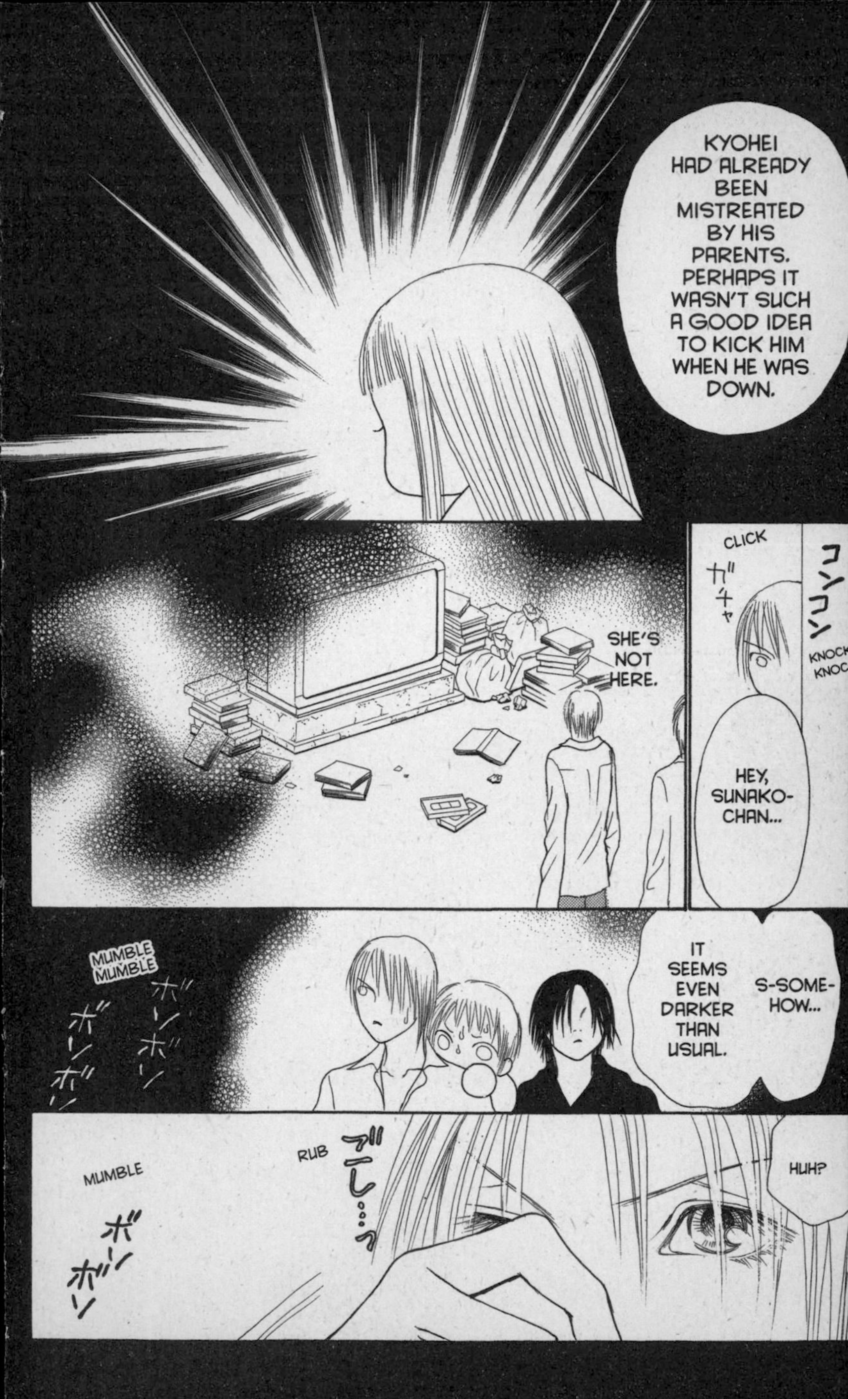
KYOHEI HAD ALREADY BEEN MISTREATED BY HIS PARENTS. PERHAPS IT WASN'T SUCH A GOOD IDEA TO KICK HIM WHEN HE WAS DOWN.
コンコン
KNOCK KNOC
ガチャ
CLICK
HEY, SUNAKO-CHAN...
SHE'S NOT HERE.
S-SOMEHOW...
IT SEEMS EVEN DARKER THAN USUAL.
ボソボソ
MUMBLE MUMBLE
HUH?
RUB
ボソボソ
MUMBLE

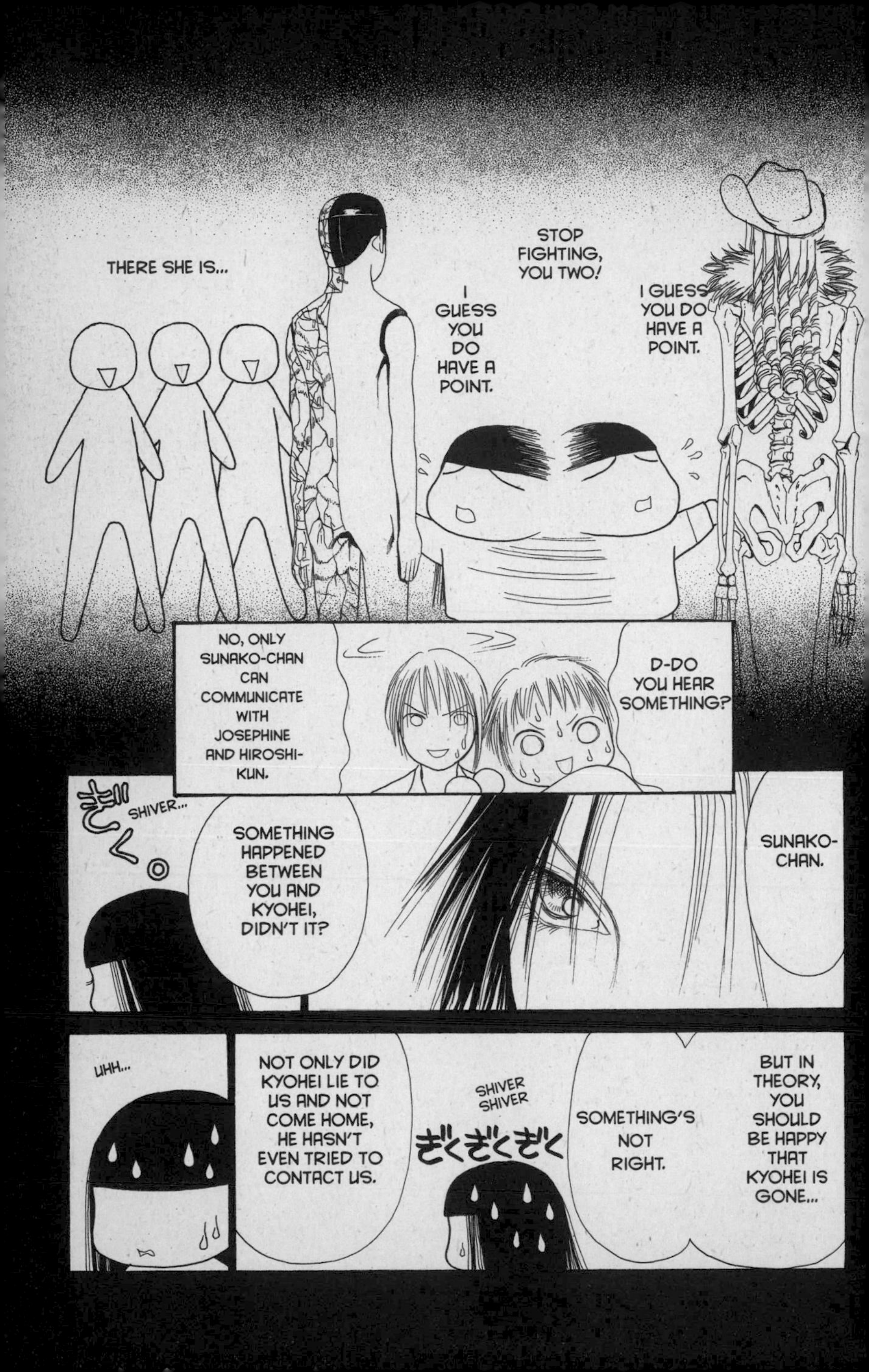
I GUESS YOU DO HAVE A POINT.
STOP FIGHTING, YOU TWO!
I GUESS YOU DO HAVE A POINT.
THERE SHE IS...
D-DO YOU HEAR SOMETHING?
NO, ONLY SUNAKO-CHAN CAN COMMUNICATE WITH JOSEPHINE AND HIROSHI-KUN.
SUNAKO-CHAN.
SOMETHING HAPPENED BETWEEN YOU AND KYOHEI, DIDN'T IT?
SHIVER...
BUT IN THEORY, YOU SHOULD BE HAPPY THAT KYOHEI IS GONE...
SOMETHING'S NOT RIGHT.
SHIVER SHIVER
ぎくぎくぎく
NOT ONLY DID KYOHEI LIE TO US AND NOT COME HOME, HE HASN'T EVEN TRIED TO CONTACT US.
UHH...

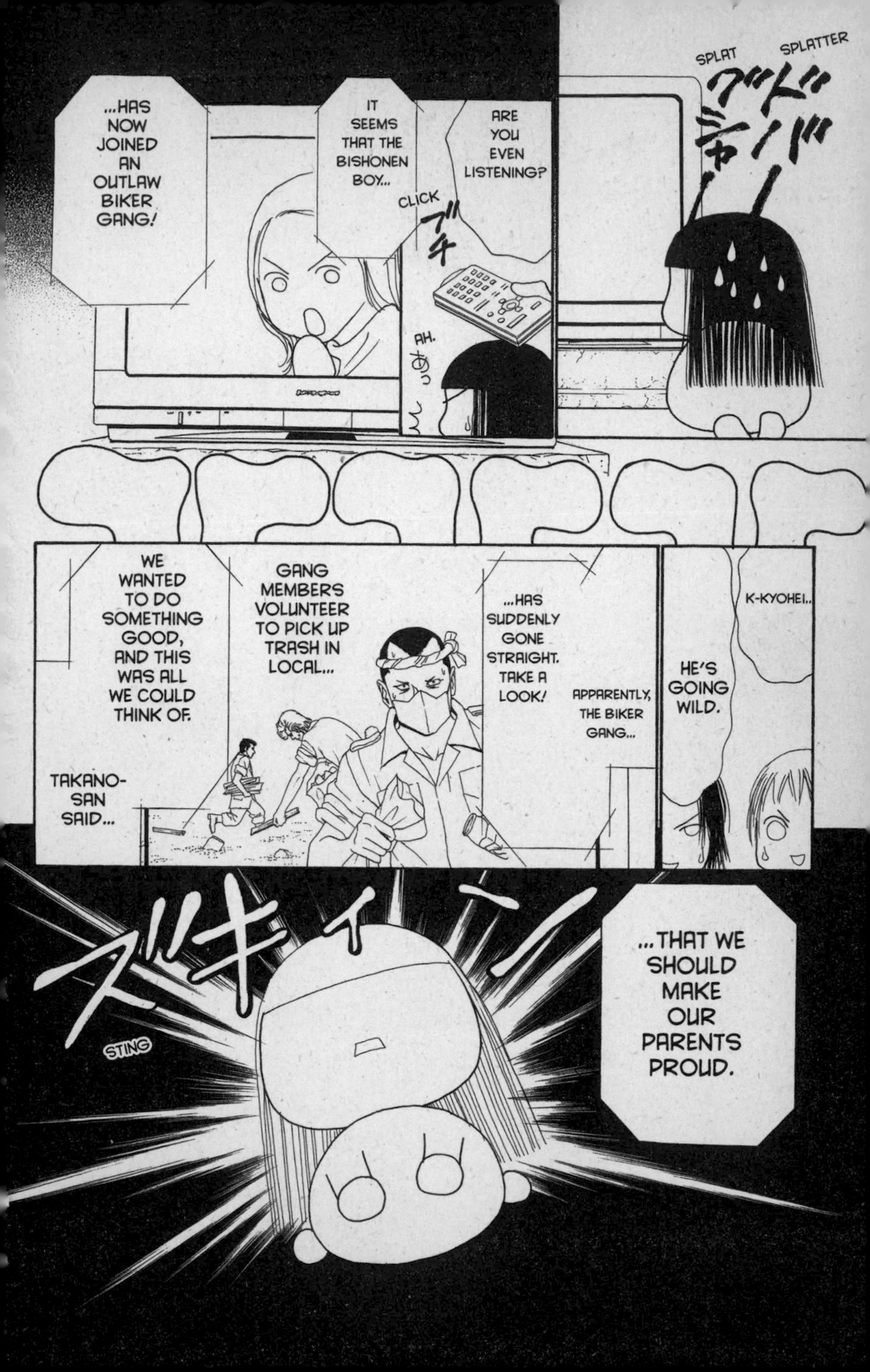
SPLATTER
SPLAT
ARE YOU EVEN LISTENING?
IT SEEMS THAT THE BISHONEN BOY...
CLICK
AH.
...HAS NOW JOINED AN OUTLAW BIKER GANG!
K-KYOHEI..
HE'S GOING WILD.
APPARENTLY, THE BIKER GANG...
...HAS SUDDENLY GONE STRAIGHT. TAKE A LOOK!
GANG MEMBERS VOLUNTEER TO PICK UP TRASH IN LOCAL...
WE WANTED TO DO SOMETHING GOOD, AND THIS WAS ALL WE COULD THINK OF.
TAKANO-SAN SAID...
...THAT WE SHOULD MAKE OUR PARENTS PROUD.
STING

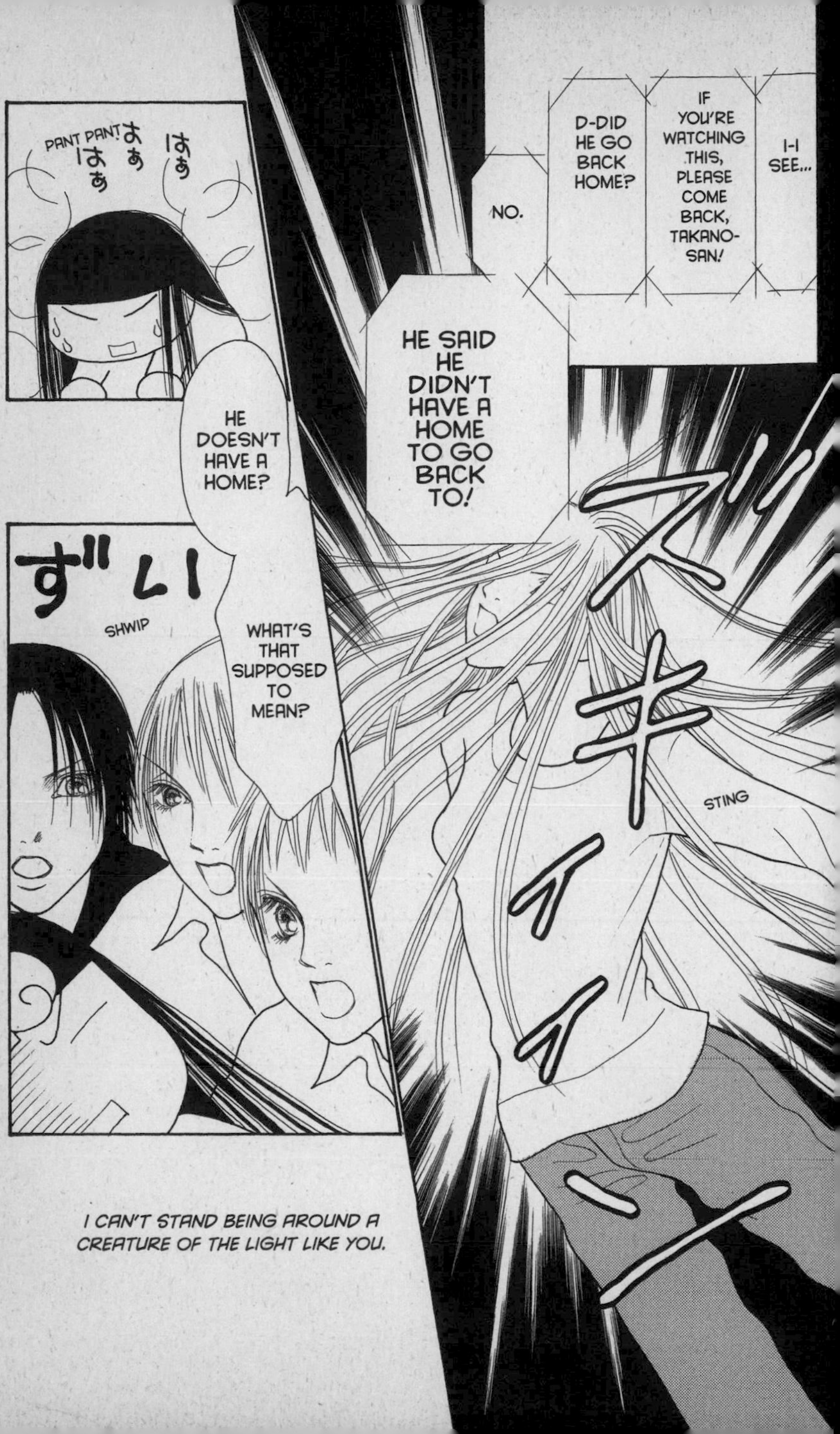
I-I SEE...
IF YOU'RE WATCHING THIS, PLEASE COME BACK, TAKANO-SAN!
D-DID HE GO BACK HOME?
NO.
HE SAID HE DIDN'T HAVE A HOME TO GO BACK TO!
はぁ はぁ
PANT PANT
HE DOESN'T HAVE A HOME?
ズキィィー
STING
ずい
SHWIP
WHAT'S THAT SUPPOSED TO MEAN?
I CAN'T STAND BEING AROUND A CREATURE OF THE LIGHT LIKE YOU.

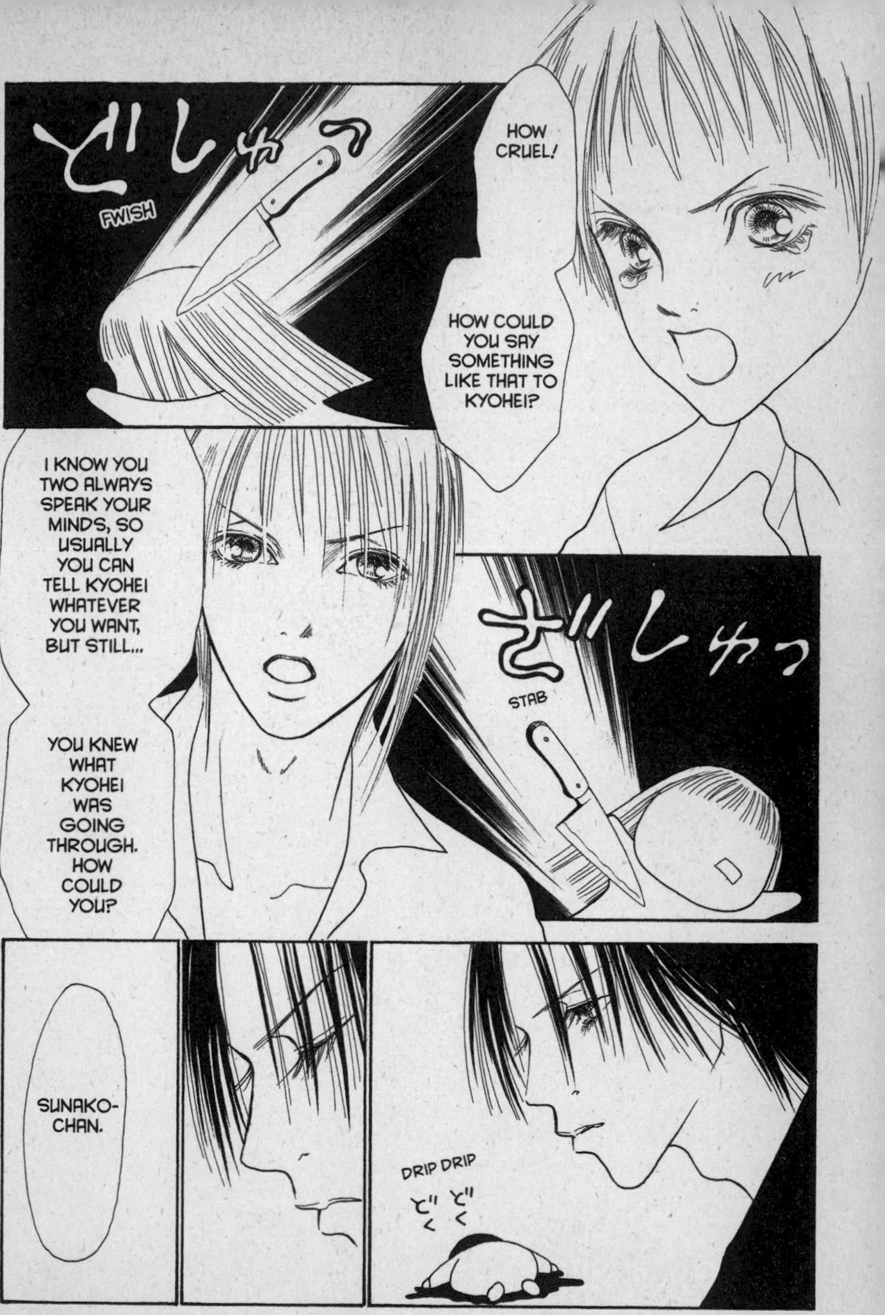
HOW CRUEL!
HOW COULD YOU SAY SOMETHING LIKE THAT TO KYOHEI?
どしゅっ
FWISH
ざしゅっ
STAB
I KNOW YOU TWO ALWAYS SPEAK YOUR MINDS, SO USUALLY YOU CAN TELL KYOHEI WHATEVER YOU WANT, BUT STILL...
YOU KNEW WHAT KYOHEI WAS GOING THROUGH. HOW COULD YOU?
DRIP DRIP
どくどく
SUNAKO-CHAN.

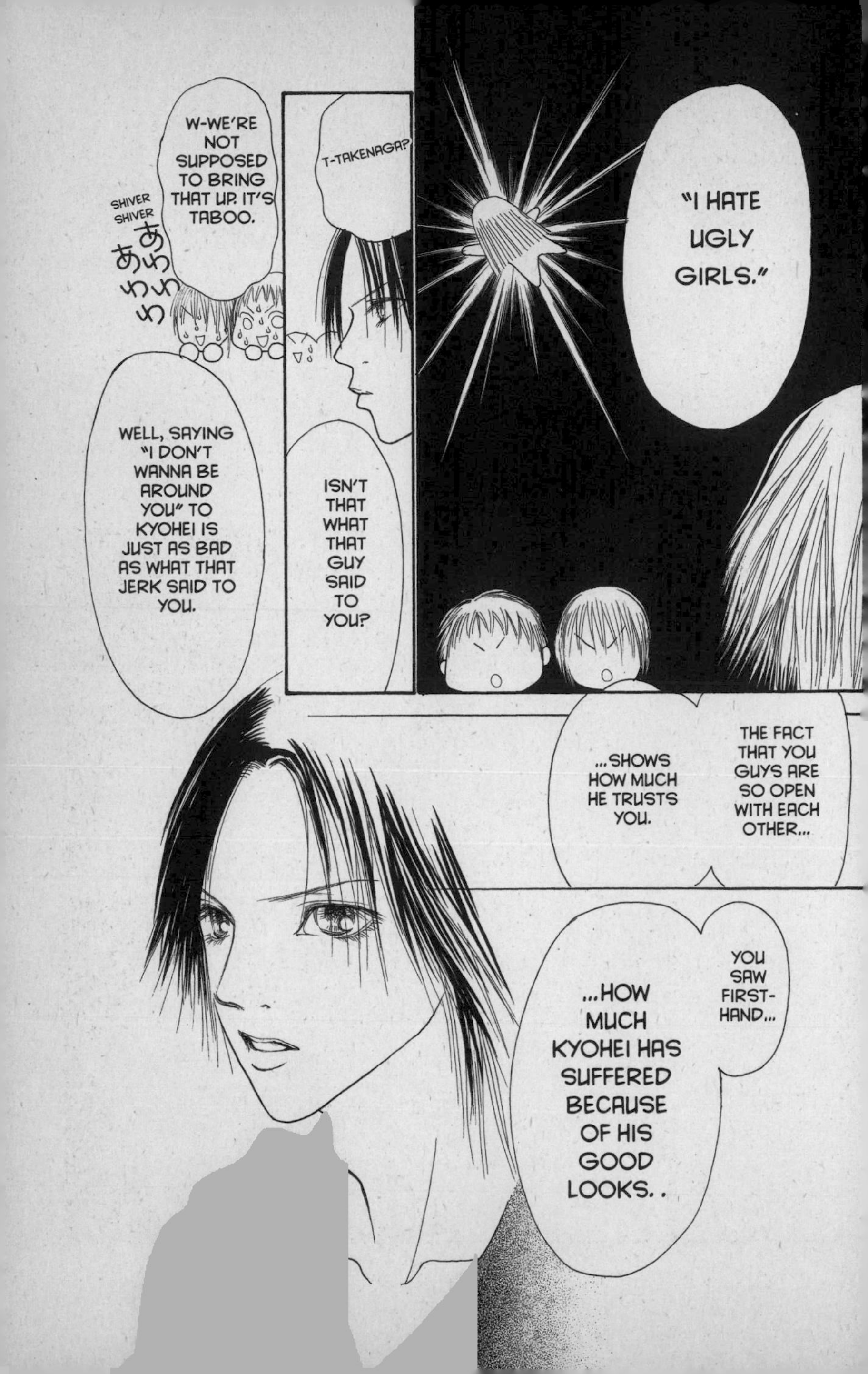
"I HATE UGLY GIRLS."
T-TAKENAGA?
ISN'T THAT WHAT THAT GUY SAID TO YOU?
W-WE'RE NOT SUPPOSED TO BRING THAT UP. IT'S TABOO.
SHIVER SHIVER
あわわ あわわ
WELL, SAYING "I DON'T WANNA BE AROUND YOU" TO KYOHEI IS JUST AS BAD AS WHAT THAT JERK SAID TO YOU.
THE FACT THAT YOU GUYS ARE SO OPEN WITH EACH OTHER...
...SHOWS HOW MUCH HE TRUSTS YOU.
YOU SAW FIRST-HAND...
...HOW MUCH KYOHEI HAS SUFFERED BECAUSE OF HIS GOOD LOOKS. .

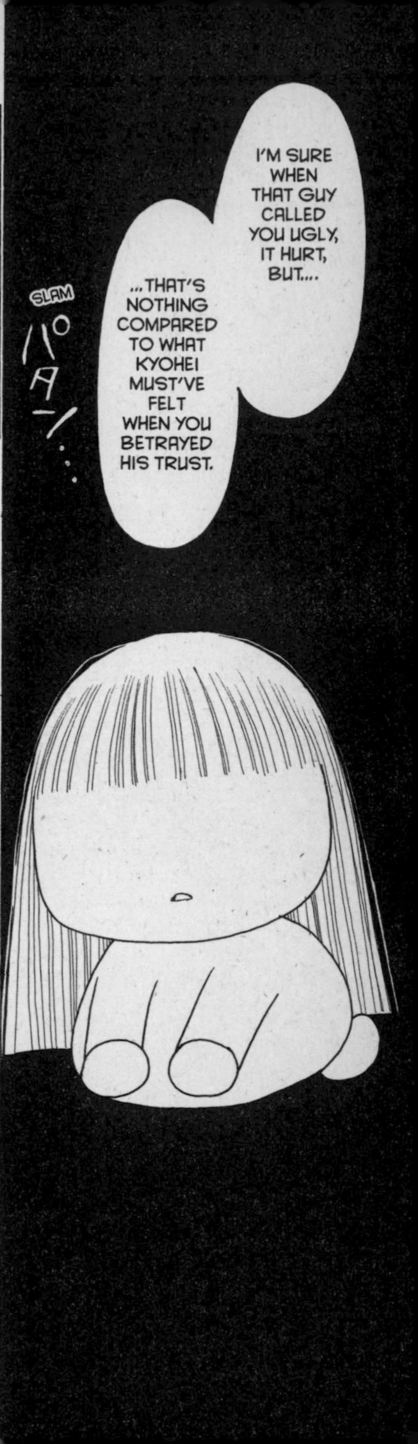
I'M SURE WHEN THAT GUY CALLED YOU UGLY, IT HURT, BUT....
...THAT'S NOTHING COMPARED TO WHAT KYOHEI MUST'VE FELT WHEN YOU BETRAYED HIS TRUST.
SLAM
パターン…

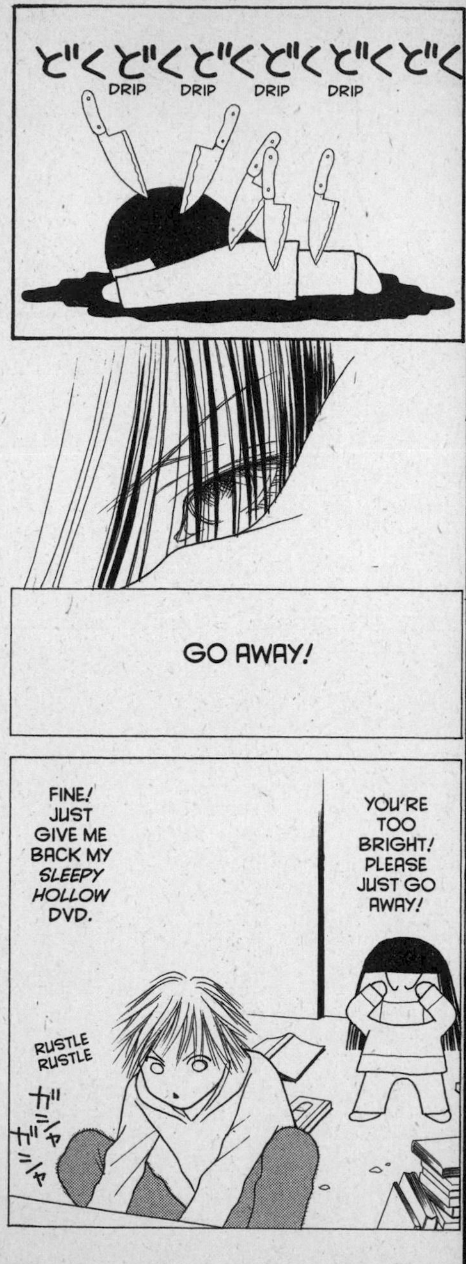
どくどくどくどくどくどく
DRIP DRIP DRIP DRIP
GO AWAY!
YOU'RE TOO BRIGHT! PLEASE JUST GO AWAY!
FINE! JUST GIVE ME BACK MY *SLEEPY HOLLOW* DVD.
RUSTLE RUSTLE
ガシャガシャ

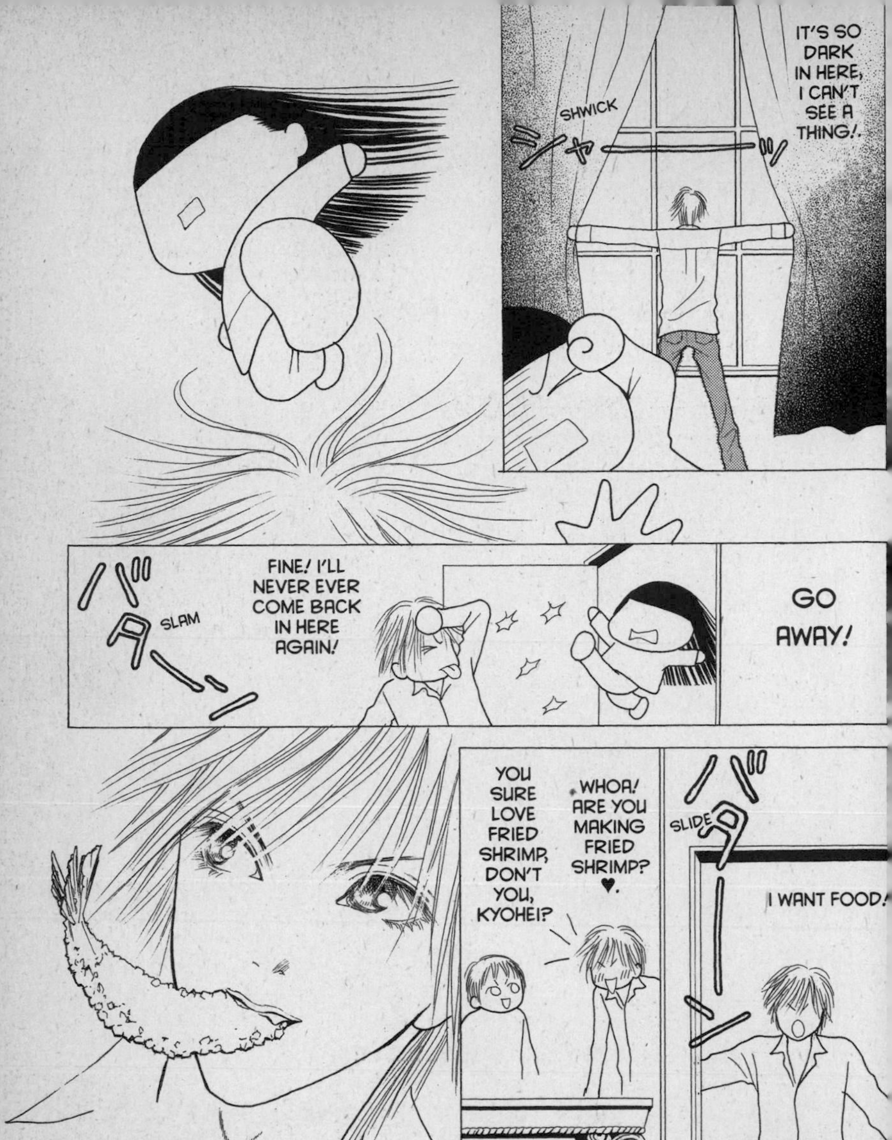

IT'S SO DARK IN HERE, I CAN'T SEE A THING!.
SHWICK
GO AWAY!
FINE! I'LL NEVER EVER COME BACK IN HERE AGAIN!
SLAM
I WANT FOOD!
SLIDE
WHOA! ARE YOU MAKING FRIED SHRIMP? ♥.
YOU SURE LOVE FRIED SHRIMP, DON'T YOU, KYOHEI?
THIS IS SO MUCH BETTER THAN WHAT THEY SERVE IN RESTAURANTS.

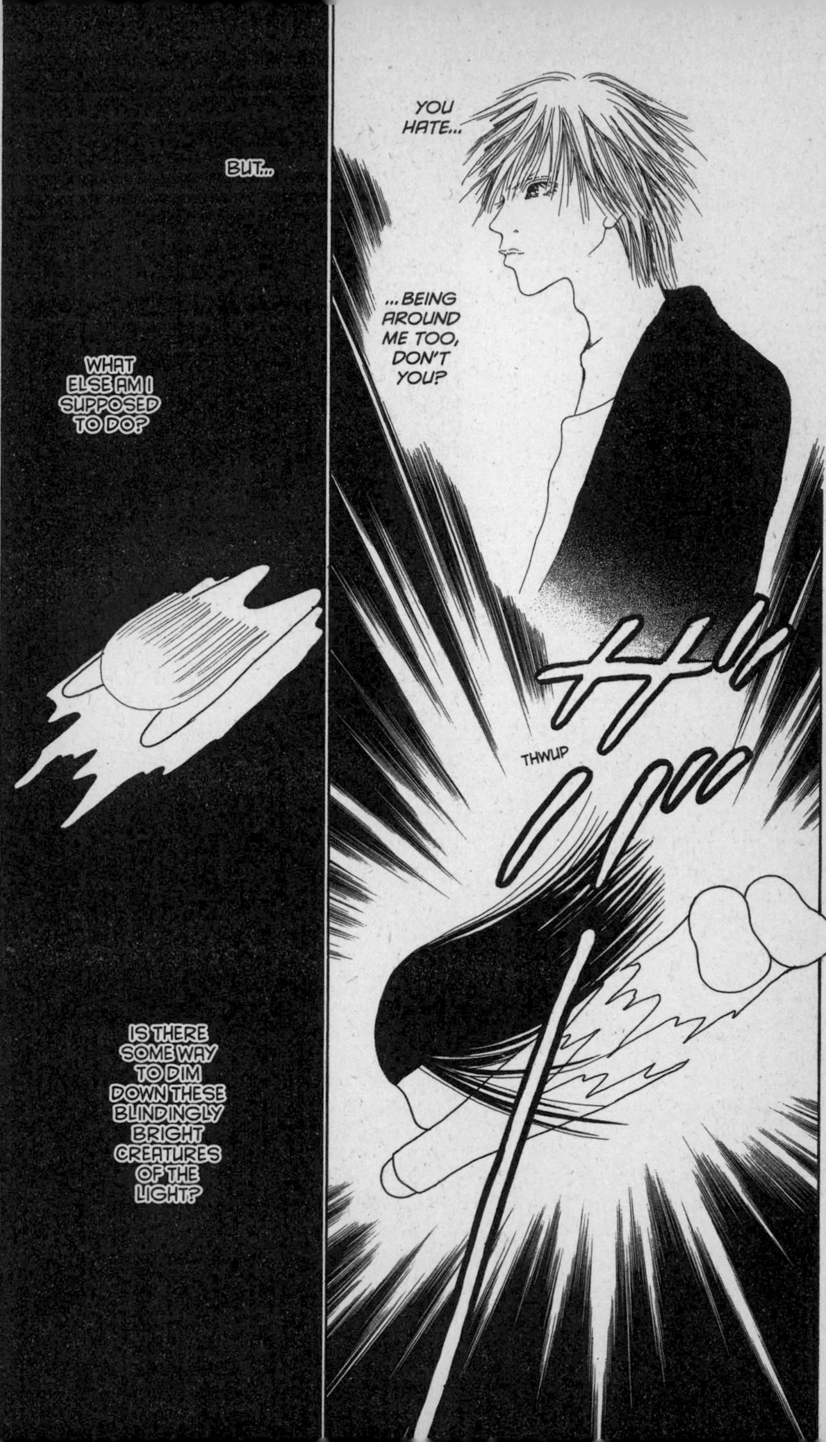
YOU HATE...
...BEING AROUND ME TOO, DON'T YOU?
THWUP
BUT...
WHAT ELSE AM I SUPPOSED TO DO?
IS THERE SOME WAY TO DIM DOWN THESE BLINDINGLY BRIGHT CREATURES OF THE LIGHT?

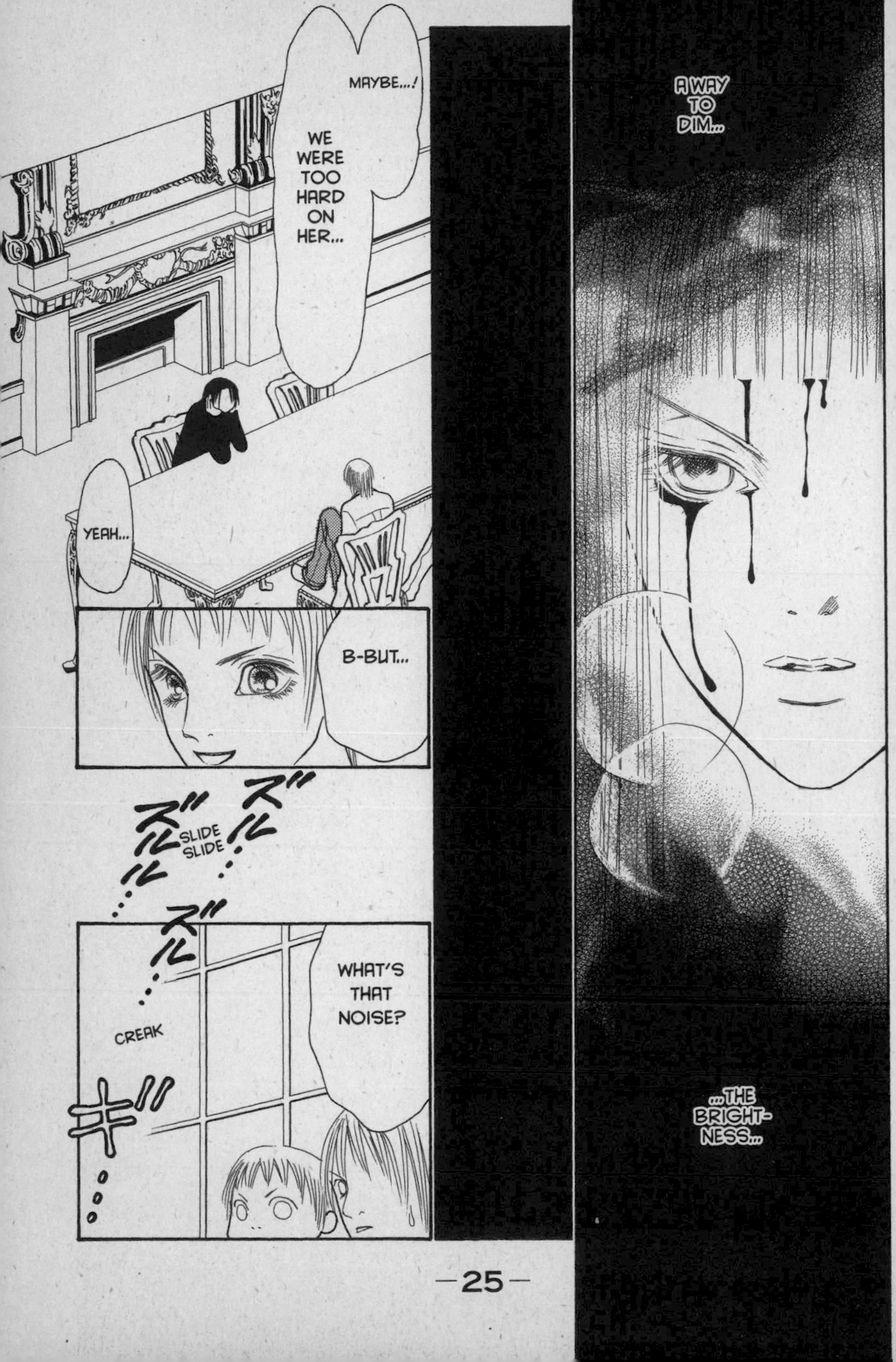
A WAY TO DIM...
...THE BRIGHTNESS...
MAYBE...!
WE WERE TOO HARD ON HER...
YEAH...
B-BUT...
ズル ズル...
SLIDE SLIDE
ズル...
WHAT'S THAT NOISE?
キ...
CREAK

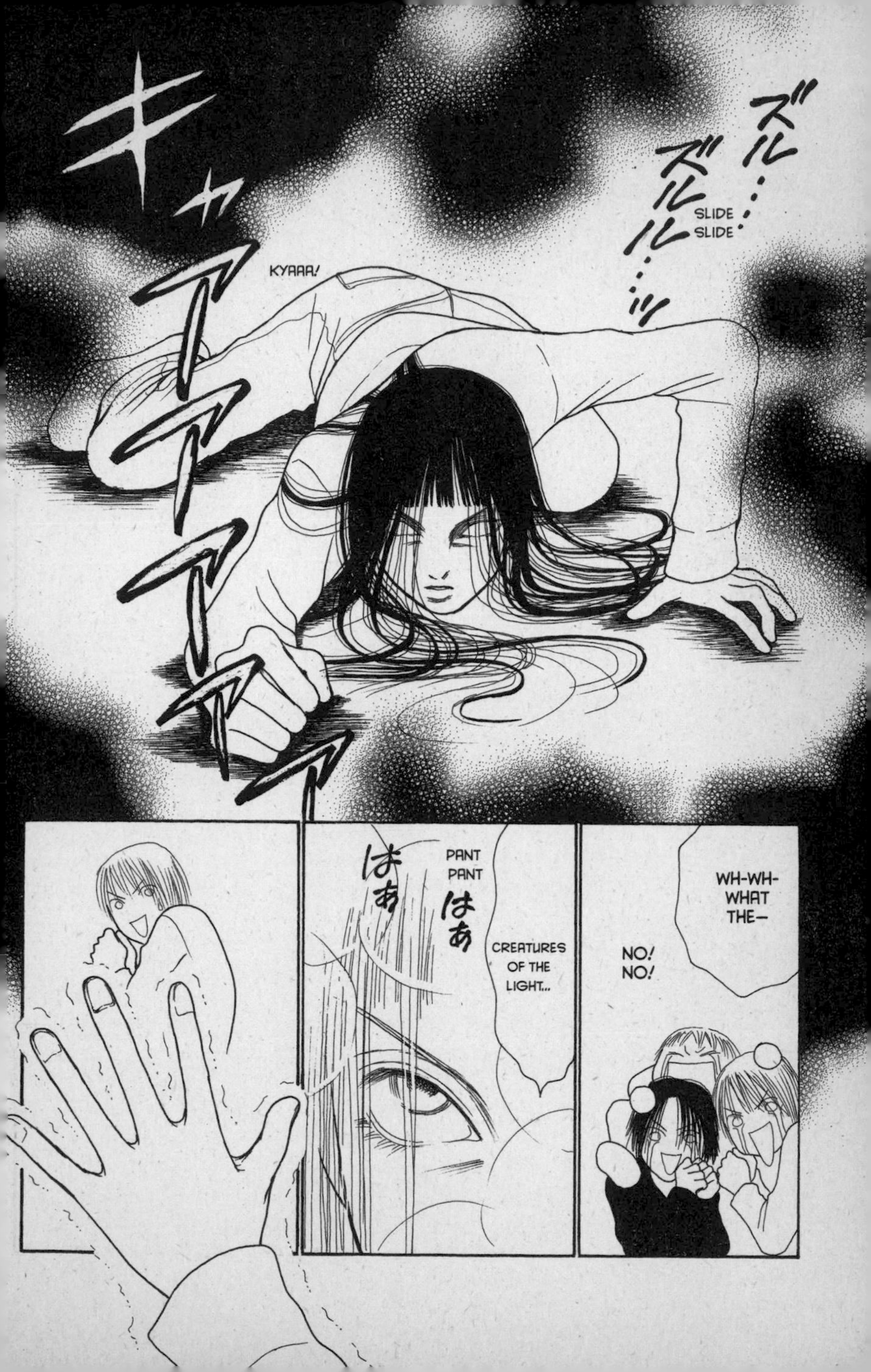
ズル…ズル…ッ
SLIDE SLIDE
キャアアアアァ
KYAAA!
WH-WH-WHAT THE—
NO! NO!
CREATURES OF THE LIGHT...
はぁ はぁ
PANT PANT

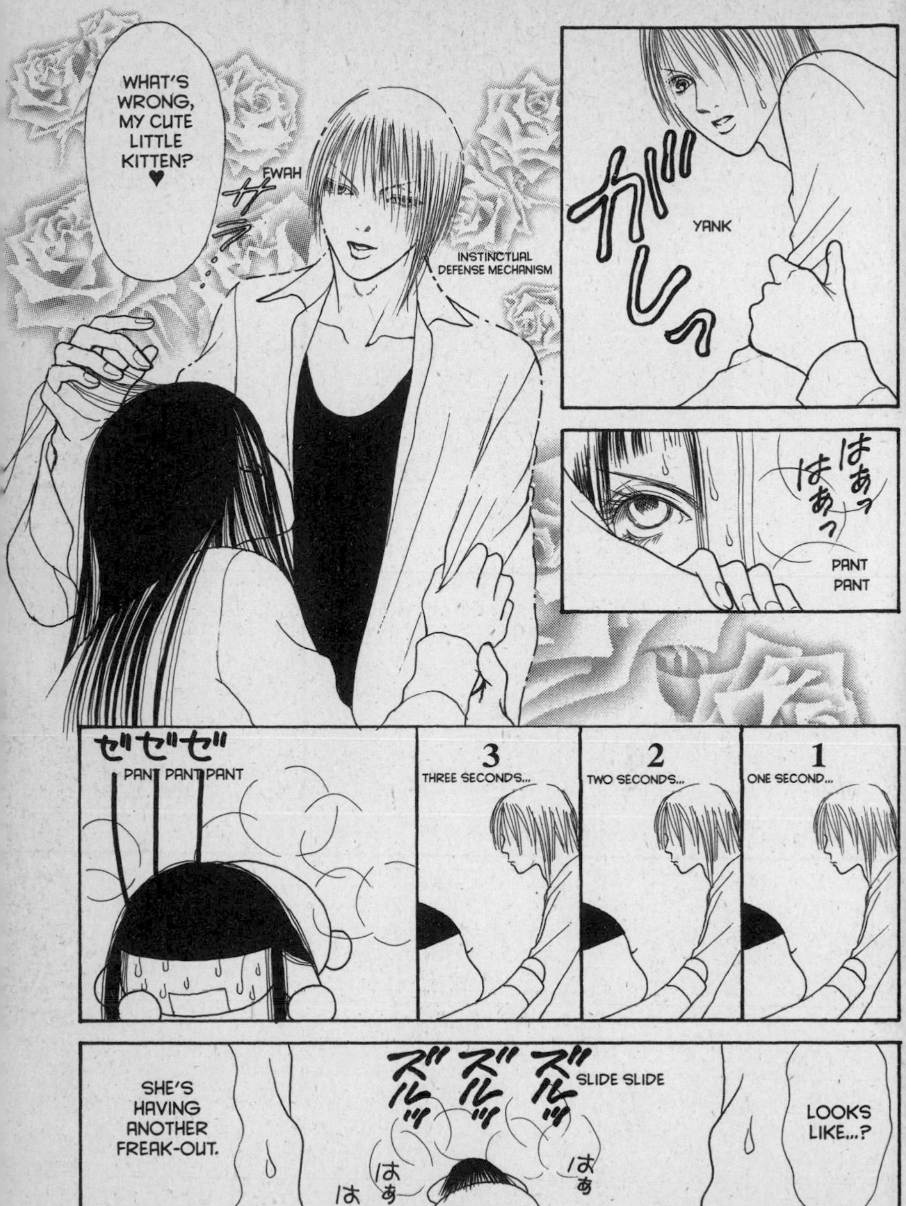
ガシッ
YANK
はあっ はあっ
PANT PANT
WHAT'S WRONG, MY CUTE LITTLE KITTEN? ♥
サラ…
FWAH
INSTINCTUAL DEFENSE MECHANISM
1
ONE SECOND...
2
TWO SECONDS...
3
THREE SECONDS...
ゼゼゼ
PANT PANT PANT
LOOKS LIKE...?
ズルッ ズルッ ズルッ
SLIDE SLIDE
はぁ はぁ はぁ
PANT PANT
SHE'S HAVING ANOTHER FREAK-OUT.

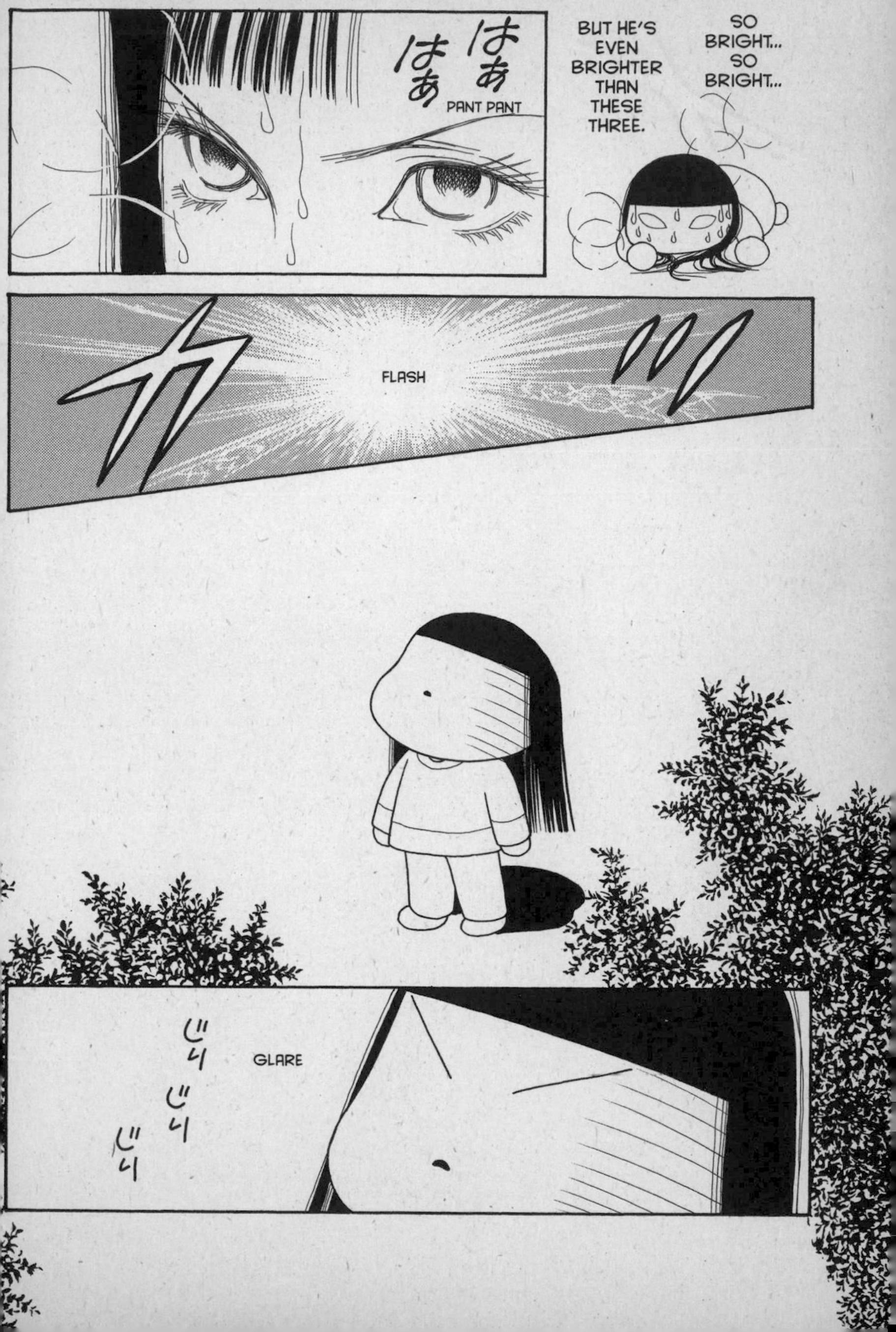
SO BRIGHT... SO BRIGHT...
BUT HE'S EVEN BRIGHTER THAN THESE THREE.
はあはあ
PANT PANT
カッ
FLASH
じぃ じぃ じぃ
GLARE

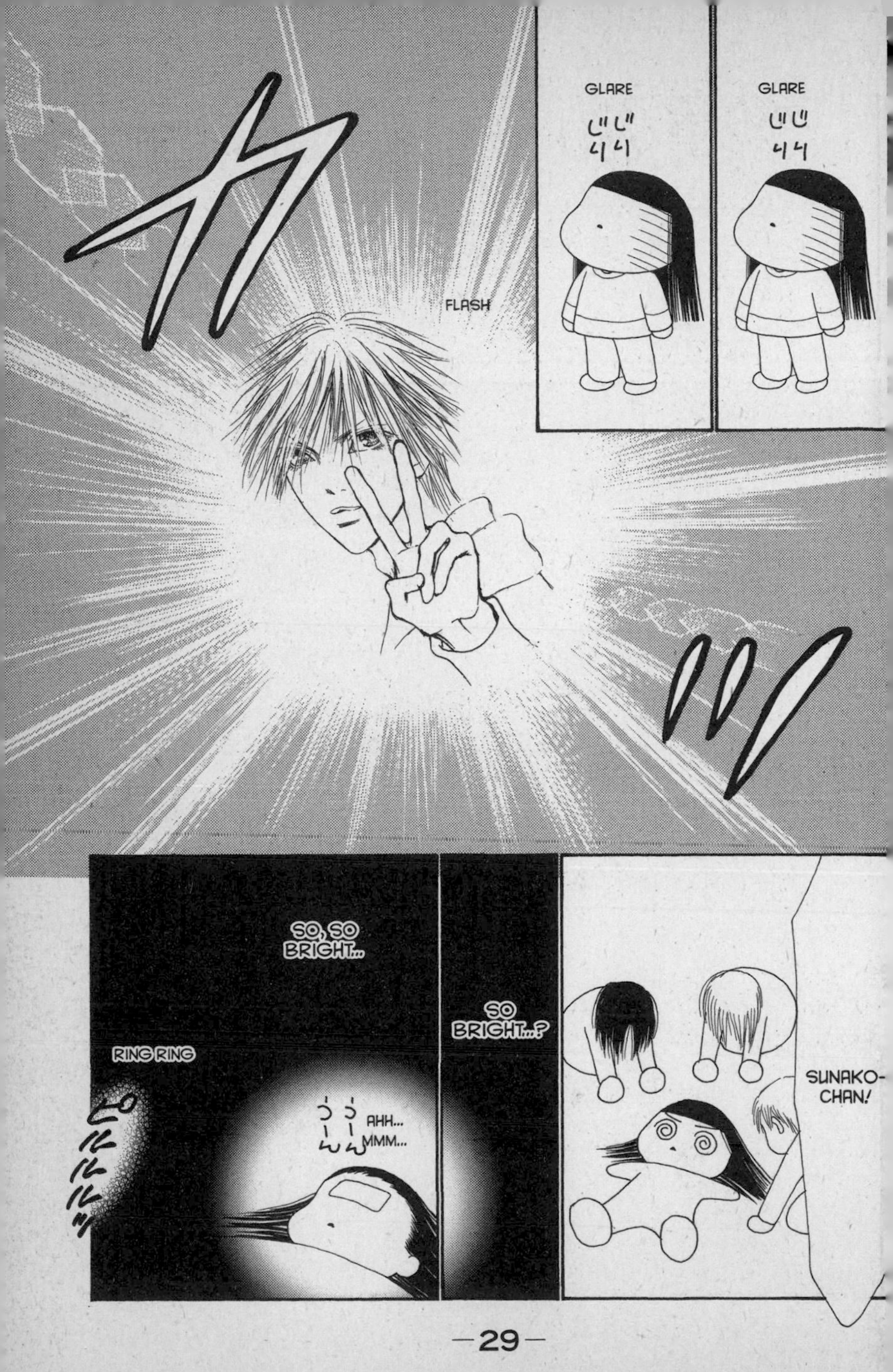
GLARE
GLARE
FLASH
SUNAKO-CHAN!
SO BRIGHT...?
SO, SO BRIGHT...
RING RING
AHH... MMM...

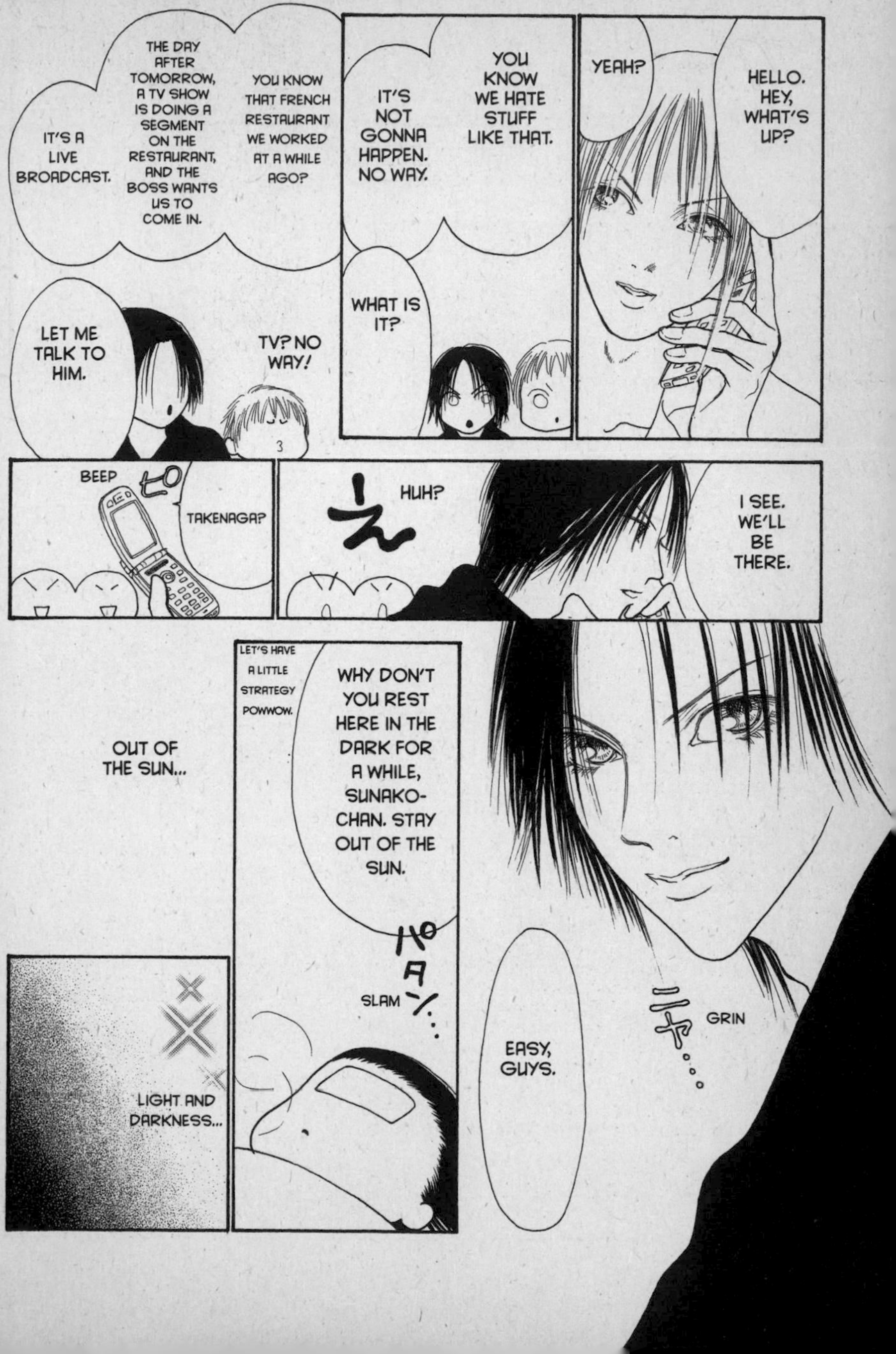

HELLO. HEY, WHAT'S UP?
YEAH?
YOU KNOW WE HATE STUFF LIKE THAT.
IT'S NOT GONNA HAPPEN. NO WAY.
WHAT IS IT?
YOU KNOW THAT FRENCH RESTAURANT WE WORKED AT A WHILE AGO?
THE DAY AFTER TOMORROW, A TV SHOW IS DOING A SEGMENT ON THE RESTAURANT, AND THE BOSS WANTS US TO COME IN.
IT'S A LIVE BROADCAST.
TV? NO WAY!
LET ME TALK TO HIM.
I SEE. WE'LL BE THERE.
え
HUH?
TAKENAGA?
BEEP
ニヤ…
GRIN
EASY, GUYS.
WHY DON'T YOU REST HERE IN THE DARK FOR A WHILE, SUNAKO-CHAN. STAY OUT OF THE SUN.
LET'S HAVE A LITTLE STRATEGY POWWOW.
SLAM
OUT OF THE SUN...
LIGHT AND DARKNESS...

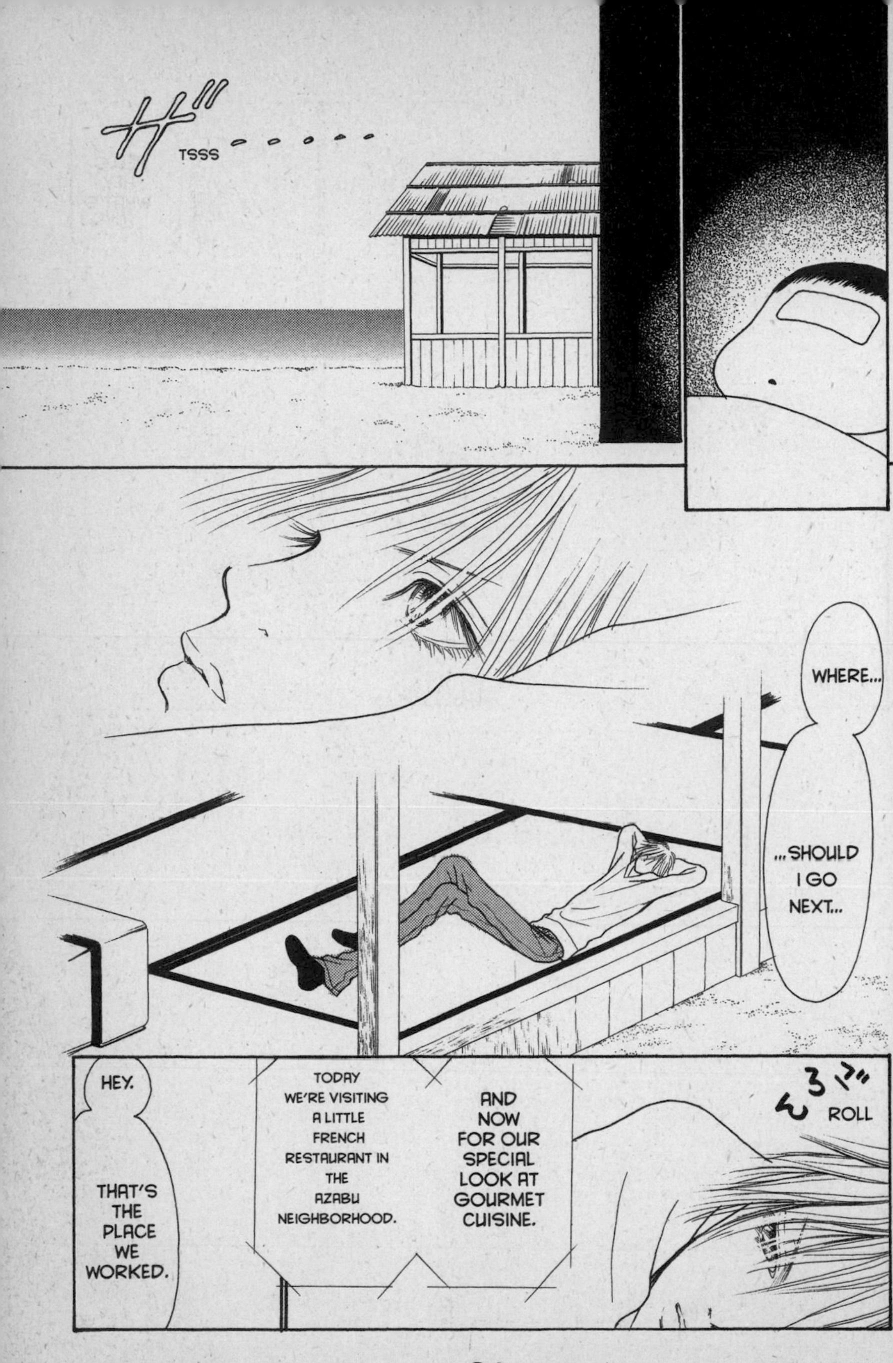
TSSS
WHERE...
...SHOULD I GO NEXT...
ROLL
AND NOW FOR OUR SPECIAL LOOK AT GOURMET CUISINE.
TODAY WE'RE VISITING A LITTLE FRENCH RESTAURANT IN THE AZABU NEIGHBORHOOD.
HEY.
THAT'S THE PLACE WE WORKED.

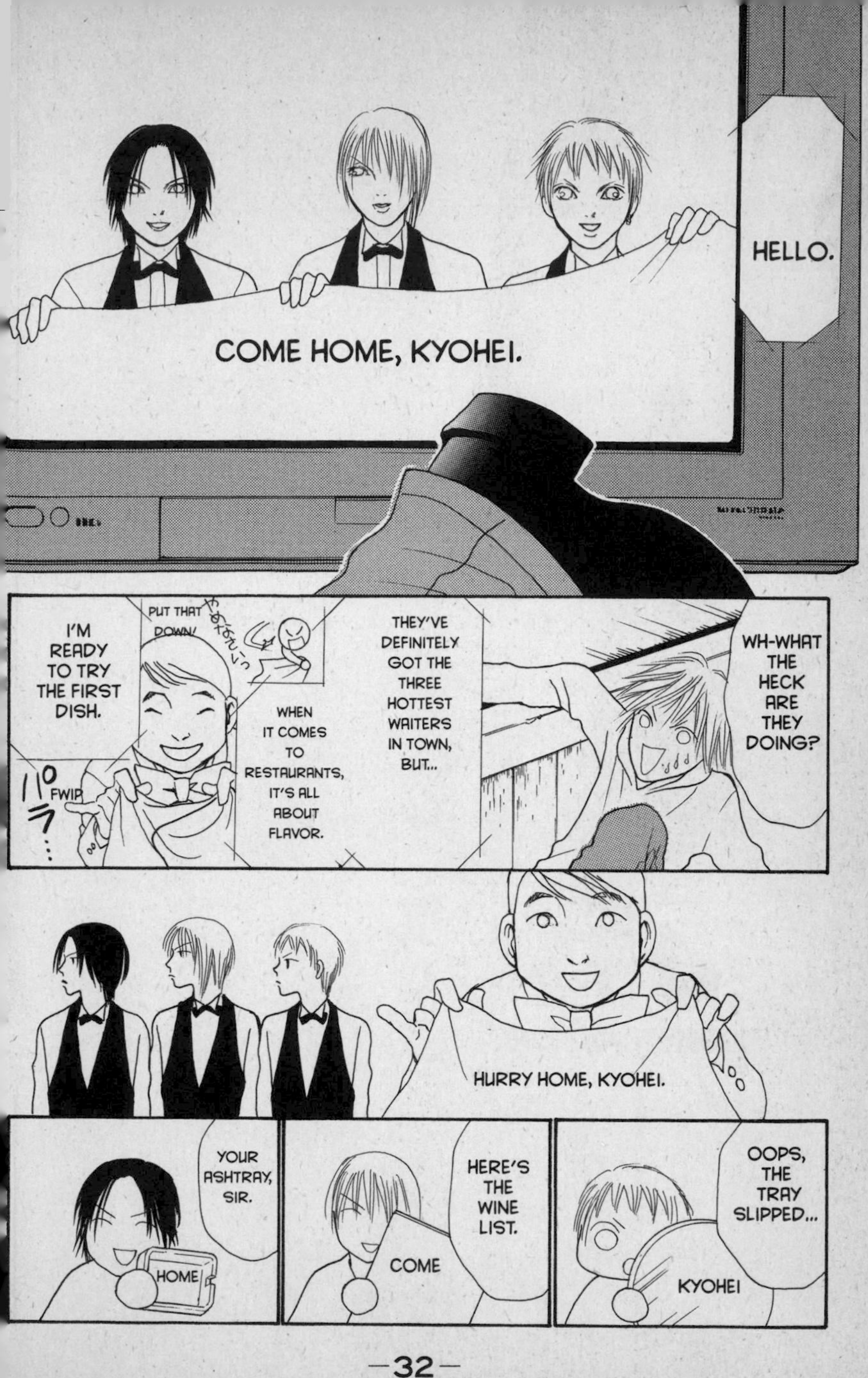
HELLO.
COME HOME, KYOHEI.
WH-WHAT THE HECK ARE THEY DOING?
THEY'VE DEFINITELY GOT THE THREE HOTTEST WAITERS IN TOWN, BUT...
WHEN IT COMES TO RESTAURANTS, IT'S ALL ABOUT FLAVOR.
PUT THAT DOWN!
I'M READY TO TRY THE FIRST DISH.
FWIP
HURRY HOME, KYOHEI.
OOPS, THE TRAY SLIPPED...
KYOHEI
HERE'S THE WINE LIST.
COME
YOUR ASHTRAY, SIR.
HOME

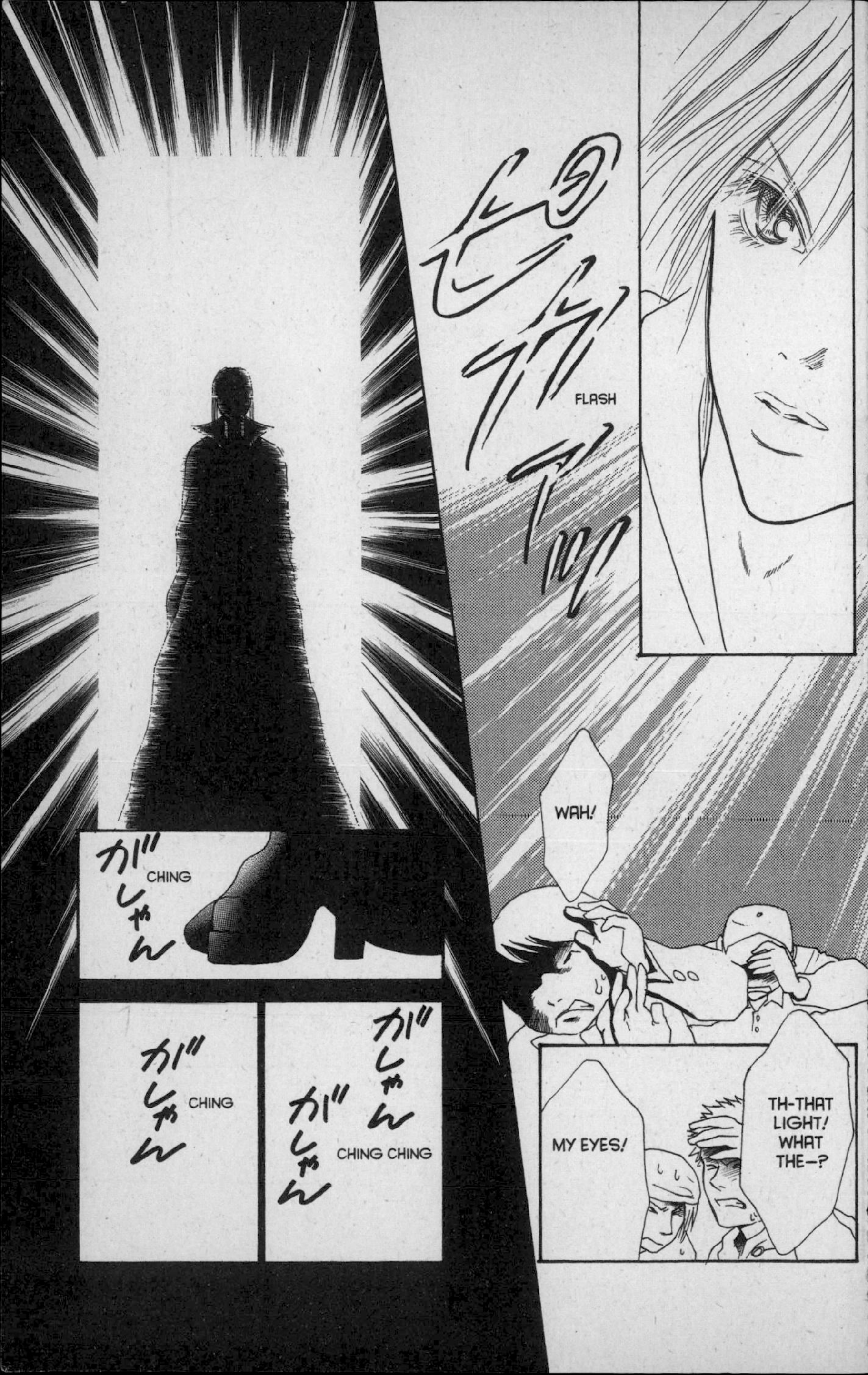
ピカァッ
FLASH
WAH!
TH-THAT LIGHT! WHAT THE—?
MY EYES!
がしゃん
CHING
がしゃん
がしゃん
CHING CHING
がしゃん
CHING

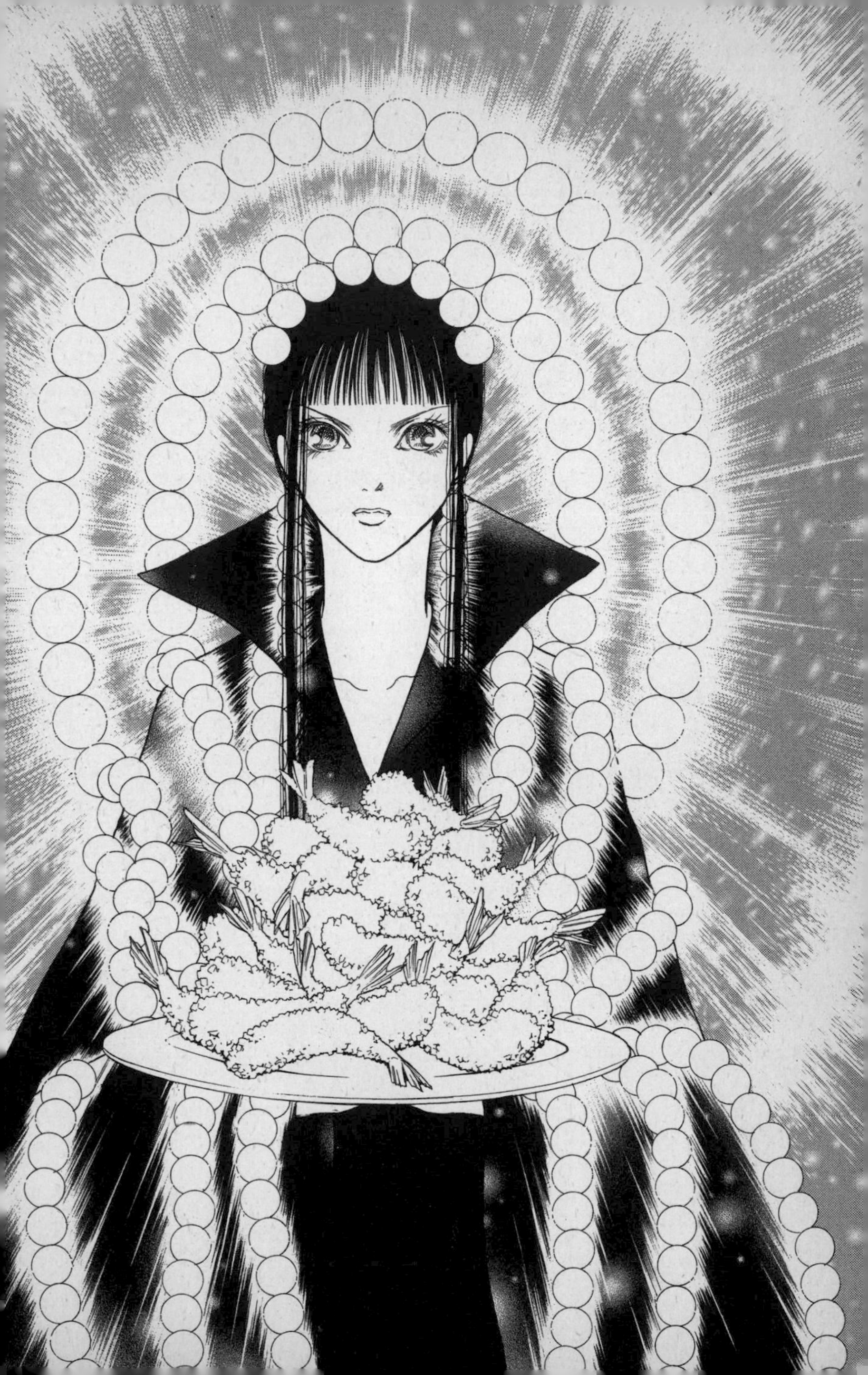

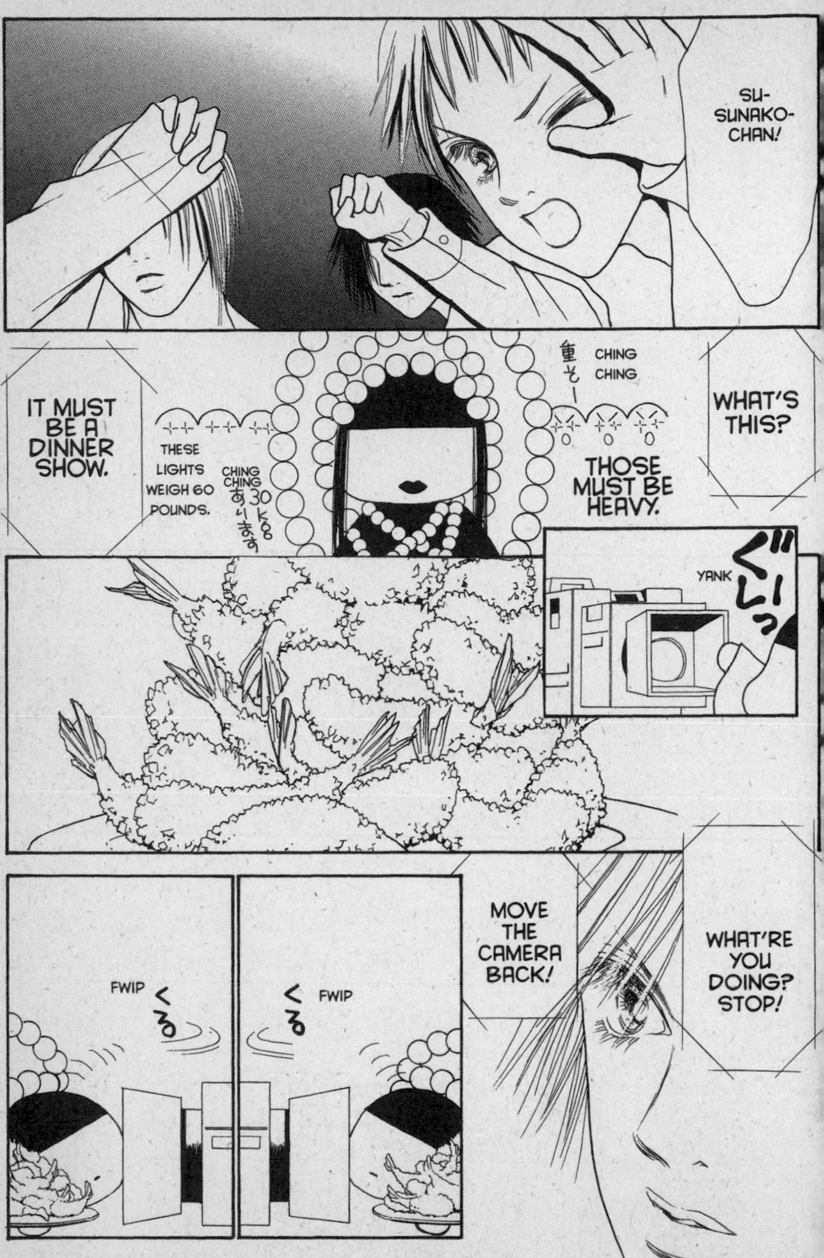

SU-SUNAKO-CHAN!
WHAT'S THIS?
THOSE MUST BE HEAVY.
CHING CHING
重そー
THESE LIGHTS WEIGH 60 POUNDS.
CHING CHING
30kgあります
IT MUST BE A DINNER SHOW.
YANK
ぐいっ
WHAT'RE YOU DOING? STOP!
MOVE THE CAMERA BACK!
FWIP
くる
FWIP
くる

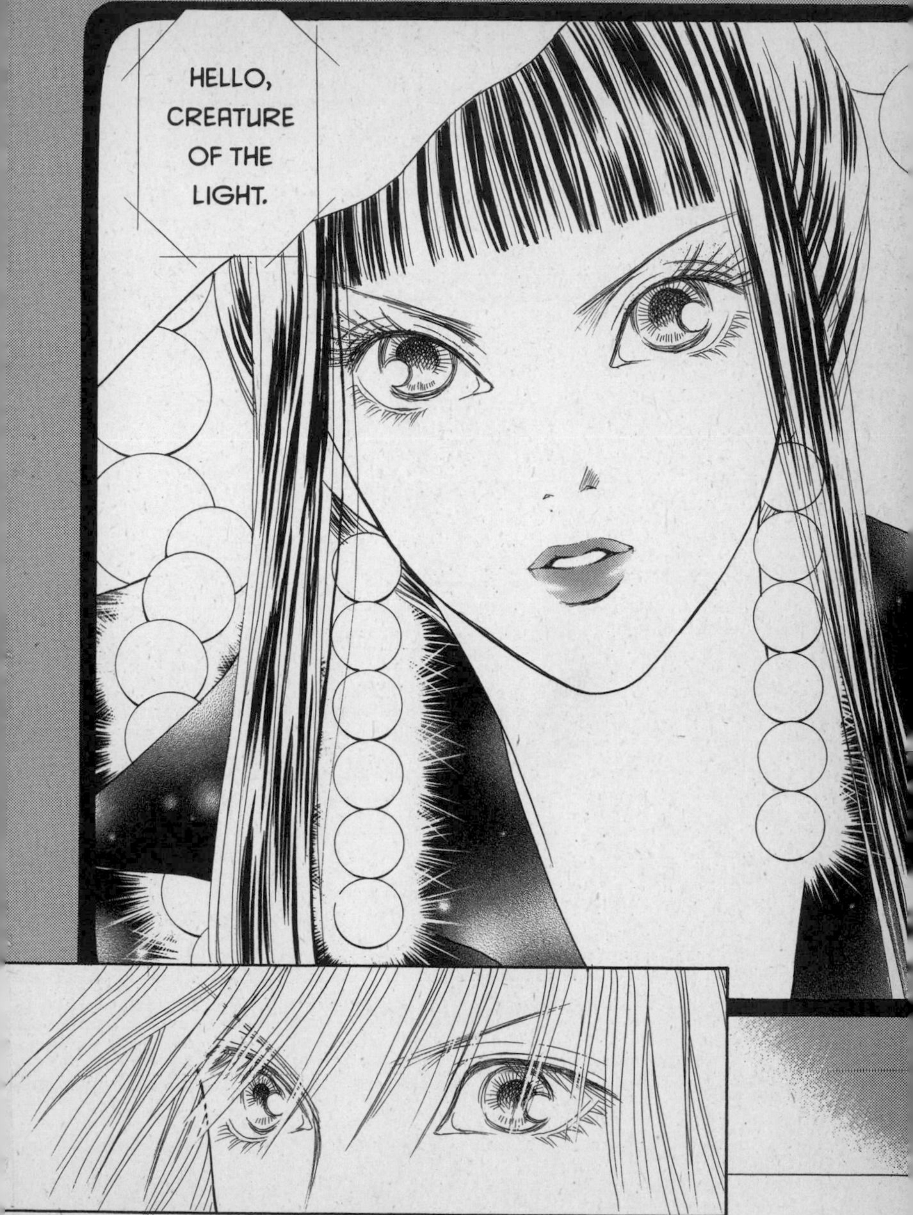
HELLO, CREATURE OF THE LIGHT.

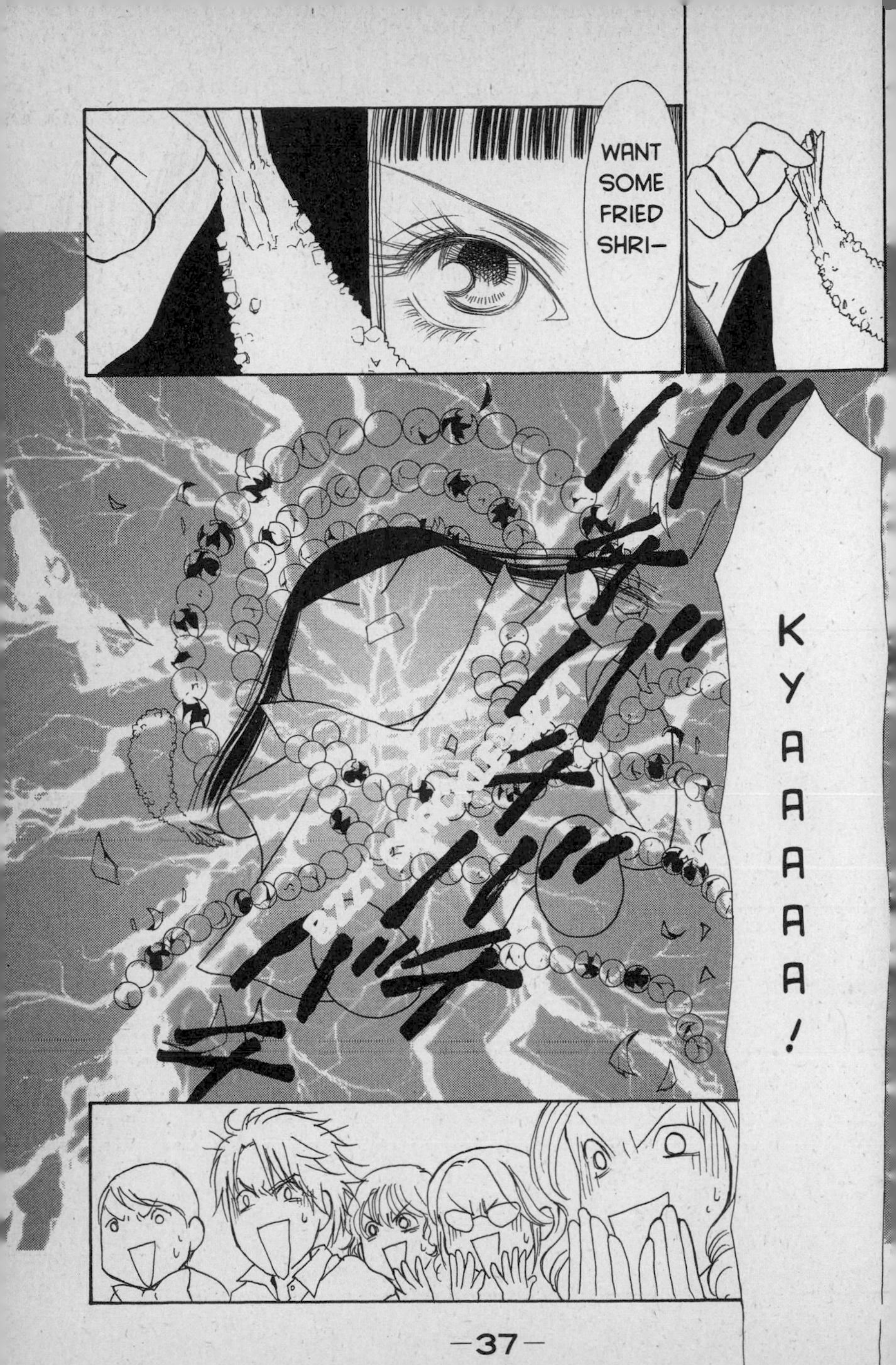
WANT SOME FRIED SHRI–
KYAAAAA!
BZZT

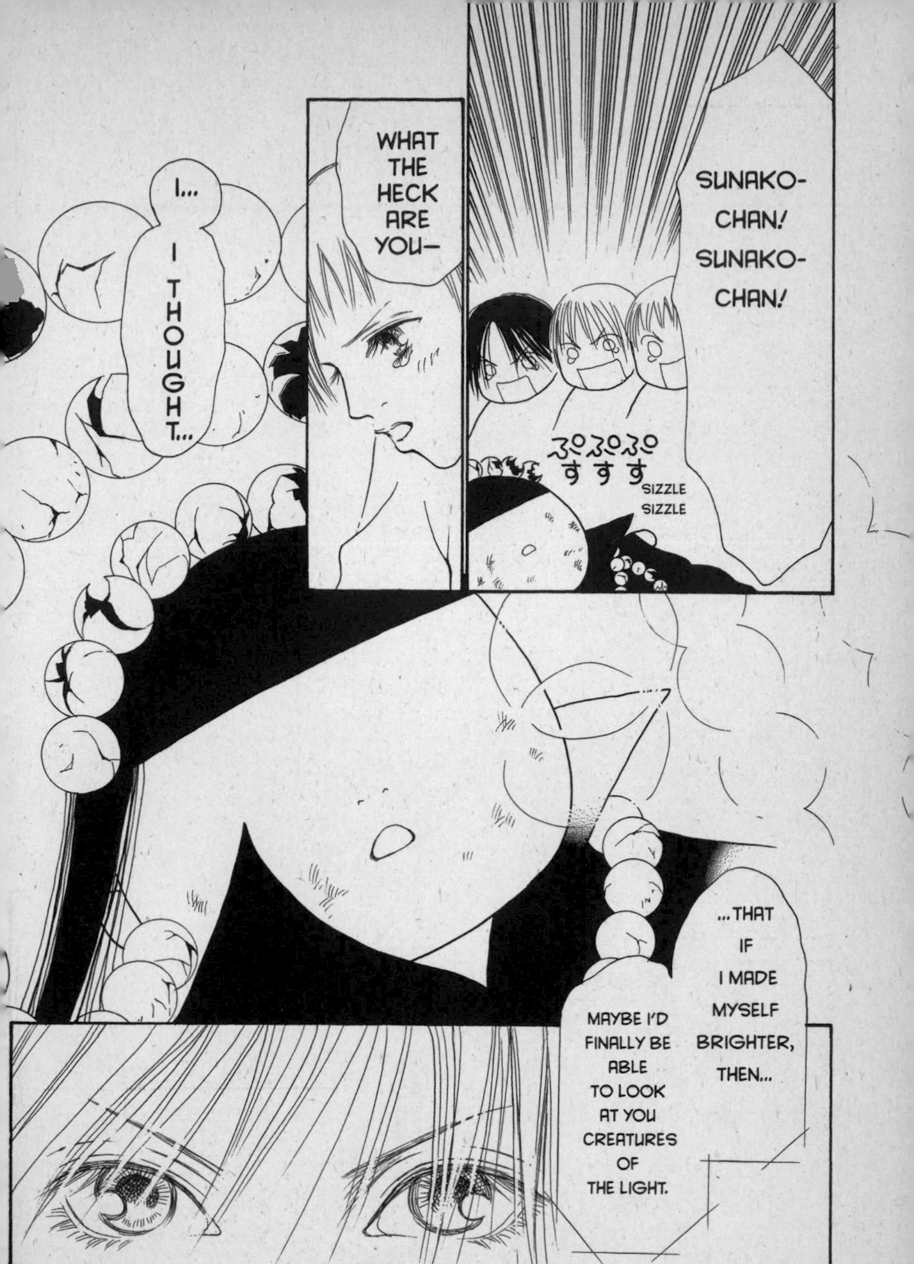
SUNAKO-CHAN! SUNAKO-CHAN!
ぷすぷすぷす
SIZZLE SIZZLE
WHAT THE HECK ARE YOU—
I...
I THOUGHT...
...THAT IF I MADE MYSELF BRIGHTER, THEN...
MAYBE I'D FINALLY BE ABLE TO LOOK AT YOU CREATURES OF THE LIGHT.

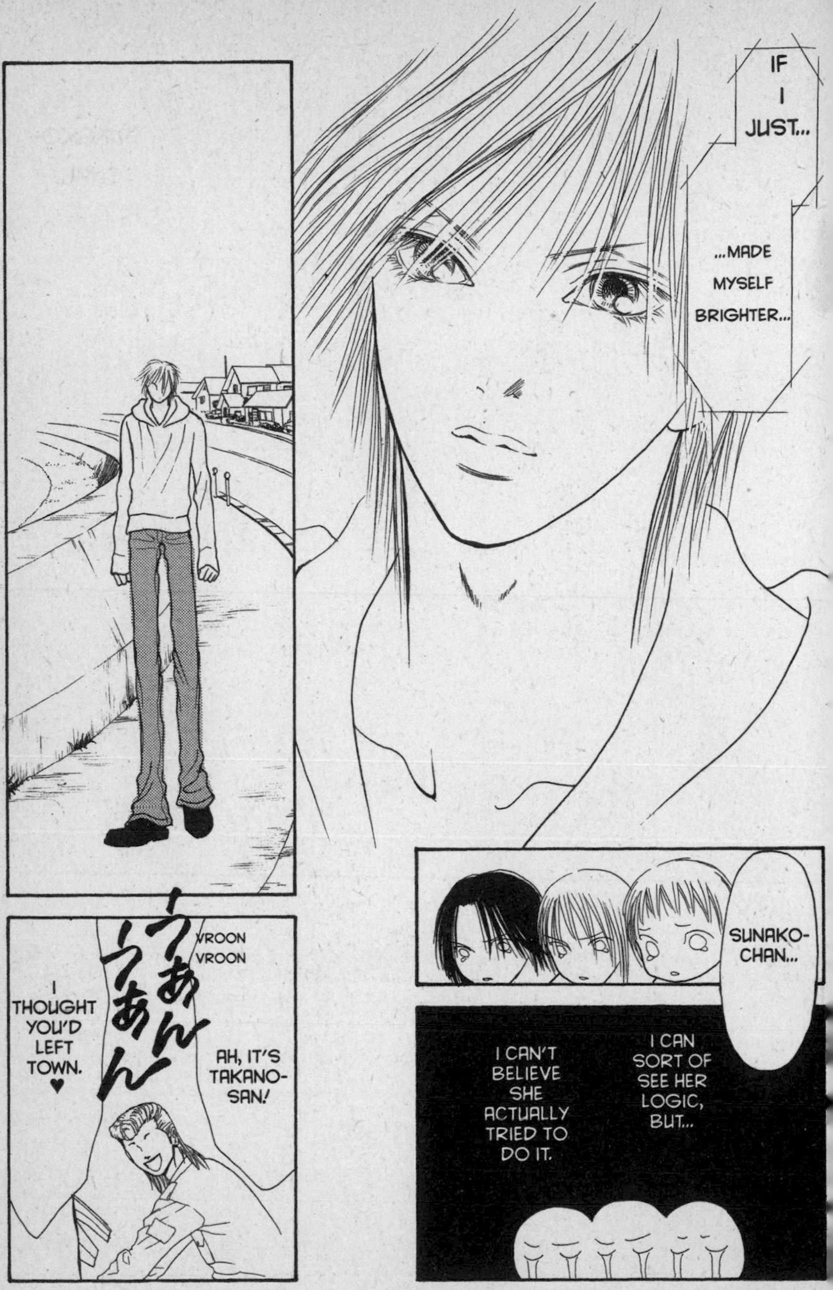
IF I JUST...
...MADE MYSELF BRIGHTER...
SUNAKO-CHAN...
I CAN SORT OF SEE HER LOGIC, BUT...
I CAN'T BELIEVE SHE ACTUALLY TRIED TO DO IT.
うあんうあん
VROON VROON
AH, IT'S TAKANO-SAN!
I THOUGHT YOU'D LEFT TOWN. ♥

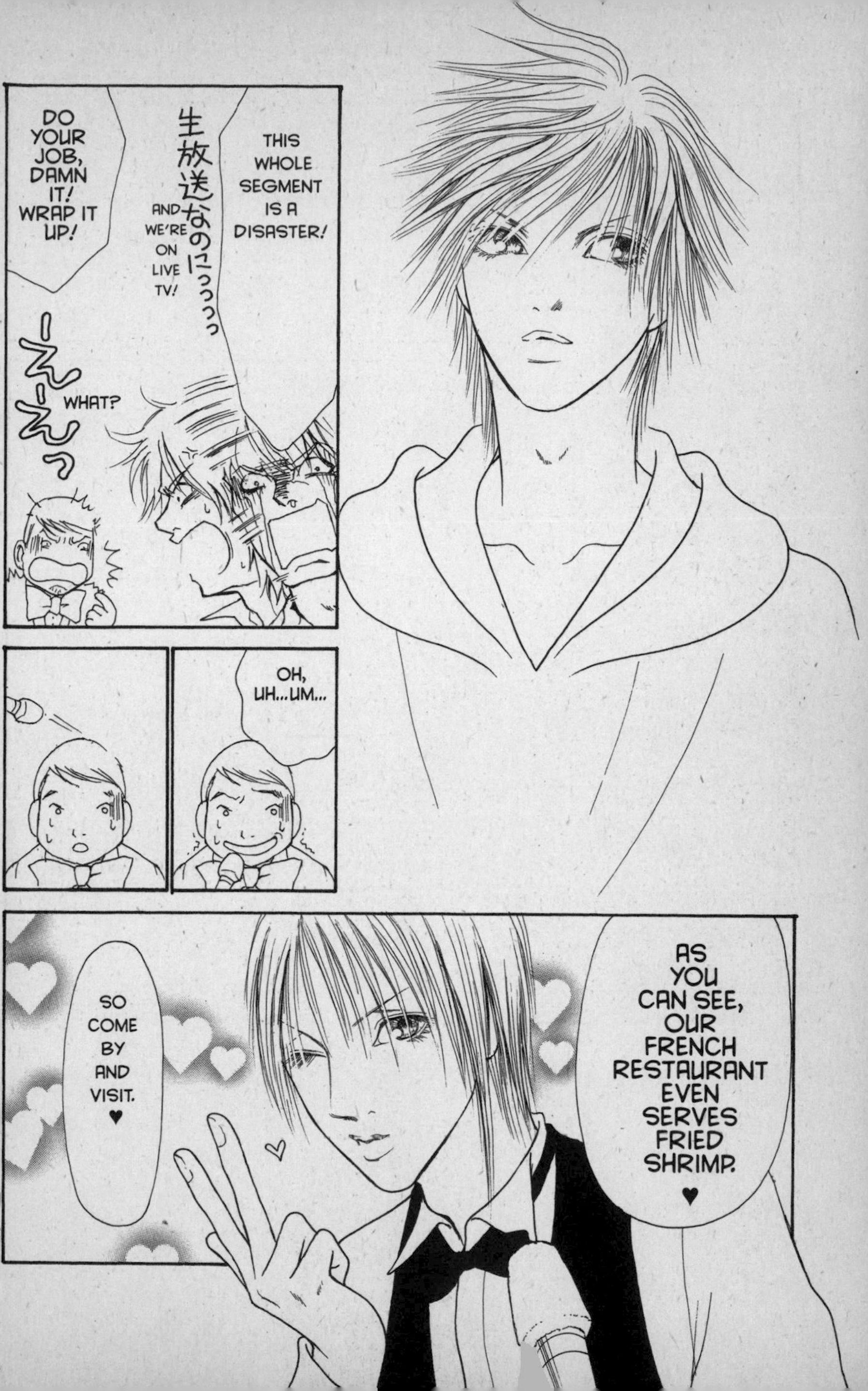
THIS WHOLE SEGMENT IS A DISASTER!
生放送なのにっっっ
AND WE'RE ON LIVE TV!
DO YOUR JOB, DAMN IT! WRAP IT UP!
えーえっ
WHAT?
OH, UH...UM...
AS YOU CAN SEE, OUR FRENCH RESTAURANT EVEN SERVES FRIED SHRIMP. ♥
SO COME BY AND VISIT. ♥

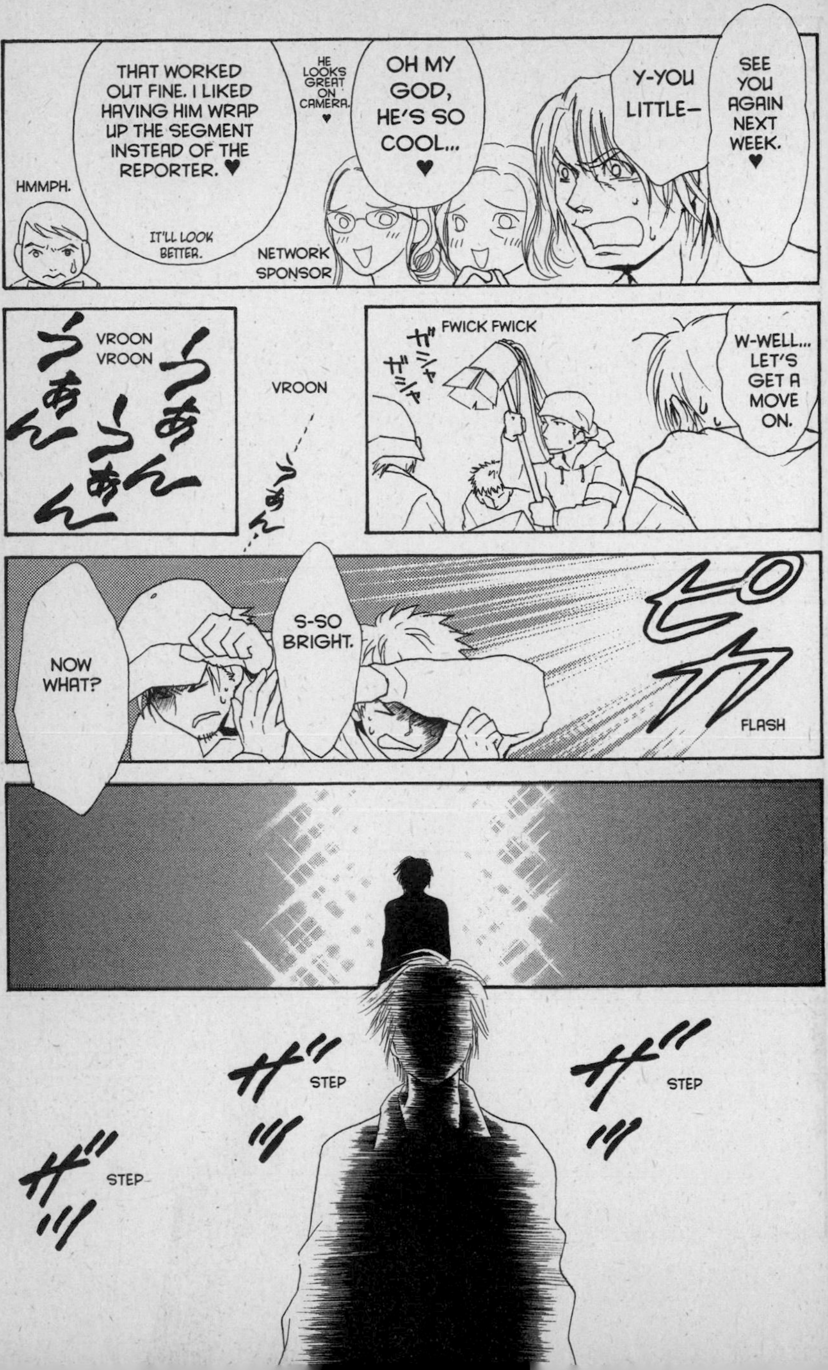
SEE YOU AGAIN NEXT WEEK. ♥
Y-YOU LITTLE—
OH MY GOD, HE'S SO COOL... ♥
HE LOOKS GREAT ON CAMERA. ♥
NETWORK SPONSOR
THAT WORKED OUT FINE. I LIKED HAVING HIM WRAP UP THE SEGMENT INSTEAD OF THE REPORTER. ♥
IT'LL LOOK BETTER.
HMMPH.
W-WELL... LET'S GET A MOVE ON.
ガシャ ガシャ
FWICK FWICK
うあん
VROON
うあん うあん うあん
VROON VROON
ピカ
FLASH
S-SO BRIGHT.
NOW WHAT?
ザッ
STEP
ザッ
STEP
ザッ
STEP-

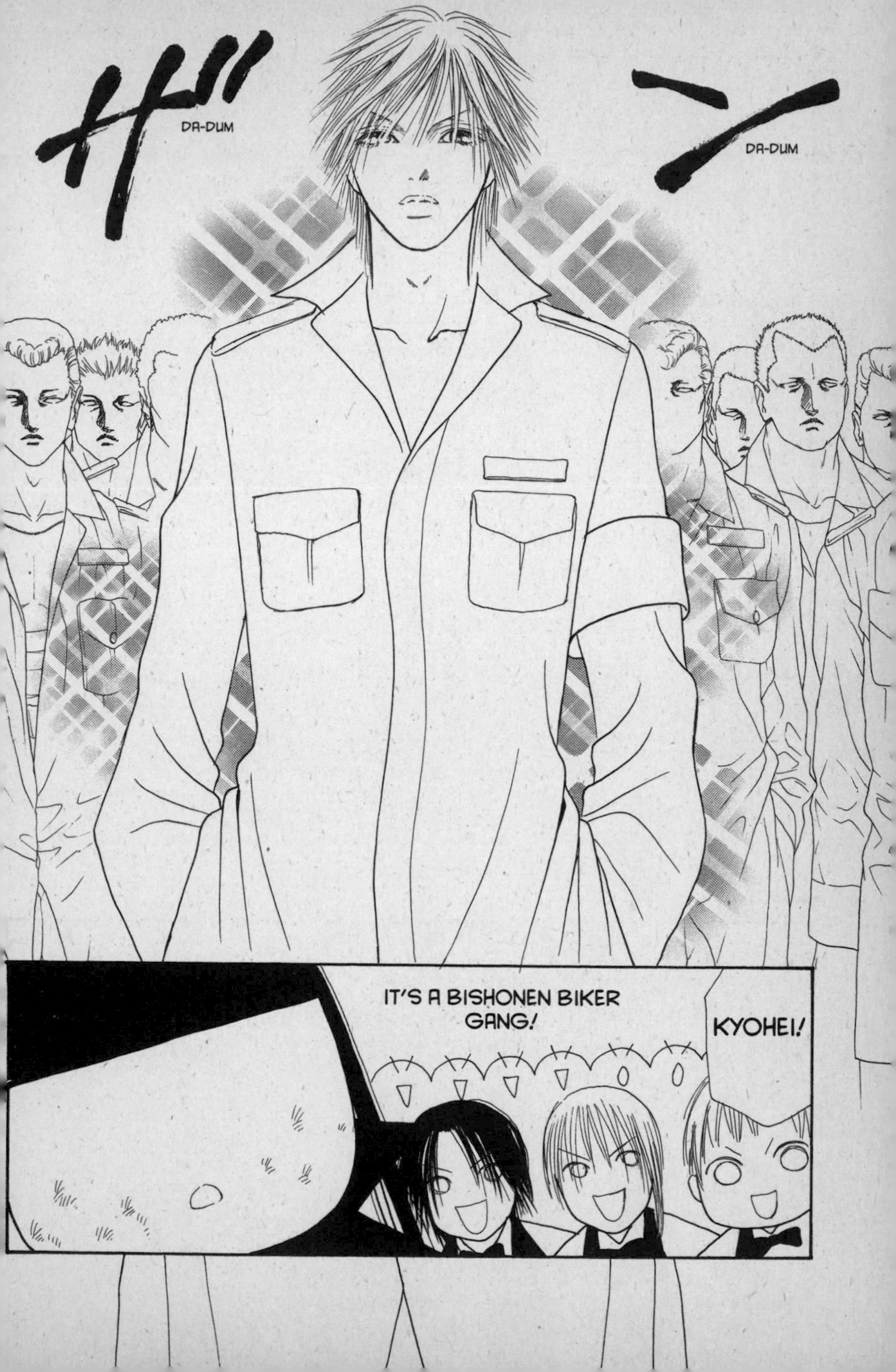
DA-DUM
DA-DUM
KYOHEI!
IT'S A BISHONEN BIKER GANG!

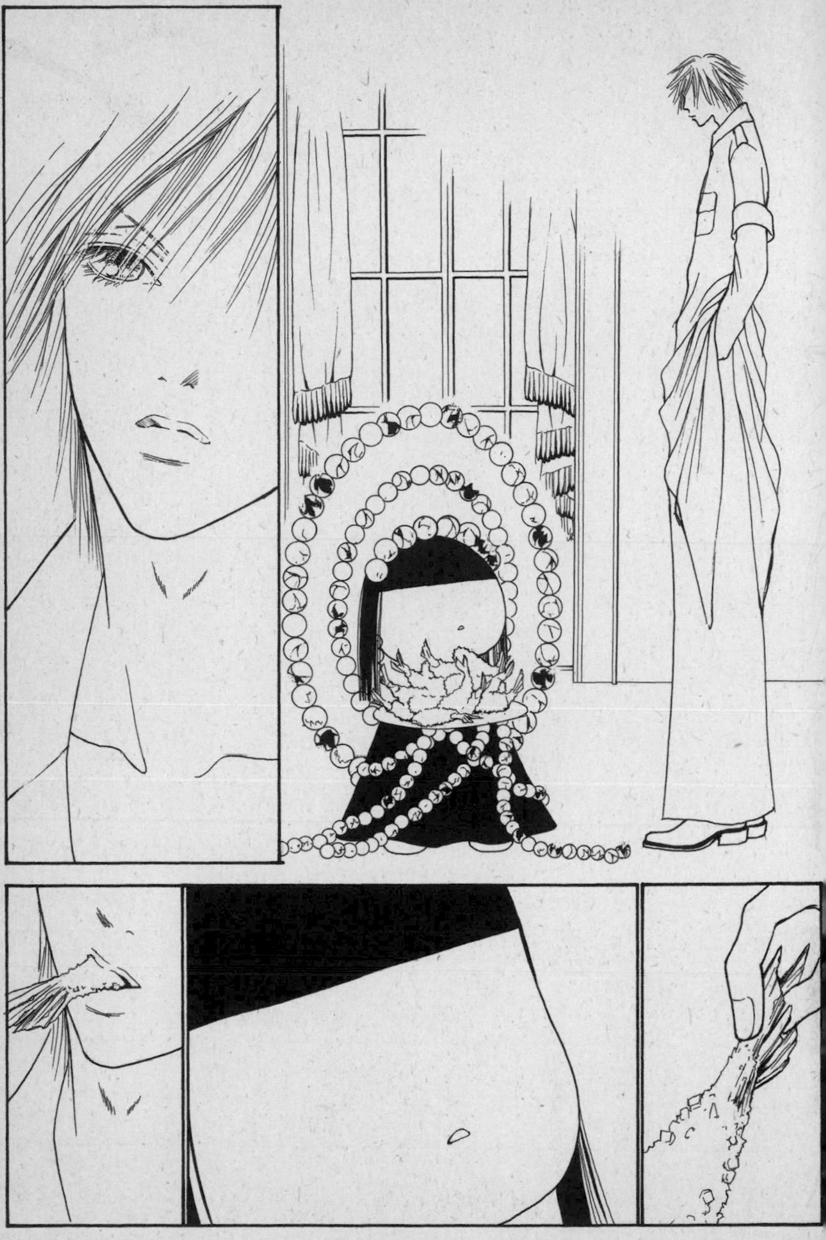

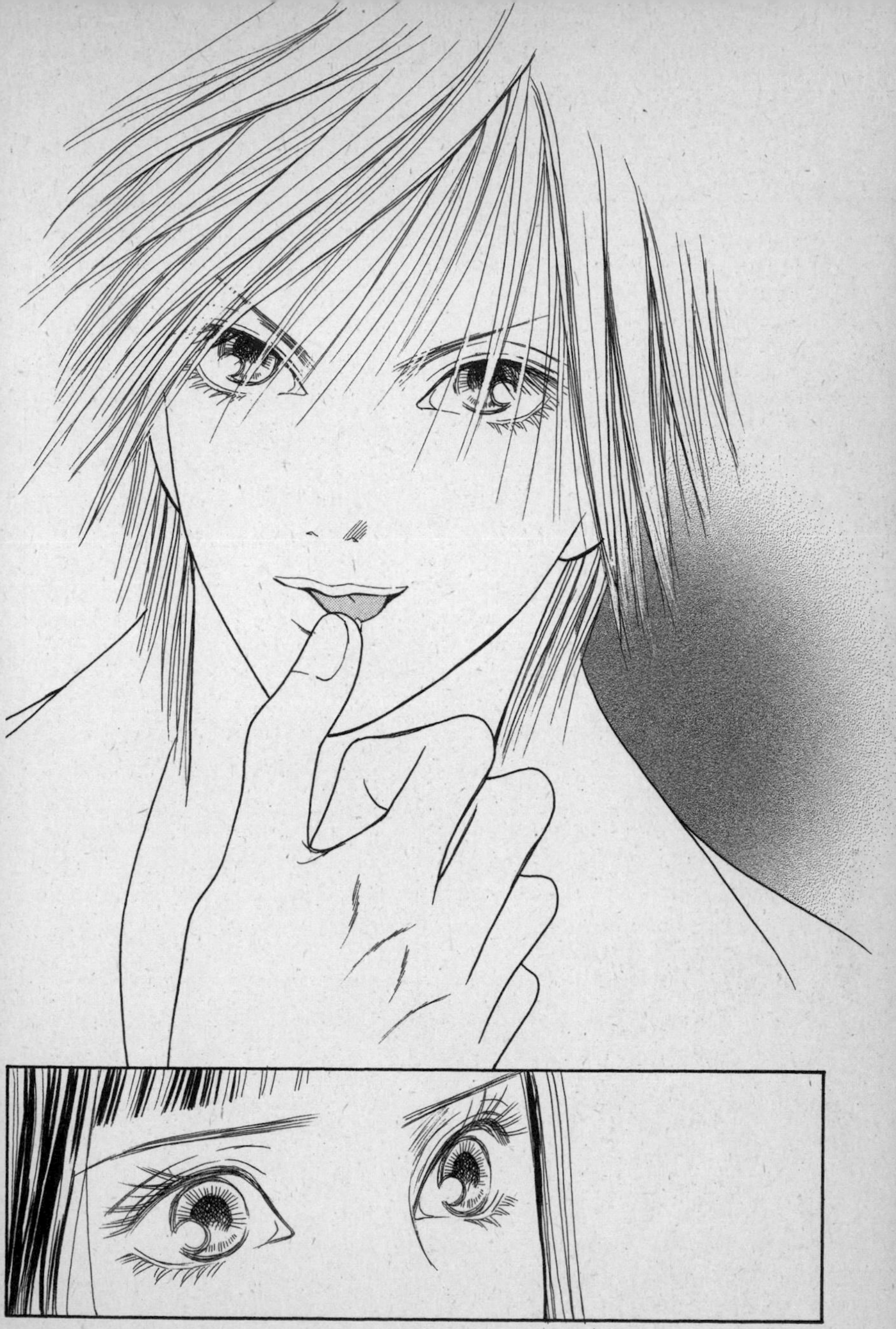

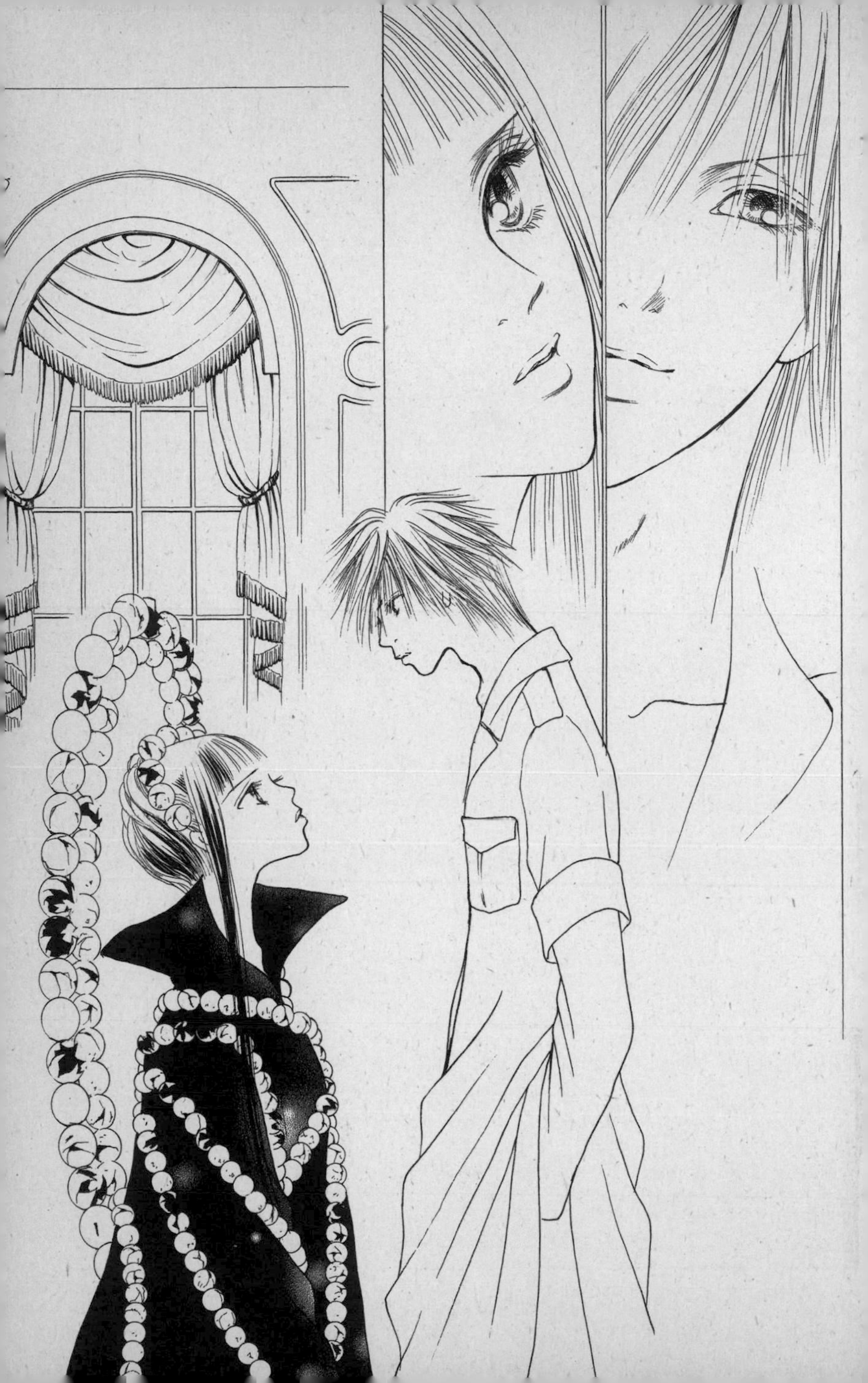

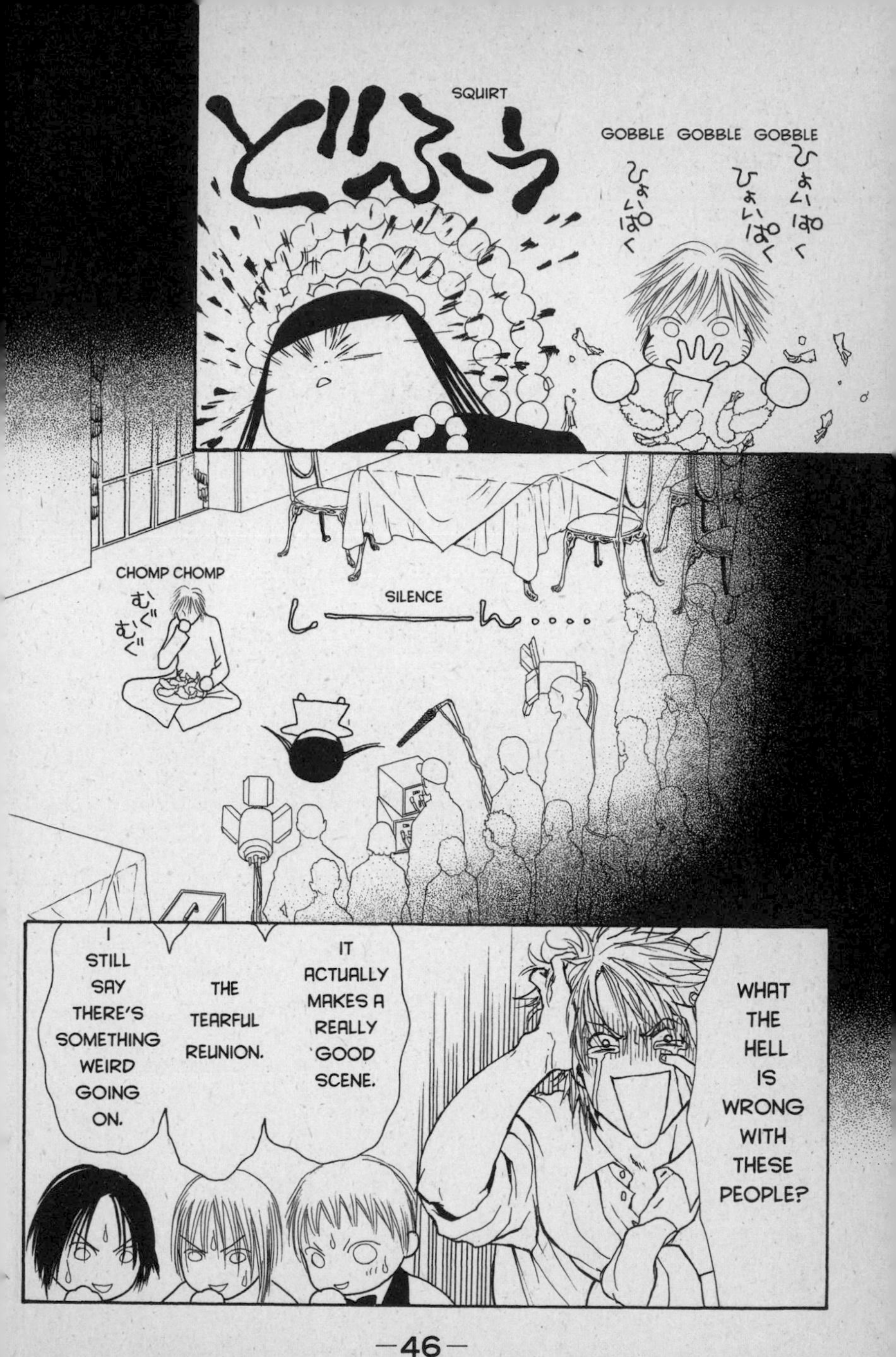
GOBBLE GOBBLE GOBBLE
ひょいぱく ひょいぱく ひょいぱく
SQUIRT
どふぅ
SILENCE
しーーん....
CHOMP CHOMP
むぐむぐ
WHAT THE HELL IS WRONG WITH THESE PEOPLE?
IT ACTUALLY MAKES A REALLY GOOD SCENE.
THE TEARFUL REUNION.
I STILL SAY THERE'S SOMETHING WEIRD GOING ON.

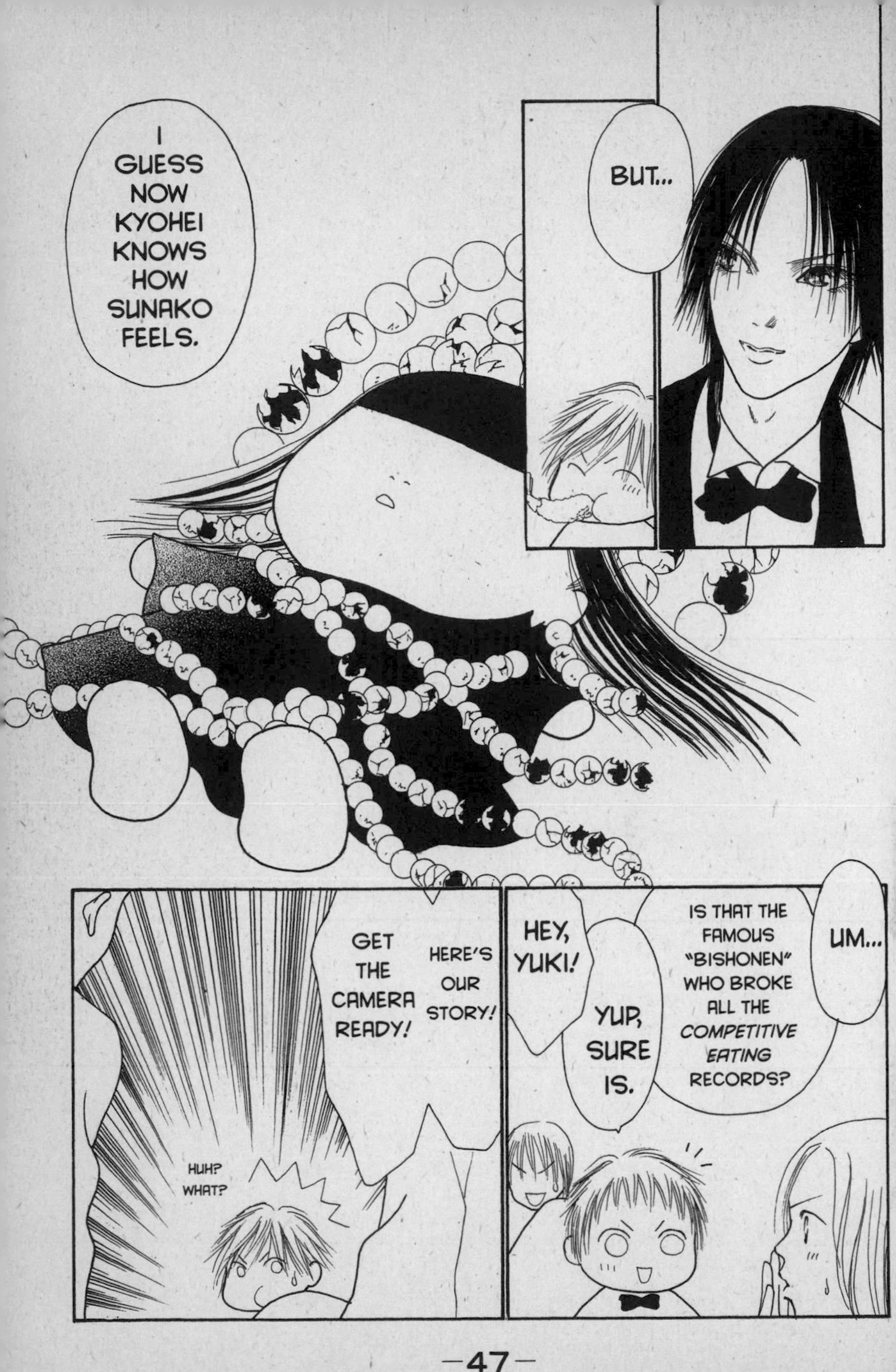
BUT...
I GUESS NOW KYOHEI KNOWS HOW SUNAKO FEELS.
UM...
IS THAT THE FAMOUS "BISHONEN" WHO BROKE ALL THE *COMPETITIVE EATING* RECORDS?
YUP, SURE IS.
HEY, YUKI!
HERE'S OUR STORY!
GET THE CAMERA READY!
HUH? WHAT?

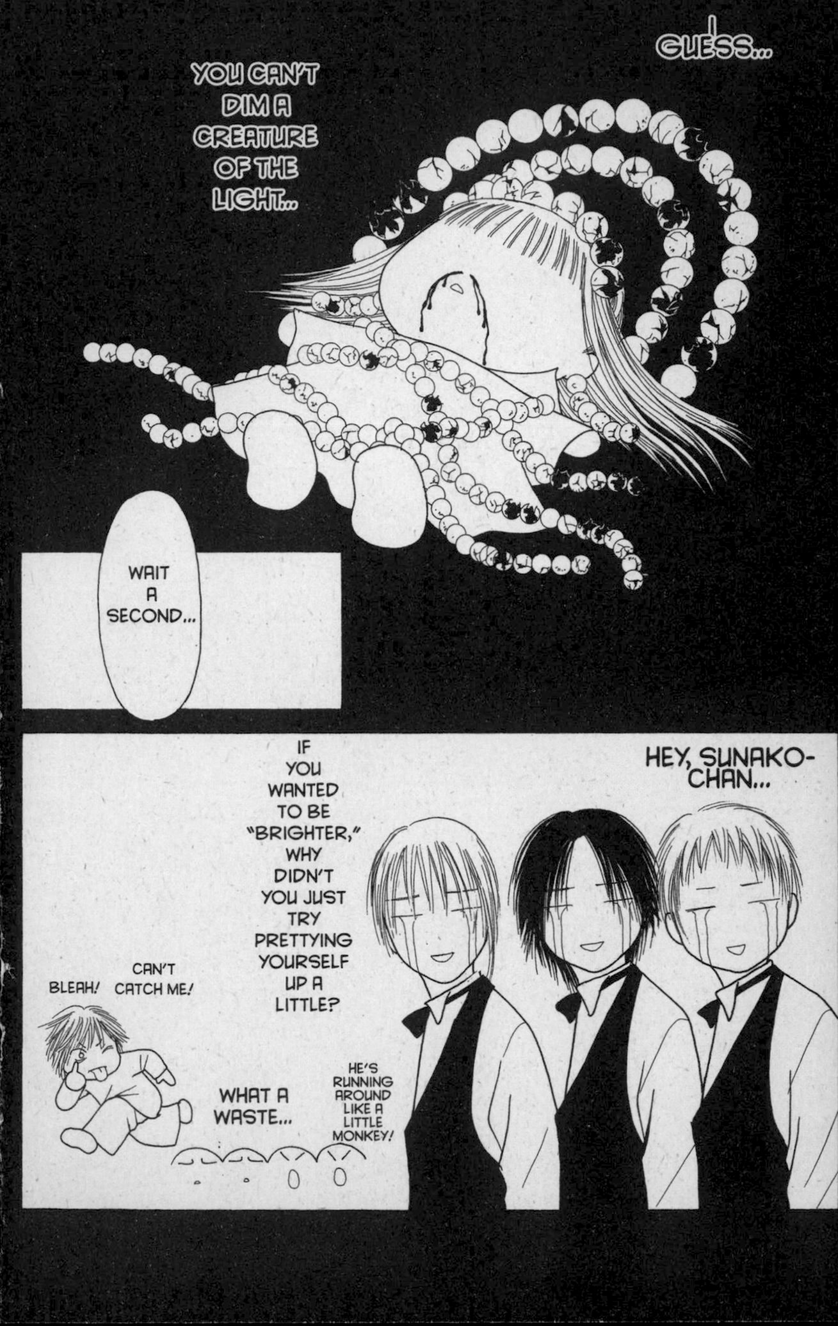
I GUESS...
YOU CAN'T DIM A CREATURE OF THE LIGHT...
WAIT A SECOND...
HEY, SUNAKO-CHAN...
IF YOU WANTED TO BE "BRIGHTER," WHY DIDN'T YOU JUST TRY PRETTYING YOURSELF UP A LITTLE?
HE'S RUNNING AROUND LIKE A LITTLE MONKEY!
WHAT A WASTE...
CAN'T CATCH ME!
BLEAH!

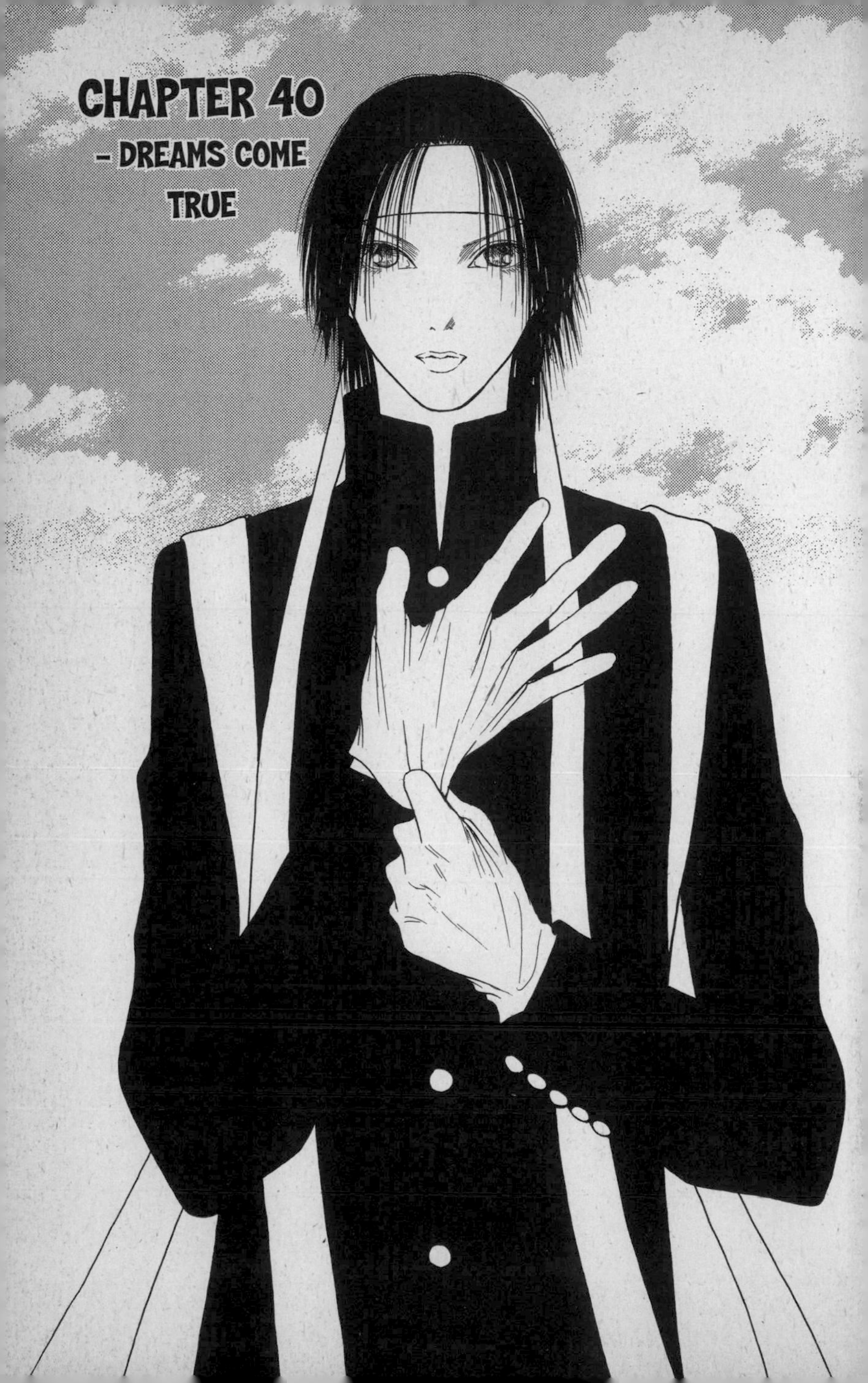
CHAPTER 40
– DREAMS COME TRUE

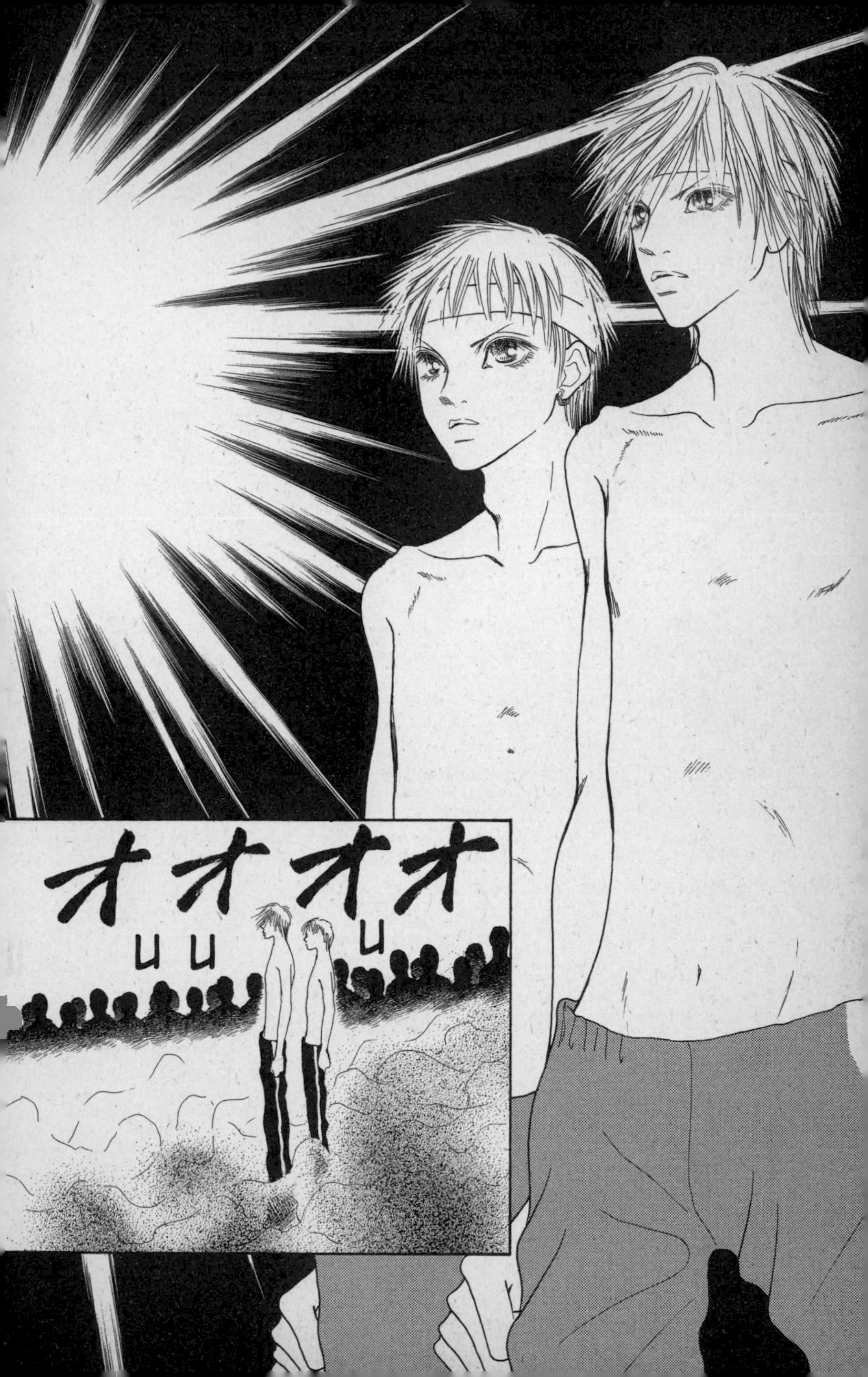
オオオオ

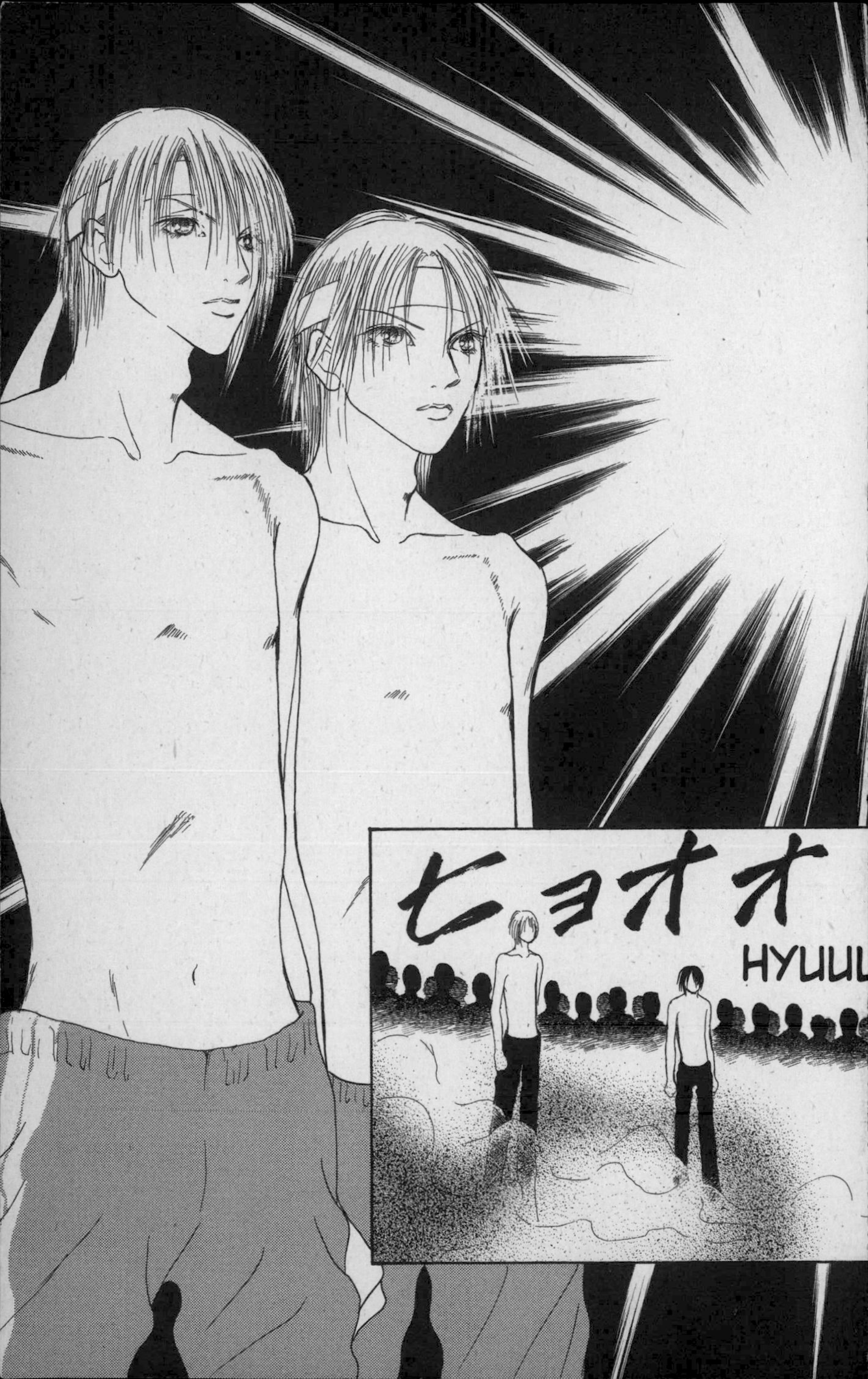
ヒョオオ
HYUUU

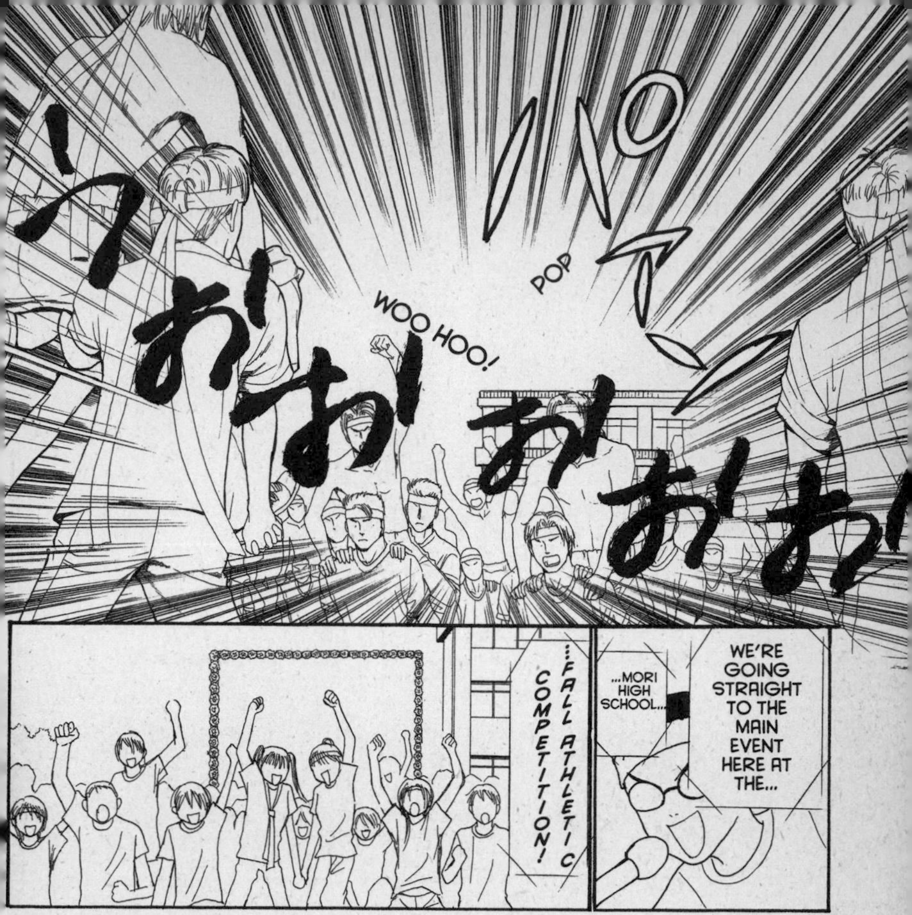
POP
WOO HOO!
WE'RE GOING STRAIGHT TO THE MAIN EVENT HERE AT THE...
...MORI HIGH SCHOOL...
...FALL ATHLETIC COMPETITION!

BEHIND THE SCENES

I KNOW, I KNOW, I ENDED UP DOING IT. "THE ATHLETIC COMPETITION." BACK IN BOOK THREE, I SAID SOMETHING ABOUT NEVER WANTING TO SHOW THE GUYS DOING EXERCISE, BUT...PEOPLE CHANGE. I REALLY ENJOYED DRAWING THE BATTLE SCENE.

AT FIRST I WAS GONNA HAVE THE FOUR GUYS BE CHEERLEADERS, BUT THEN I REALIZED THAT IT WAS UNNECESSARY, SO I CUT IT. I WANTED TO DRESS THEM UP IN TRADITIONAL MALE SPIRIT LEADER GARB...REALLY HIGH GETA SHOES, BANDANAS, LONG-TAILED SHIRTS, AND DOKAN PANTS, BUT IT DIDN'T HAPPEN (EXCEPT FOR TAKENAGA).

I ALSO WANTED TO DO A REALLY VIOLENT GAME OF CAPTURE THE FLAG, AND A COSPLAY RELAY RACE. ♥

*LONG-TAILED SHIRTS ⇦ EXTRA-LONG UNIFORM SHIRTS. DOKAN PANTS ⇦ SUPER-WIDE, PUFFY PANTS.

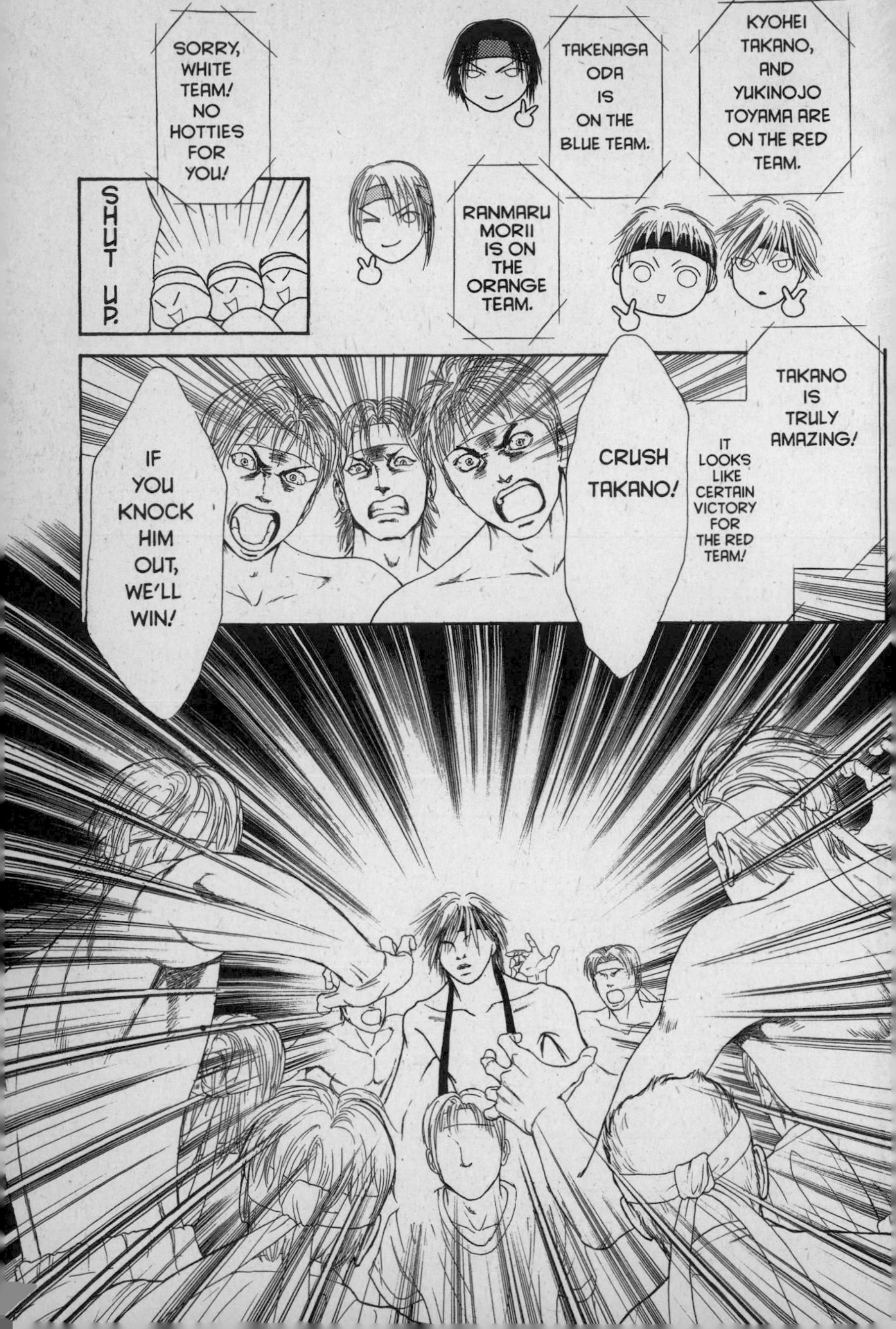
KYOHEI TAKANO, AND YUKINOJO TOYAMA ARE ON THE RED TEAM.
TAKENAGA ODA IS ON THE BLUE TEAM.
RANMARU MORII IS ON THE ORANGE TEAM.
SORRY, WHITE TEAM! NO HOTTIES FOR YOU!
SHUT UP.
TAKANO IS TRULY AMAZING!
IT LOOKS LIKE CERTAIN VICTORY FOR THE RED TEAM!
CRUSH TAKANO!
IF YOU KNOCK HIM OUT, WE'LL WIN!

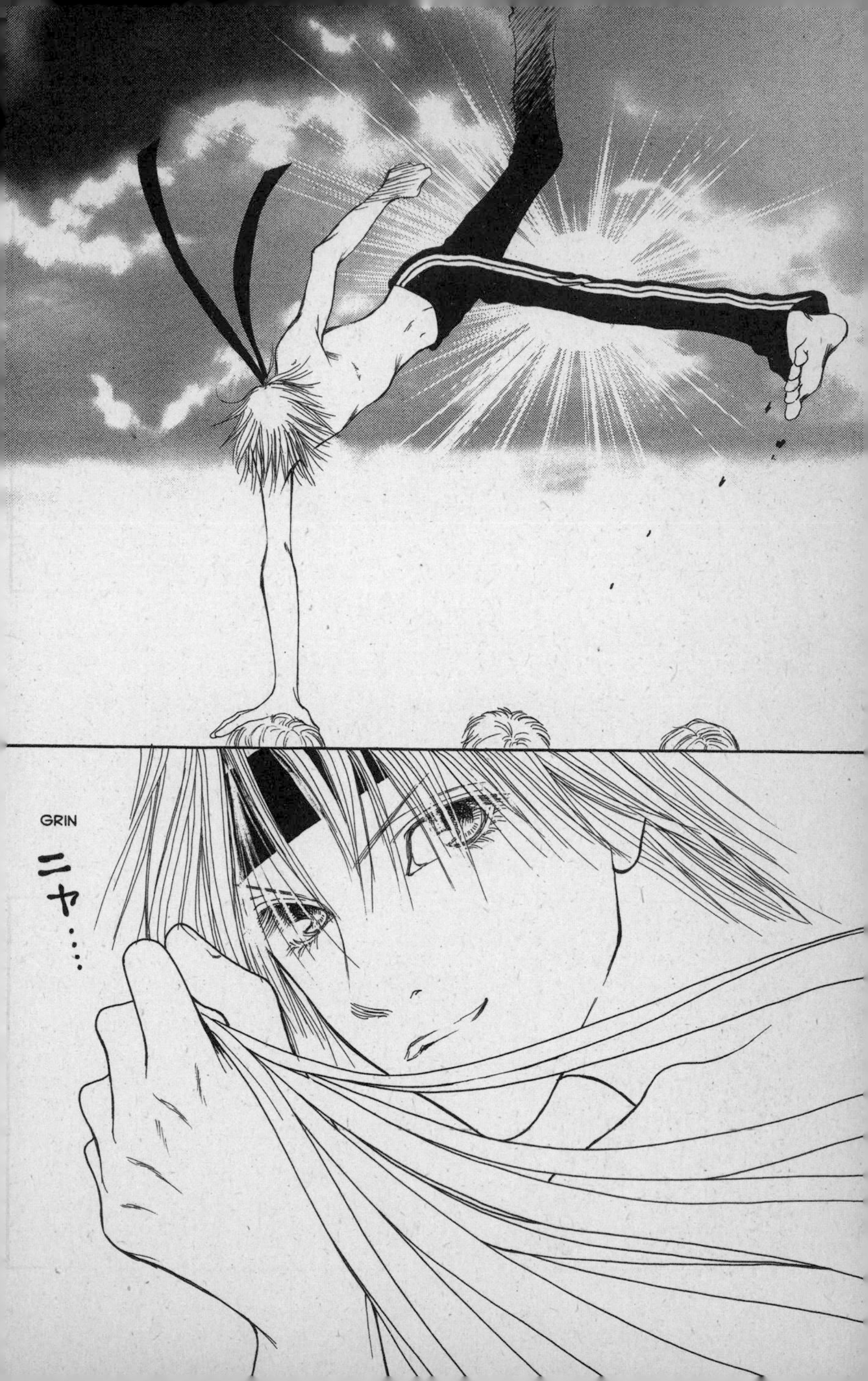
GRIN
ニヤ…

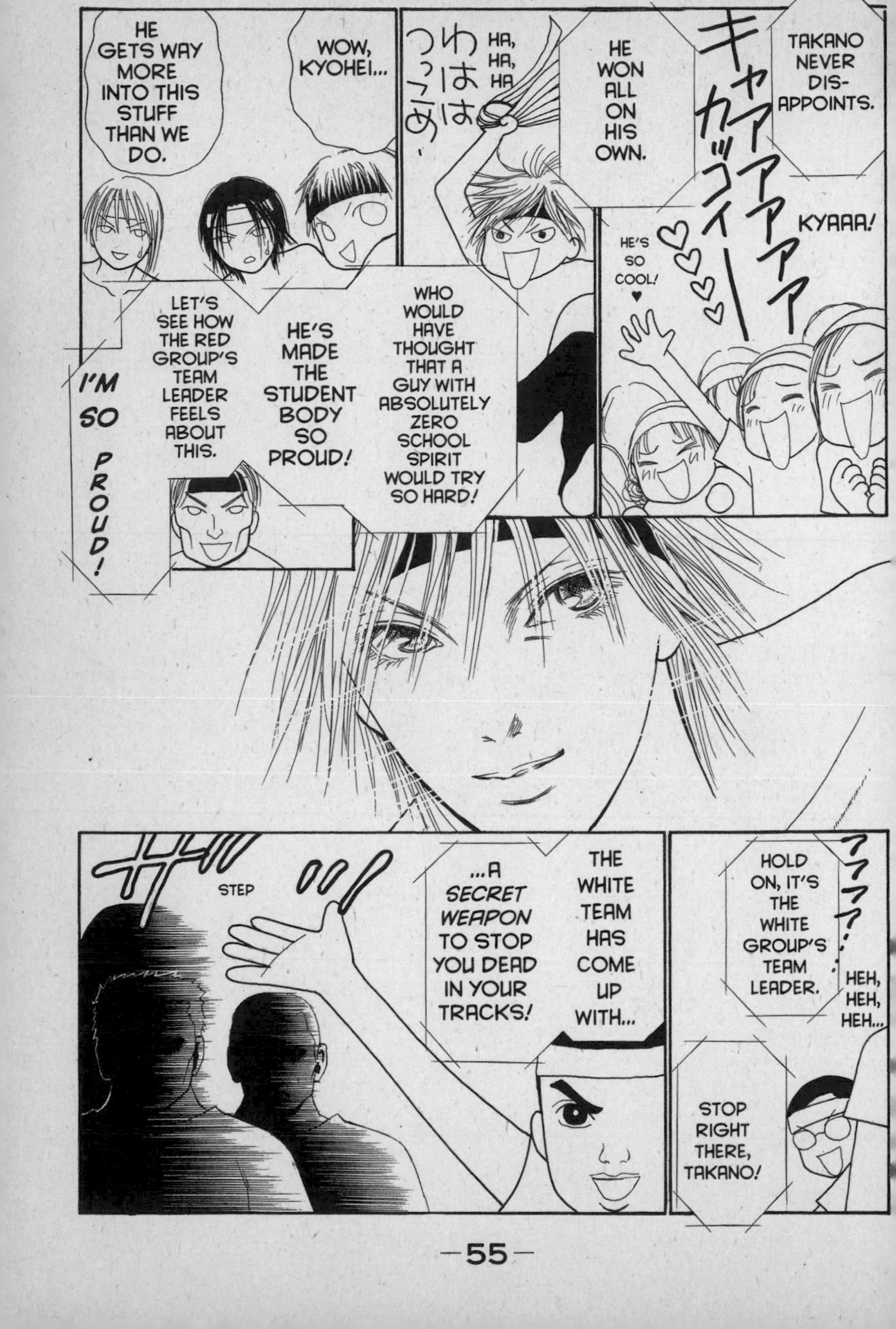
TAKANO NEVER DIS-APPOINTS.
キャアアアア
カッコイイー
KYAAA!
HE'S SO COOL! ♥
HE WON ALL ON HIS OWN.
HA, HA, HA
WOW, KYOHEI...
HE GETS WAY MORE INTO THIS STUFF THAN WE DO.
WHO WOULD HAVE THOUGHT THAT A GUY WITH ABSOLUTELY ZERO SCHOOL SPIRIT WOULD TRY SO HARD!
HE'S MADE THE STUDENT BODY SO PROUD!
LET'S SEE HOW THE RED GROUP'S TEAM LEADER FEELS ABOUT THIS.
I'M SO PROUD!
HEH, HEH, HEH...
HOLD ON, IT'S THE WHITE GROUP'S TEAM LEADER.
STOP RIGHT THERE, TAKANO!
THE WHITE TEAM HAS COME UP WITH...
...A SECRET WEAPON TO STOP YOU DEAD IN YOUR TRACKS!
STEP

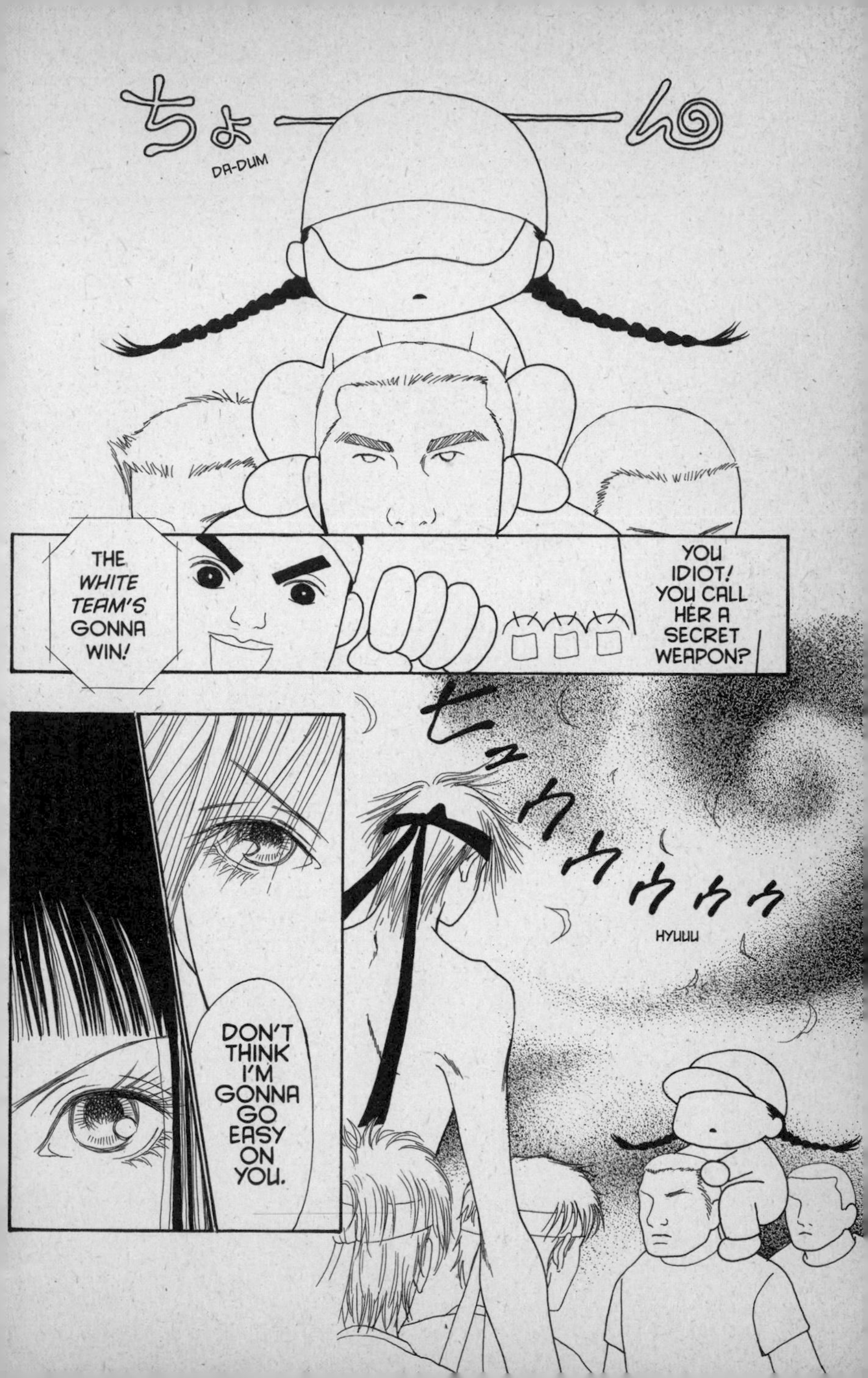
ちょーーーーん
DA-DUM
YOU IDIOT! YOU CALL HER A SECRET WEAPON?
THE *WHITE* TEAM'S GONNA WIN!
ヒュウウウウウウ
HYUUU
DON'T THINK I'M GONNA GO EASY ON YOU.

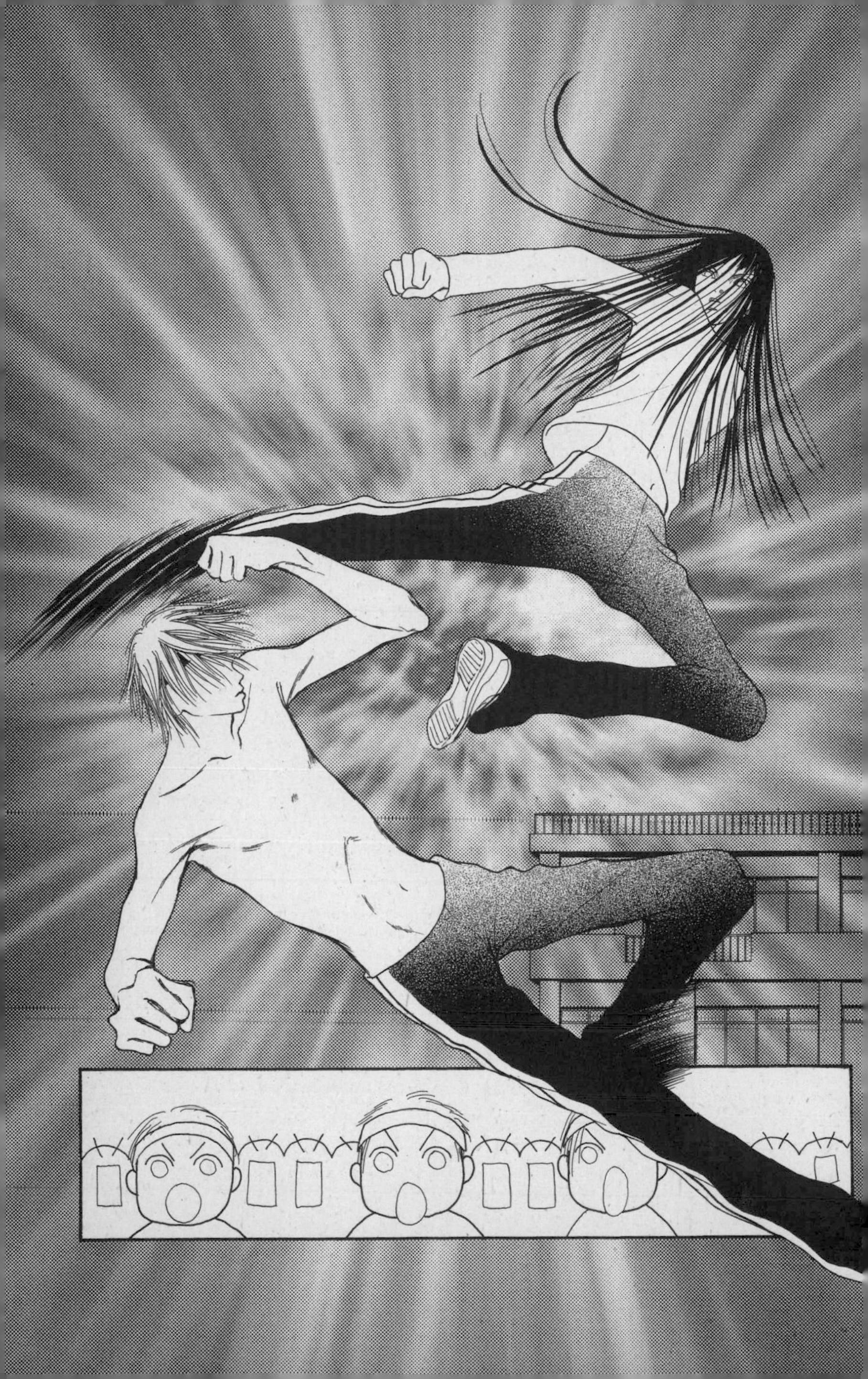

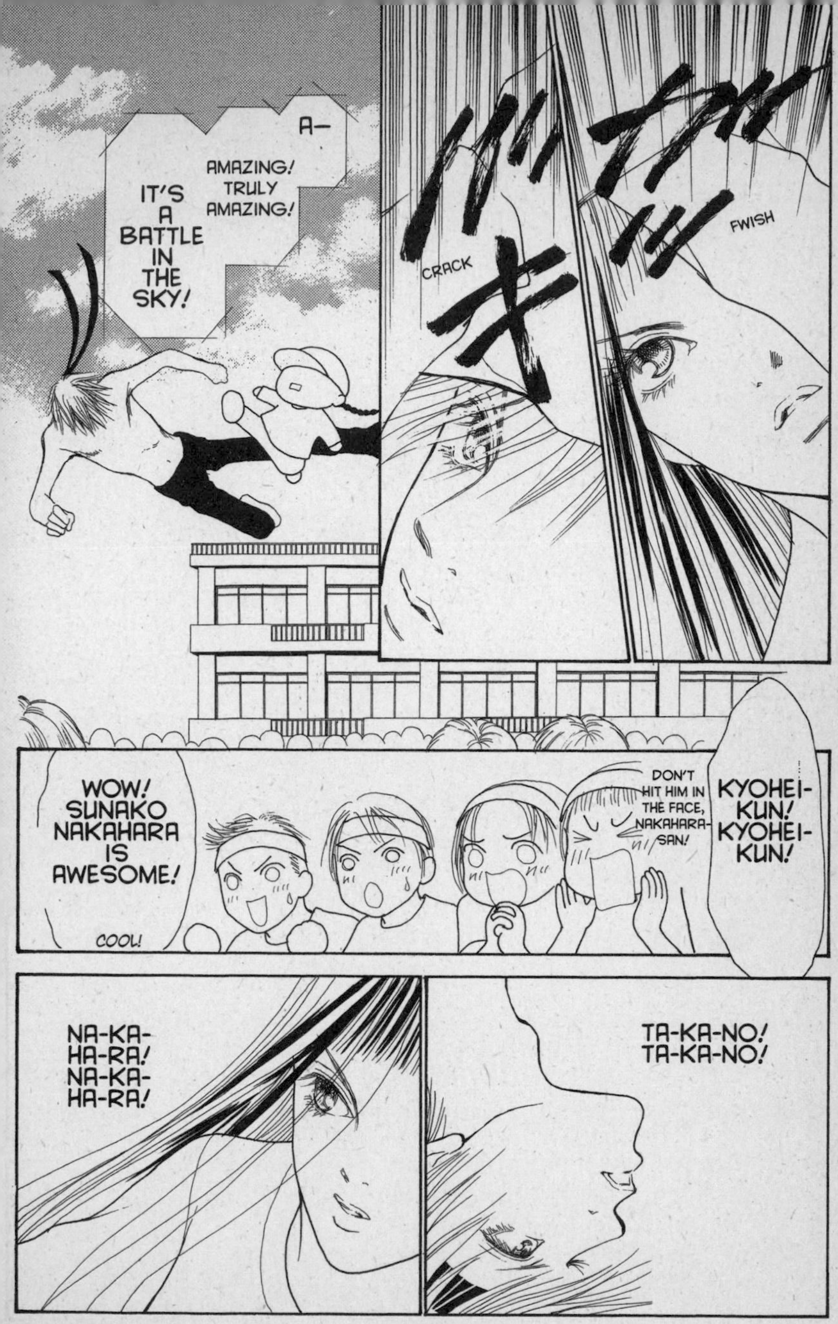
CRACK
FWISH
A—
AMAZING! TRULY AMAZING!
IT'S A BATTLE IN THE SKY!
KYOHEI-KUN! KYOHEI-KUN!
DON'T HIT HIM IN THE FACE, NAKAHARA-SAN!
WOW! SUNAKO NAKAHARA IS AWESOME!
COOL!
TA-KA-NO! TA-KA-NO!
NA-KA-HA-RA! NA-KA-HA-RA!

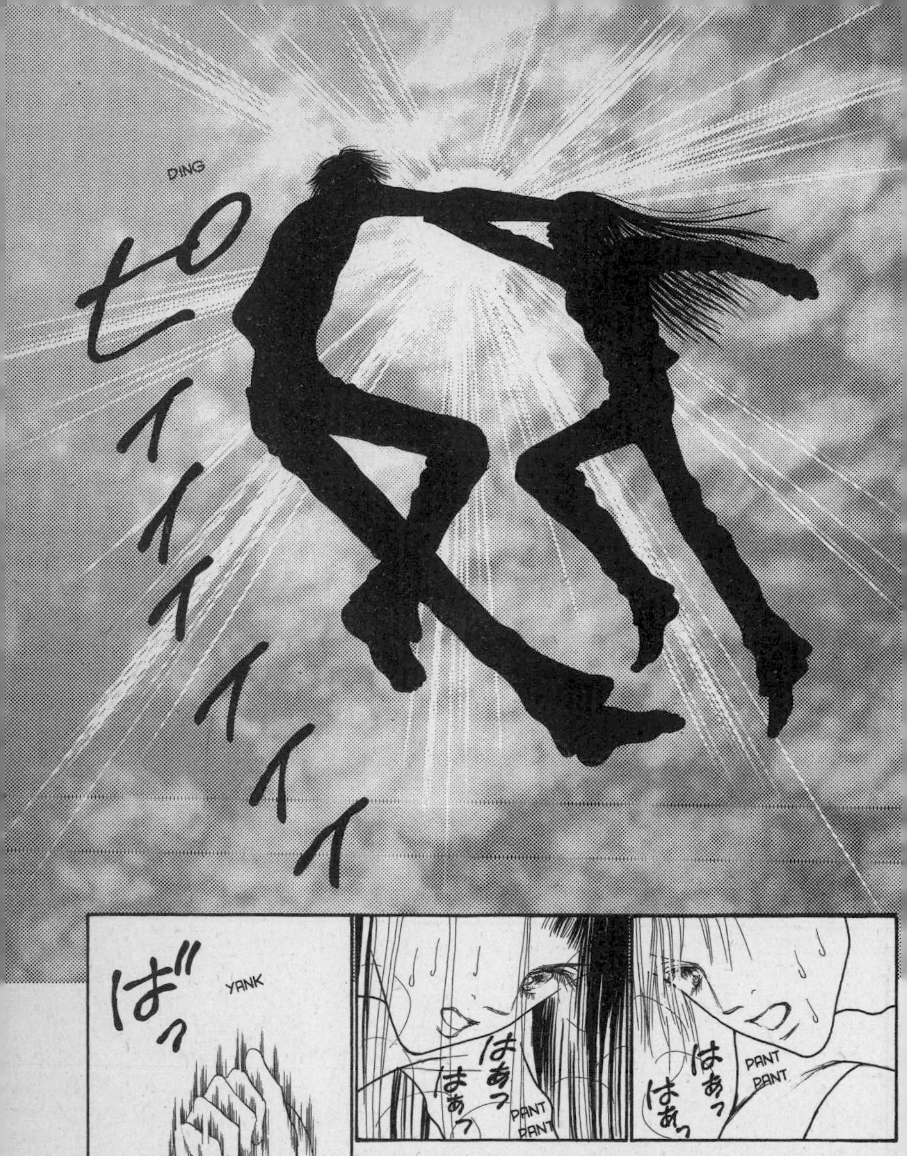
ピイイイイイ
DING
はあっ はあっ
PANT PANT
はあっ はあっ
PANT PANT
WH—
WHO WON?
ばっ
YANK

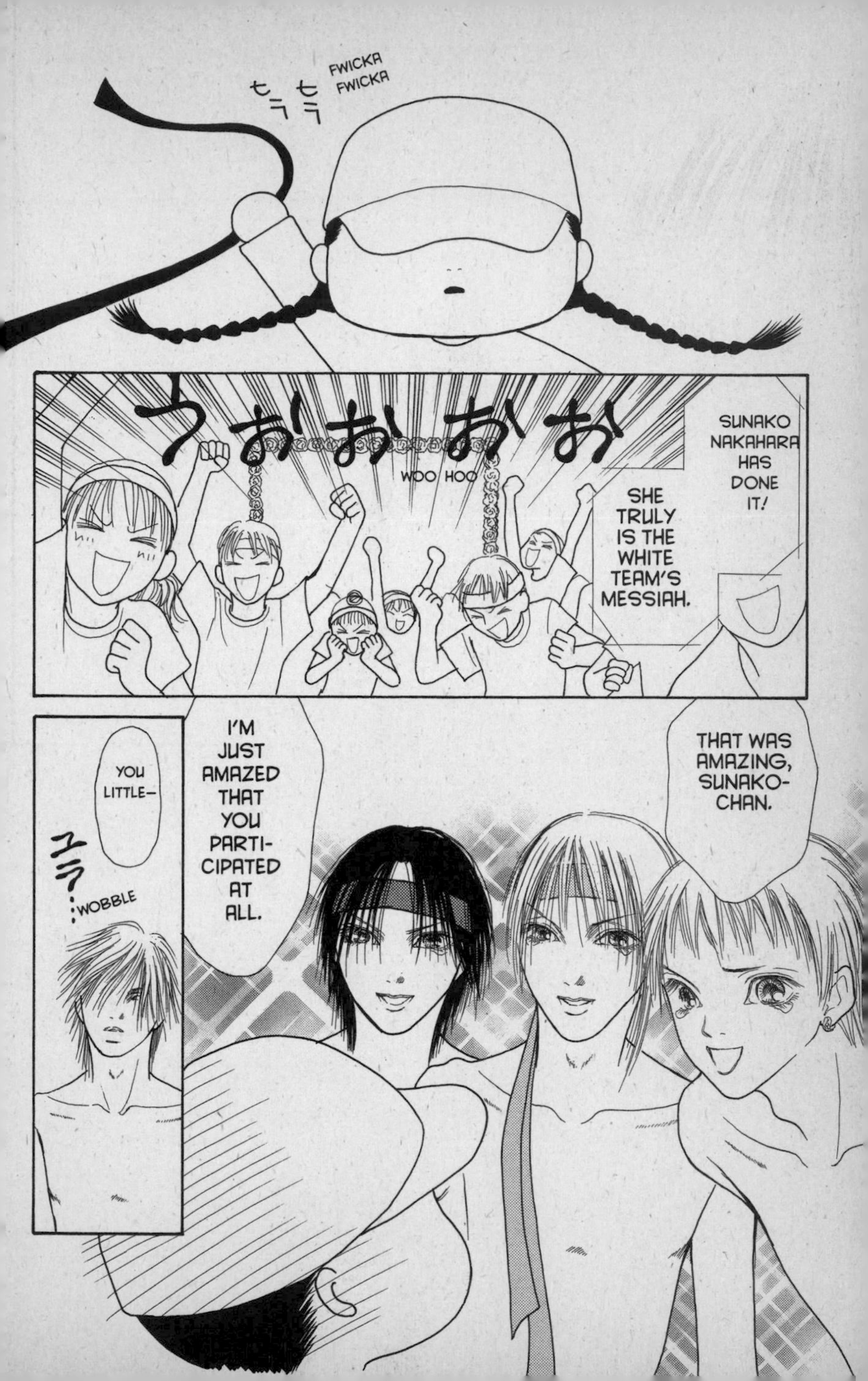
ヒラヒラ
FWICKA FWICKA
うおおおお
WOO HOO
SUNAKO NAKAHARA HAS DONE IT!
SHE TRULY IS THE WHITE TEAM'S MESSIAH.
THAT WAS AMAZING, SUNAKO-CHAN.
I'M JUST AMAZED THAT YOU PARTICIPATED AT ALL.
YOU LITTLE—
ユラ…
WOBBLE

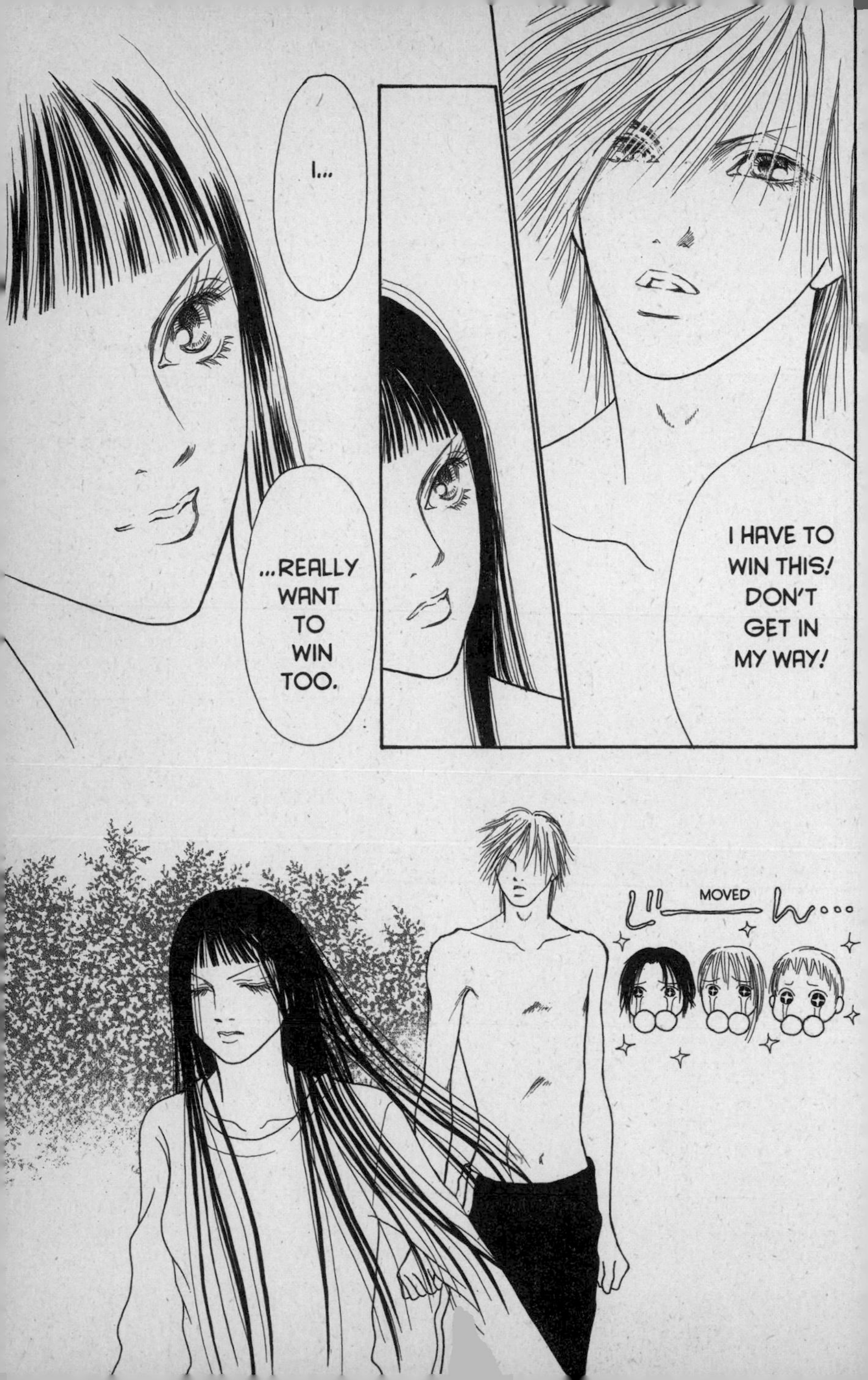
I HAVE TO WIN THIS! DON'T GET IN MY WAY!
I...
...REALLY WANT TO WIN TOO.
じーん…
MOVED

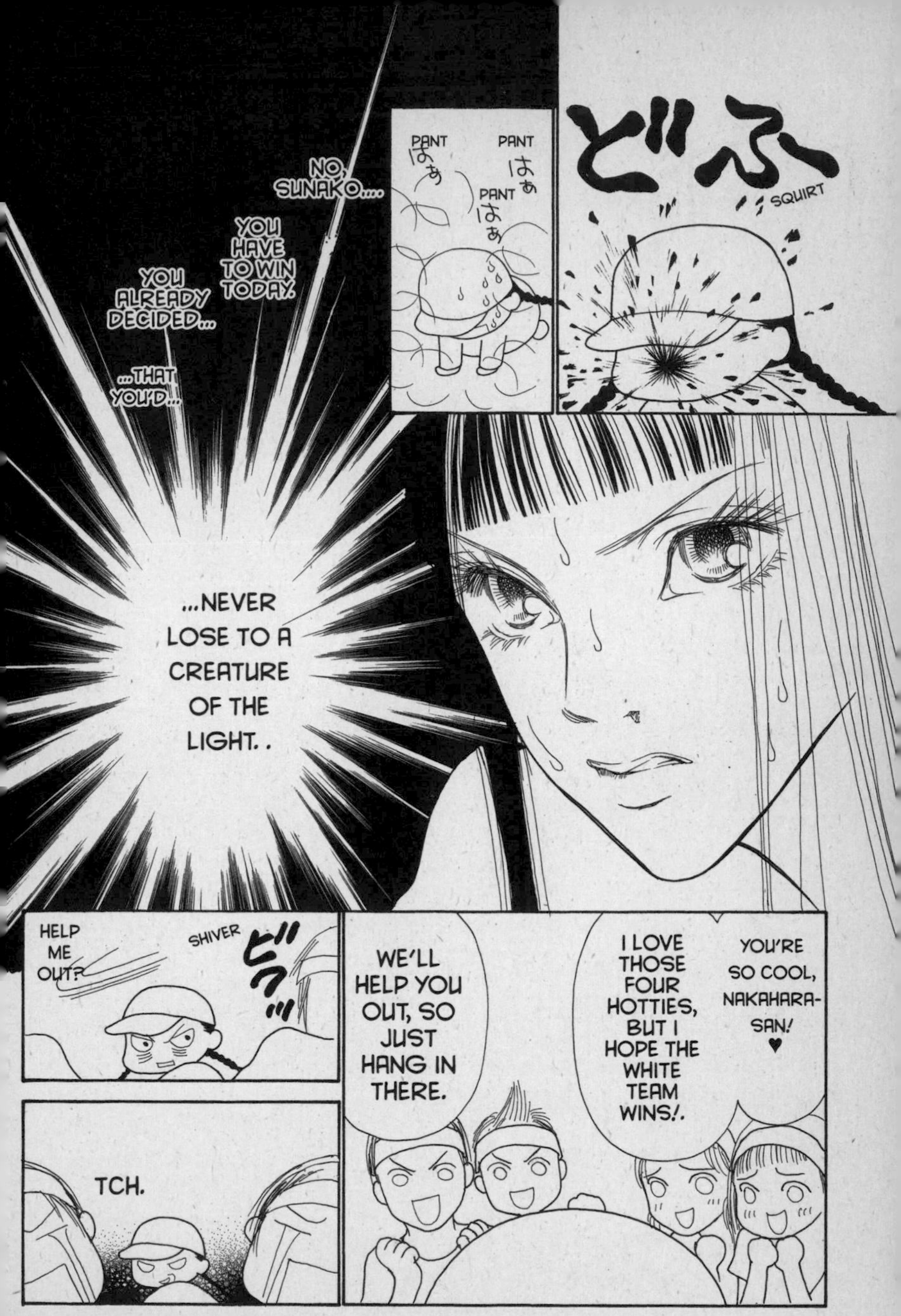
どふ
SQUIRT
PANT はぁ
PANT はぁ
PANT はぁ
NO, SUNAKO....
YOU HAVE TO WIN TODAY.
YOU ALREADY DECIDED...
...THAT YOU'D...
...NEVER LOSE TO A CREATURE OF THE LIGHT. .
YOU'RE SO COOL, NAKAHARA-SAN! ♥
I LOVE THOSE FOUR HOTTIES, BUT I HOPE THE WHITE TEAM WINS!.
WE'LL HELP YOU OUT, SO JUST HANG IN THERE.
SHIVER ビクッ
HELP ME OUT?
TCH.

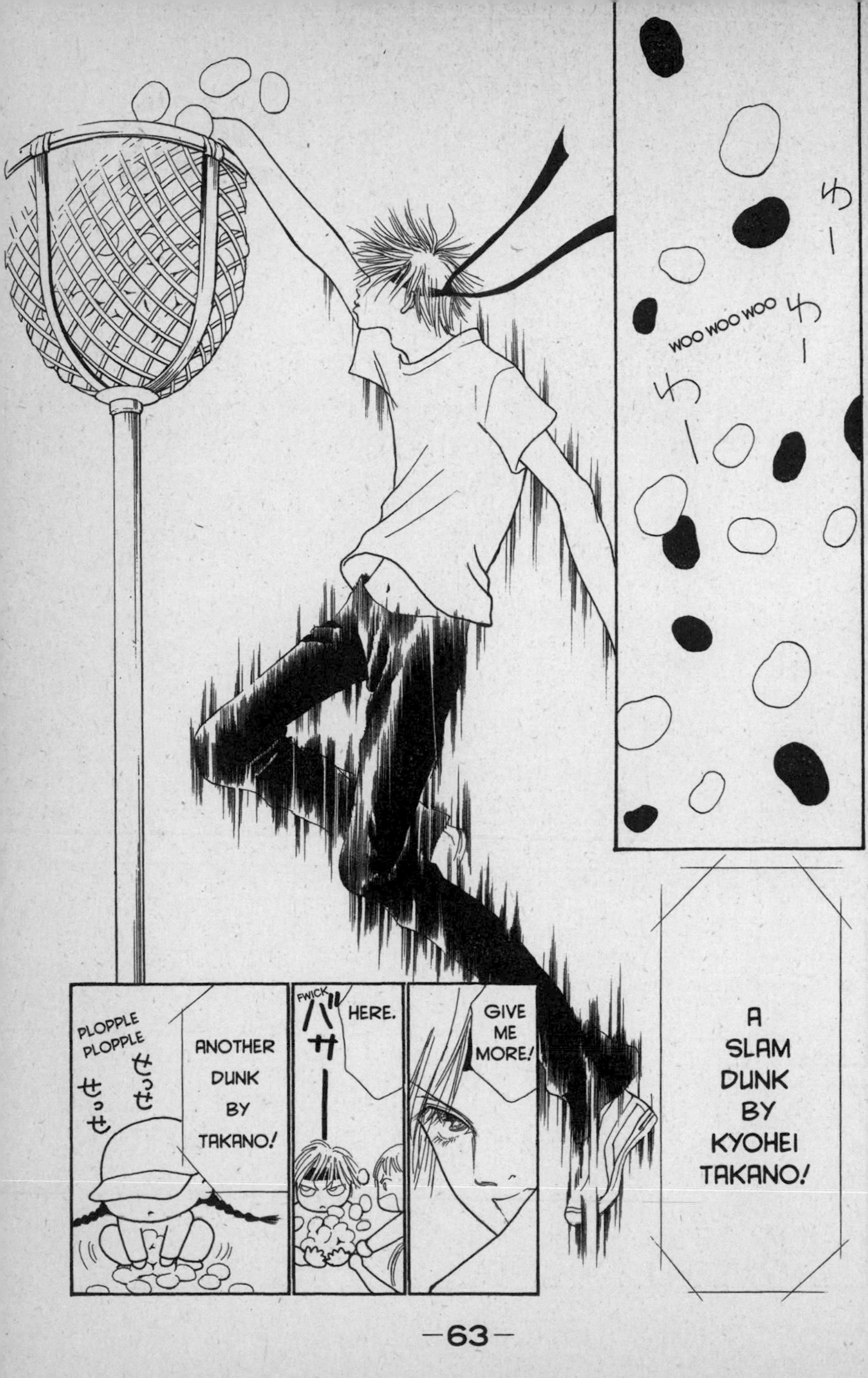
ゆー
ゆー
ゆー
WOO WOO WOO
A SLAM DUNK BY KYOHEI TAKANO!
GIVE ME MORE!
HERE.
FWICK
バサー
ANOTHER DUNK BY TAKANO!
PLOPPLE PLOPPLE
せっせ
せっせ

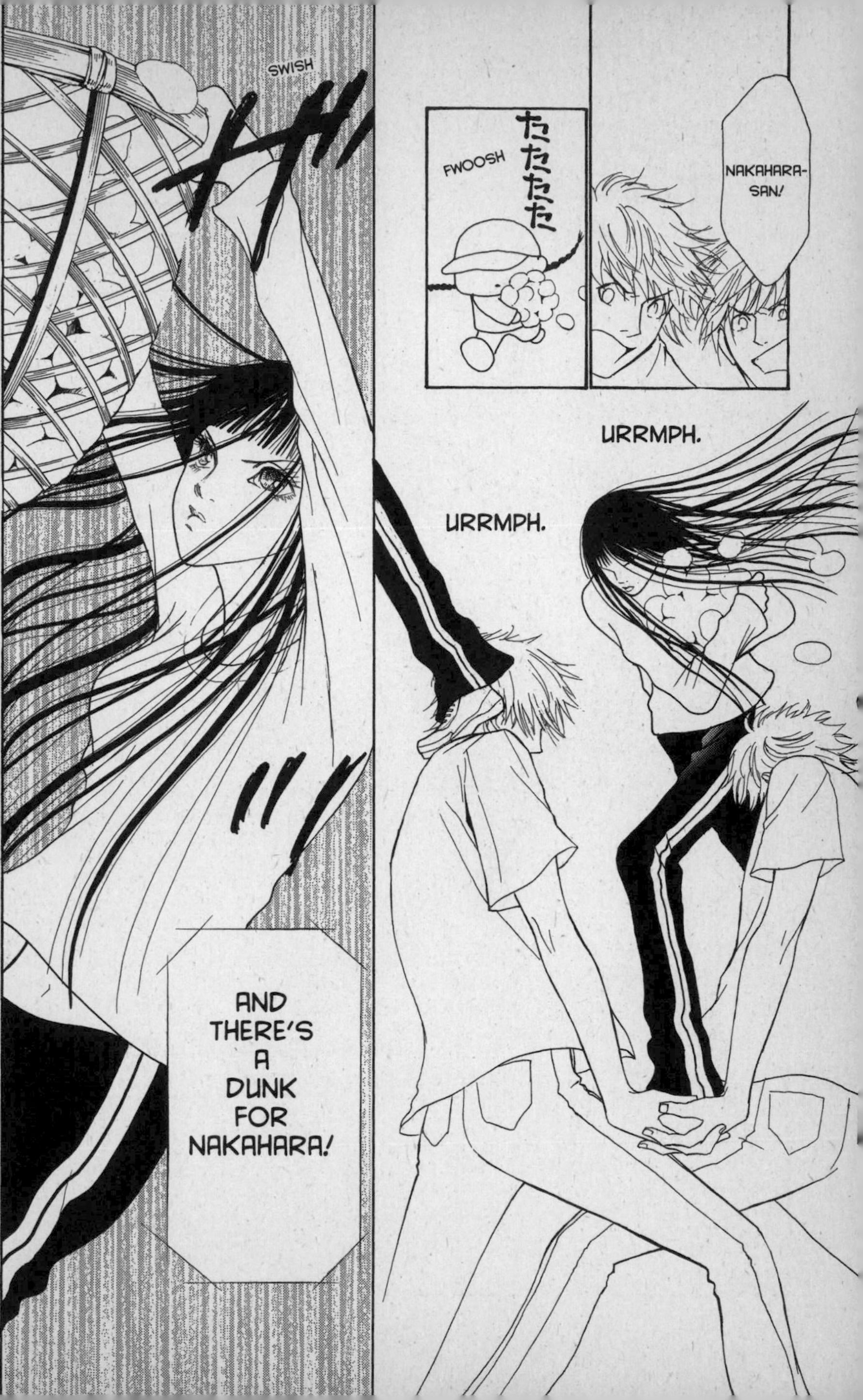
NAKAHARA-SAN!
たたたた
FWOOSH
URRMPH.
URRMPH.
SWISH
AND THERE'S A DUNK FOR NAKAHARA!

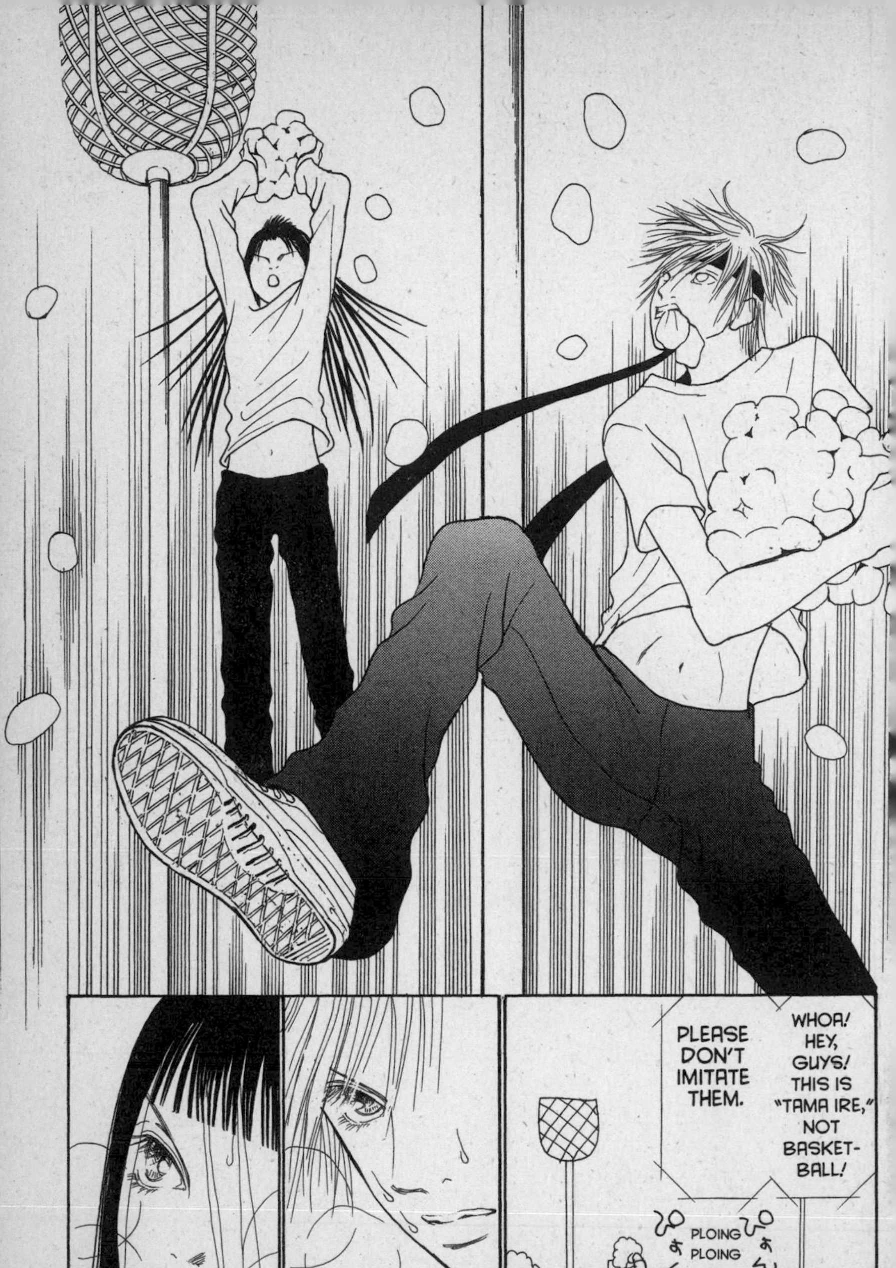
WHOA! HEY, GUYS! THIS IS "TAMA IRE," NOT BASKET-BALL!
PLEASE DON'T IMITATE THEM.
ぴょん
PLOING PLOING
ぴょん

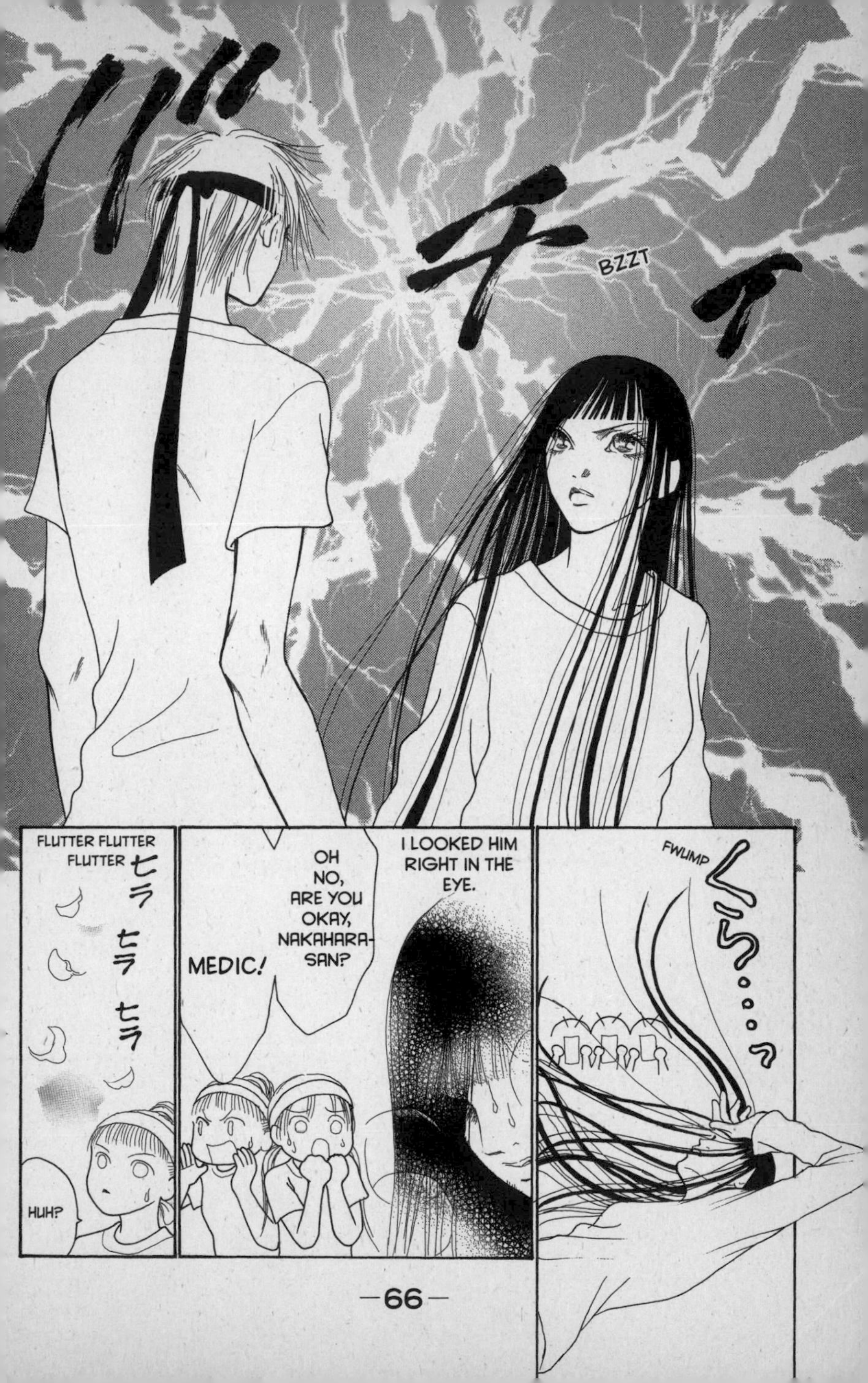

BZZT
FWUMP
くら。。。
I LOOKED HIM RIGHT IN THE EYE.
OH NO, ARE YOU OKAY, NAKAHARA-SAN?
MEDIC!
FLUTTER FLUTTER FLUTTER
ヒラ ヒラ ヒラ
HUH?

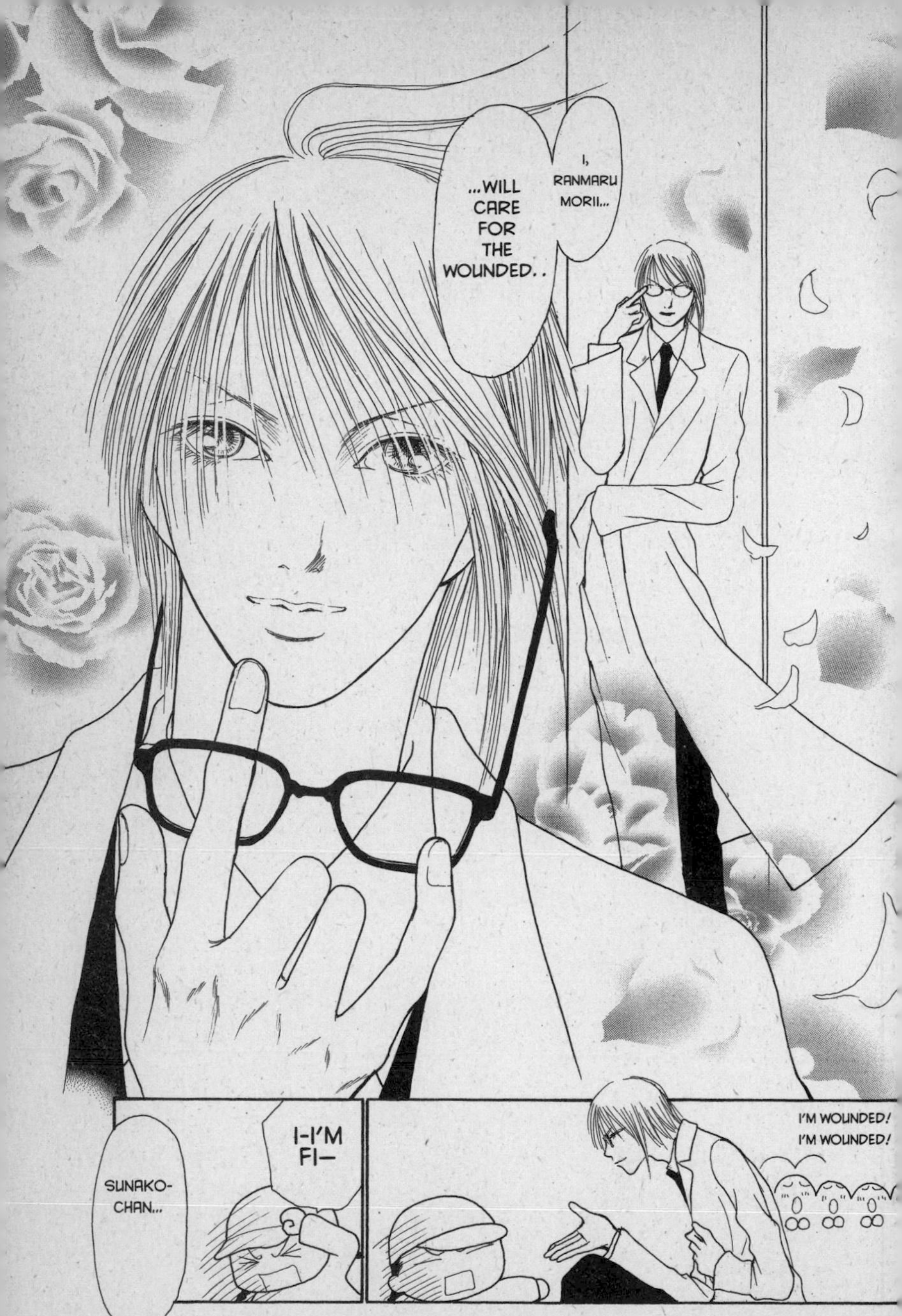
I, RANMARU MORII...
...WILL CARE FOR THE WOUNDED..
I'M WOUNDED! I'M WOUNDED!
I-I'M FI—
SUNAKO-CHAN...

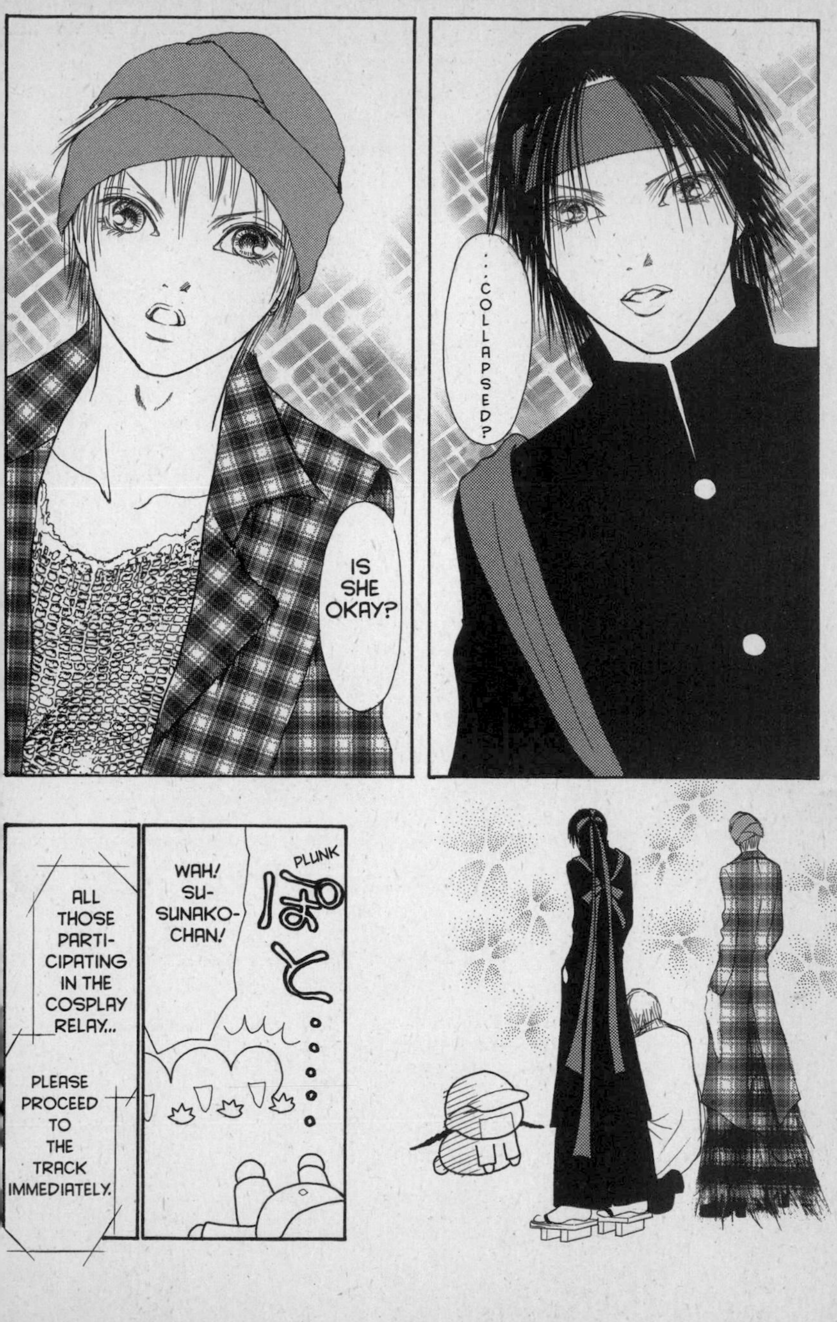
...COLLAPSED?
IS SHE OKAY?
PLUNK
WAH! SU-SUNAKO-CHAN!
ALL THOSE PARTICIPATING IN THE COSPLAY RELAY...
PLEASE PROCEED TO THE TRACK IMMEDIATELY.

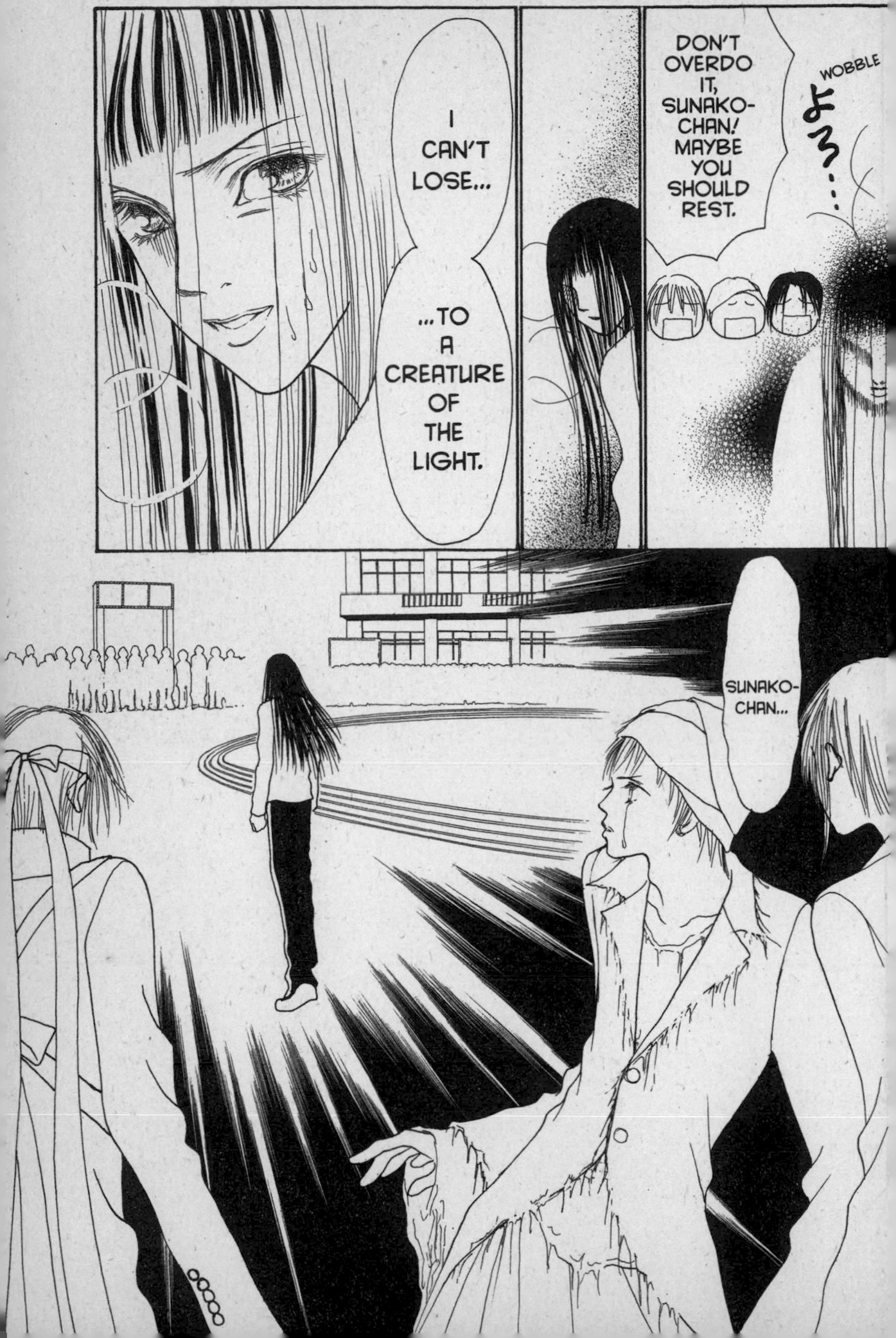
DON'T OVERDO IT, SUNAKO-CHAN! MAYBE YOU SHOULD REST.
WOBBLE
よろ…
I CAN'T LOSE...
...TO A CREATURE OF THE LIGHT.
SUNAKO-CHAN...

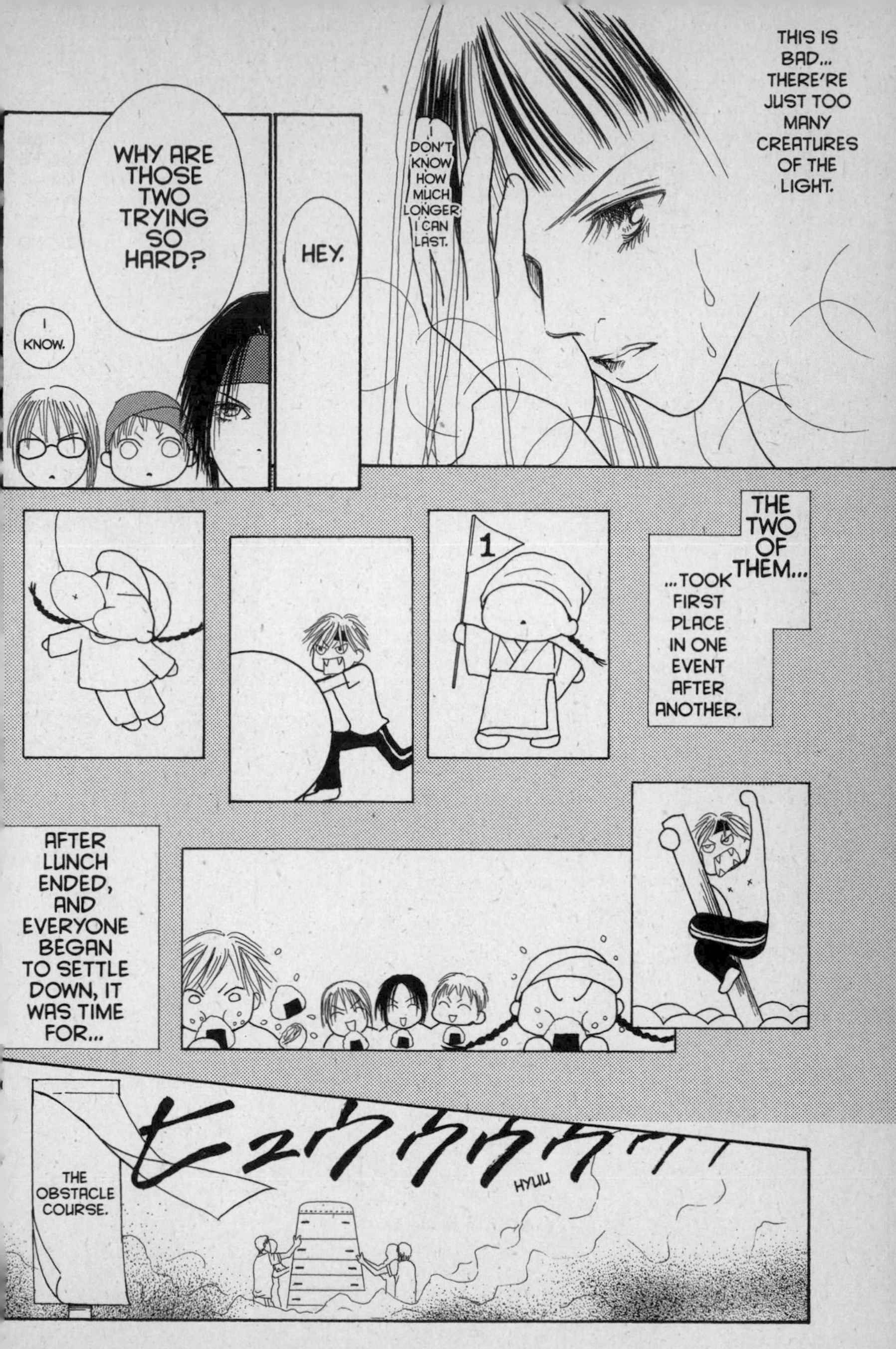
THIS IS BAD... THERE'RE JUST TOO MANY CREATURES OF THE LIGHT.
I DON'T KNOW HOW MUCH LONGER I CAN LAST.
HEY.
WHY ARE THOSE TWO TRYING SO HARD?
I KNOW.
THE TWO OF THEM...
...TOOK FIRST PLACE IN ONE EVENT AFTER ANOTHER.
1
AFTER LUNCH ENDED, AND EVERYONE BEGAN TO SETTLE DOWN, IT WAS TIME FOR...
HYUU
THE OBSTACLE COURSE.

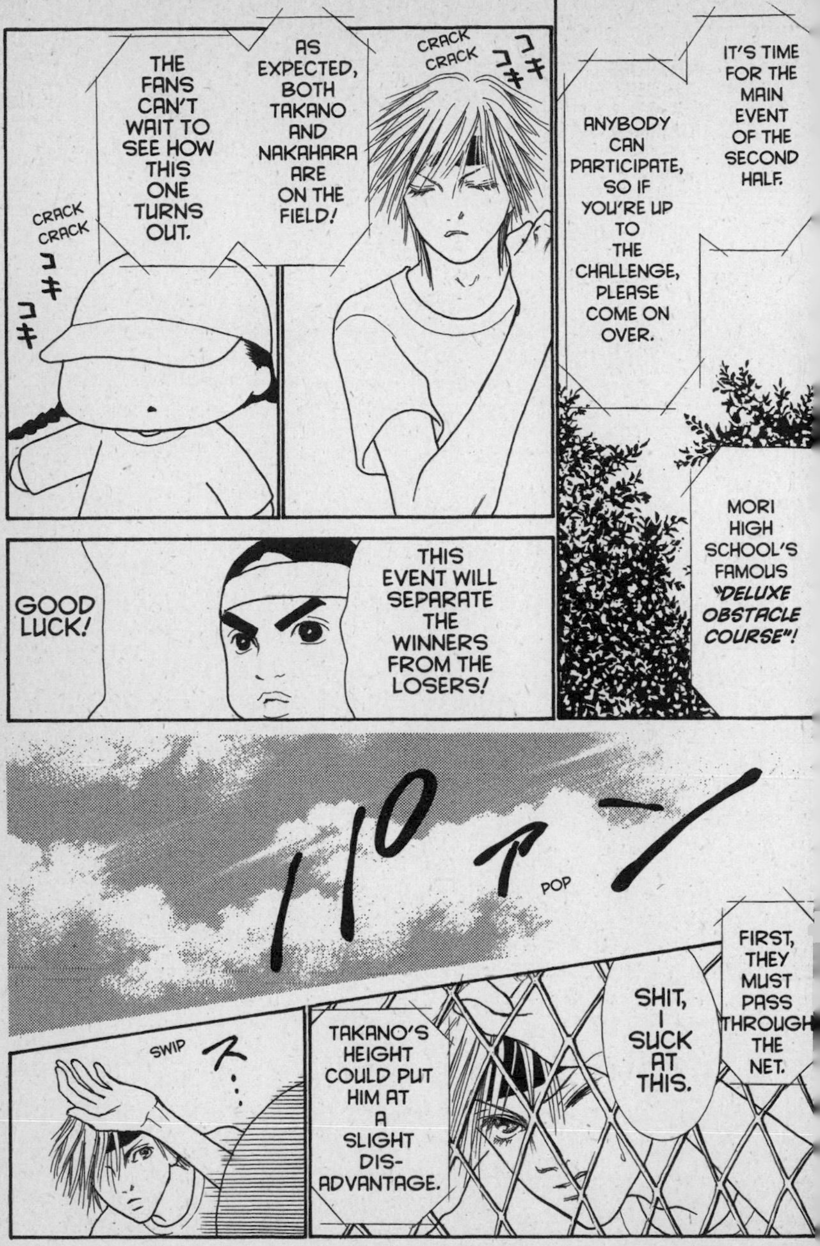
IT'S TIME FOR THE MAIN EVENT OF THE SECOND HALF.
ANYBODY CAN PARTICIPATE, SO IF YOU'RE UP TO THE CHALLENGE, PLEASE COME ON OVER.
MORI HIGH SCHOOL'S FAMOUS "DELUXE OBSTACLE COURSE"!
CRACK CRACK
コキ コキ
AS EXPECTED, BOTH TAKANO AND NAKAHARA ARE ON THE FIELD!
THE FANS CAN'T WAIT TO SEE HOW THIS ONE TURNS OUT.
CRACK CRACK
コキ コキ
THIS EVENT WILL SEPARATE THE WINNERS FROM THE LOSERS!
GOOD LUCK!
パァーン
POP
FIRST, THEY MUST PASS THROUGH THE NET.
SHIT, I SUCK AT THIS.
TAKANO'S HEIGHT COULD PUT HIM AT A SLIGHT DIS-ADVANTAGE.
SWIP
ス…

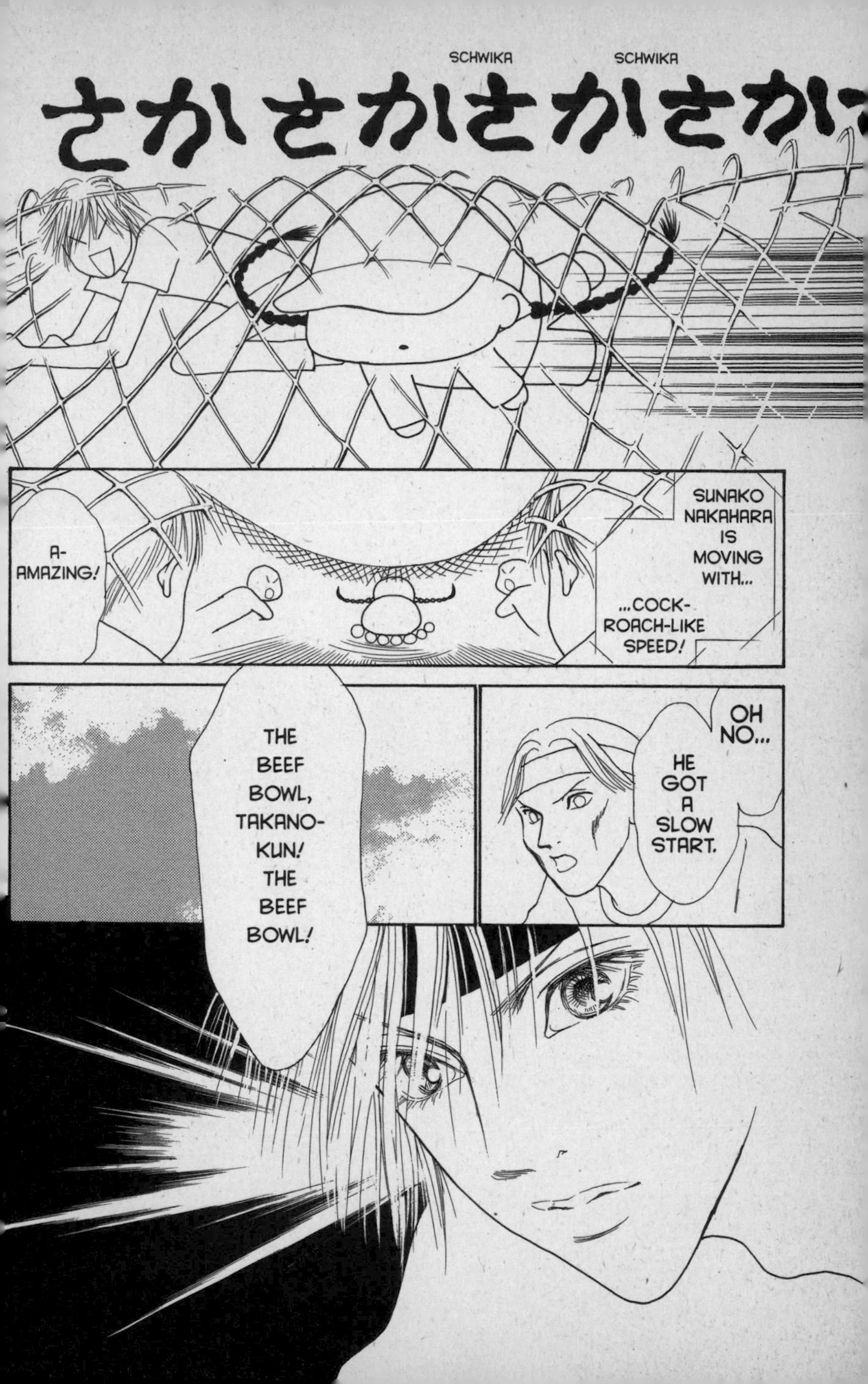
SCHWIKA SCHWIKA
さかさかさかさ
SUNAKO NAKAHARA IS MOVING WITH...
...COCK-ROACH-LIKE SPEED!
A-AMAZING!
OH NO...
HE GOT A SLOW START.
THE BEEF BOWL, TAKANO-KUN! THE BEEF BOWL!

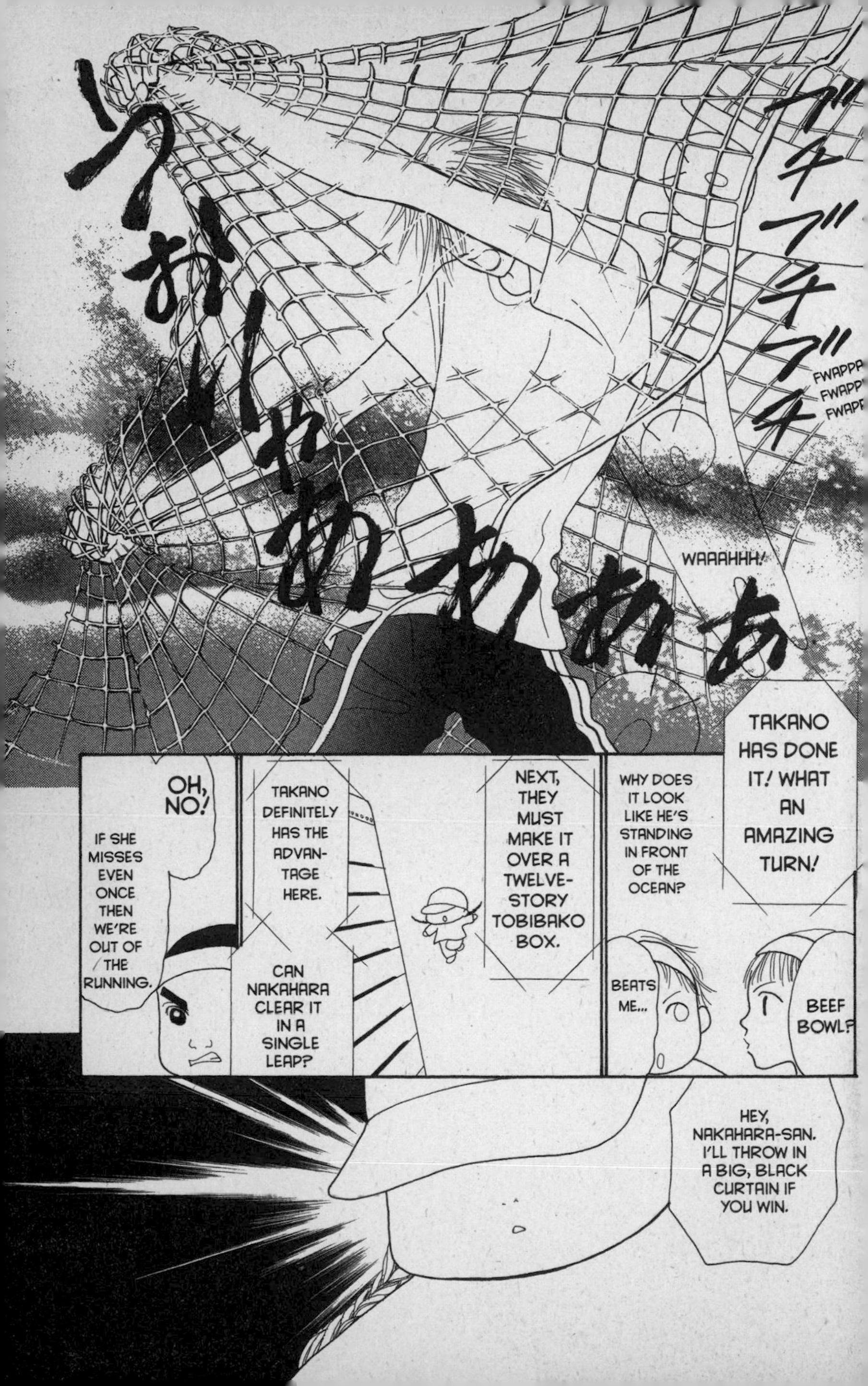

ブチブチブチ
FWAPP
FWAPP
FWAPP
うおりゃああああ
WAAAHHH!
TAKANO HAS DONE IT! WHAT AN AMAZING TURN!
WHY DOES IT LOOK LIKE HE'S STANDING IN FRONT OF THE OCEAN?
BEEF BOWL?
BEATS ME...
NEXT, THEY MUST MAKE IT OVER A TWELVE-STORY TOBIBAKO BOX.
TAKANO DEFINITELY HAS THE ADVANTAGE HERE.
CAN NAKAHARA CLEAR IT IN A SINGLE LEAP?
OH, NO!
IF SHE MISSES EVEN ONCE THEN WE'RE OUT OF THE RUNNING.
HEY, NAKAHARA-SAN. I'LL THROW IN A BIG, BLACK CURTAIN IF YOU WIN.

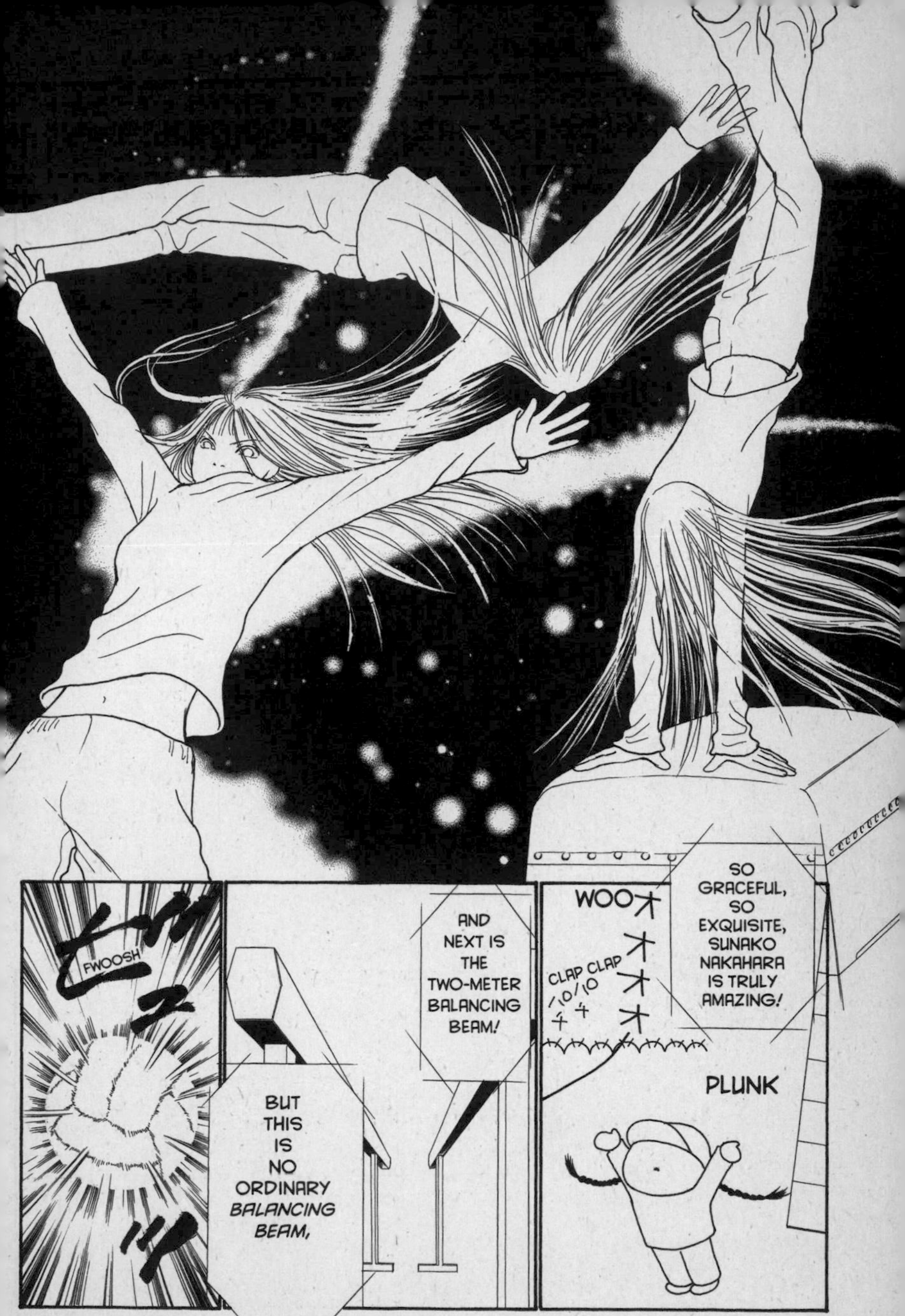
SO GRACEFUL, SO EXQUISITE, SUNAKO NAKAHARA IS TRULY AMAZING!
WOO
CLAP CLAP
PLUNK
AND NEXT IS THE TWO-METER BALANCING BEAM!
BUT THIS IS NO ORDINARY *BALANCING BEAM*,
FWOOSH

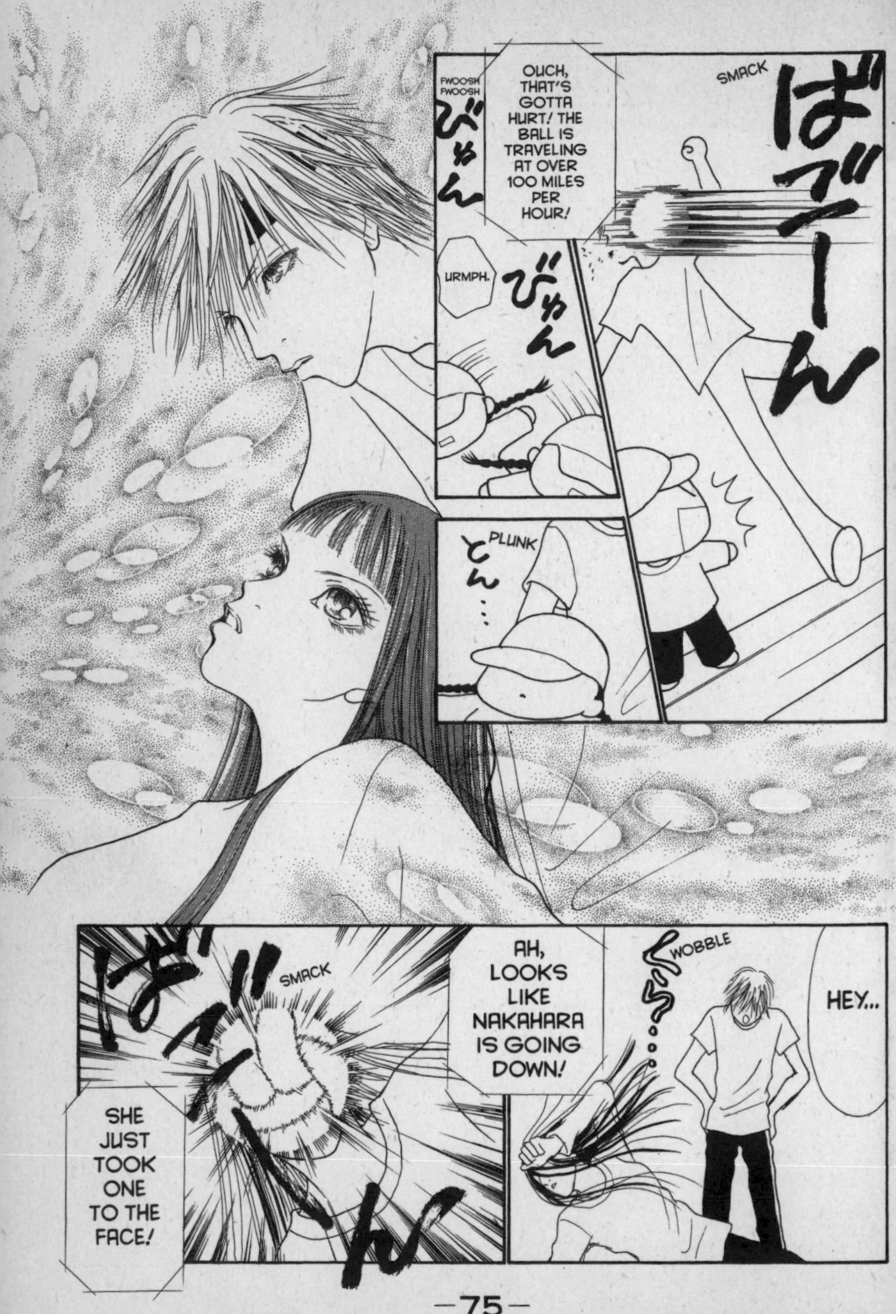

SMACK
ばーん
FWOOSH FWOOSH
びゅん
OUCH, THAT'S GOTTA HURT! THE BALL IS TRAVELING AT OVER 100 MILES PER HOUR!
URMPH.
びゅん
PLUNK
とん…
HEY...
WOBBLE
AH, LOOKS LIKE NAKAHARA IS GOING DOWN!
SMACK
ばーん
SHE JUST TOOK ONE TO THE FACE!

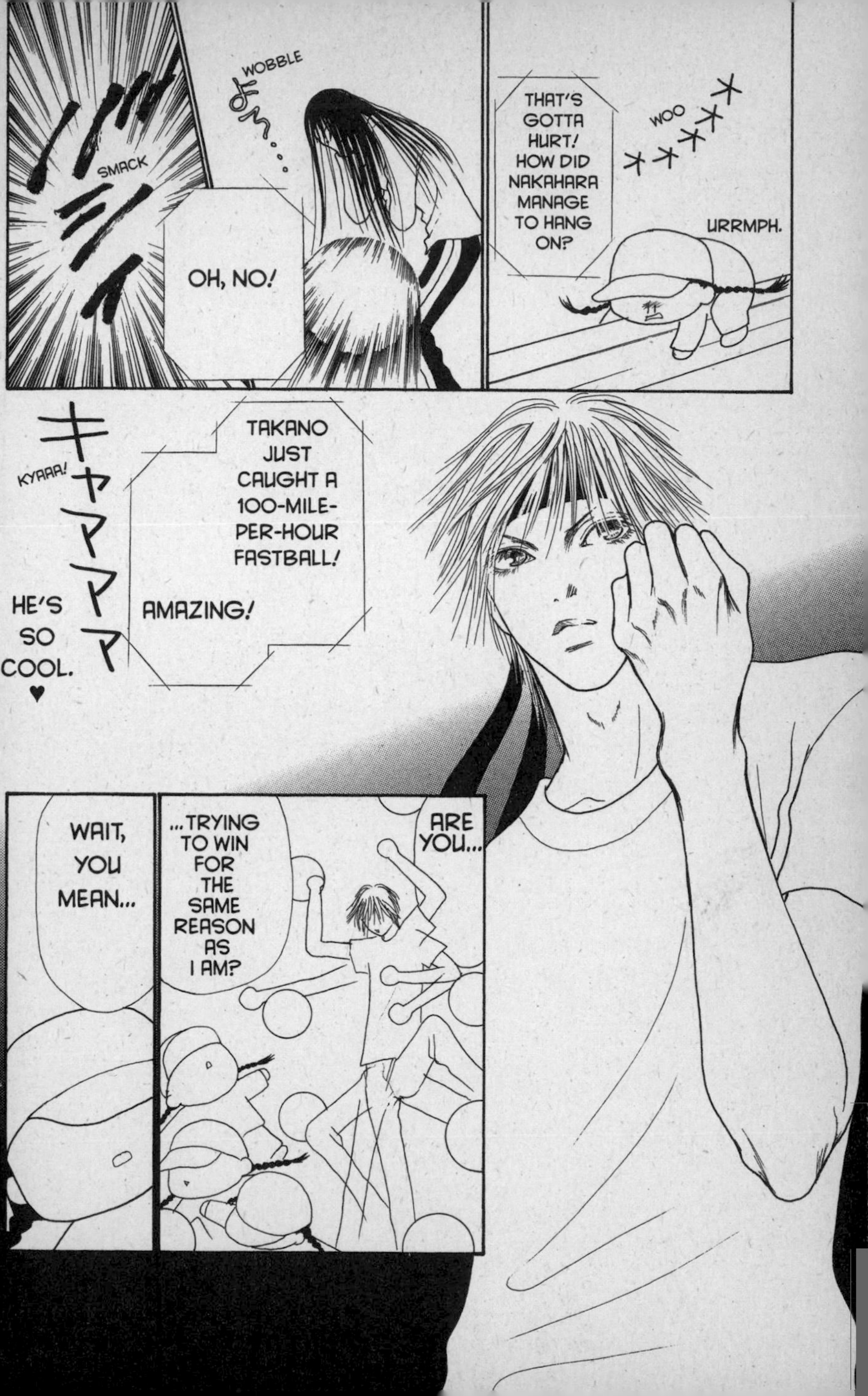
WOO
THAT'S GOTTA HURT! HOW DID NAKAHARA MANAGE TO HANG ON?
URRMPH.
WOBBLE
SMACK
OH, NO!
TAKANO JUST CAUGHT A 100-MILE-PER-HOUR FASTBALL!
AMAZING!
KYAAA!
HE'S SO COOL. ♥
ARE YOU...
...TRYING TO WIN FOR THE SAME REASON AS I AM?
WAIT, YOU MEAN...

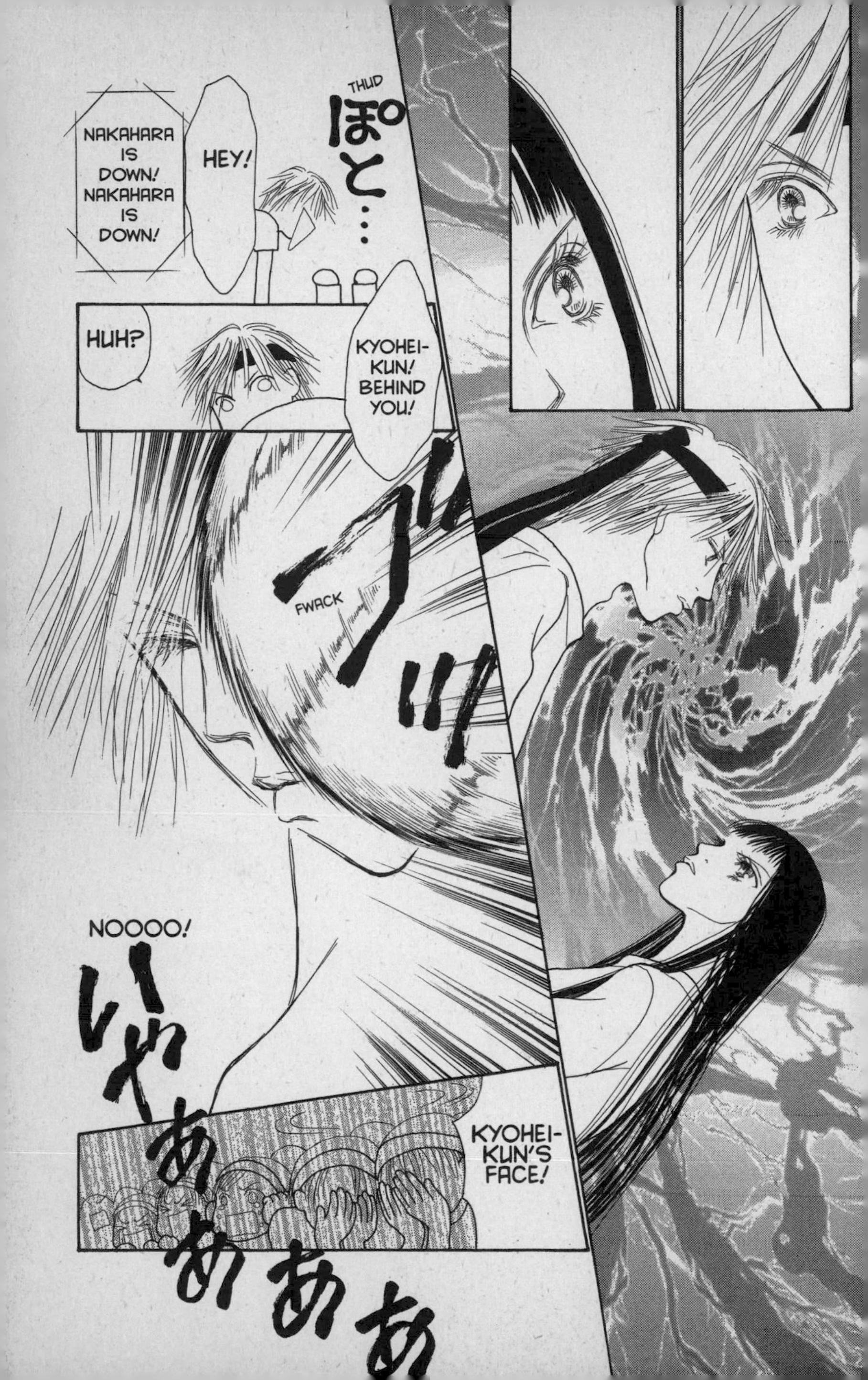
THUD
ぽと…
HEY!
NAKAHARA IS DOWN! NAKAHARA IS DOWN!
KYOHEI-KUN! BEHIND YOU!
HUH?
FWACK
KYOHEI-KUN'S FACE!
NOOOO!
いやあああ

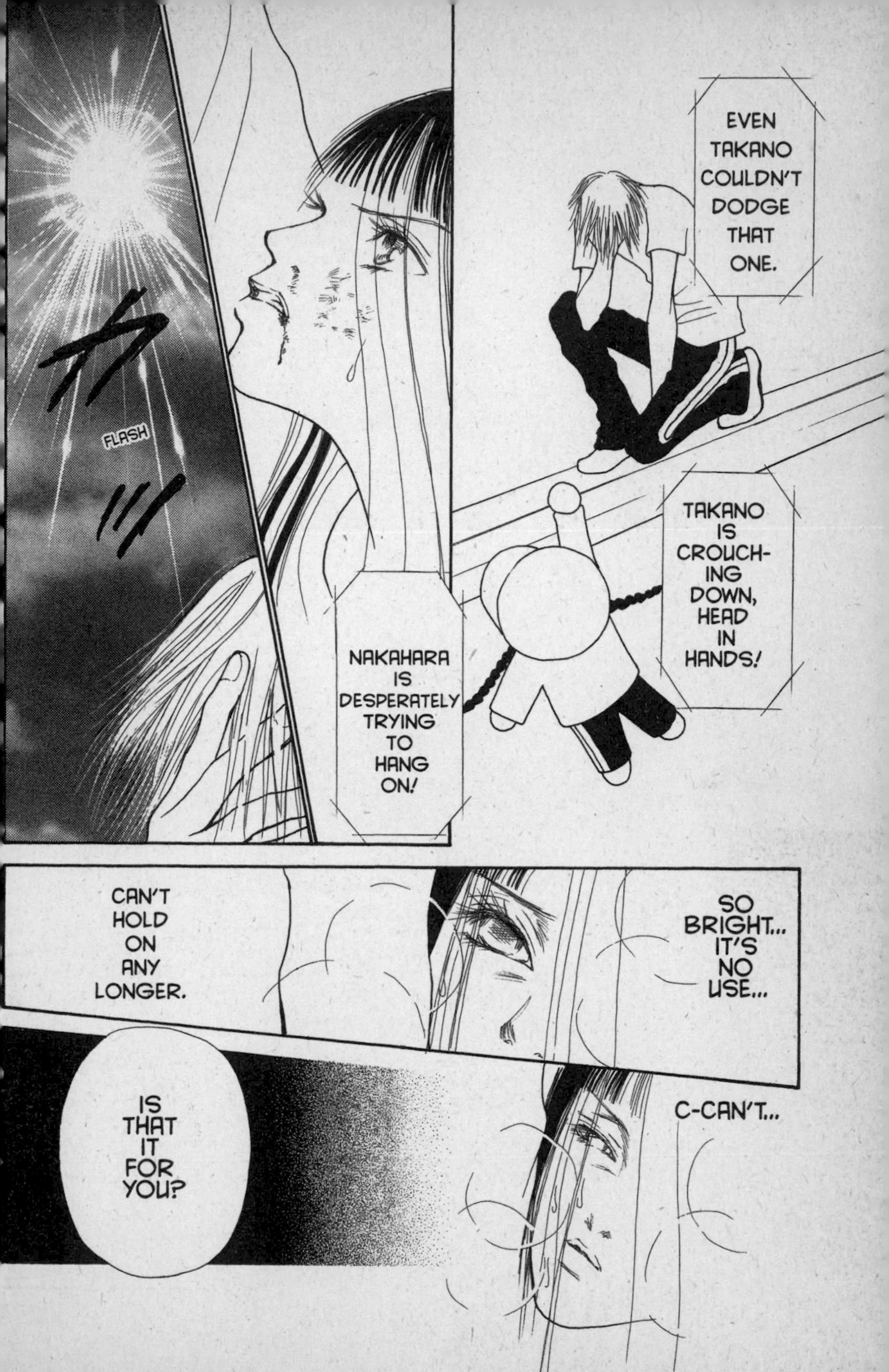
EVEN TAKANO COULDN'T DODGE THAT ONE.
TAKANO IS CROUCHING DOWN, HEAD IN HANDS!
NAKAHARA IS DESPERATELY TRYING TO HANG ON!
FLASH
SO BRIGHT... IT'S NO USE...
CAN'T HOLD ON ANY LONGER.
C-CAN'T...
IS THAT IT FOR YOU?

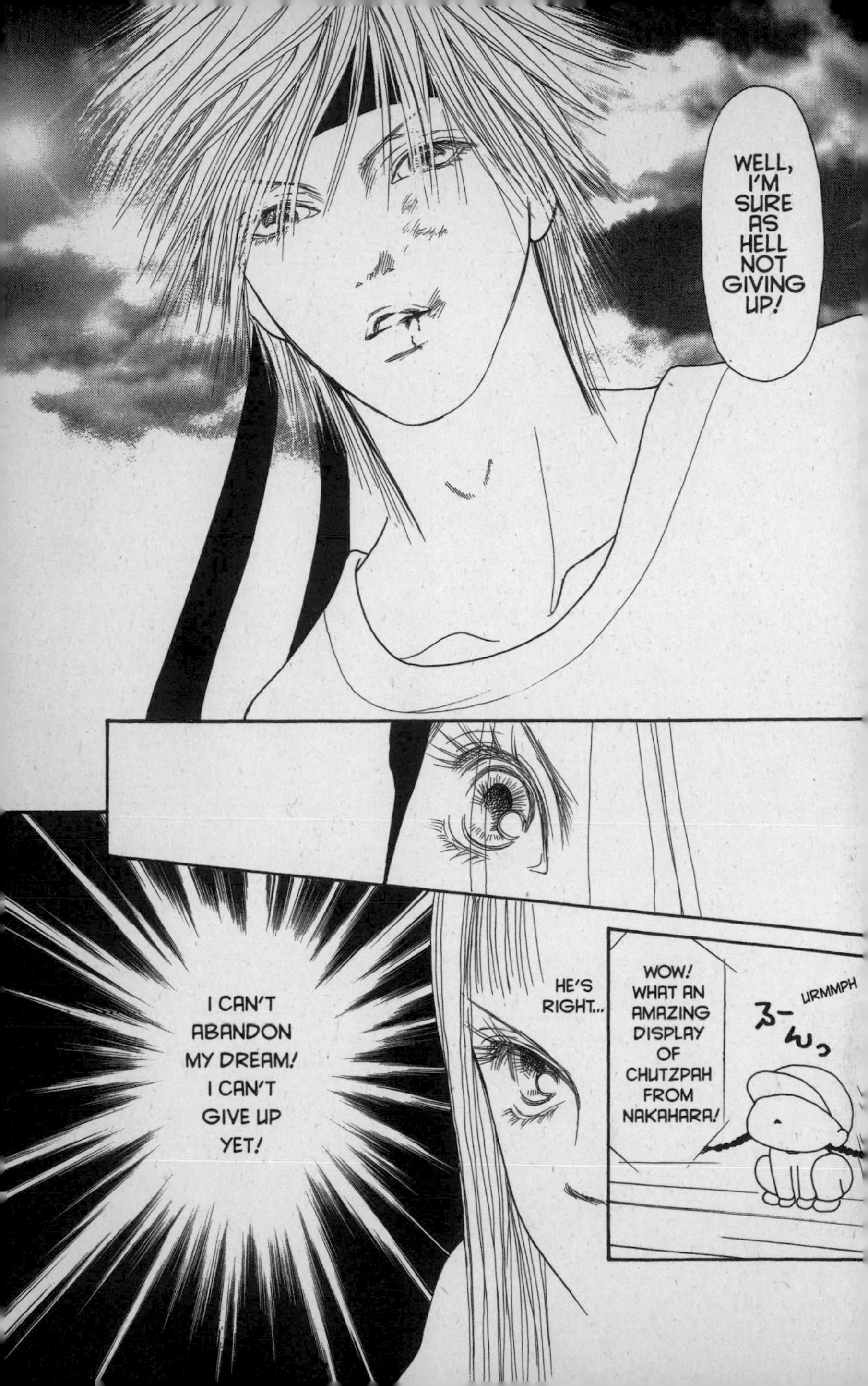
WELL, I'M SURE AS HELL NOT GIVING UP!
URMMPH
ふーんっ
WOW! WHAT AN AMAZING DISPLAY OF CHUTZPAH FROM NAKAHARA!
HE'S RIGHT...
I CAN'T ABANDON MY DREAM! I CAN'T GIVE UP YET!

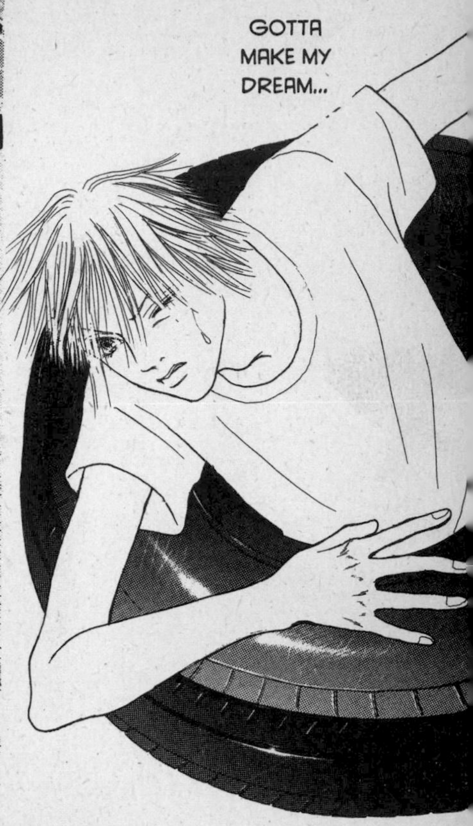
GOTTA MAKE MY DREAM...
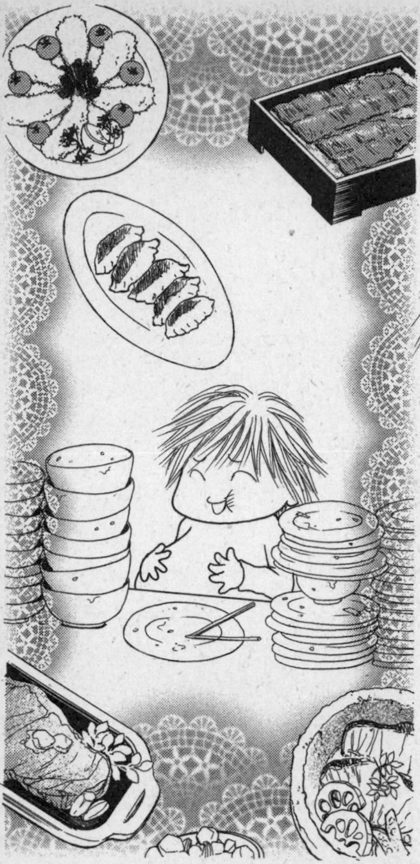
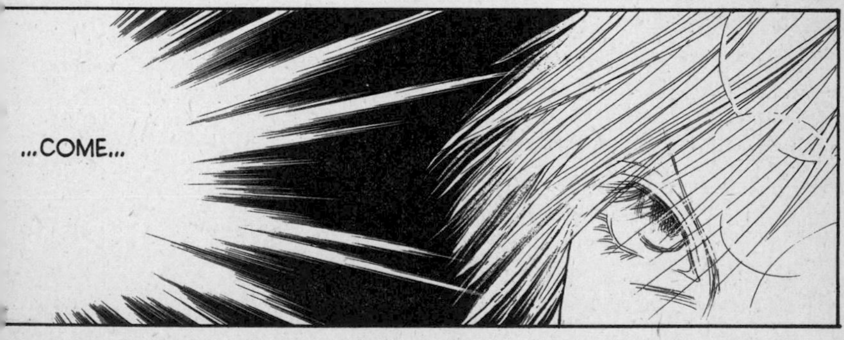
...COME...

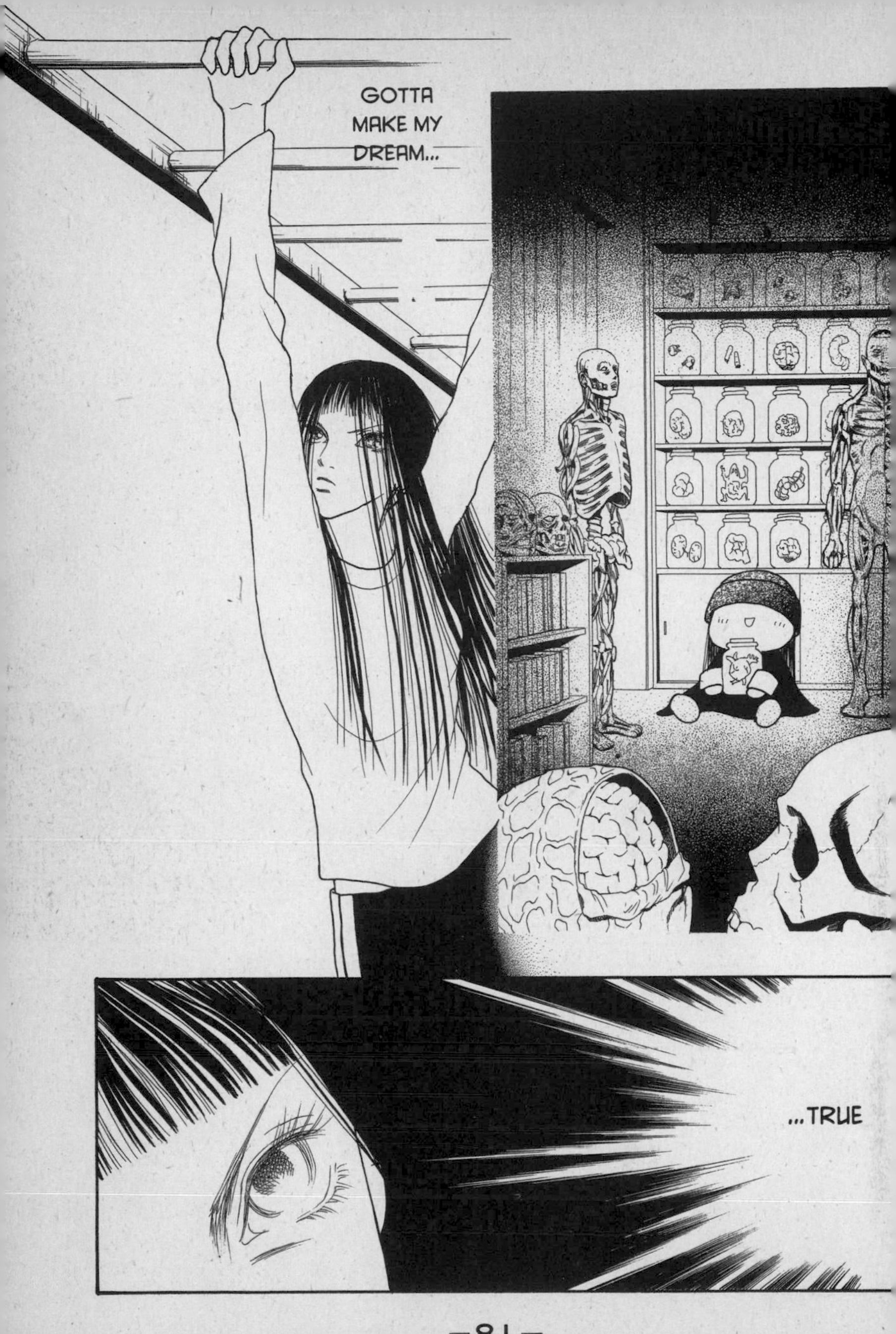
GOTTA MAKE MY DREAM...
...TRUE

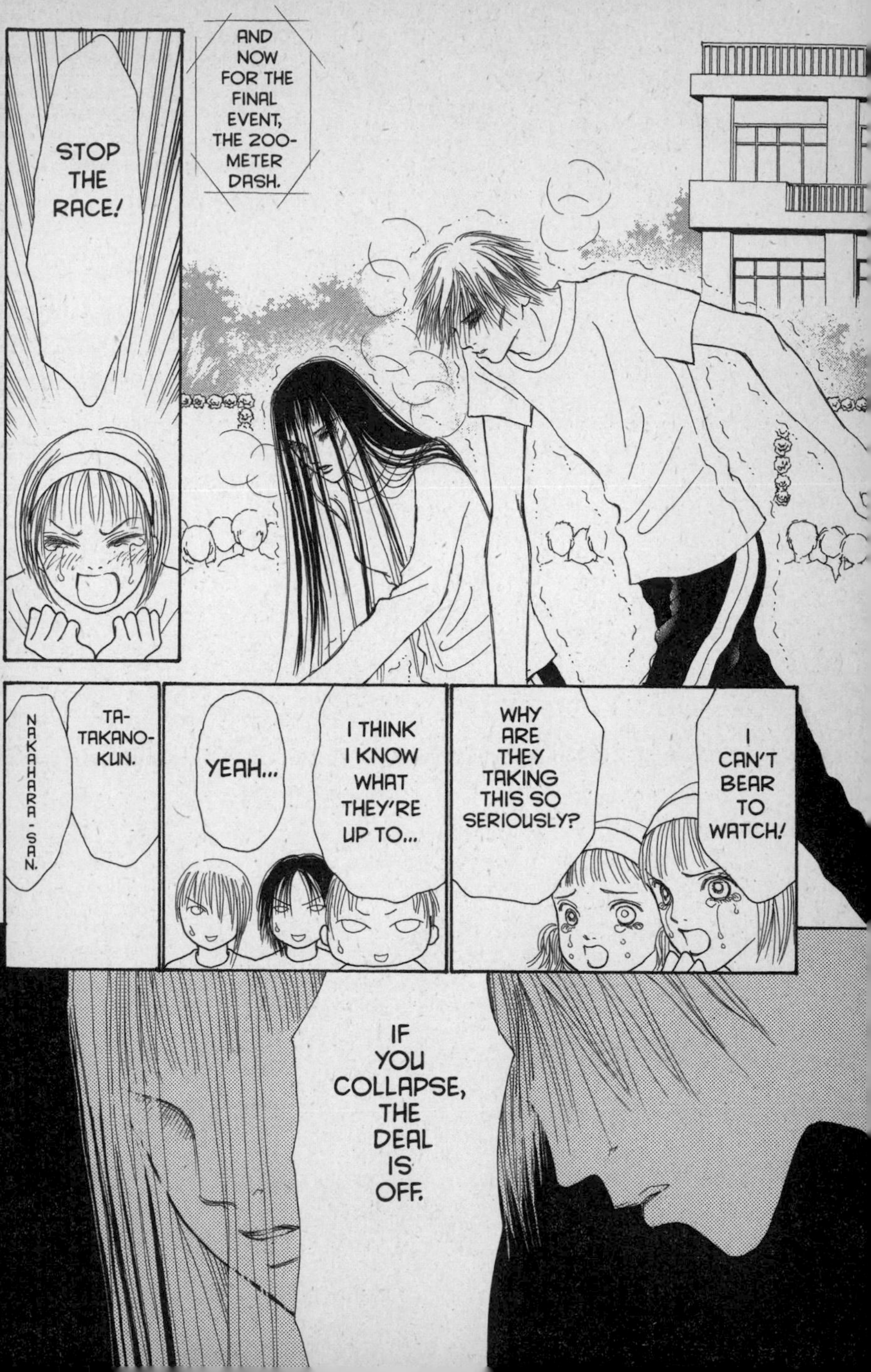
AND NOW FOR THE FINAL EVENT, THE 200-METER DASH.
STOP THE RACE!
I CAN'T BEAR TO WATCH!
WHY ARE THEY TAKING THIS SO SERIOUSLY?
I THINK I KNOW WHAT THEY'RE UP TO...
YEAH...
TA-TAKANO-KUN.
NAKAHARA-SAN.
IF YOU COLLAPSE, THE DEAL IS OFF.

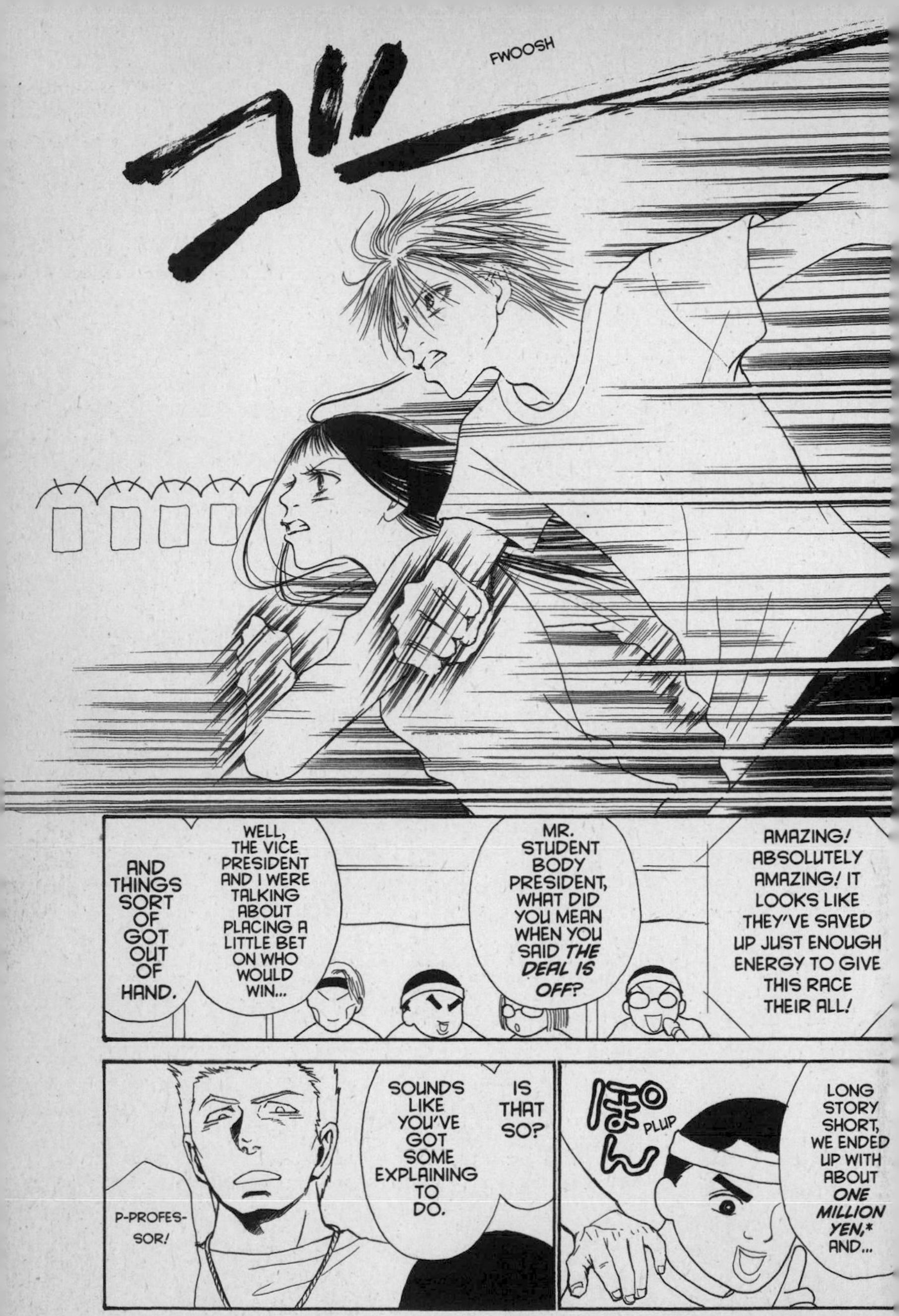
ゴ
FWOOSH
AMAZING! ABSOLUTELY AMAZING! IT LOOKS LIKE THEY'VE SAVED UP JUST ENOUGH ENERGY TO GIVE THIS RACE THEIR ALL!
MR. STUDENT BODY PRESIDENT, WHAT DID YOU MEAN WHEN YOU SAID *THE DEAL IS OFF*?
WELL, THE VICE PRESIDENT AND I WERE TALKING ABOUT PLACING A LITTLE BET ON WHO WOULD WIN...
AND THINGS SORT OF GOT OUT OF HAND.
ぽん
PLUP
LONG STORY SHORT, WE ENDED UP WITH ABOUT *ONE MILLION YEN,** AND...
IS THAT SO?
SOUNDS LIKE YOU'VE GOT SOME EXPLAINING TO DO.
P-PROFES-SOR!

*$10,000

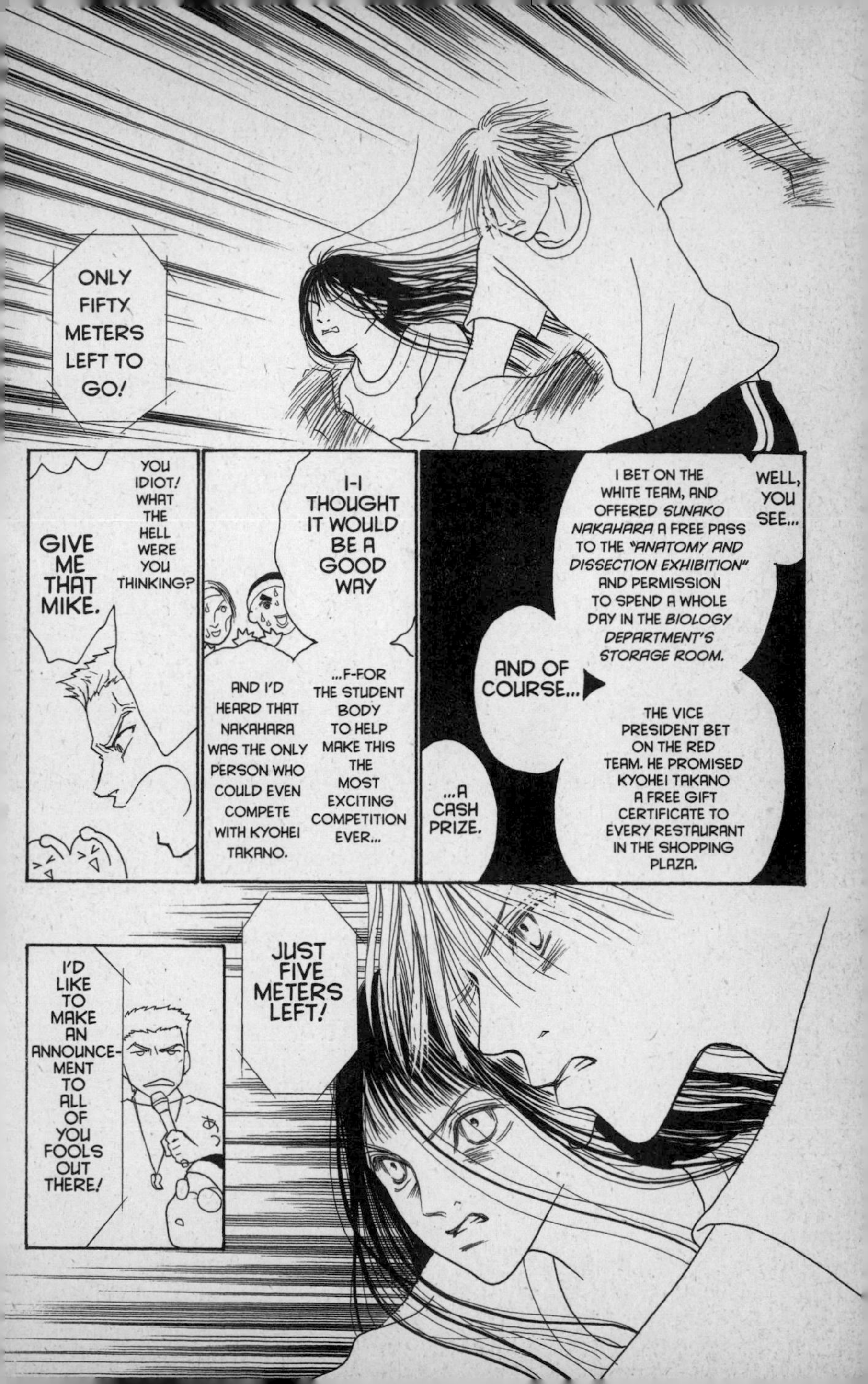
ONLY FIFTY METERS LEFT TO GO!
WELL, YOU SEE...
I BET ON THE WHITE TEAM, AND OFFERED *SUNAKO NAKAHARA* A FREE PASS TO THE *"ANATOMY AND DISSECTION EXHIBITION"* AND PERMISSION TO SPEND A WHOLE DAY IN THE *BIOLOGY DEPARTMENT'S* STORAGE ROOM.
THE VICE PRESIDENT BET ON THE RED TEAM. HE PROMISED KYOHEI TAKANO A FREE GIFT CERTIFICATE TO EVERY RESTAURANT IN THE SHOPPING PLAZA.
AND OF COURSE...
...A CASH PRIZE.
I-I THOUGHT IT WOULD BE A GOOD WAY
...F-FOR THE STUDENT BODY TO HELP MAKE THIS THE MOST EXCITING COMPETITION EVER...
AND I'D HEARD THAT NAKAHARA WAS THE ONLY PERSON WHO COULD EVEN COMPETE WITH KYOHEI TAKANO.
YOU IDIOT! WHAT THE HELL WERE YOU THINKING?
GIVE ME THAT MIKE.
JUST FIVE METERS LEFT!
I'D LIKE TO MAKE AN ANNOUNCEMENT TO ALL OF YOU FOOLS OUT THERE!

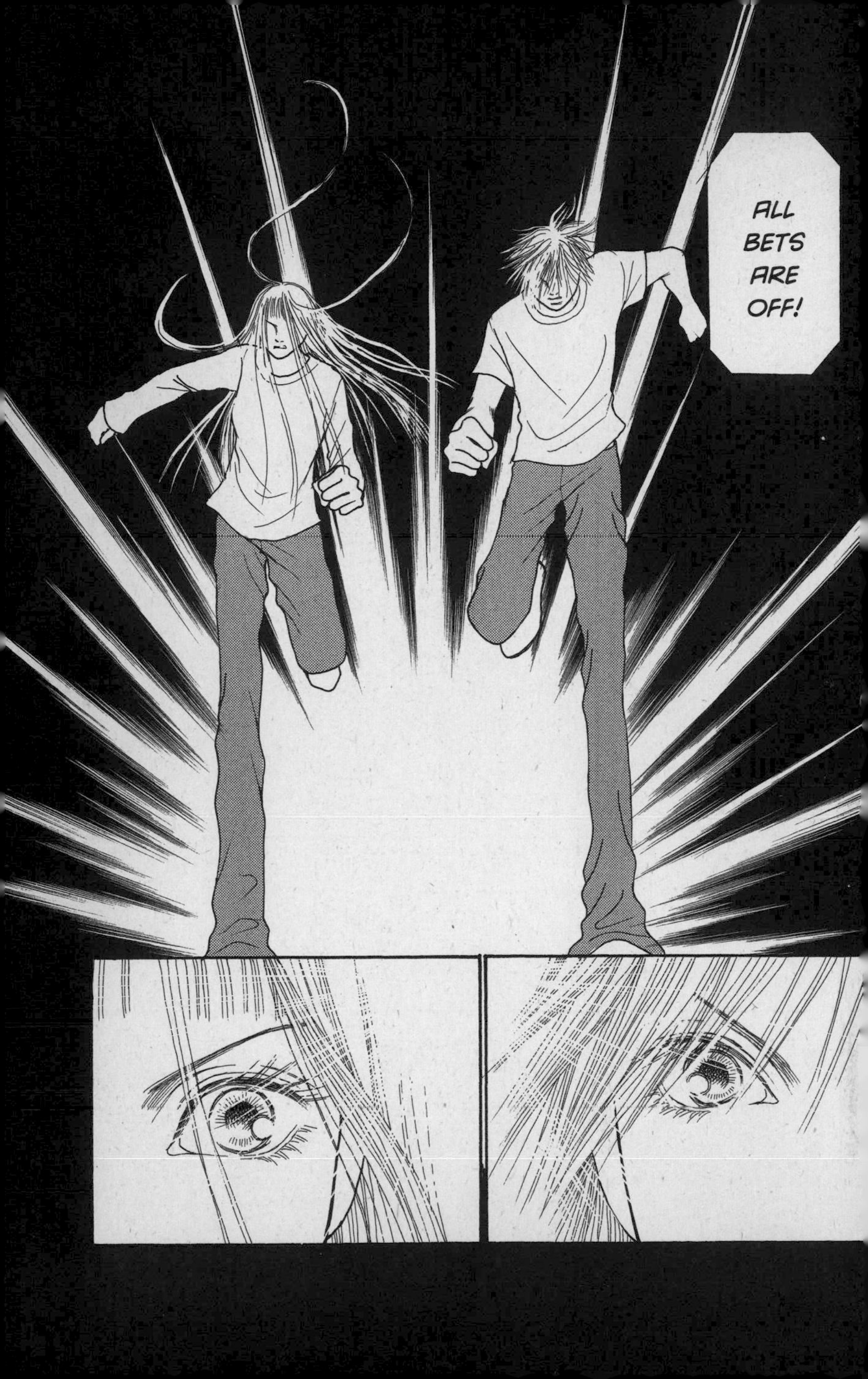
ALL BETS ARE OFF!

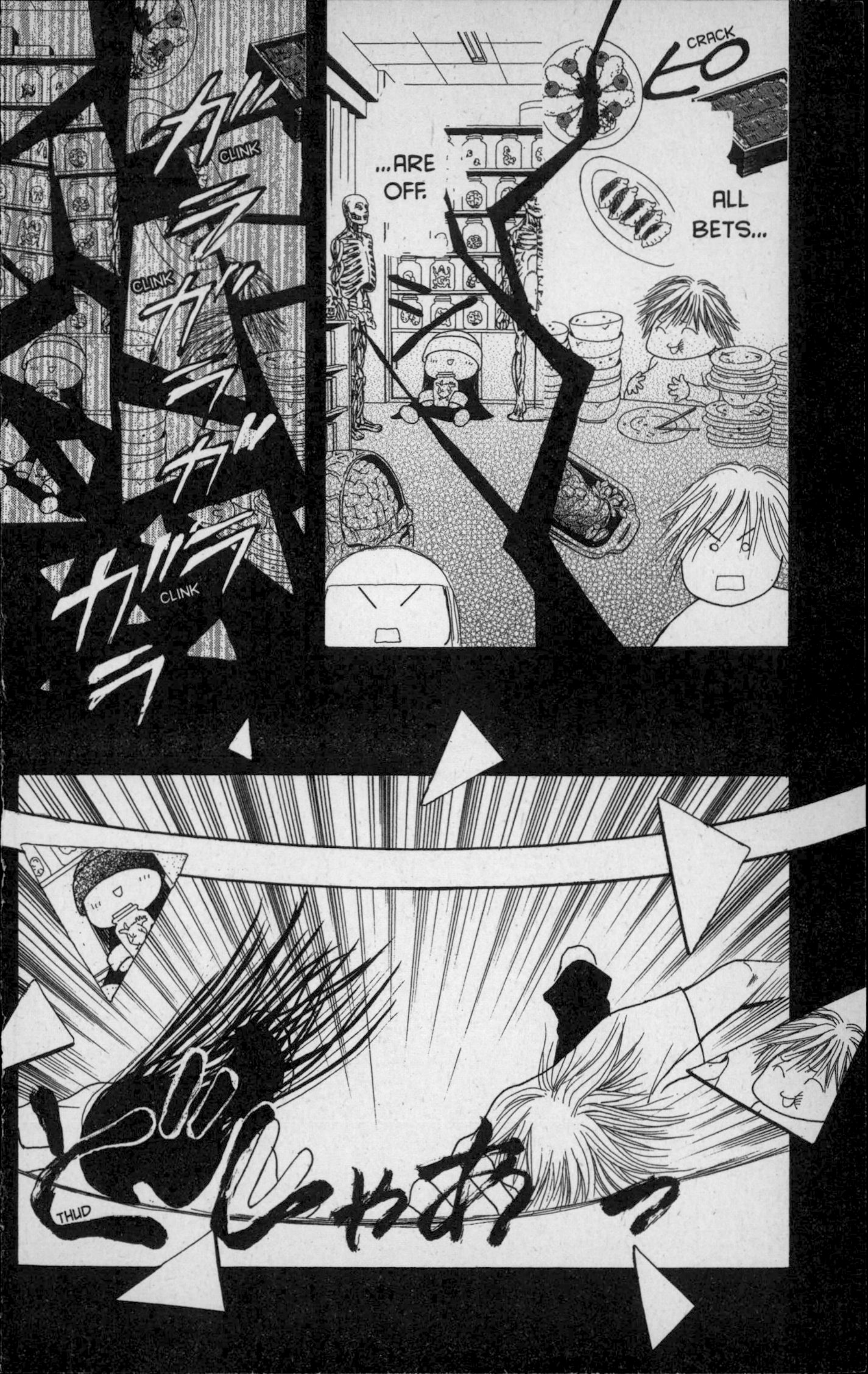

CRACK
ALL BETS...
...ARE OFF.
CLINK
CLINK
CLINK
THUD

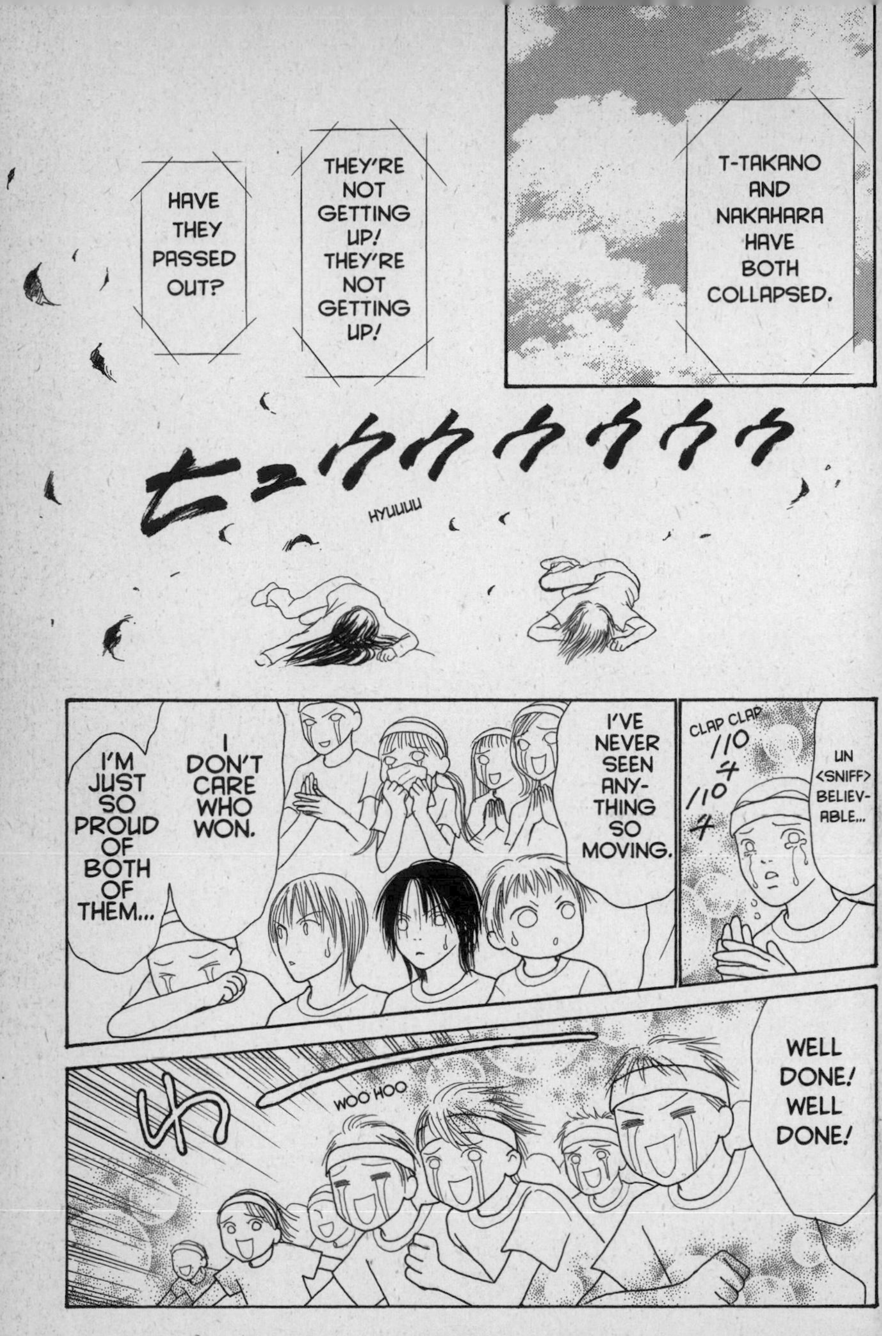

T-TAKANO AND NAKAHARA HAVE BOTH COLLAPSED.
THEY'RE NOT GETTING UP! THEY'RE NOT GETTING UP!
HAVE THEY PASSED OUT?
ヒュウウウウウウ
HYUUUU
CLAP CLAP
UN <SNIFF> BELIEVABLE...
I'VE NEVER SEEN ANYTHING SO MOVING.
I DON'T CARE WHO WON.
I'M JUST SO PROUD OF BOTH OF THEM...
WELL DONE! WELL DONE!
WOO HOO
わ

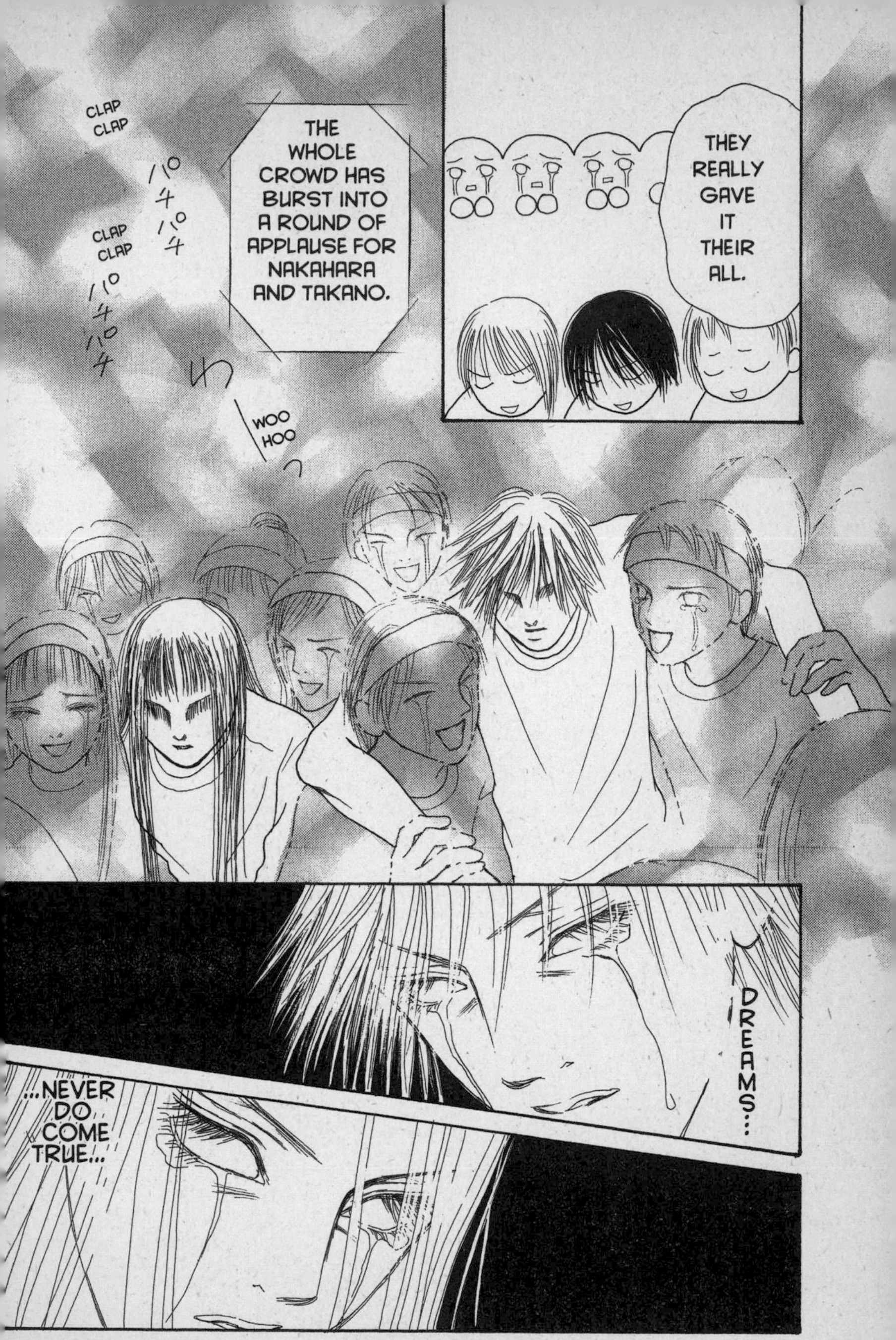
THEY REALLY GAVE IT THEIR ALL.
THE WHOLE CROWD HAS BURST INTO A ROUND OF APPLAUSE FOR NAKAHARA AND TAKANO.
CLAP CLAP
パチパチ
CLAP CLAP
パチパチ
わっ
WOO HOO
DREAMS...
...NEVER DO COME TRUE...

CHAPTER 41 – THE SLEEPING PRINCESS

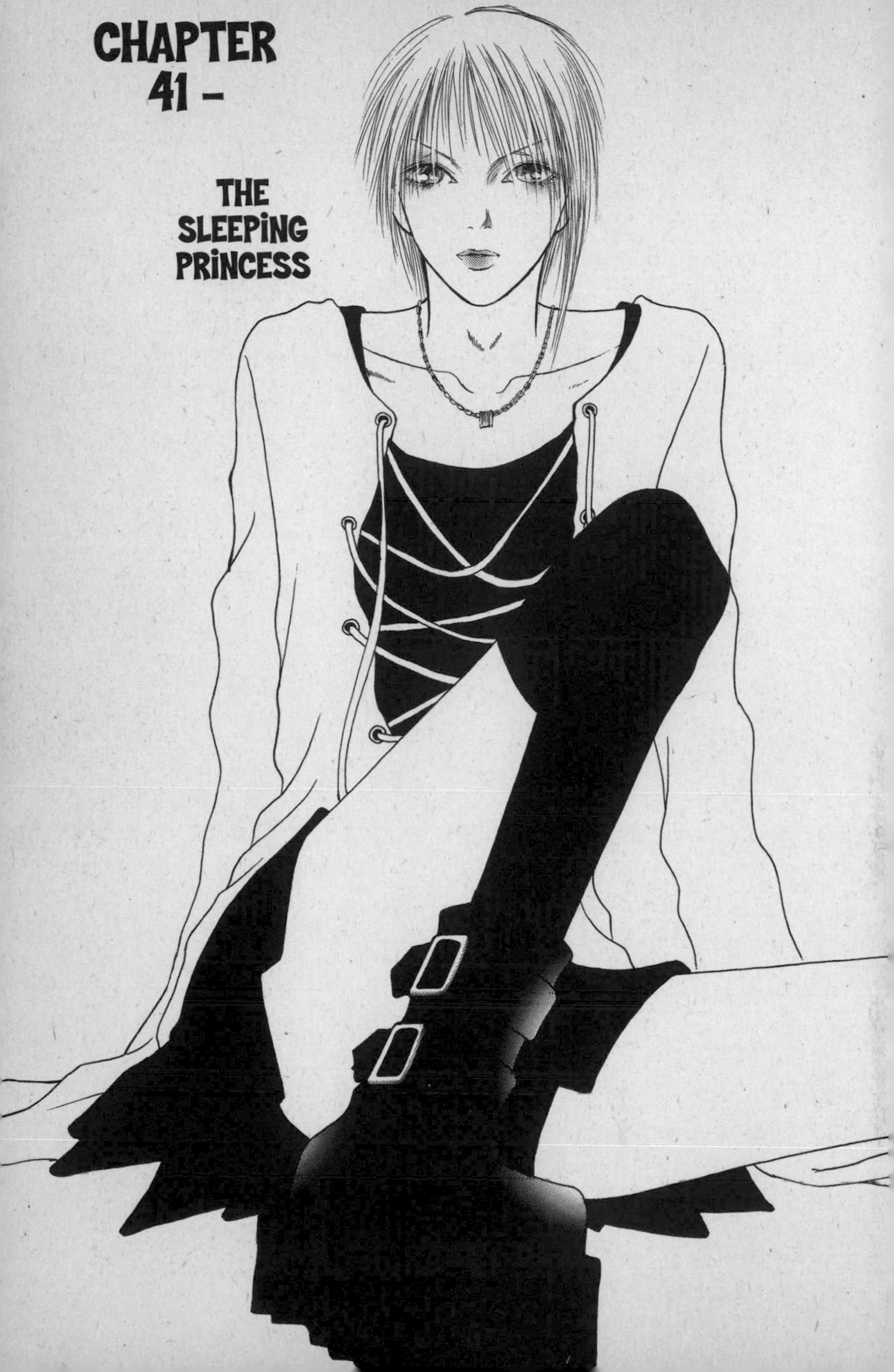

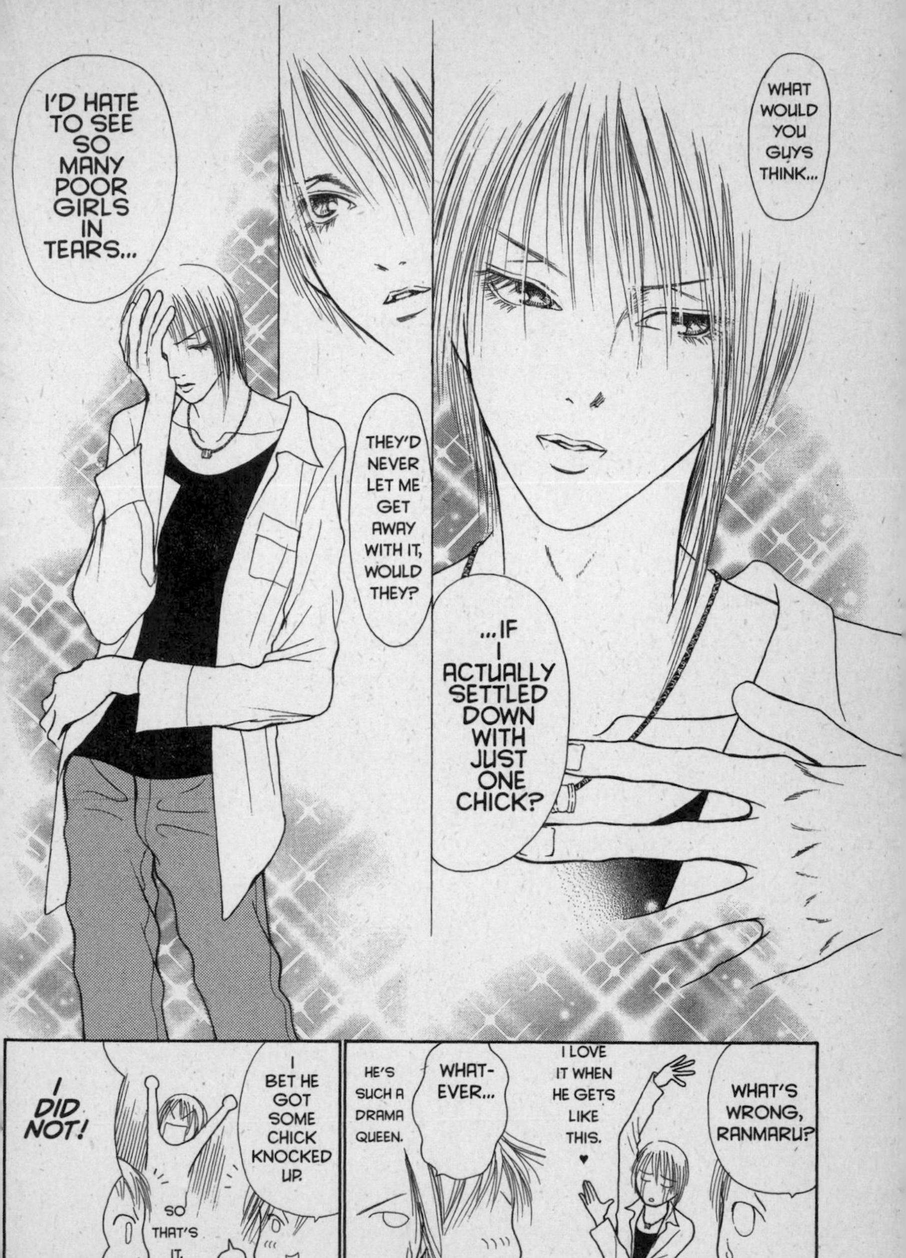
WHAT WOULD YOU GUYS THINK...
...IF I ACTUALLY SETTLED DOWN WITH JUST ONE CHICK?
THEY'D NEVER LET ME GET AWAY WITH IT, WOULD THEY?
I'D HATE TO SEE SO MANY POOR GIRLS IN TEARS...
WHAT'S WRONG, RANMARU?
I LOVE IT WHEN HE GETS LIKE THIS. ♥
WHAT-EVER...
HE'S SUCH A DRAMA QUEEN.
I BET HE GOT SOME CHICK KNOCKED UP.
SO THAT'S IT.
I DID NOT!

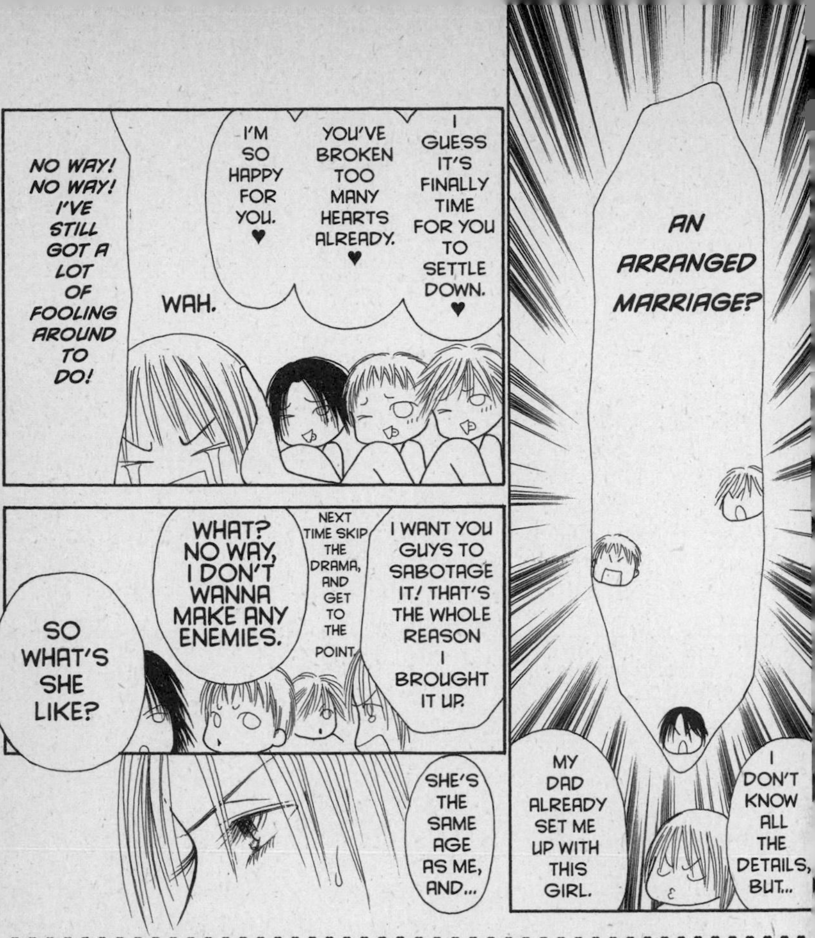
AN ARRANGED MARRIAGE?
I DON'T KNOW ALL THE DETAILS, BUT...
MY DAD ALREADY SET ME UP WITH THIS GIRL.
I GUESS IT'S FINALLY TIME FOR YOU TO SETTLE DOWN. ♥
YOU'VE BROKEN TOO MANY HEARTS ALREADY. ♥
I'M SO HAPPY FOR YOU. ♥
WAH.
NO WAY! NO WAY! I'VE STILL GOT A LOT OF FOOLING AROUND TO DO!
I WANT YOU GUYS TO SABOTAGE IT! THAT'S THE WHOLE REASON I BROUGHT IT UP.
NEXT TIME SKIP THE DRAMA, AND GET TO THE POINT.
WHAT? NO WAY, I DON'T WANNA MAKE ANY ENEMIES.
SO WHAT'S SHE LIKE?
SHE'S THE SAME AGE AS ME, AND...

BEHIND THE SCENES

I WROTE THIS STORY CAUSE I'D BEEN THINKING "IT'S ABOUT TIME I FOUND A GIRLFRIEND FOR RANMARU," BUT I HAD A REALLY HARD TIME COMING UP WITH THE RIGHT GIRL FOR HIM. I KIND OF KNEW WHAT TYPE OF GIRLS RANMARU WOULD BE ATTRACTED TO, BUT I WANTED SOMETHING FRESH. I ASKED MY CHIEF EDITOR WHAT SHE THOUGHT, AND SHE SAID, "WHAT ABOUT I-SAN, IN THE EDITING DEPARTMENT." AND THEN EVERYTHING FELL INTO PLACE. I TRIED TO KEEP IT A SECRET FROM I-SAN, BUT SHE TOTALLY KNEW WHAT I WAS UP TO. I GUESS IT KIND OF MADE HER DEPRESSED. SORRY, I-SAN...

"THE PRINCESS" DOESN'T HAVE A NAME YET. I'M STILL THINKING. ← HEY!

I'M THINKING THAT A NAME THAT ENDS IN "O" WOULD FIT HER...LIKE "TAMAO" OR "YASUYO." ARE THEY REALLY GONNA HOOK UP? EVEN I DON'T KNOW THE ANSWER TO THAT ONE.

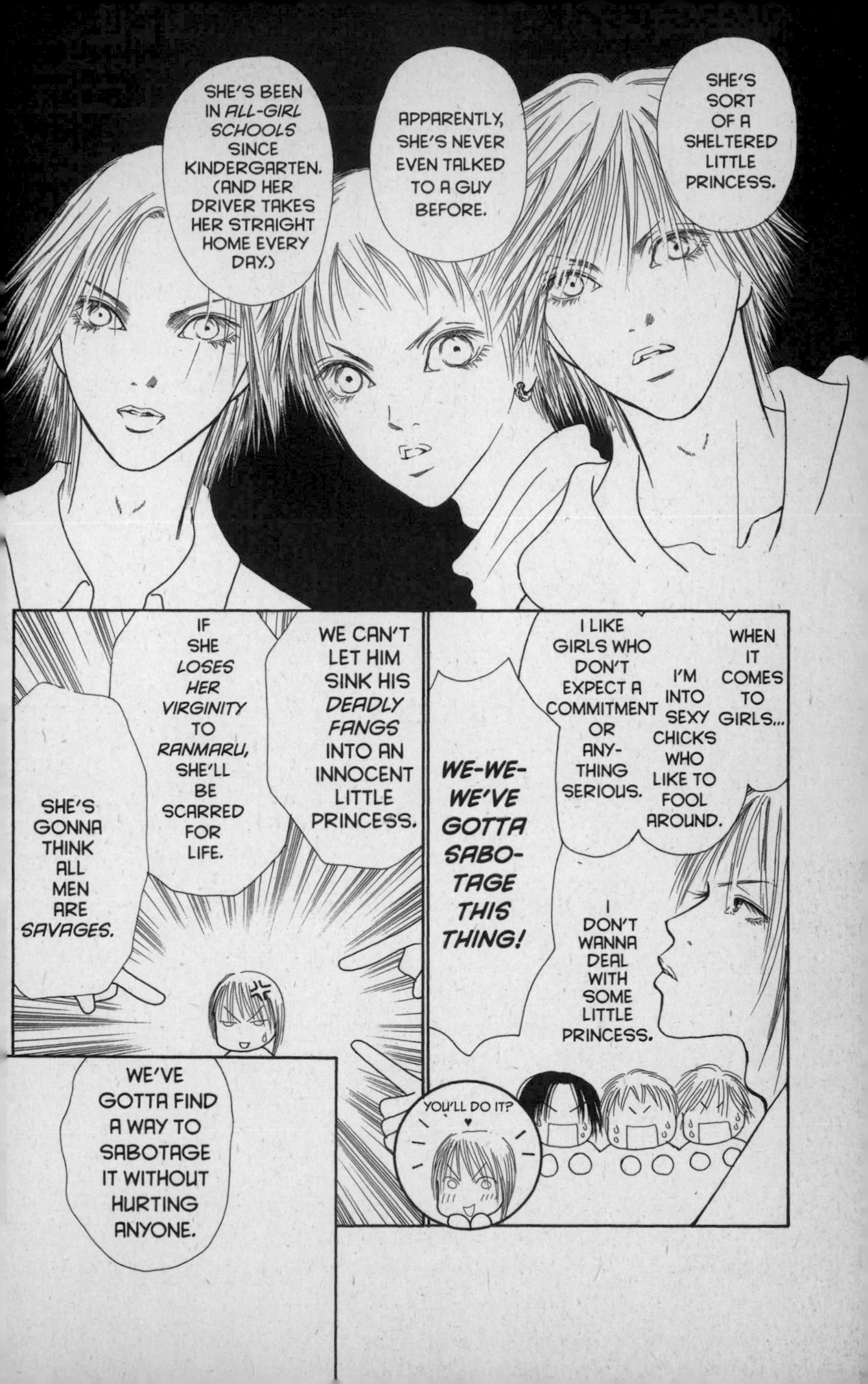

SHE'S SORT OF A SHELTERED LITTLE PRINCESS.
APPARENTLY, SHE'S NEVER EVEN TALKED TO A GUY BEFORE.
SHE'S BEEN IN *ALL-GIRL SCHOOLS* SINCE KINDERGARTEN. (AND HER DRIVER TAKES HER STRAIGHT HOME EVERY DAY.)
WHEN IT COMES TO GIRLS...
I'M INTO SEXY CHICKS WHO LIKE TO FOOL AROUND.
I LIKE GIRLS WHO DON'T EXPECT A COMMITMENT OR ANY-THING SERIOUS.
I DON'T WANNA DEAL WITH SOME LITTLE PRINCESS.
WE-WE-WE'VE GOTTA SABO-TAGE THIS THING!
YOU'LL DO IT?
WE CAN'T LET HIM SINK HIS *DEADLY FANGS* INTO AN INNOCENT LITTLE PRINCESS.
IF SHE *LOSES HER VIRGINITY* TO *RANMARU,* SHE'LL BE SCARRED FOR LIFE.
SHE'S GONNA THINK ALL MEN ARE *SAVAGES.*
WE'VE GOTTA FIND A WAY TO SABOTAGE IT WITHOUT HURTING ANYONE.

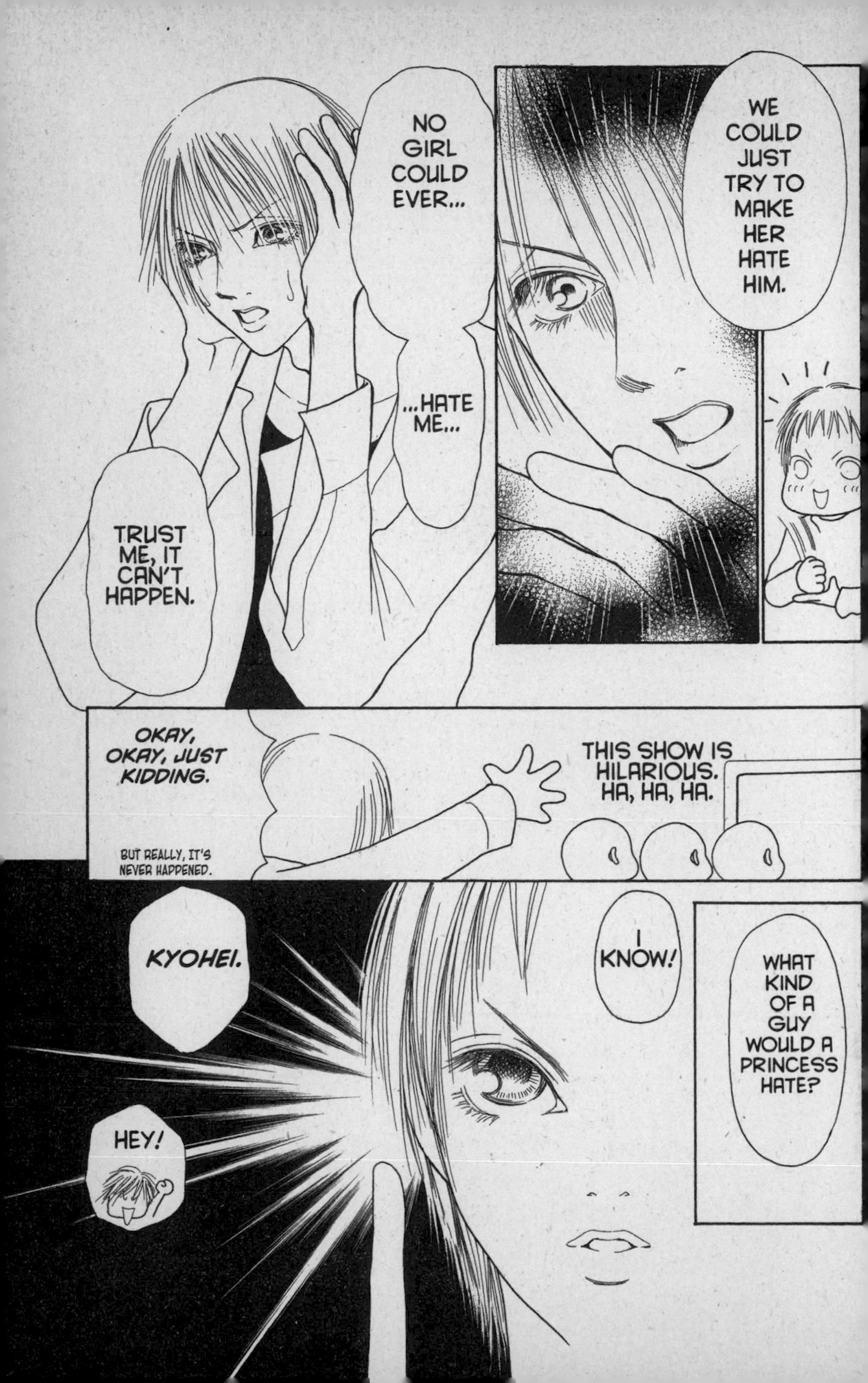
WE COULD JUST TRY TO MAKE HER HATE HIM.
NO GIRL COULD EVER...
...HATE ME...
TRUST ME, IT CAN'T HAPPEN.
THIS SHOW IS HILARIOUS. HA, HA, HA.
OKAY, OKAY, JUST KIDDING.
BUT REALLY, IT'S NEVER HAPPENED.
WHAT KIND OF A GUY WOULD A PRINCESS HATE?
I KNOW!
KYOHEI.
HEY!

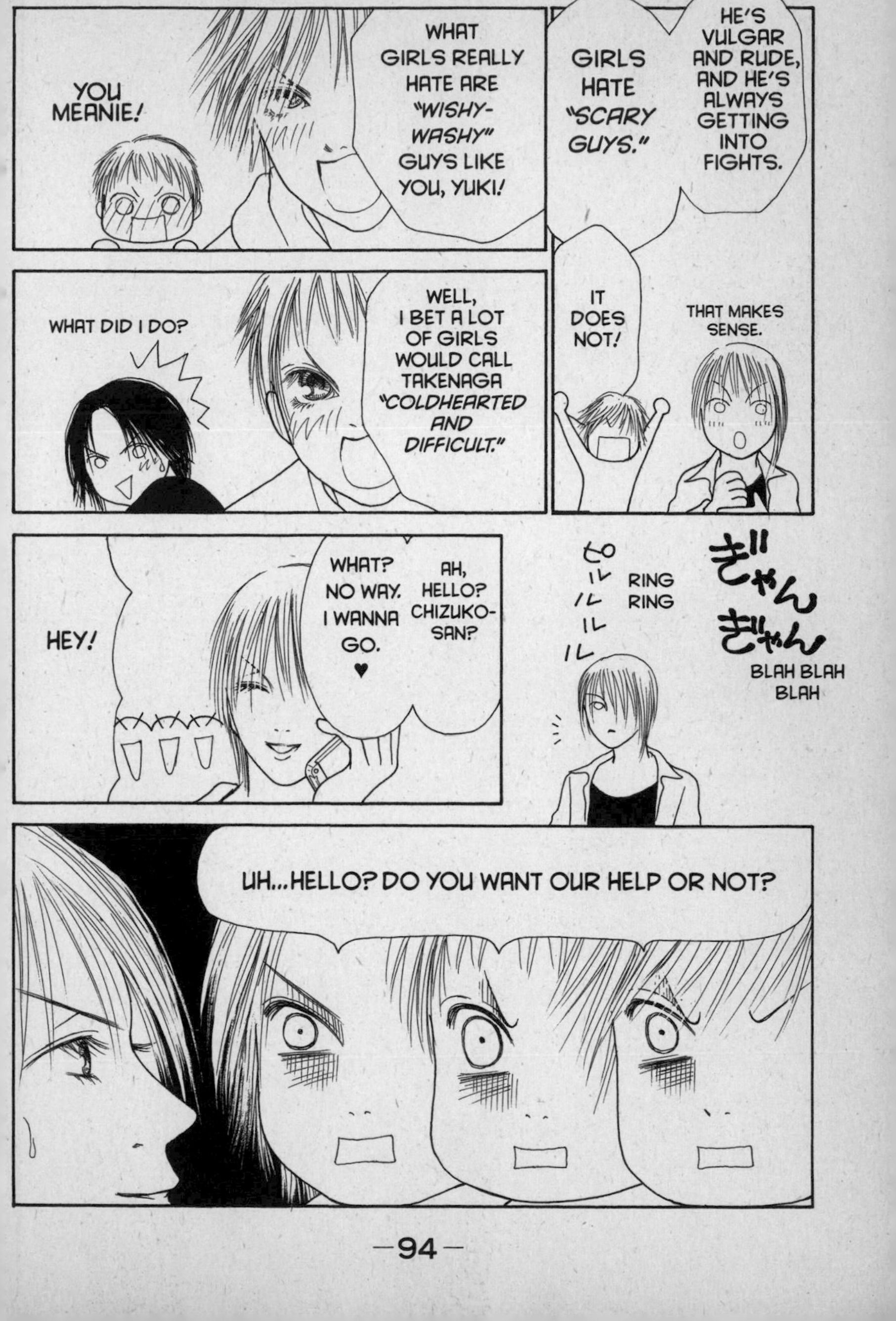
HE'S VULGAR AND RUDE, AND HE'S ALWAYS GETTING INTO FIGHTS.
GIRLS HATE "SCARY GUYS."
WHAT GIRLS REALLY HATE ARE "WISHY-WASHY" GUYS LIKE YOU, YUKI!
YOU MEANIE!
THAT MAKES SENSE.
IT DOES NOT!
WELL, I BET A LOT OF GIRLS WOULD CALL TAKENAGA "COLDHEARTED AND DIFFICULT."
WHAT DID I DO?
ぎゃんぎゃん
BLAH BLAH BLAH
ピルルル
RING RING
AH, HELLO? CHIZUKO-SAN?
WHAT? NO WAY. I WANNA GO. ♥
HEY!
UH...HELLO? DO YOU WANT OUR HELP OR NOT?

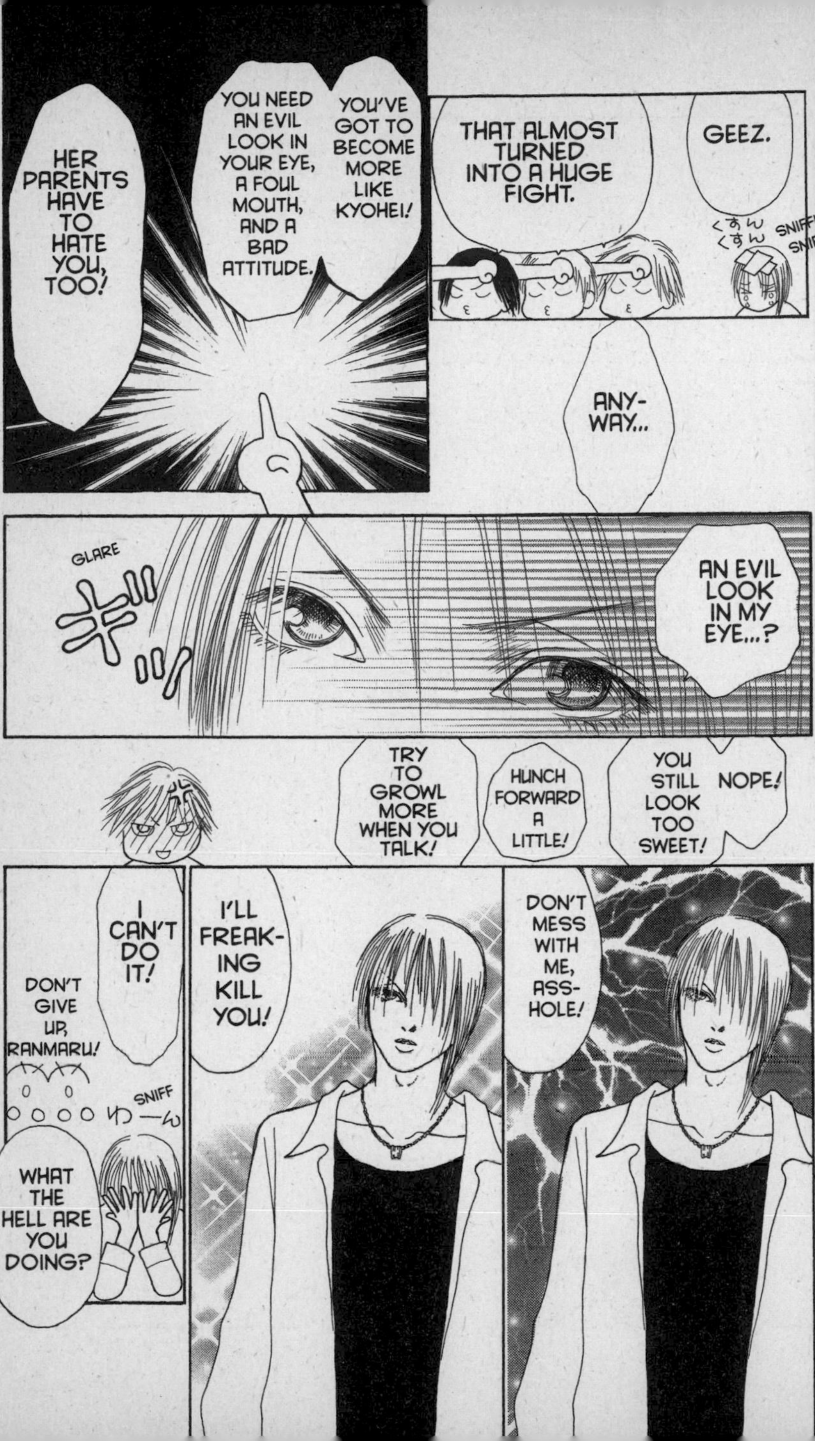
GEEZ.
THAT ALMOST TURNED INTO A HUGE FIGHT.
くすん くすん
SNIFFL
SNIFF
ANY-WAY...
YOU'VE GOT TO BECOME MORE LIKE KYOHEI!
YOU NEED AN EVIL LOOK IN YOUR EYE, A FOUL MOUTH, AND A BAD ATTITUDE.
HER PARENTS HAVE TO HATE YOU, TOO!
AN EVIL LOOK IN MY EYE...?
GLARE
NOPE!
YOU STILL LOOK TOO SWEET!
HUNCH FORWARD A LITTLE!
TRY TO GROWL MORE WHEN YOU TALK!
DON'T MESS WITH ME, ASS-HOLE!
I'LL FREAKING KILL YOU!
I CAN'T DO IT!
DON'T GIVE UP, RANMARU!
わーん
SNIFF
WHAT THE HELL ARE YOU DOING?

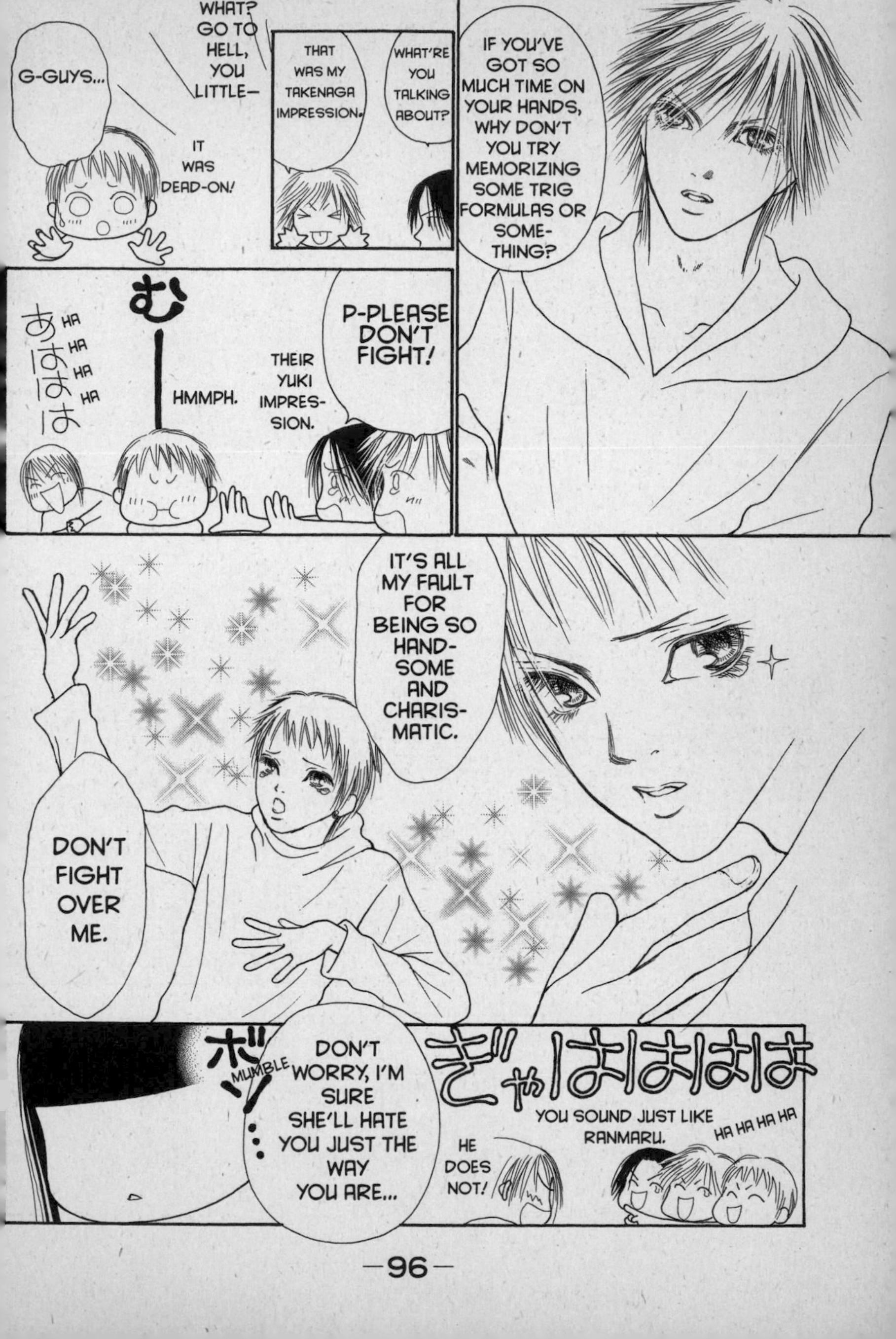
IF YOU'VE GOT SO MUCH TIME ON YOUR HANDS, WHY DON'T YOU TRY MEMORIZING SOME TRIG FORMULAS OR SOMETHING?
WHAT'RE YOU TALKING ABOUT?
THAT WAS MY TAKENAGA IMPRESSION.
WHAT? GO TO HELL, YOU LITTLE—
G-GUYS...
IT WAS DEAD-ON!
P-PLEASE DON'T FIGHT!
THEIR YUKI IMPRESSION.
むー
HMMPH.
あははは
HA HA HA HA
IT'S ALL MY FAULT FOR BEING SO HANDSOME AND CHARISMATIC.
DON'T FIGHT OVER ME.
ぎゃははははは
YOU SOUND JUST LIKE RANMARU.
HA HA HA HA
HE DOES NOT!
DON'T WORRY, I'M SURE SHE'LL HATE YOU JUST THE WAY YOU ARE...
ボソ
MUMBLE

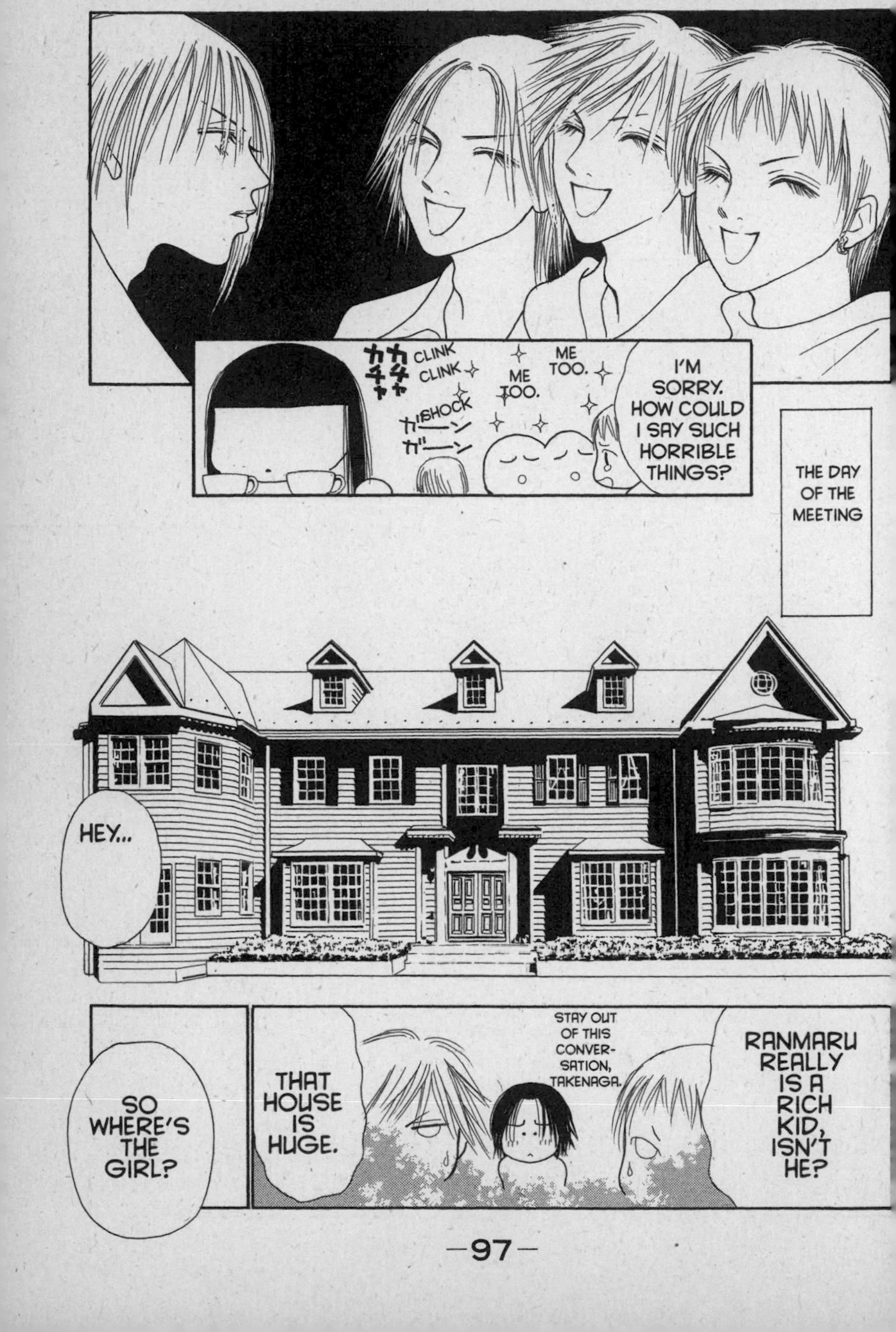
I'M SORRY. HOW COULD I SAY SUCH HORRIBLE THINGS?
ME TOO.
ME TOO.
カチャカチャ CLINK CLINK
ガーン ガーン SHOCK
THE DAY OF THE MEETING
HEY...
RANMARU REALLY IS A RICH KID, ISN'T HE?
STAY OUT OF THIS CONVERSATION, TAKENAGA.
THAT HOUSE IS HUGE.
SO WHERE'S THE GIRL?

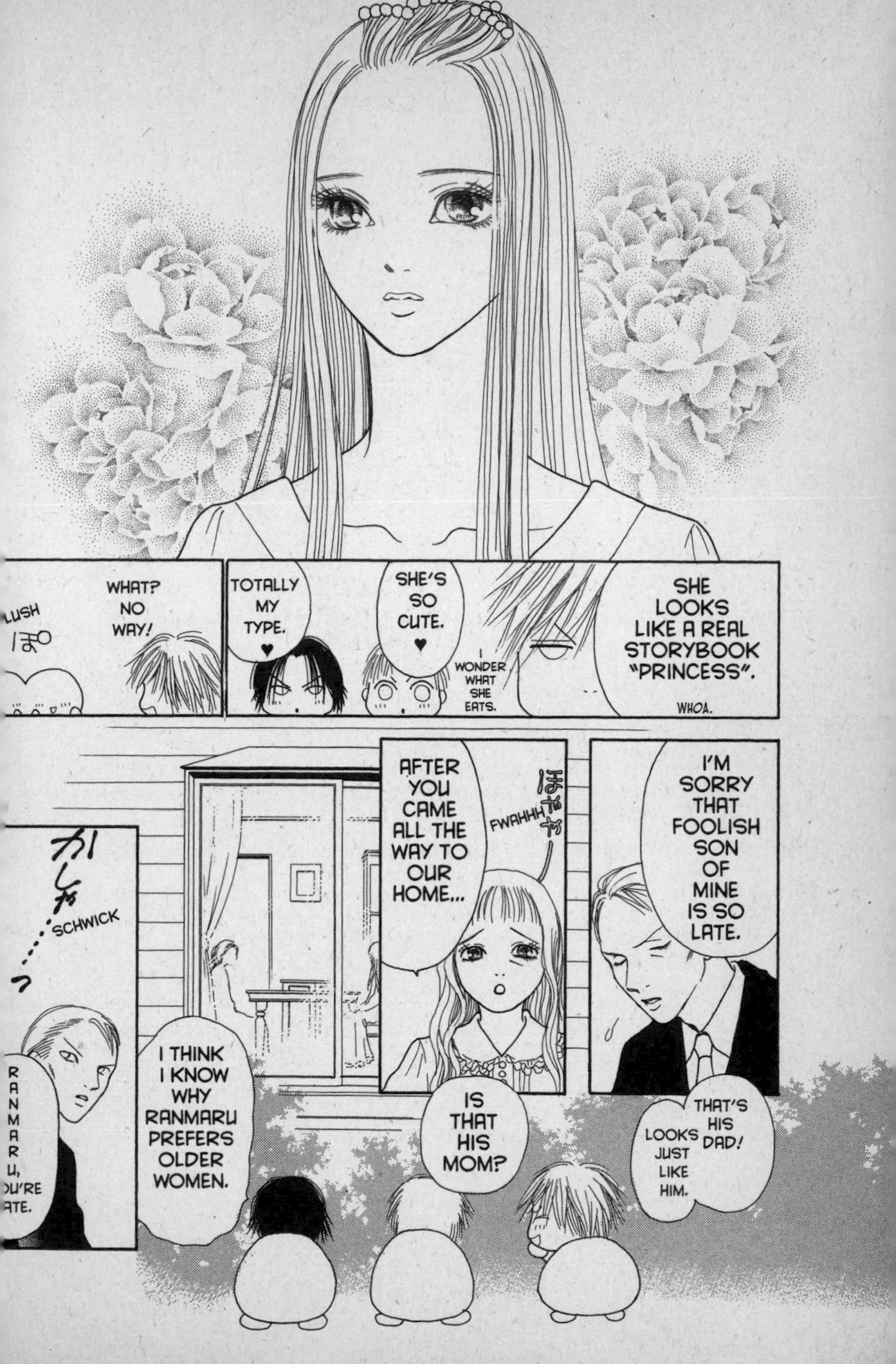
SHE LOOKS LIKE A REAL STORYBOOK "PRINCESS".
WHOA.
I WONDER WHAT SHE EATS.
SHE'S SO CUTE. ♥
TOTALLY MY TYPE. ♥
WHAT? NO WAY!
I'M SORRY THAT FOOLISH SON OF MINE IS SO LATE.
ほわわ
FWAHHH
AFTER YOU CAME ALL THE WAY TO OUR HOME...
THAT'S HIS DAD!
LOOKS JUST LIKE HIM.
IS THAT HIS MOM?
I THINK I KNOW WHY RANMARU PREFERS OLDER WOMEN.
SCHWICK
RANMARU,

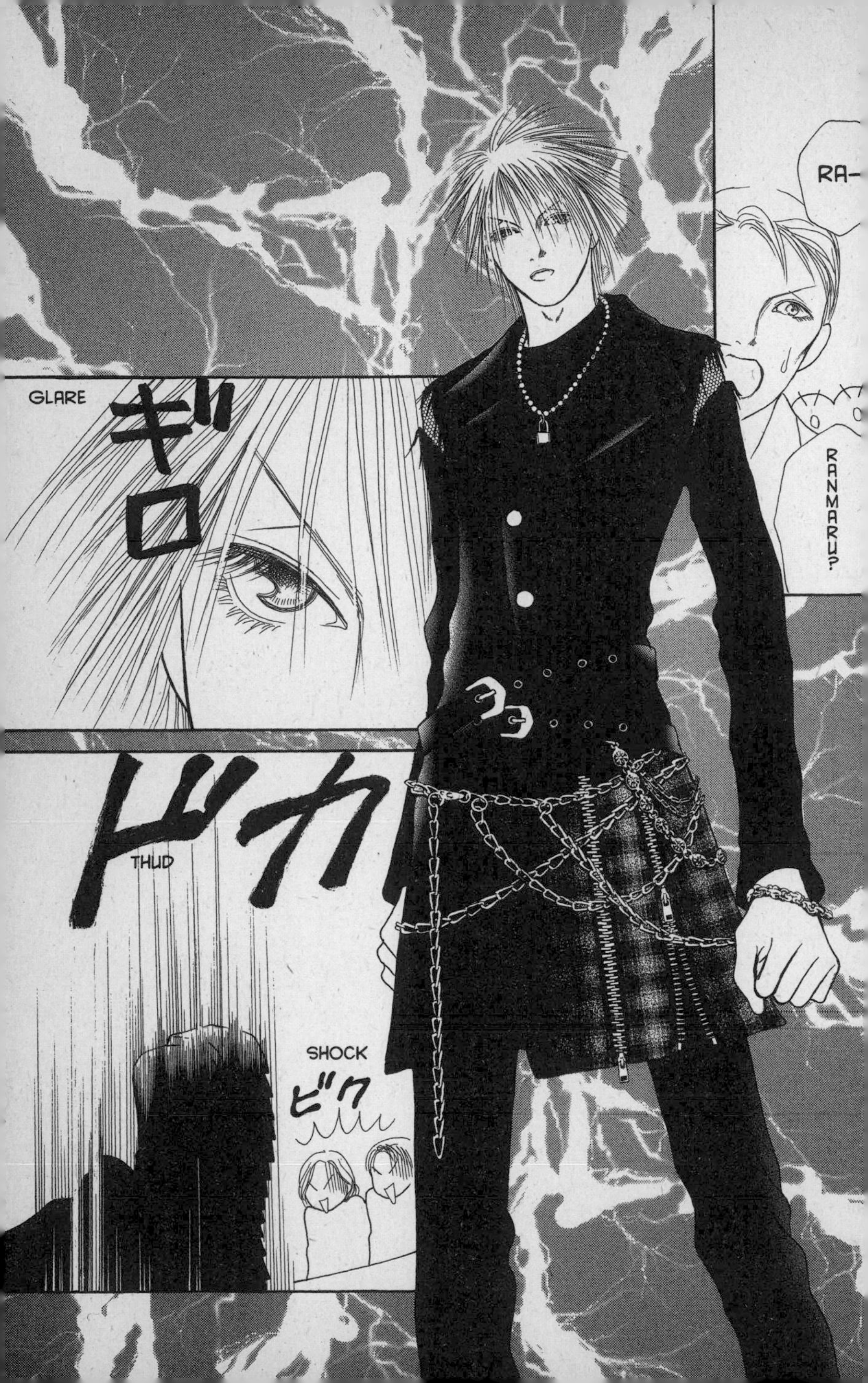
RA-
RANMARU?
GLARE
ギロ
THUD
ドカ
SHOCK
ビク

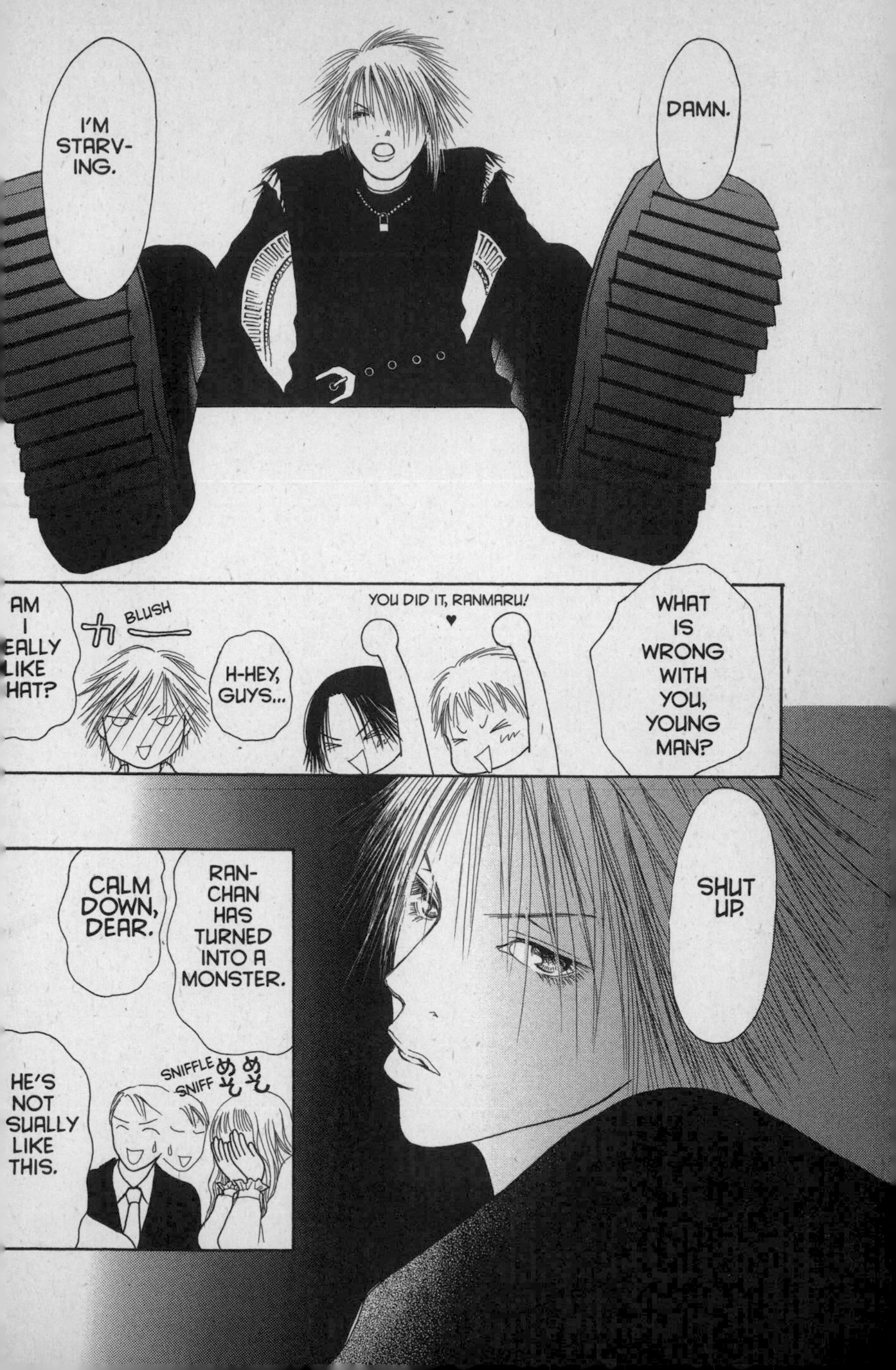
DAMN.
I'M STARV-ING.
WHAT IS WRONG WITH YOU, YOUNG MAN?
YOU DID IT, RANMARU!
H-HEY, GUYS...
BLUSH
AM I EALLY LIKE HAT?
SHUT UP.
RAN-CHAN HAS TURNED INTO A MONSTER.
CALM DOWN, DEAR.
SNIFFLE SNIFF
めそめそ
HE'S NOT SUALLY LIKE THIS.

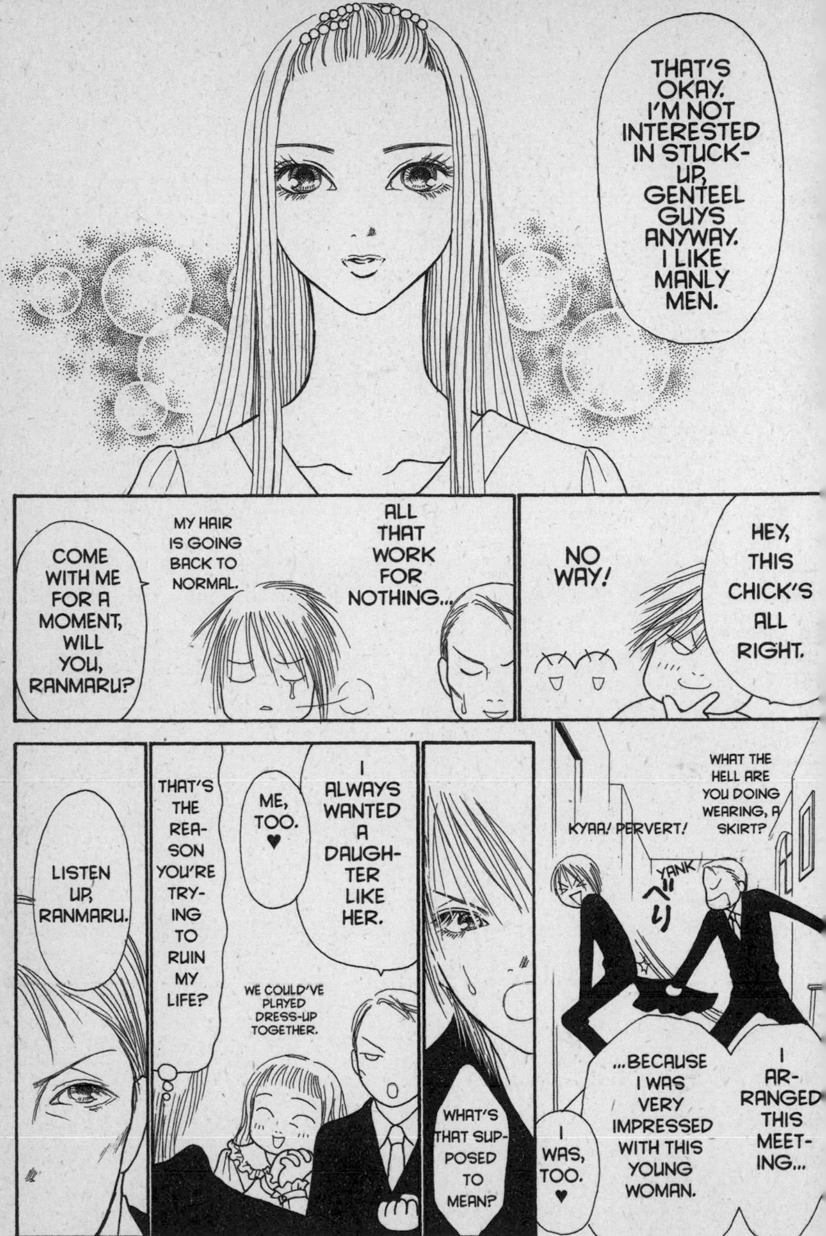
THAT'S OKAY. I'M NOT INTERESTED IN STUCK-UP, GENTEEL GUYS ANYWAY. I LIKE MANLY MEN.
HEY, THIS CHICK'S ALL RIGHT.
NO WAY!
ALL THAT WORK FOR NOTHING...
MY HAIR IS GOING BACK TO NORMAL.
COME WITH ME FOR A MOMENT, WILL YOU, RANMARU?
I ARRANGED THIS MEETING...
...BECAUSE I WAS VERY IMPRESSED WITH THIS YOUNG WOMAN.
I WAS, TOO. ♥
WHAT THE HELL ARE YOU DOING WEARING, A SKIRT?
KYAA! PERVERT!
YANK
WHAT'S THAT SUPPOSED TO MEAN?
I ALWAYS WANTED A DAUGHTER LIKE HER.
ME, TOO. ♥
WE COULD'VE PLAYED DRESS-UP TOGETHER.
THAT'S THE REASON YOU'RE TRYING TO RUIN MY LIFE?
LISTEN UP, RANMARU.

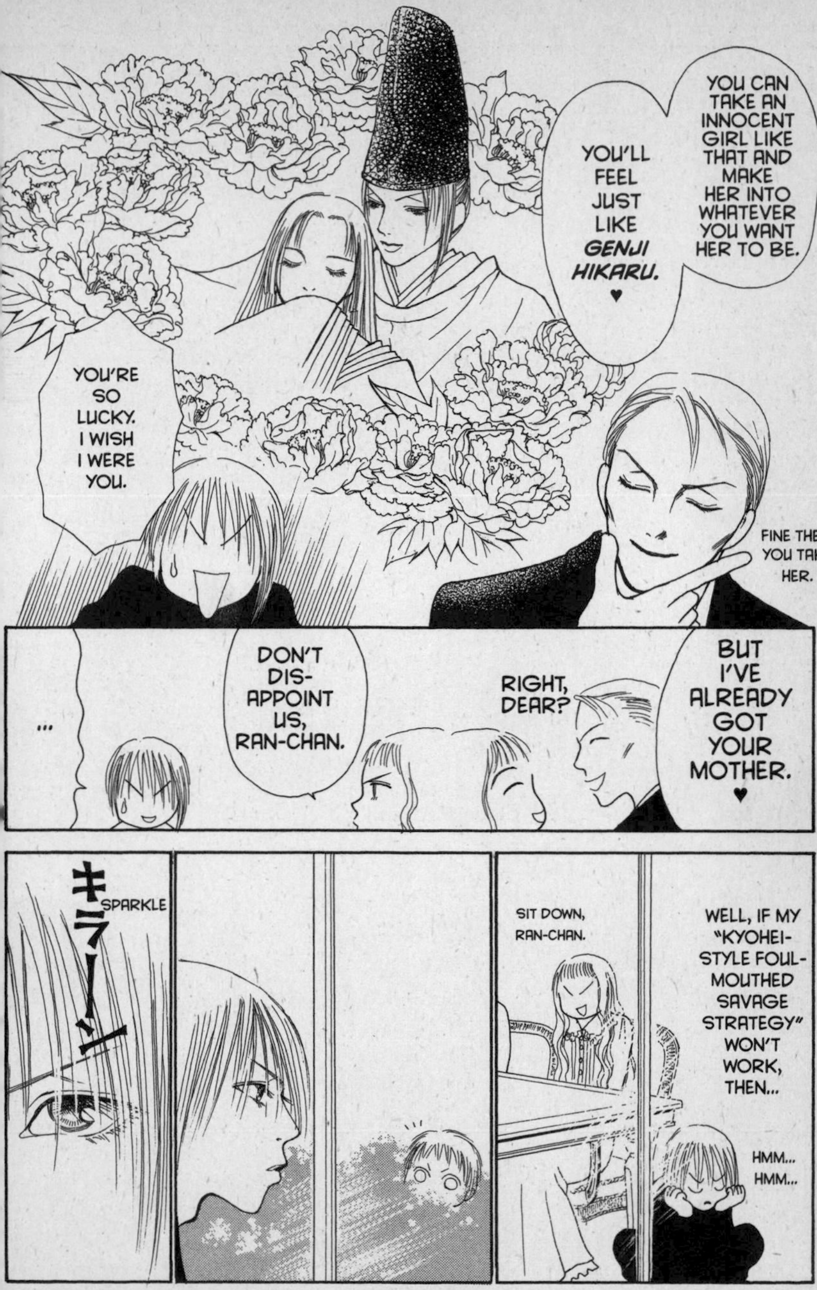
YOU CAN TAKE AN INNOCENT GIRL LIKE THAT AND MAKE HER INTO WHATEVER YOU WANT HER TO BE.
YOU'LL FEEL JUST LIKE *GENJI HIKARU.* ♥
YOU'RE SO LUCKY. I WISH I WERE YOU.
FINE THEN. YOU TAKE HER.
BUT I'VE ALREADY GOT YOUR MOTHER. ♥
RIGHT, DEAR?
DON'T DIS-APPOINT US, RAN-CHAN.
...
WELL, IF MY "KYOHEI-STYLE FOUL-MOUTHED SAVAGE STRATEGY" WON'T WORK, THEN...
SIT DOWN, RAN-CHAN.
HMM... HMM...
キラーン
SPARKLE

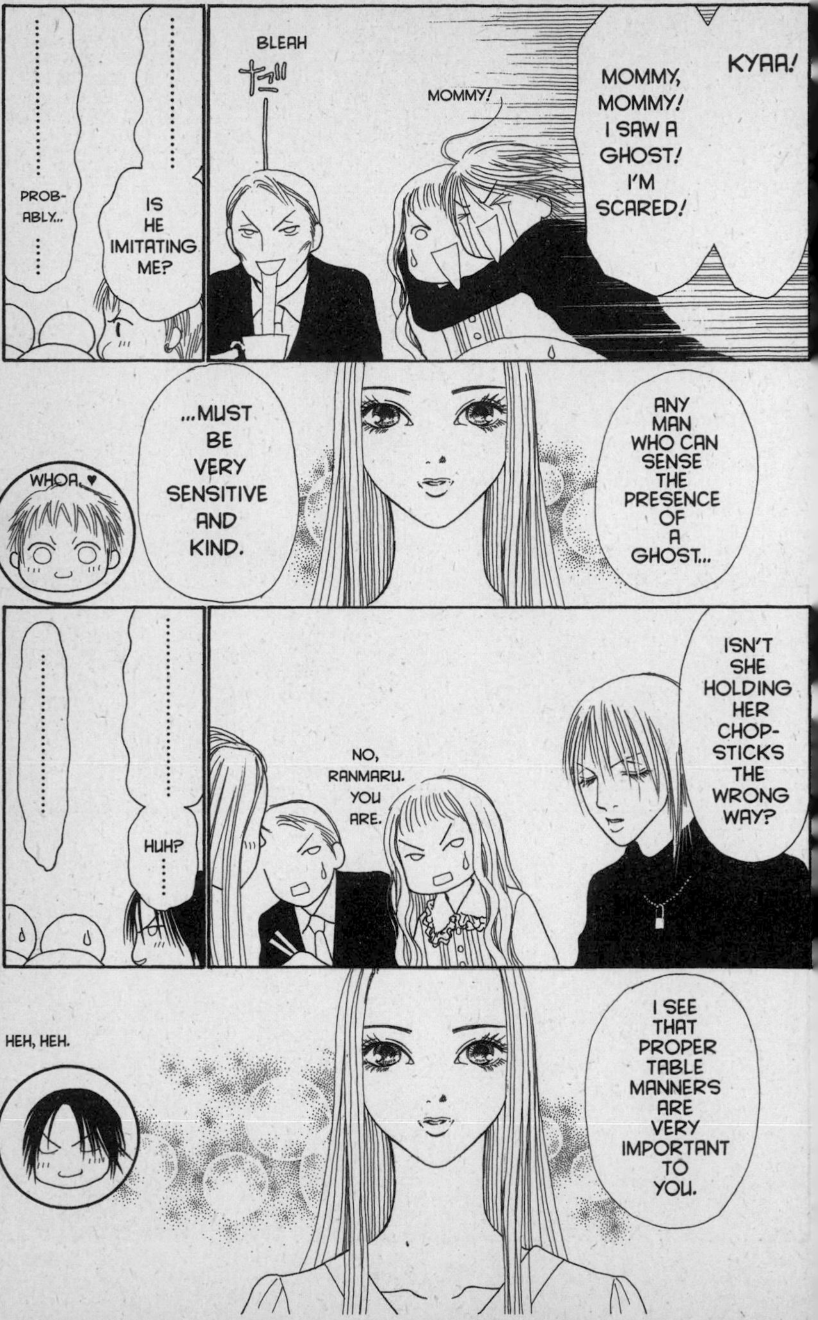
KYAA!
MOMMY, MOMMY! I SAW A GHOST! I'M SCARED!
MOMMY!
BLEAH
......IS HE IMITATING ME?
......PROBABLY......
ANY MAN WHO CAN SENSE THE PRESENCE OF A GHOST...
...MUST BE VERY SENSITIVE AND KIND.
WHOA.♥
ISN'T SHE HOLDING HER CHOPSTICKS THE WRONG WAY?
NO, RANMARU. YOU ARE.
......HUH?...
......
I SEE THAT PROPER TABLE MANNERS ARE VERY IMPORTANT TO YOU.
HEH, HEH.

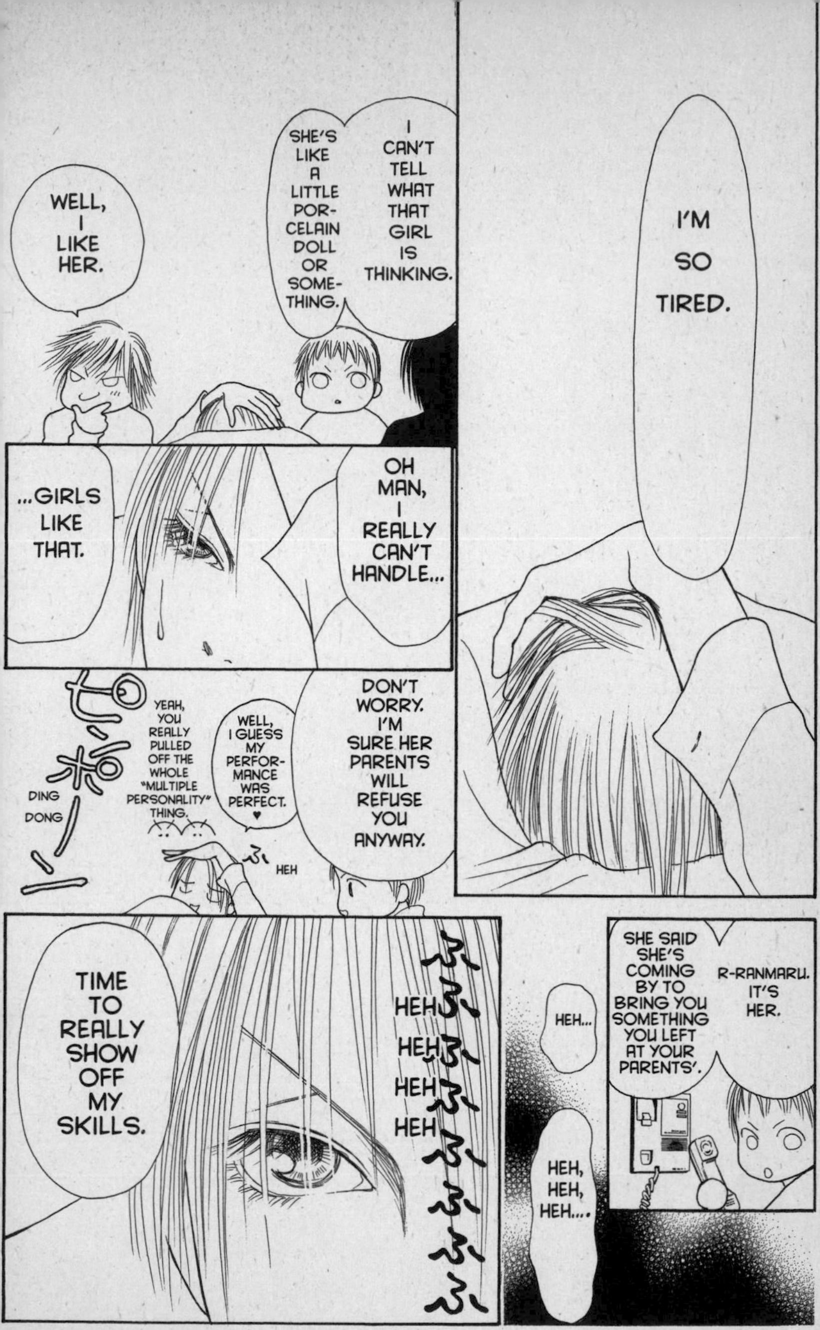

I'M SO TIRED.
I CAN'T TELL WHAT THAT GIRL IS THINKING.
SHE'S LIKE A LITTLE PORCELAIN DOLL OR SOMETHING.
WELL, I LIKE HER.
OH MAN, I REALLY CAN'T HANDLE...
...GIRLS LIKE THAT.
DON'T WORRY. I'M SURE HER PARENTS WILL REFUSE YOU ANYWAY.
WELL, I GUESS MY PERFORMANCE WAS PERFECT. ♥
YEAH, YOU REALLY PULLED OFF THE WHOLE "MULTIPLE PERSONALITY" THING.
HEH
DING DONG
R-RANMARU. IT'S HER.
SHE SAID SHE'S COMING BY TO BRING YOU SOMETHING YOU LEFT AT YOUR PARENTS'.
HEH...
HEH, HEH, HEH....
HEH HEH HEH HEH
TIME TO REALLY SHOW OFF MY SKILLS.

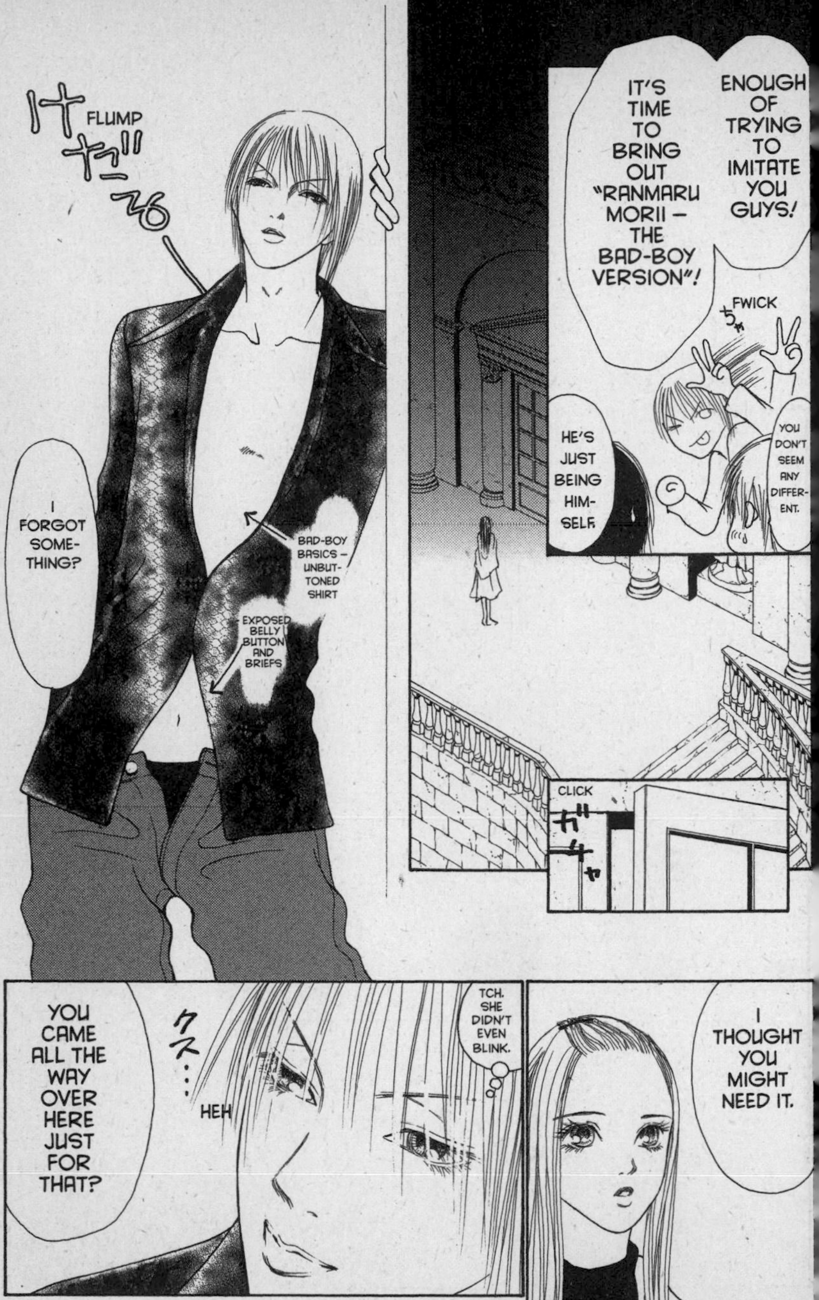

ENOUGH OF TRYING TO IMITATE YOU GUYS!
IT'S TIME TO BRING OUT "RANMARU MORII – THE BAD-BOY VERSION"!
FWICK
YOU DON'T SEEM ANY DIFFER-ENT.
HE'S JUST BEING HIM-SELF.
CLICK
FLUMP
I FORGOT SOME-THING?
BAD-BOY BASICS – UNBUT-TONED SHIRT
EXPOSED BELLY BUTTON AND BRIEFS
I THOUGHT YOU MIGHT NEED IT.
TCH. SHE DIDN'T EVEN BLINK.
HEH
YOU CAME ALL THE WAY OVER HERE JUST FOR THAT?

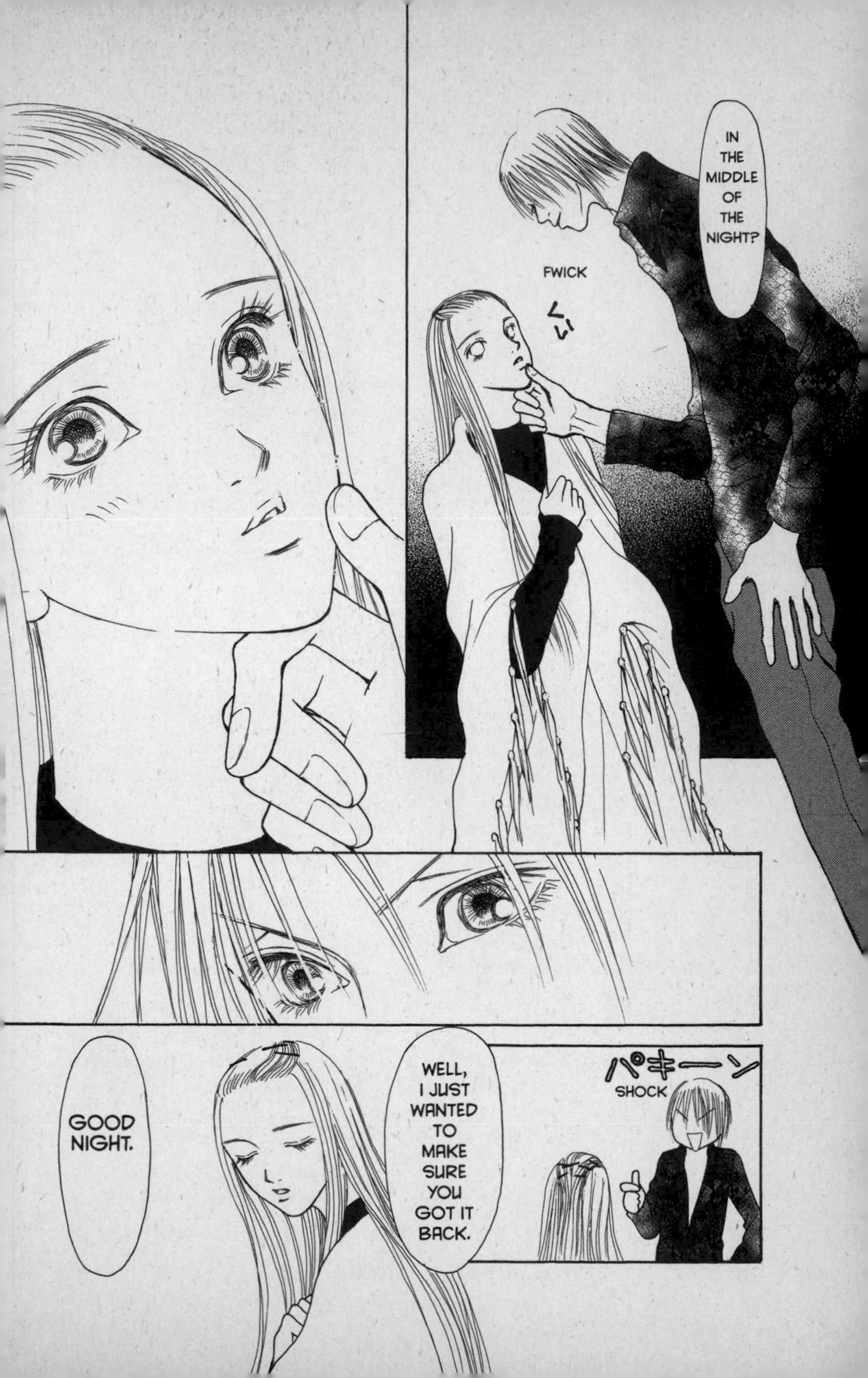
IN THE MIDDLE OF THE NIGHT?
くい
FWICK
パキーン
SHOCK
WELL, I JUST WANTED TO MAKE SURE YOU GOT IT BACK.
GOOD NIGHT.

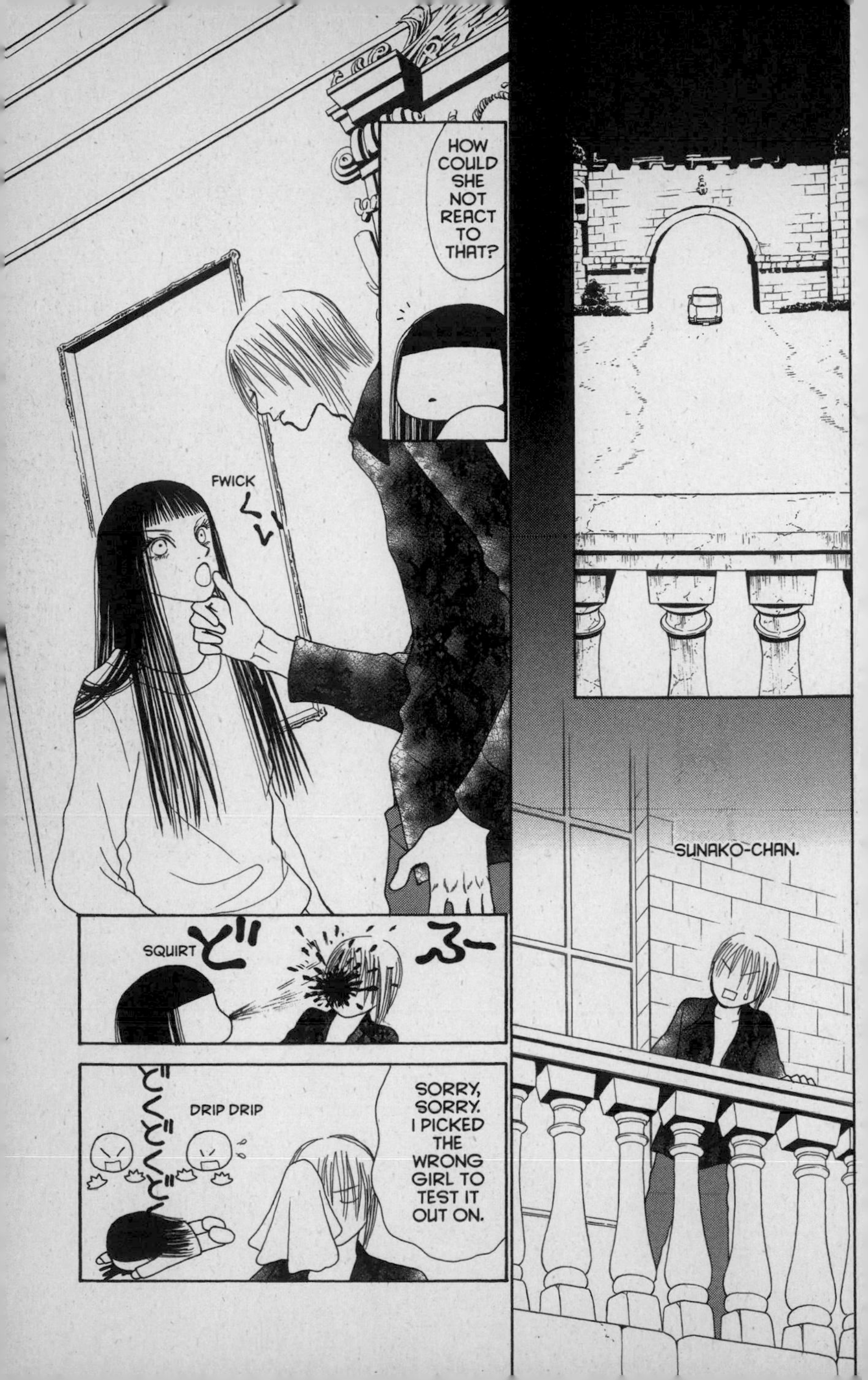
SUNAKO-CHAN.
HOW COULD SHE NOT REACT TO THAT?
FWICK
くい
ふー
SQUIRT
ど
SORRY, SORRY. I PICKED THE WRONG GIRL TO TEST IT OUT ON.
DRIP DRIP

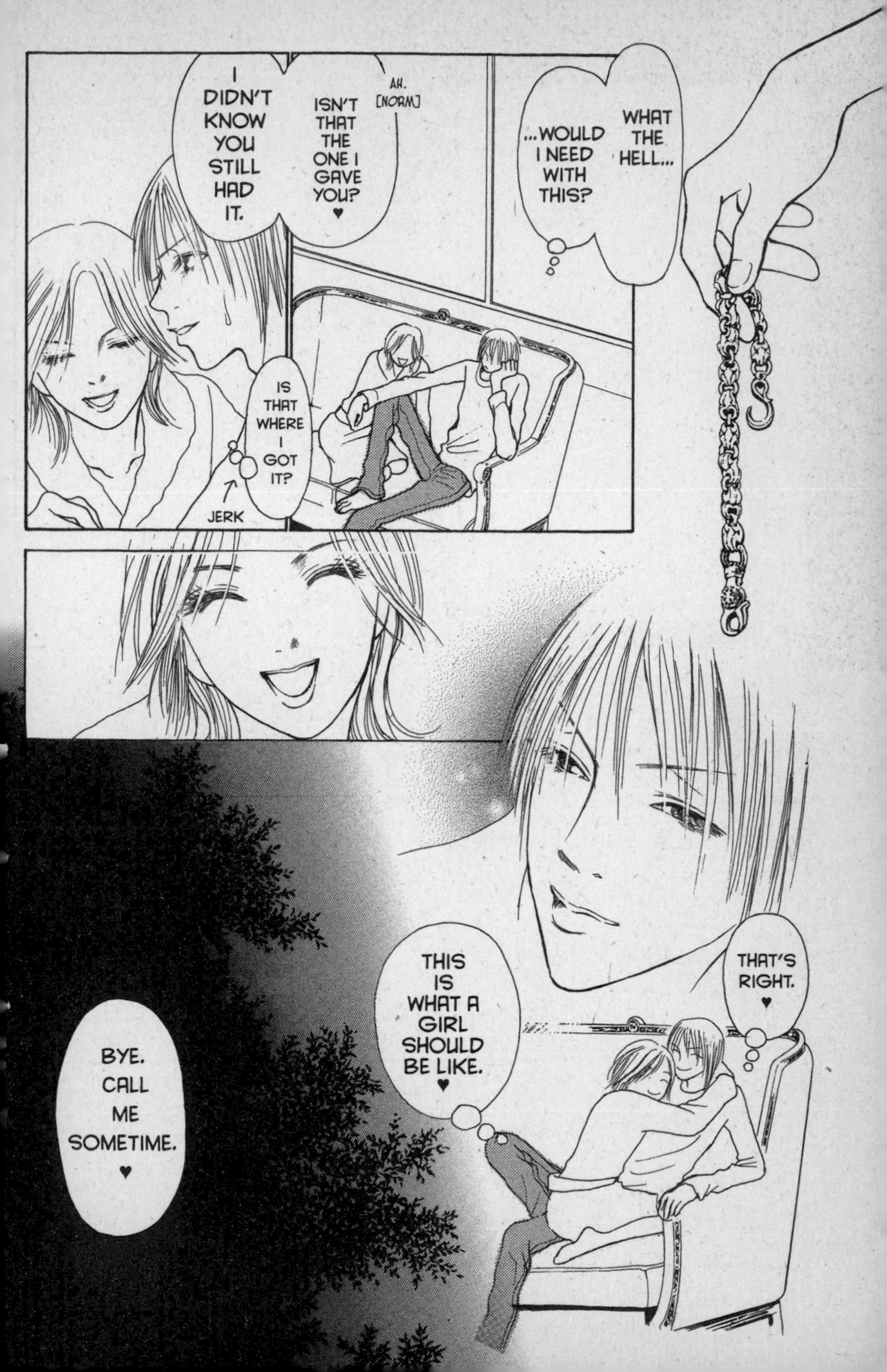
WHAT THE HELL...
...WOULD I NEED WITH THIS?
ISN'T THAT THE ONE I GAVE YOU? ♥
AH. [NORM]
I DIDN'T KNOW YOU STILL HAD IT.
IS THAT WHERE I GOT IT?
JERK
THAT'S RIGHT. ♥
THIS IS WHAT A GIRL SHOULD BE LIKE. ♥
BYE. CALL ME SOMETIME. ♥

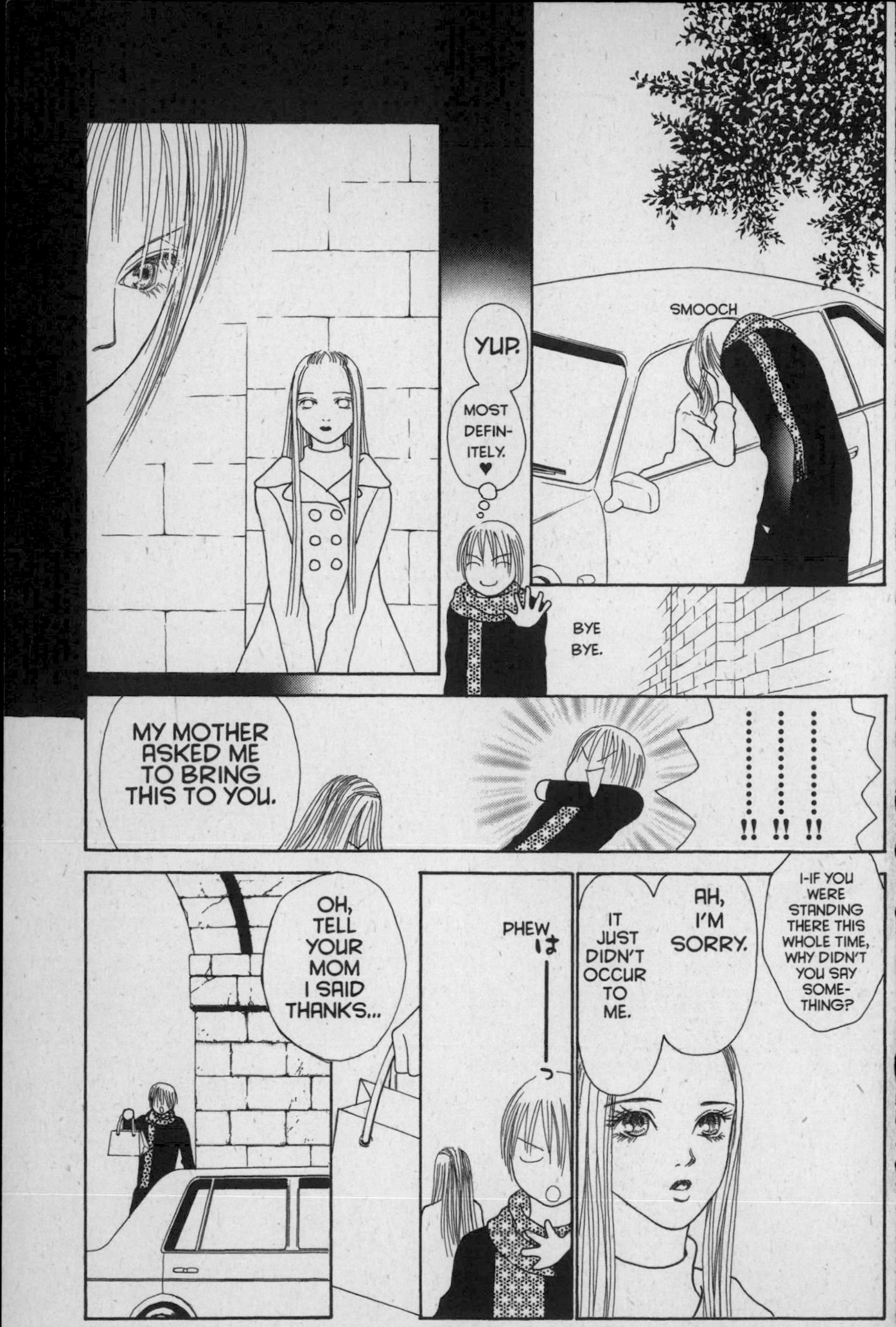
SMOOCH
YUP.
MOST DEFIN-ITELY. ♥
BYE BYE.
......!! ......!! ......!!
MY MOTHER ASKED ME TO BRING THIS TO YOU.
I-IF YOU WERE STANDING THERE THIS WHOLE TIME, WHY DIDN'T YOU SAY SOME-THING?
AH, I'M SORRY.
IT JUST DIDN'T OCCUR TO ME.
PHEW は―っ
OH, TELL YOUR MOM I SAID THANKS...

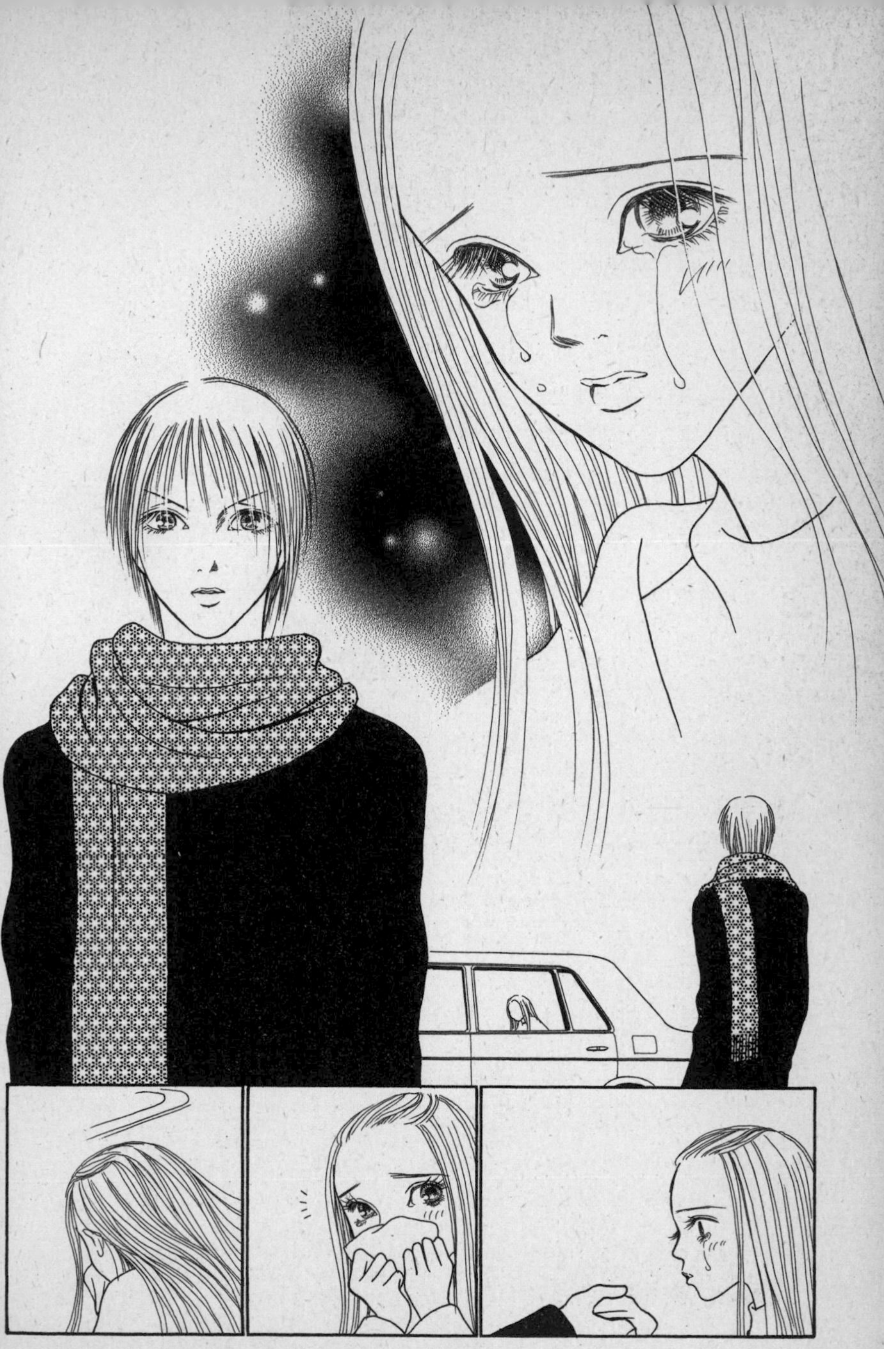

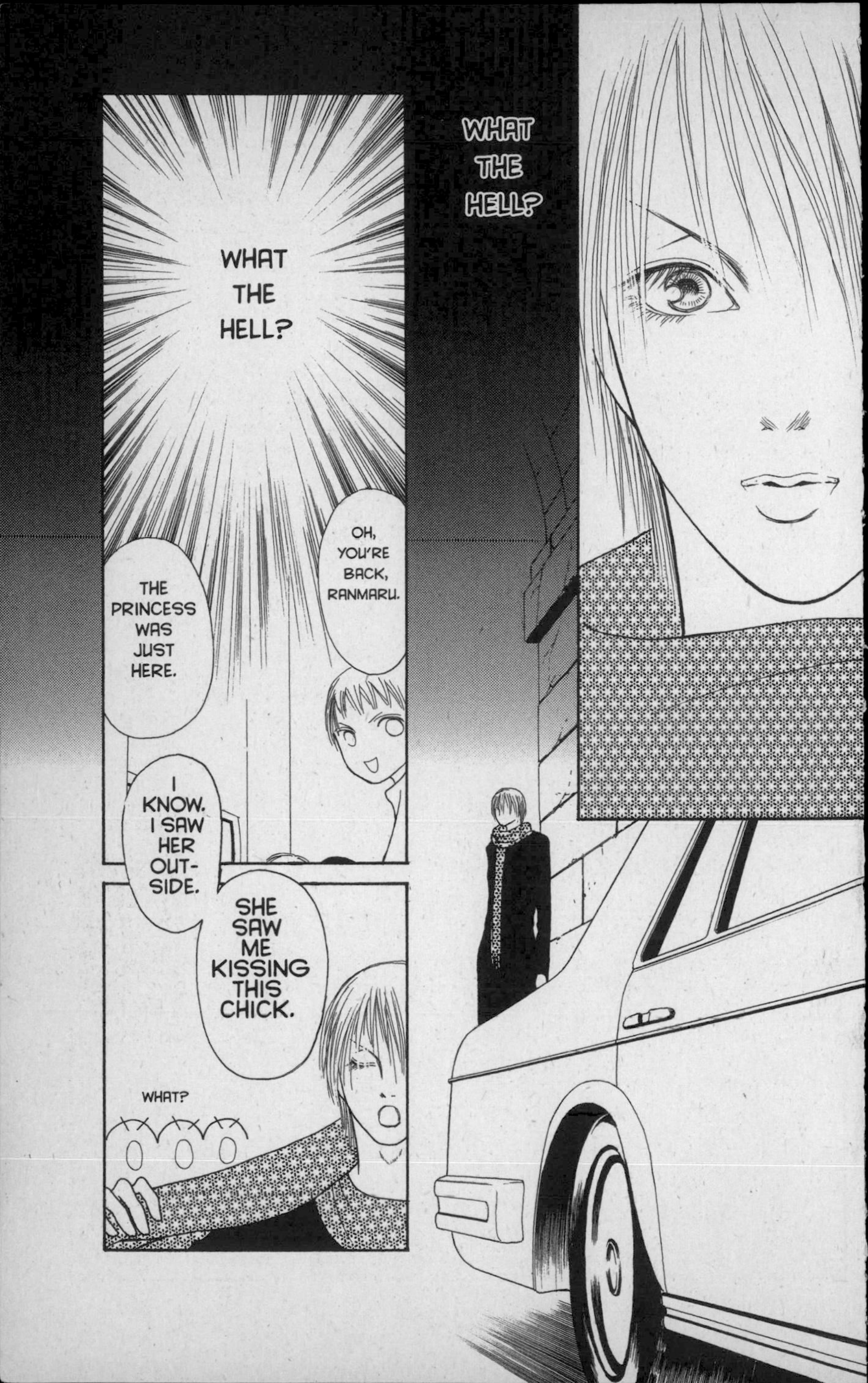
WHAT THE HELL?
WHAT THE HELL?
OH, YOU'RE BACK, RANMARU.
THE PRINCESS WAS JUST HERE.
I KNOW. I SAW HER OUT-SIDE.
SHE SAW ME KISSING THIS CHICK.
WHAT?

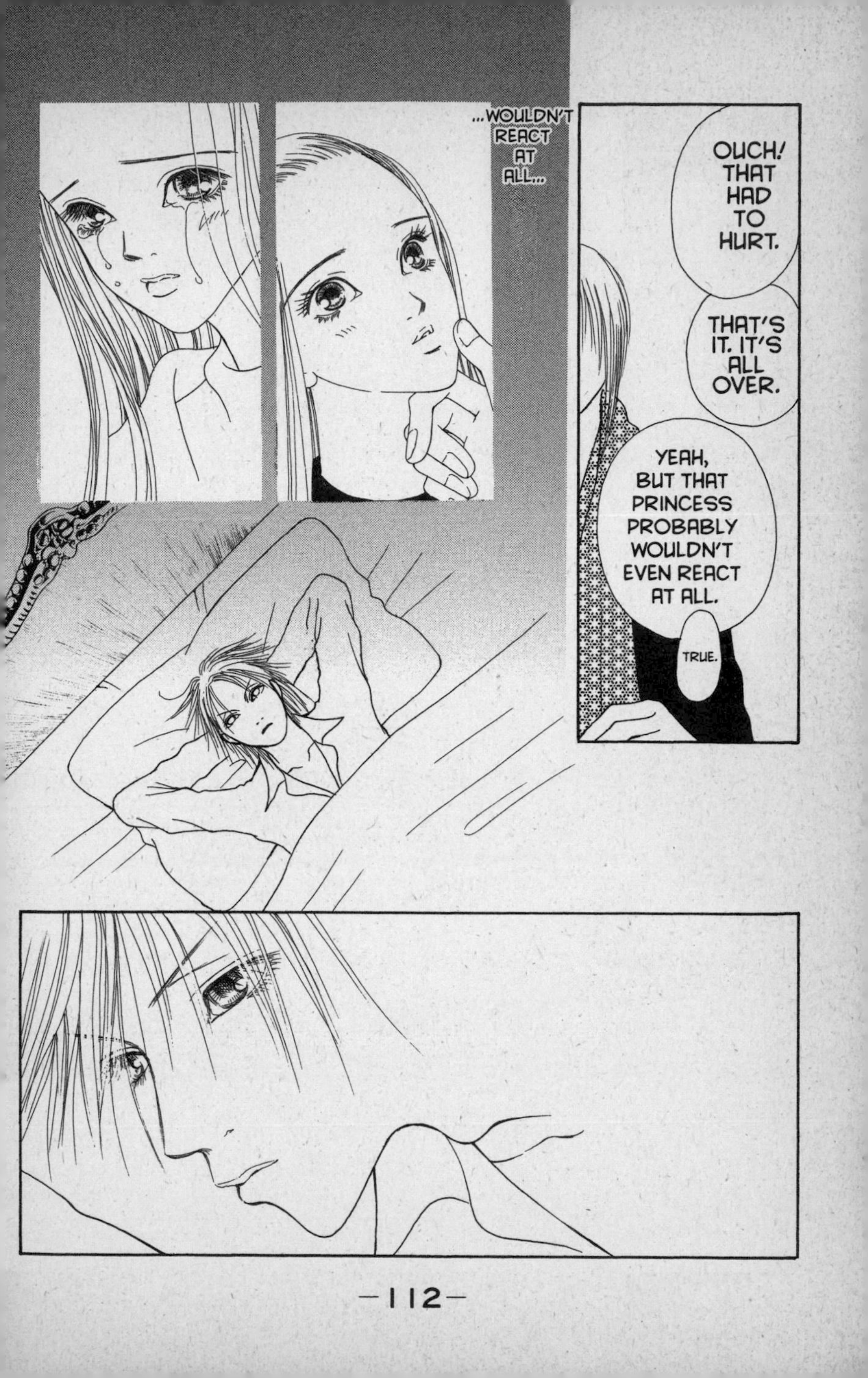
OUCH! THAT HAD TO HURT.
THAT'S IT. IT'S ALL OVER.
YEAH, BUT THAT PRINCESS PROBABLY WOULDN'T EVEN REACT AT ALL.
TRUE.
...WOULDN'T REACT AT ALL...

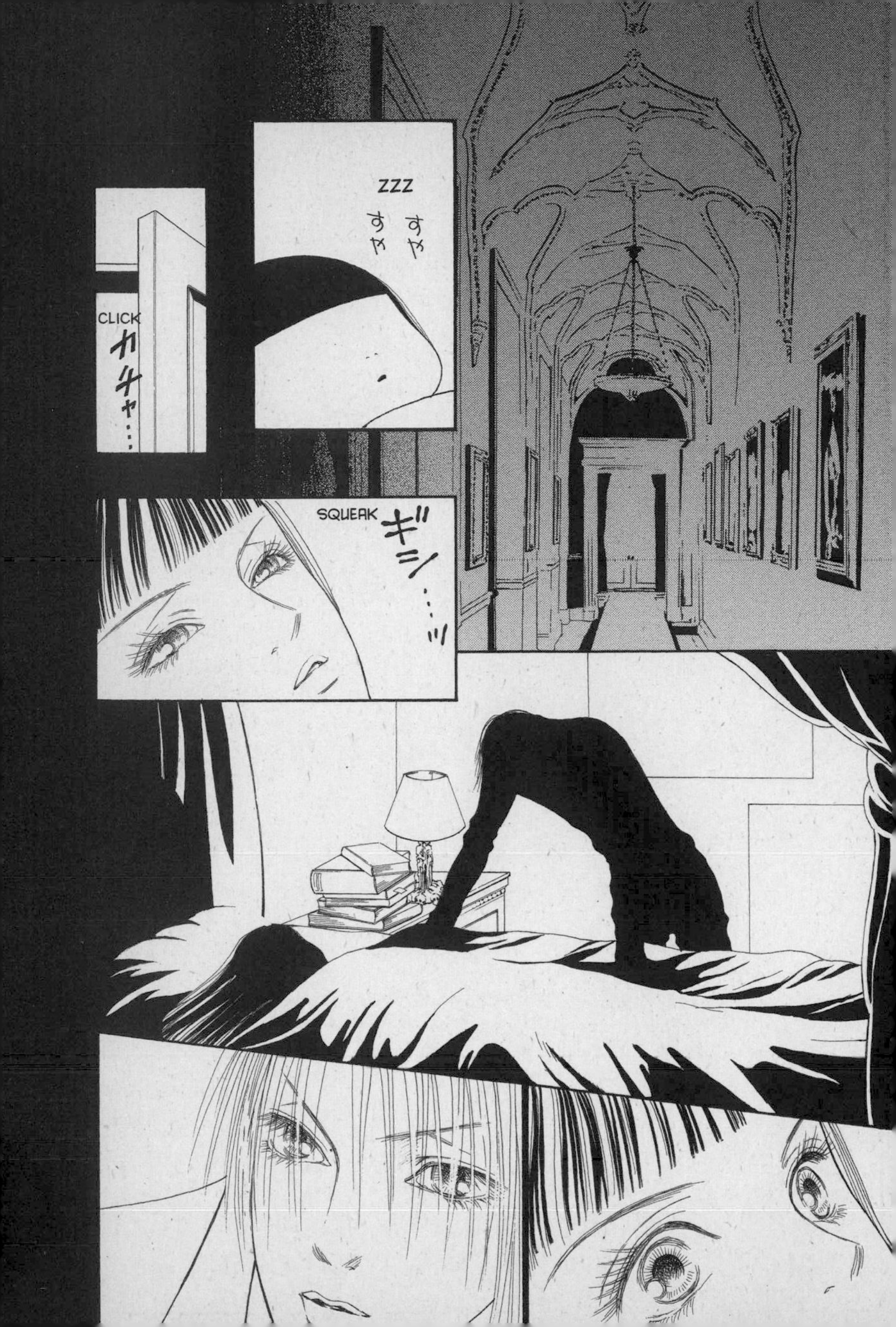
ZZZ
すやすや
CLICK
カチャ…
SQUEAK
ギシ…ッ

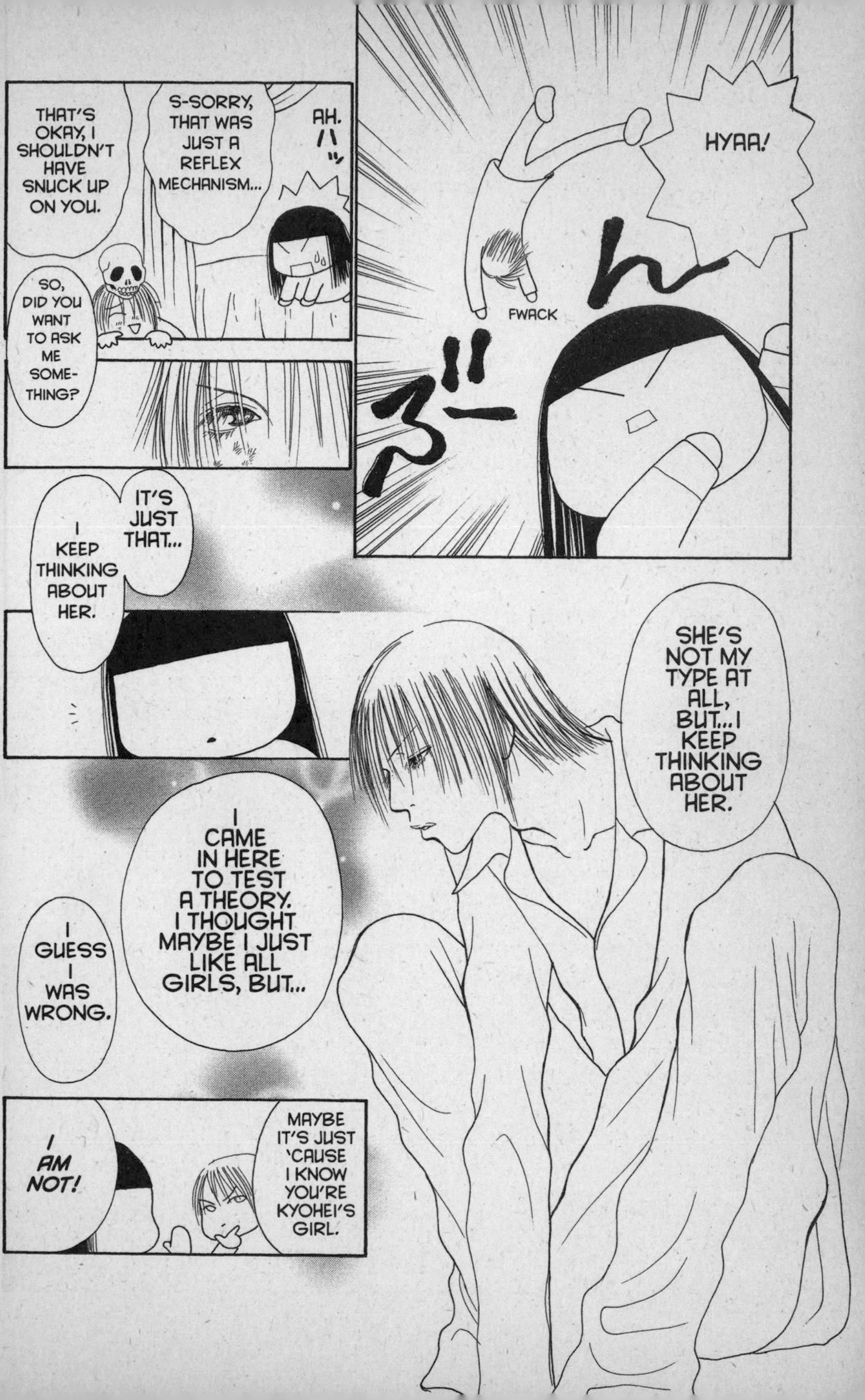

HYAA!
ぶーん
FWACK
AH.
S-SORRY, THAT WAS JUST A REFLEX MECHANISM...
THAT'S OKAY, I SHOULDN'T HAVE SNUCK UP ON YOU.
SO, DID YOU WANT TO ASK ME SOME-THING?
IT'S JUST THAT...
I KEEP THINKING ABOUT HER.
SHE'S NOT MY TYPE AT ALL, BUT...I KEEP THINKING ABOUT HER.
I CAME IN HERE TO TEST A THEORY. I THOUGHT MAYBE I JUST LIKE ALL GIRLS, BUT...
I GUESS I WAS WRONG.
MAYBE IT'S JUST 'CAUSE I KNOW YOU'RE KYOHEI'S GIRL.
I AM NOT!

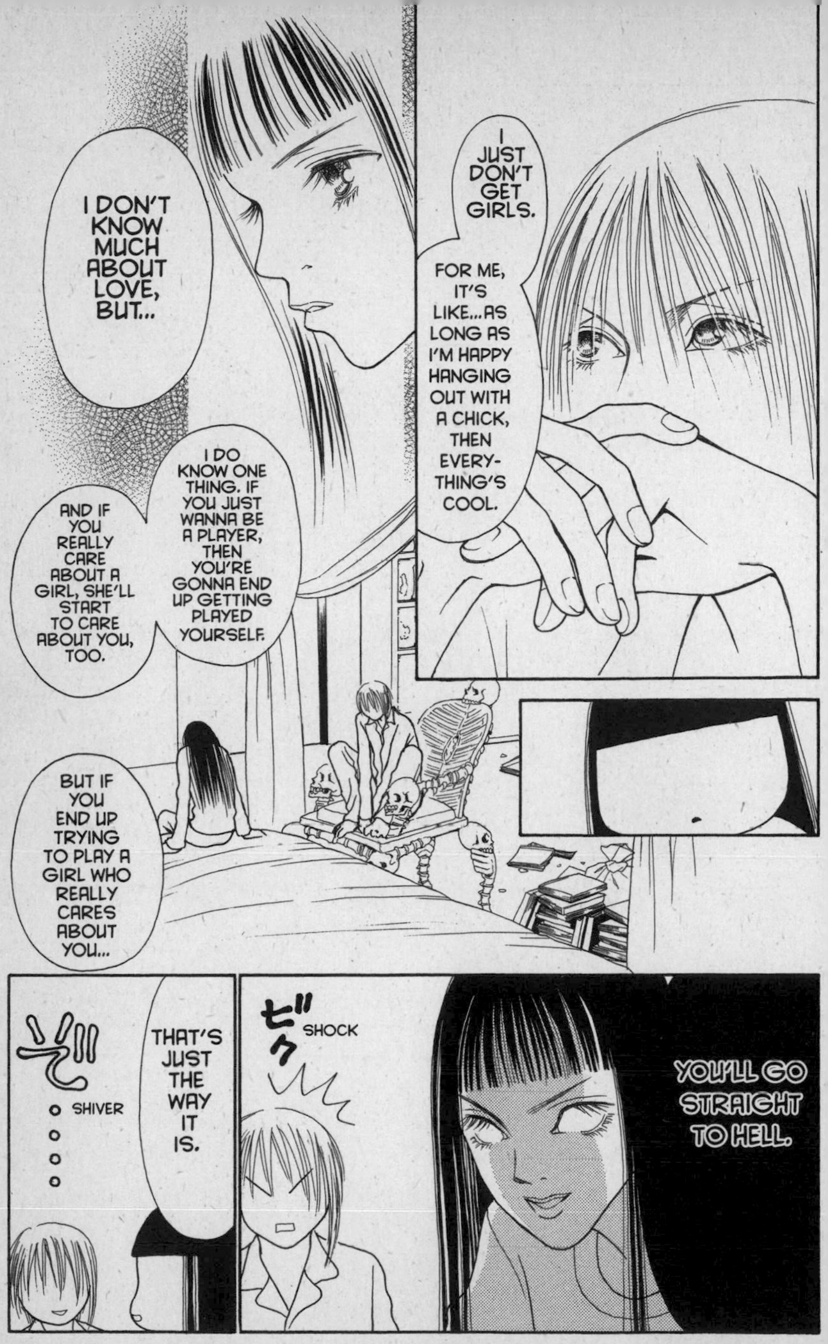
I JUST DON'T GET GIRLS.
FOR ME, IT'S LIKE...AS LONG AS I'M HAPPY HANGING OUT WITH A CHICK, THEN EVERY-THING'S COOL.
I DON'T KNOW MUCH ABOUT LOVE, BUT...
I DO KNOW ONE THING. IF YOU JUST WANNA BE A PLAYER, THEN YOU'RE GONNA END UP GETTING PLAYED YOURSELF.
AND IF YOU REALLY CARE ABOUT A GIRL, SHE'LL START TO CARE ABOUT YOU, TOO.
BUT IF YOU END UP TRYING TO PLAY A GIRL WHO REALLY CARES ABOUT YOU...
YOU'LL GO STRAIGHT TO HELL.
ビク
SHOCK
THAT'S JUST THE WAY IT IS.
ゾ
SHIVER

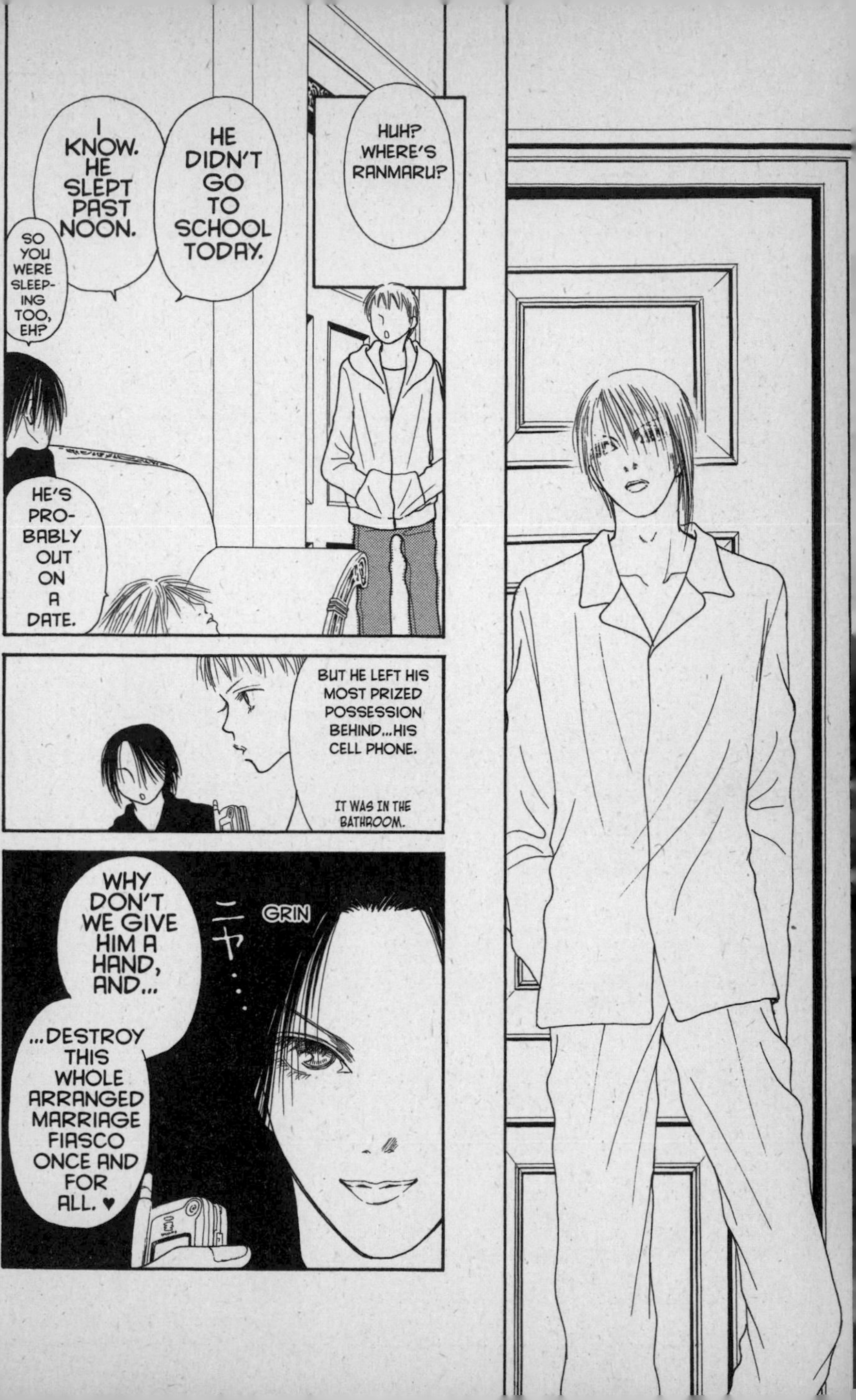
HUH? WHERE'S RANMARU?
HE DIDN'T GO TO SCHOOL TODAY.
I KNOW. HE SLEPT PAST NOON.
SO YOU WERE SLEEP-ING TOO, EH?
HE'S PRO-BABLY OUT ON A DATE.
BUT HE LEFT HIS MOST PRIZED POSSESSION BEHIND...HIS CELL PHONE.
IT WAS IN THE BATHROOM.
ニヤ…
GRIN
WHY DON'T WE GIVE HIM A HAND, AND...
...DESTROY THIS WHOLE ARRANGED MARRIAGE FIASCO ONCE AND FOR ALL. ♥

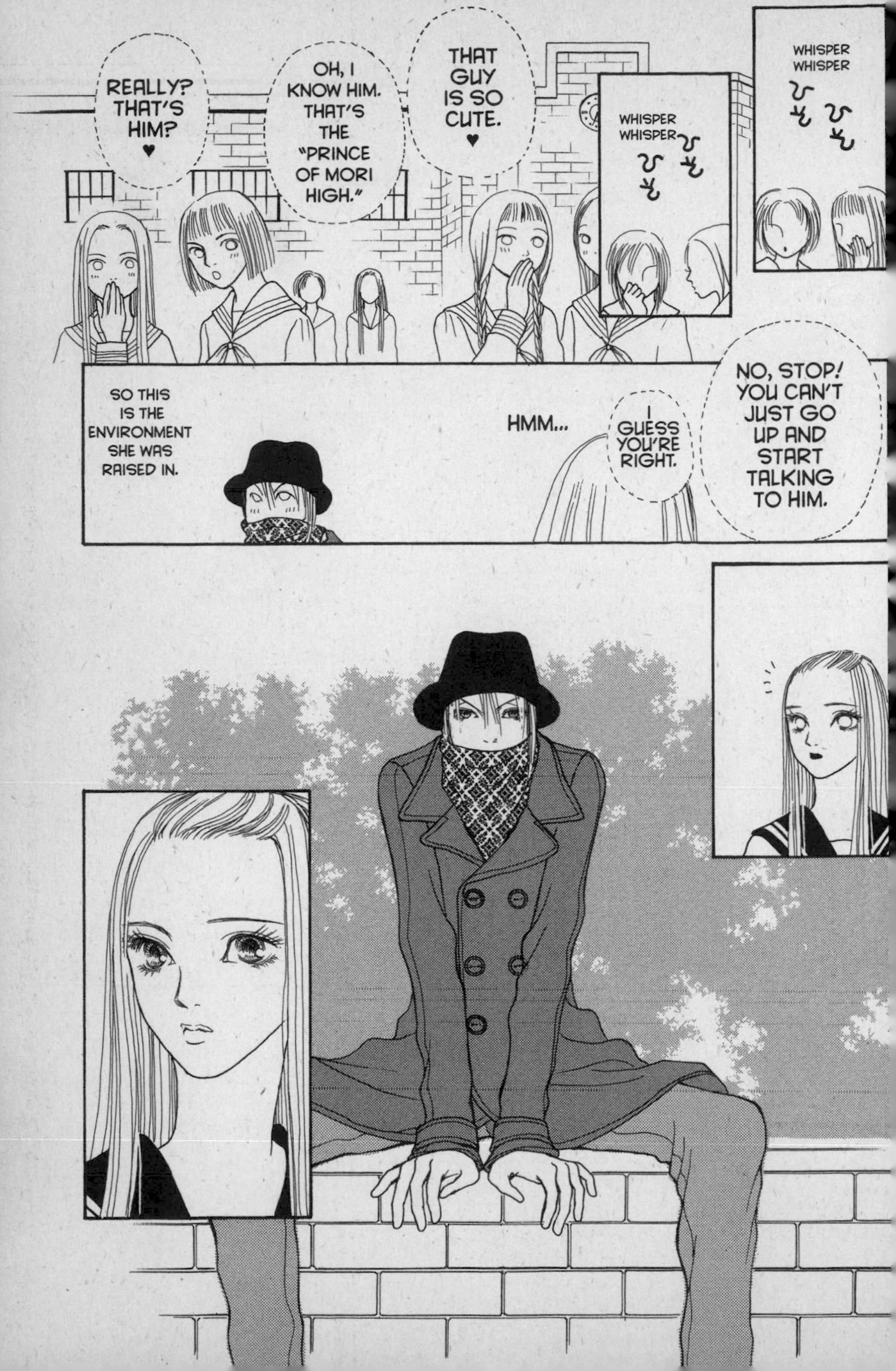
WHISPER WHISPER
WHISPER WHISPER
THAT GUY IS SO CUTE. ♥
OH, I KNOW HIM. THAT'S THE "PRINCE OF MORI HIGH."
REALLY? THAT'S HIM? ♥
NO, STOP! YOU CAN'T JUST GO UP AND START TALKING TO HIM.
I GUESS YOU'RE RIGHT.
HMM...
SO THIS IS THE ENVIRONMENT SHE WAS RAISED IN.

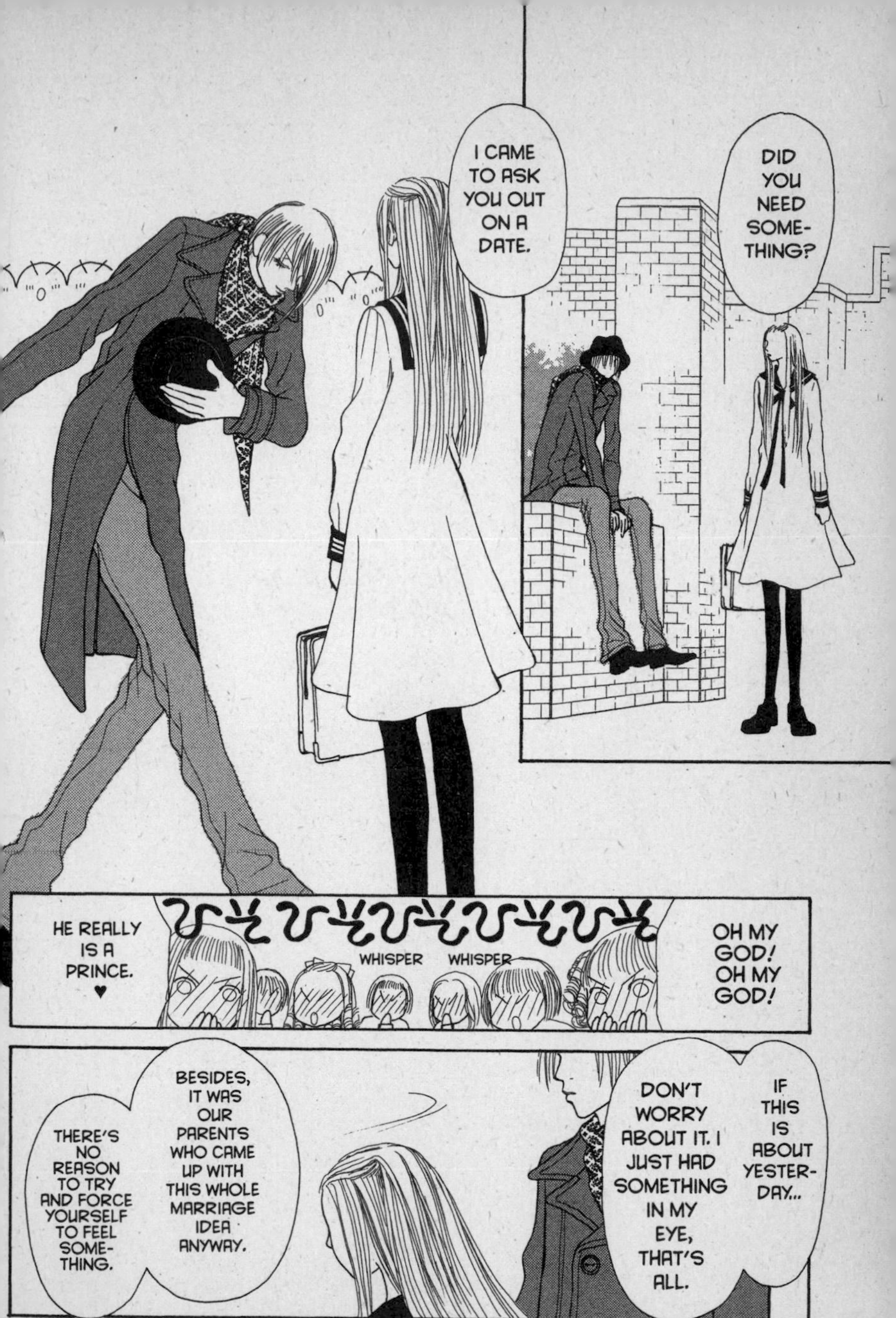
DID YOU NEED SOME-THING?
I CAME TO ASK YOU OUT ON A DATE.
OH MY GOD! OH MY GOD!
WHISPER WHISPER
HE REALLY IS A PRINCE. ♥
IF THIS IS ABOUT YESTER-DAY...
DON'T WORRY ABOUT IT. I JUST HAD SOMETHING IN MY EYE, THAT'S ALL.
BESIDES, IT WAS OUR PARENTS WHO CAME UP WITH THIS WHOLE MARRIAGE IDEA ANYWAY.
THERE'S NO REASON TO TRY AND FORCE YOURSELF TO FEEL SOME-THING.

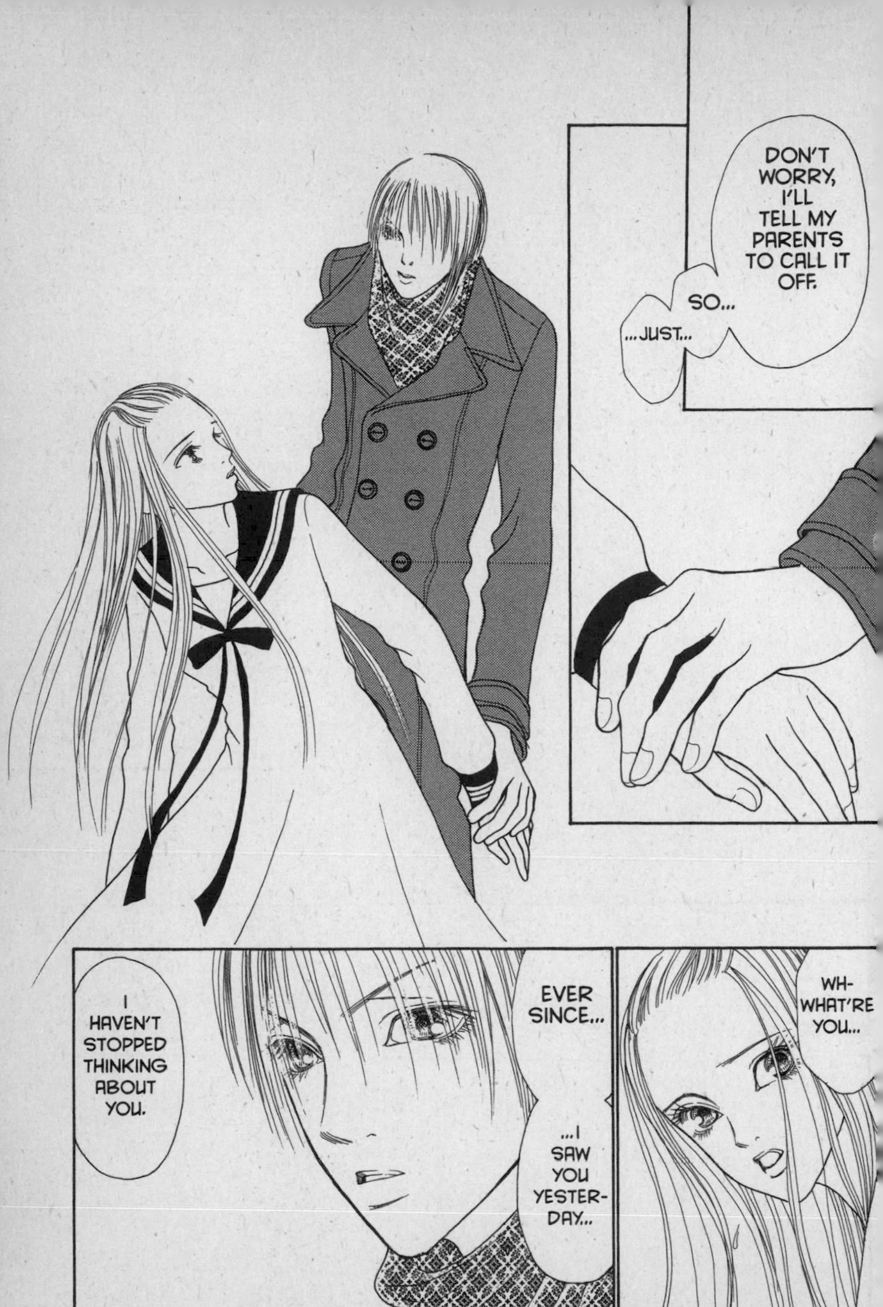
DON'T WORRY, I'LL TELL MY PARENTS TO CALL IT OFF.
SO...
...JUST...
WH-WHAT'RE YOU...
EVER SINCE...
...I SAW YOU YESTER-DAY...
I HAVEN'T STOPPED THINKING ABOUT YOU.

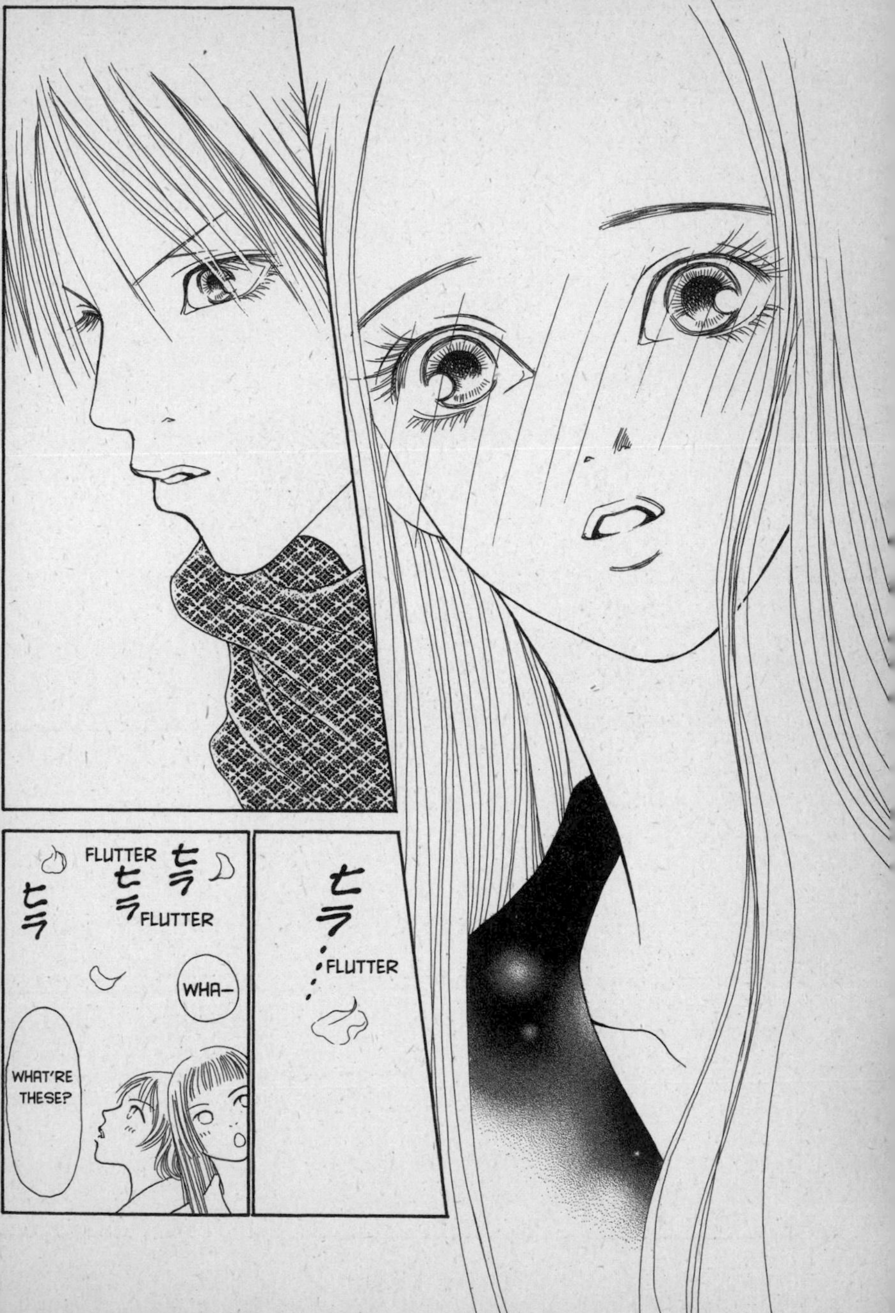
ヒラ
FLUTTER
ヒラ
FLUTTER
ヒラ
FLUTTER
ヒラ
WHA-
WHAT'RE THESE?

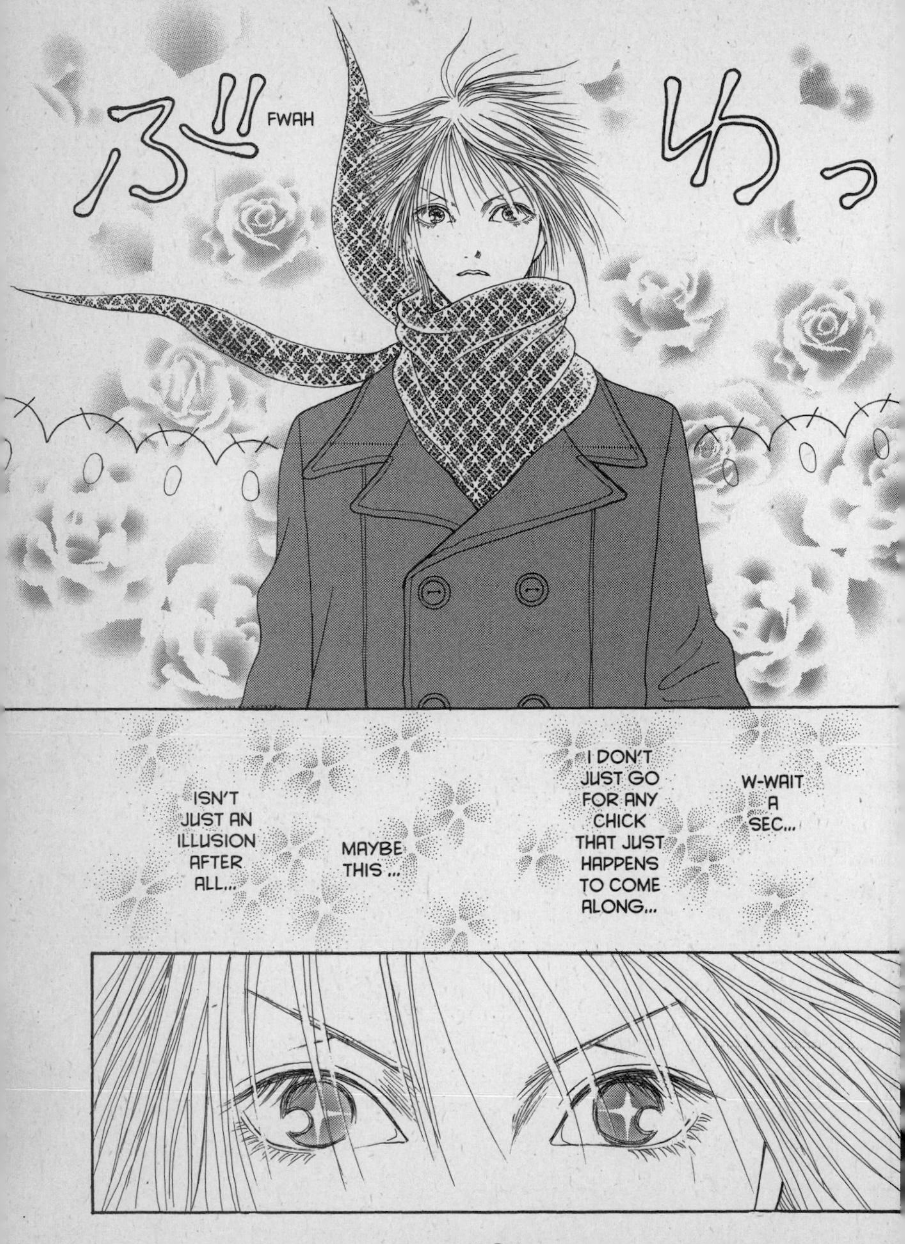
ふわっ
FWAH
W-WAIT A SEC...
I DON'T JUST GO FOR ANY CHICK THAT JUST HAPPENS TO COME ALONG...
MAYBE THIS ...
ISN'T JUST AN ILLUSION AFTER ALL...

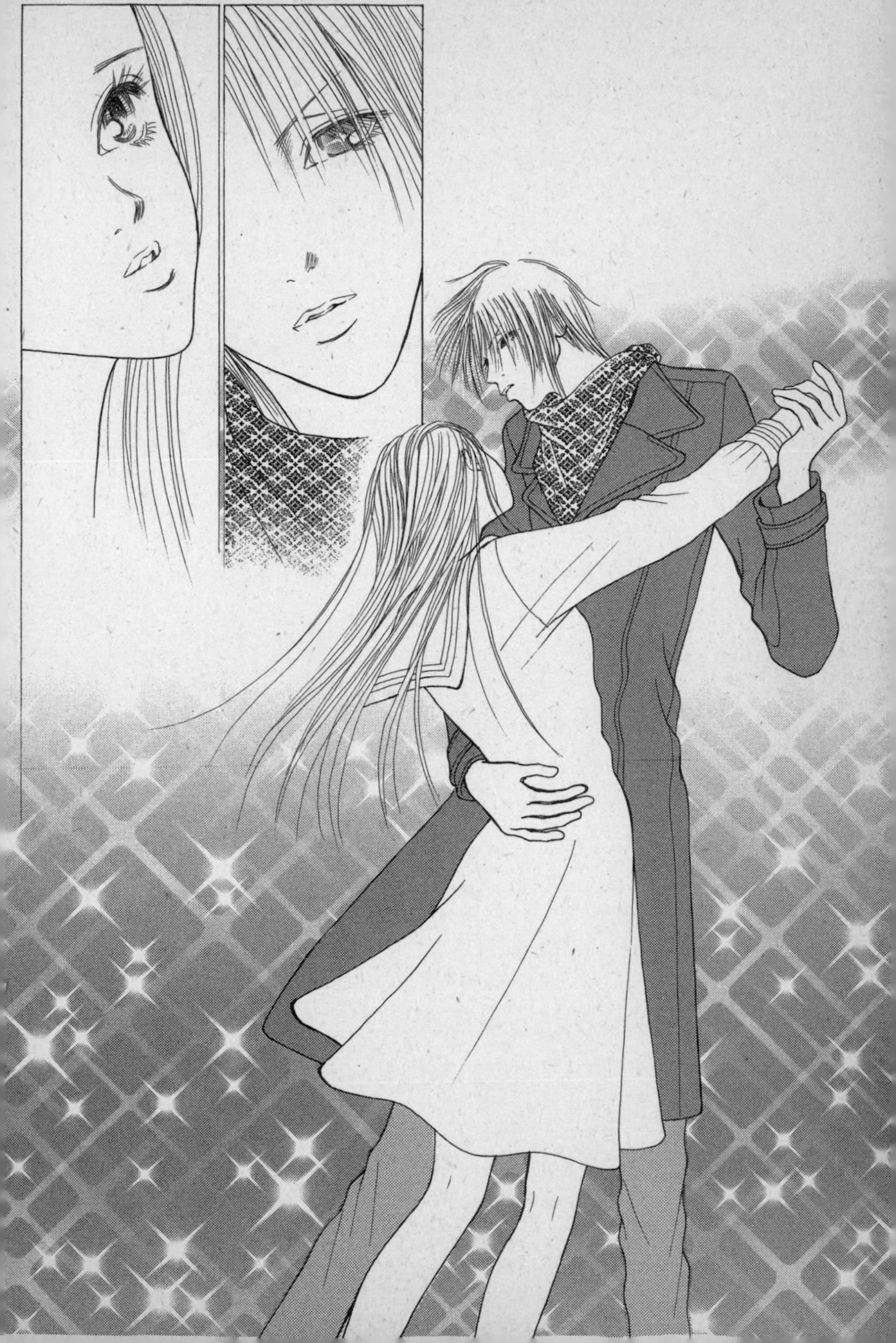

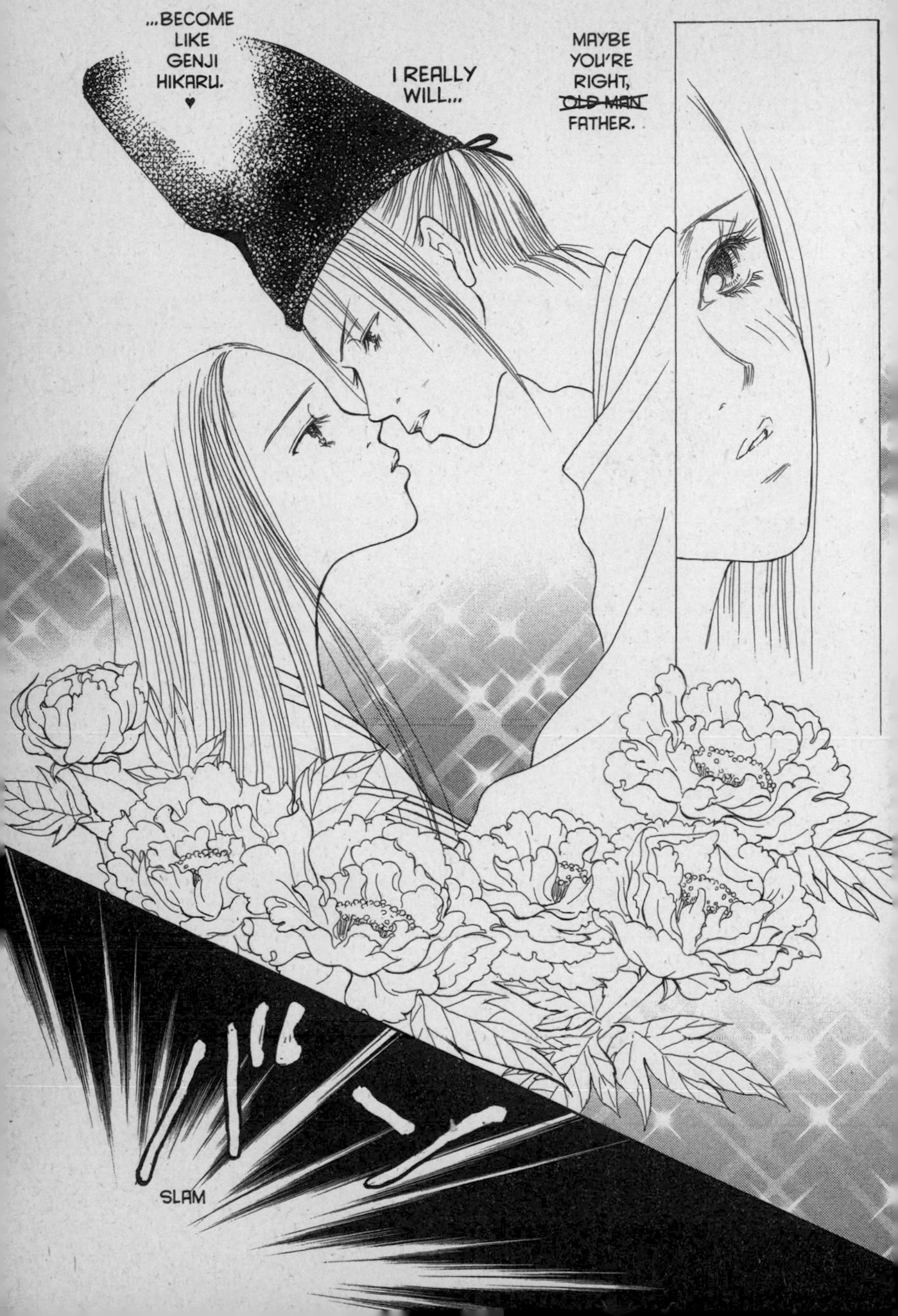
MAYBE YOU'RE RIGHT, ~~OLD MAN~~ FATHER.
I REALLY WILL...
...BECOME LIKE GENJI HIKARU. ♥
SLAM

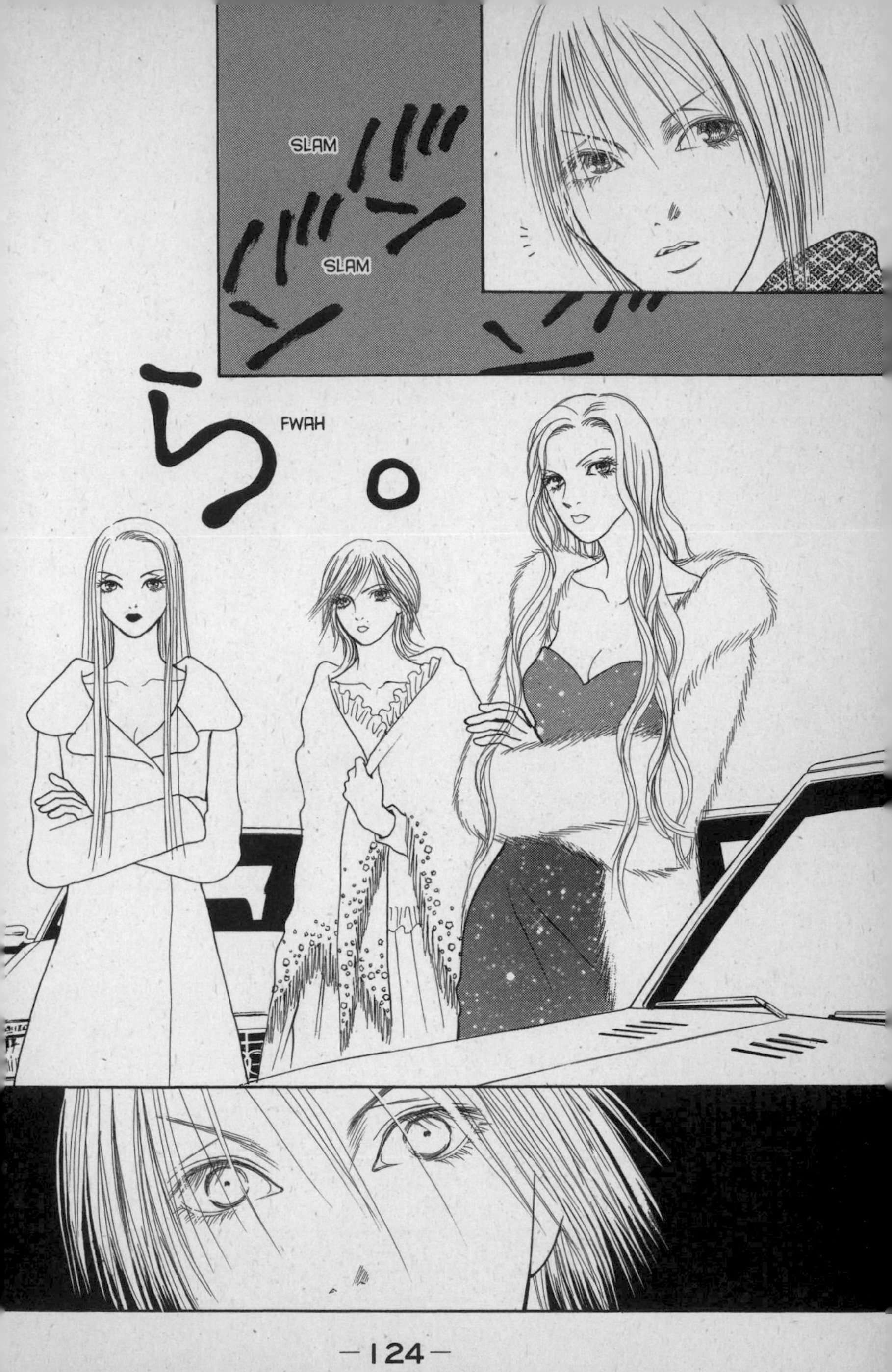
SLAM
SLAM
FWAH

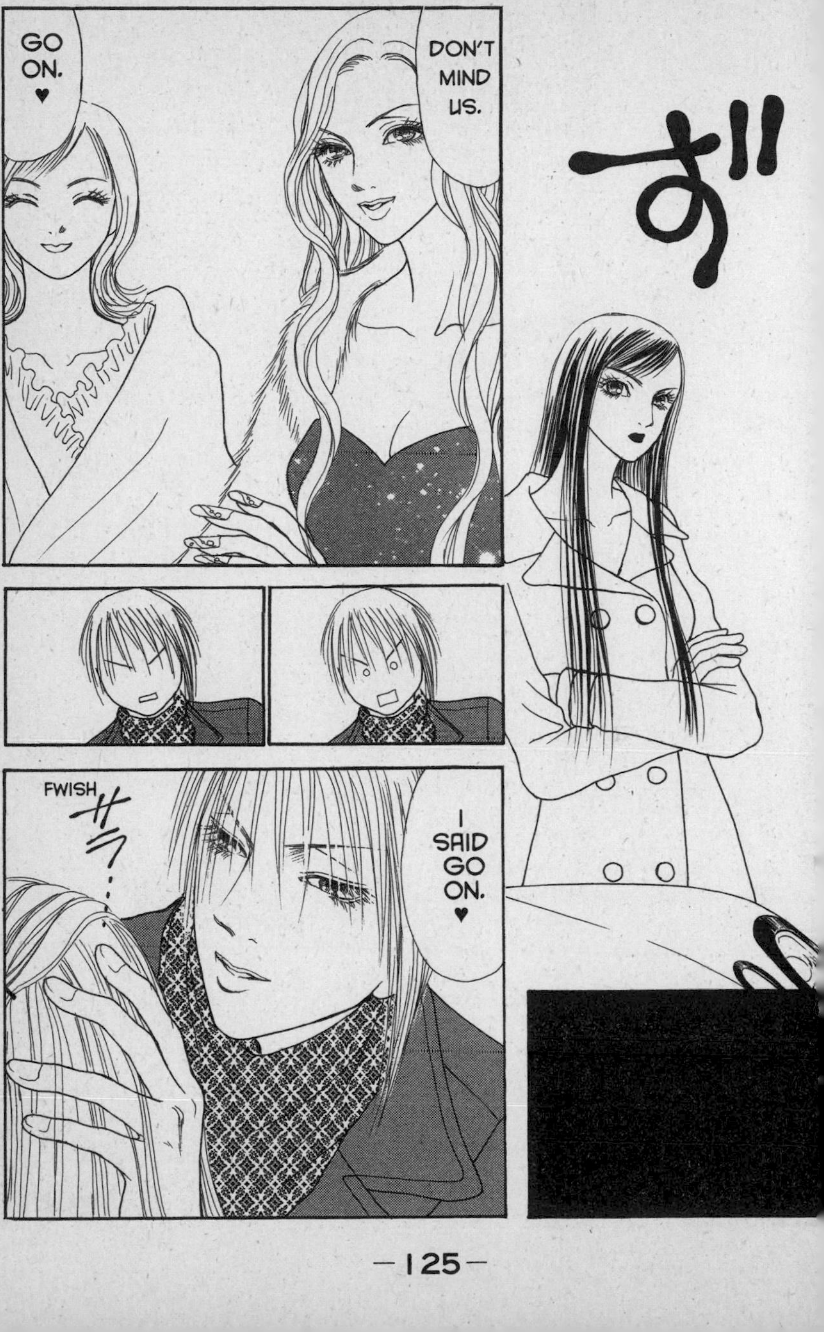
ず"
DON'T MIND US.
GO ON. ♥
I SAID GO ON. ♥
FWISH
サラ…

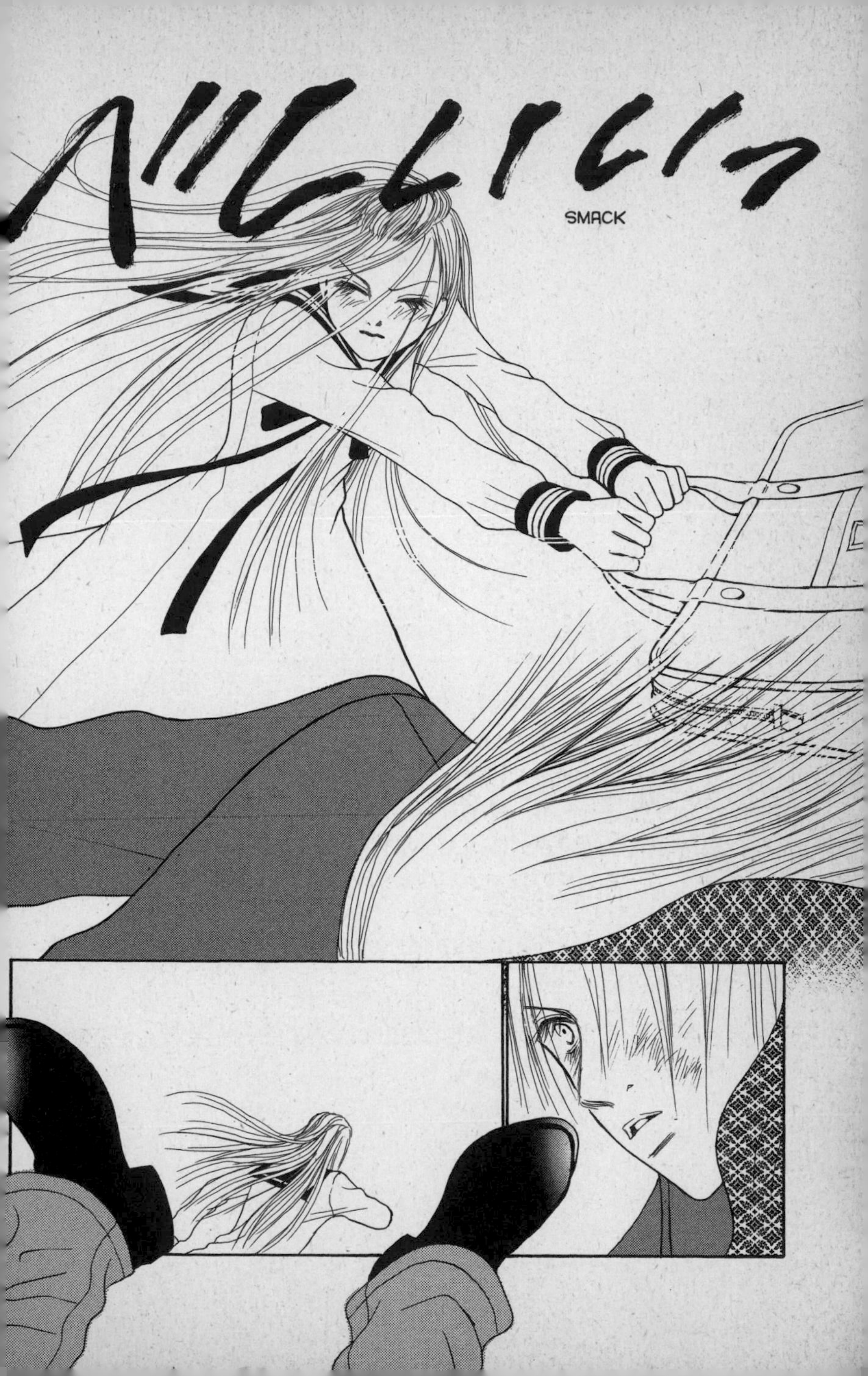
SMACK

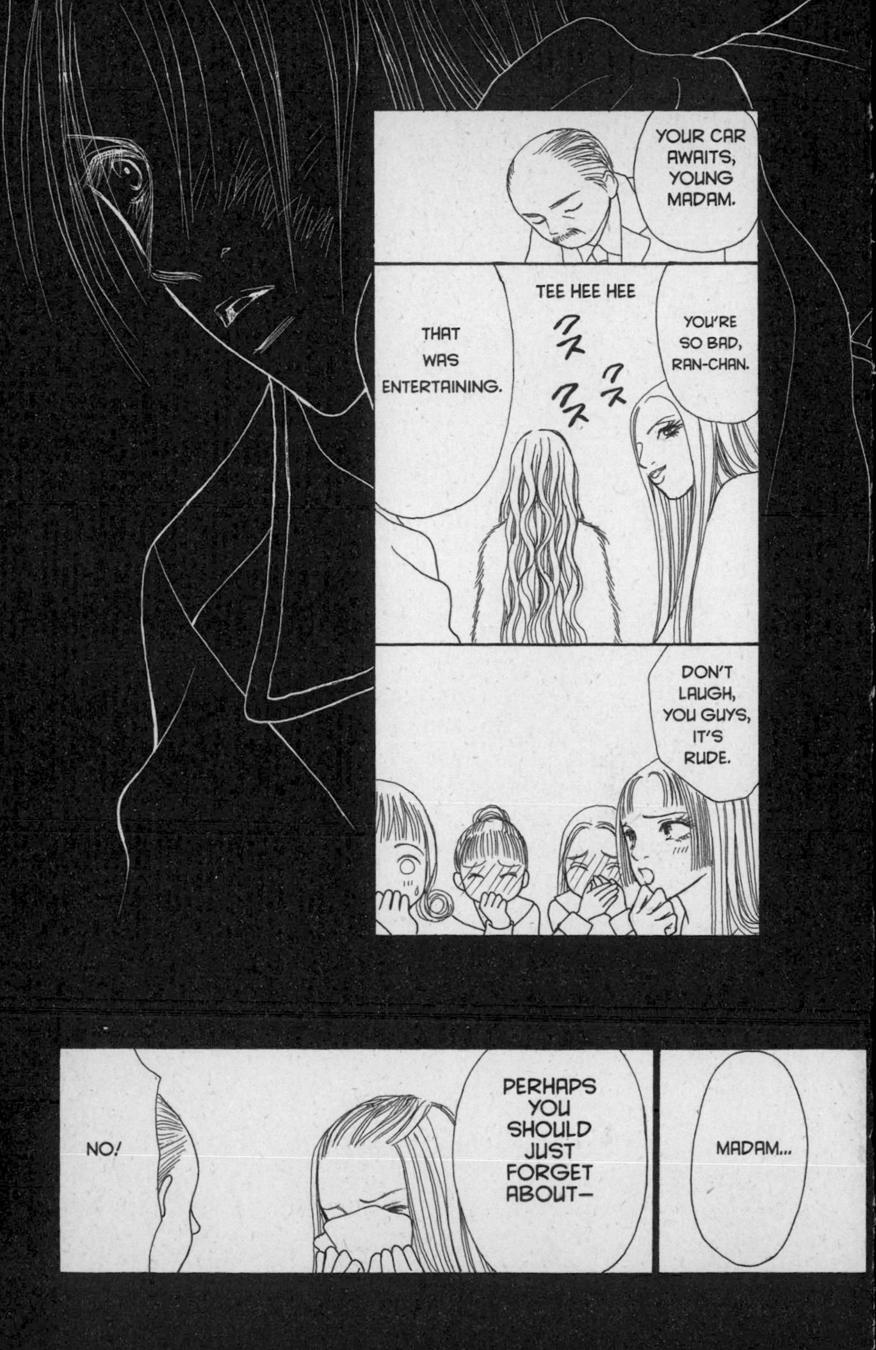
YOUR CAR AWAITS, YOUNG MADAM.
YOU'RE SO BAD, RAN-CHAN.
TEE HEE HEE
クス クス クス
THAT WAS ENTERTAINING.
DON'T LAUGH, YOU GUYS, IT'S RUDE.
MADAM...
PERHAPS YOU SHOULD JUST FORGET ABOUT—
NO!

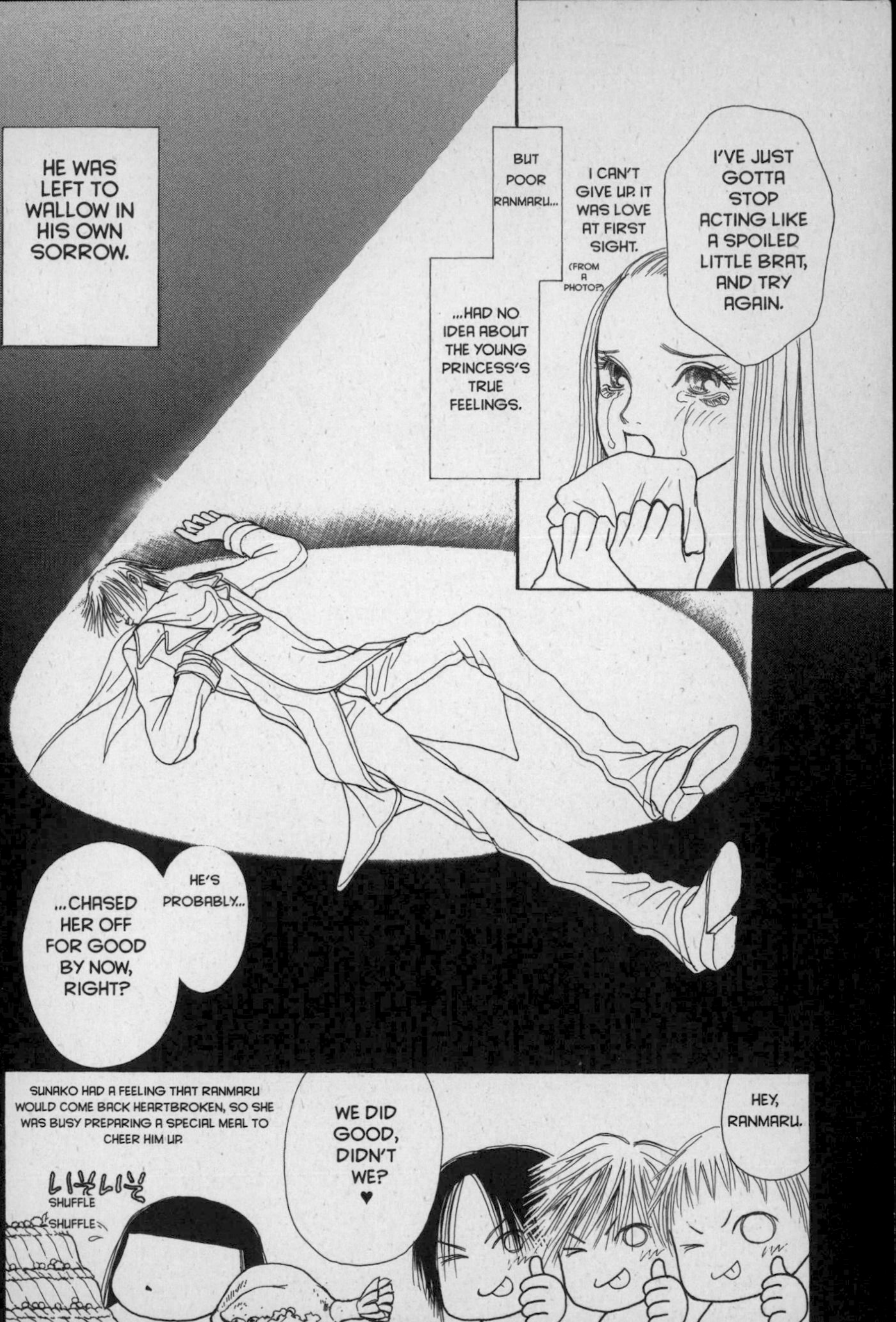
I'VE JUST GOTTA STOP ACTING LIKE A SPOILED LITTLE BRAT, AND TRY AGAIN.
I CAN'T GIVE UP. IT WAS LOVE AT FIRST SIGHT.
(FROM A PHOTO?)
BUT POOR RANMARU...
...HAD NO IDEA ABOUT THE YOUNG PRINCESS'S TRUE FEELINGS.
HE WAS LEFT TO WALLOW IN HIS OWN SORROW.
HE'S PROBABLY...
...CHASED HER OFF FOR GOOD BY NOW, RIGHT?
HEY, RANMARU.
WE DID GOOD, DIDN'T WE? ♥
SUNAKO HAD A FEELING THAT RANMARU WOULD COME BACK HEARTBROKEN, SO SHE WAS BUSY PREPARING A SPECIAL MEAL TO CHEER HIM UP.
SHUFFLE
SHUFFLE

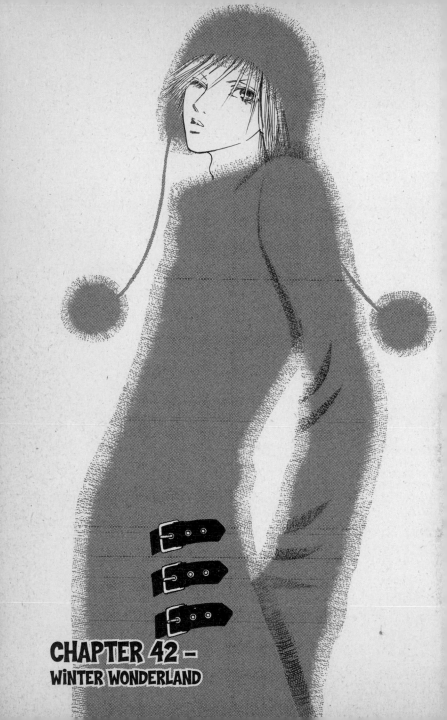

CHAPTER 42 –
WINTER WONDERLAND

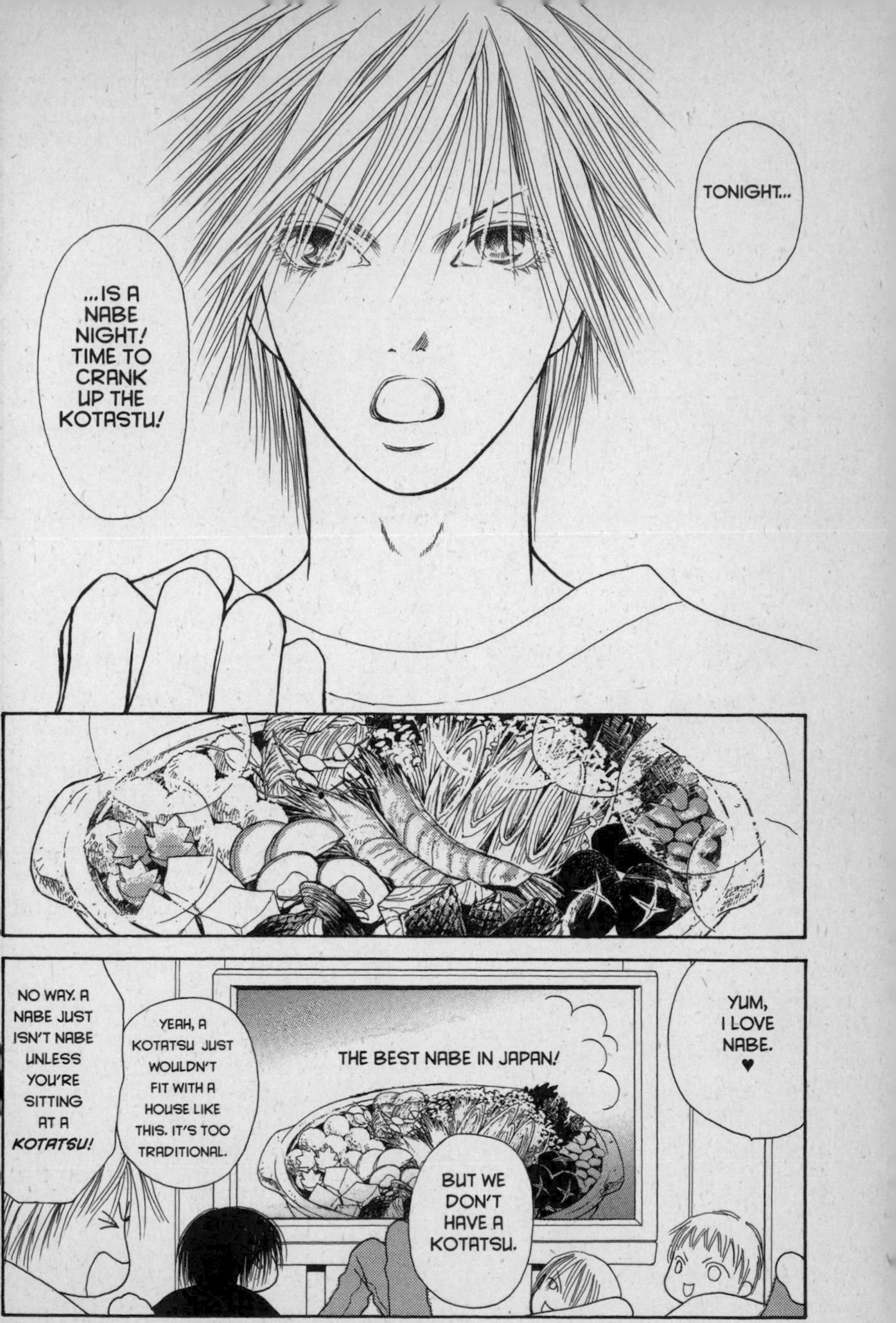
TONIGHT...
...IS A NABE NIGHT! TIME TO CRANK UP THE KOTASTU!
YUM, I LOVE NABE. ♥
THE BEST NABE IN JAPAN!
BUT WE DON'T HAVE A KOTATSU.
YEAH, A KOTATSU JUST WOULDN'T FIT WITH A HOUSE LIKE THIS. IT'S TOO TRADITIONAL.
NO WAY. A NABE JUST ISN'T NABE UNLESS YOU'RE SITTING AT A *KOTATSU!*

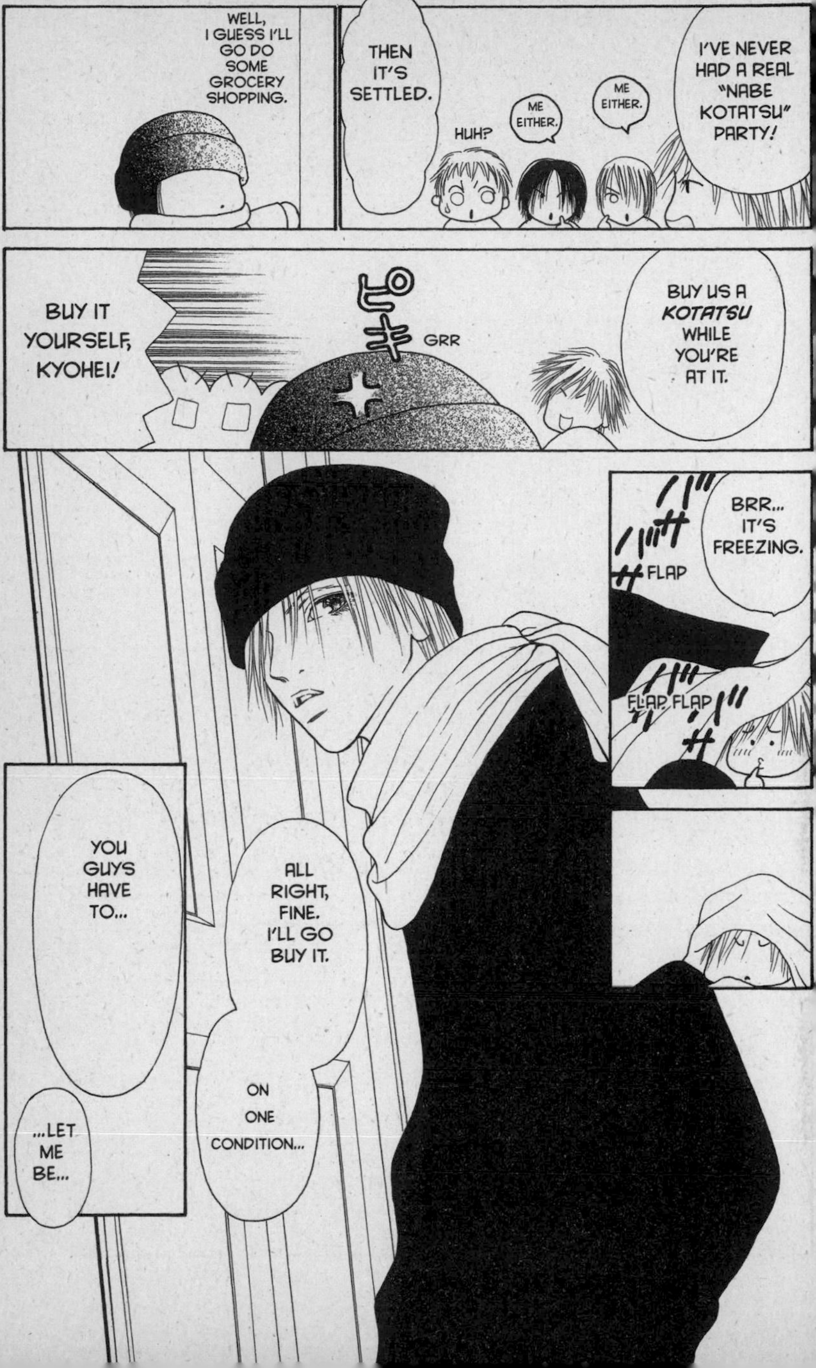
I'VE NEVER HAD A REAL "NABE KOTATSU" PARTY!
ME EITHER.
ME EITHER.
HUH?
THEN IT'S SETTLED.
WELL, I GUESS I'LL GO DO SOME GROCERY SHOPPING.
BUY US A *KOTATSU* WHILE YOU'RE AT IT.
ピキ
GRR
BUY IT YOURSELF, KYOHEI!
BRR... IT'S FREEZING.
FLAP
FLAP FLAP
ALL RIGHT, FINE. I'LL GO BUY IT.
ON ONE CONDITION...
YOU GUYS HAVE TO...
...LET ME BE...

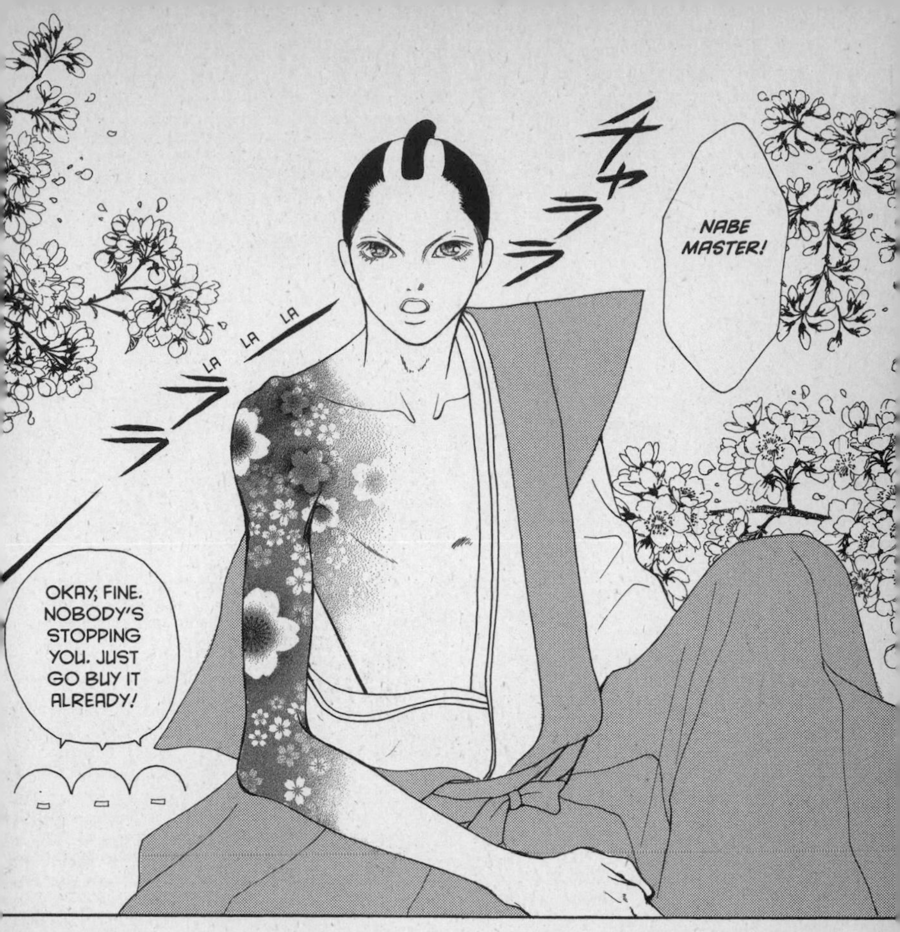
NABE MASTER!
チャララ
LA LA LA
ララ
OKAY, FINE. NOBODY'S STOPPING YOU. JUST GO BUY IT ALREADY!

BEHIND THE SCENES

A "KOTATSU NABE" PARTY... SOUNDS GOOD. IT'S BEEN YEARS SINCE I'VE DONE SOMETHING LIKE THAT. I DON'T HAVE A KOTATSU AT MY HOUSE, AND I NEVER GO BACK TO MY FAMILY'S HOME IN THE WINTER. I LOVE EATING TANGERINES WHILE SITTING AT A WARM KOTATSU. MAYBE I'LL BUY A KOTATSU. BUT IT REALLY WOULDN'T GO WITH MY ROOM. MY LIVING ROOM IS FULL OF SKELETONS. I'VE GOT A HUGE RED RUG AND BLACK VELVET CURTAINS. I ALSO HAVE A BIG CAT TOWER, AND THERE ARE CAT TOYS SCATTERED EVERYWHERE. A KOTATSU JUST WOULDN'T FIT IN.

➡ THE BACKGROUND MUSIC PLAYING IN THE ABOVE PANEL IS SUPPOSED TO BE THE THEME FROM THAT TV SHOW "TOOYAMA NO KIN-SAN." IT'S THE MUSIC THAT PLAYS DURING THAT SCENE WITH HIROKI MATSUKATA. SO PLEASE IMAGINE THAT YOU'RE HEARING IT WHILE YOU READ. I LIKE THAT SHOW, BUT RIGHT NOW I'M REALLY INTO "OOKA ECHIZEN." I'VE BEEN WATCHING THE WHOLE SERIES FROM THE VERY BEGINNING. (I COPIED IT ON VIDEO BACK WHEN THEY RERAN IT.) I WATCH IT ALL THE TIME. GOU-SAMA (GOU KATOU-SAMA) IS SO COOL. ♥ MASAYO UTUNOMIYA IS PERFECT FOR THE ROLE OF YUKIE-SAN. ♥ I HOPE THEY COME OUT WITH IT ON DVD.♥ I LIKE SANJI-SAN AND MASTER MURAKAMI.♥

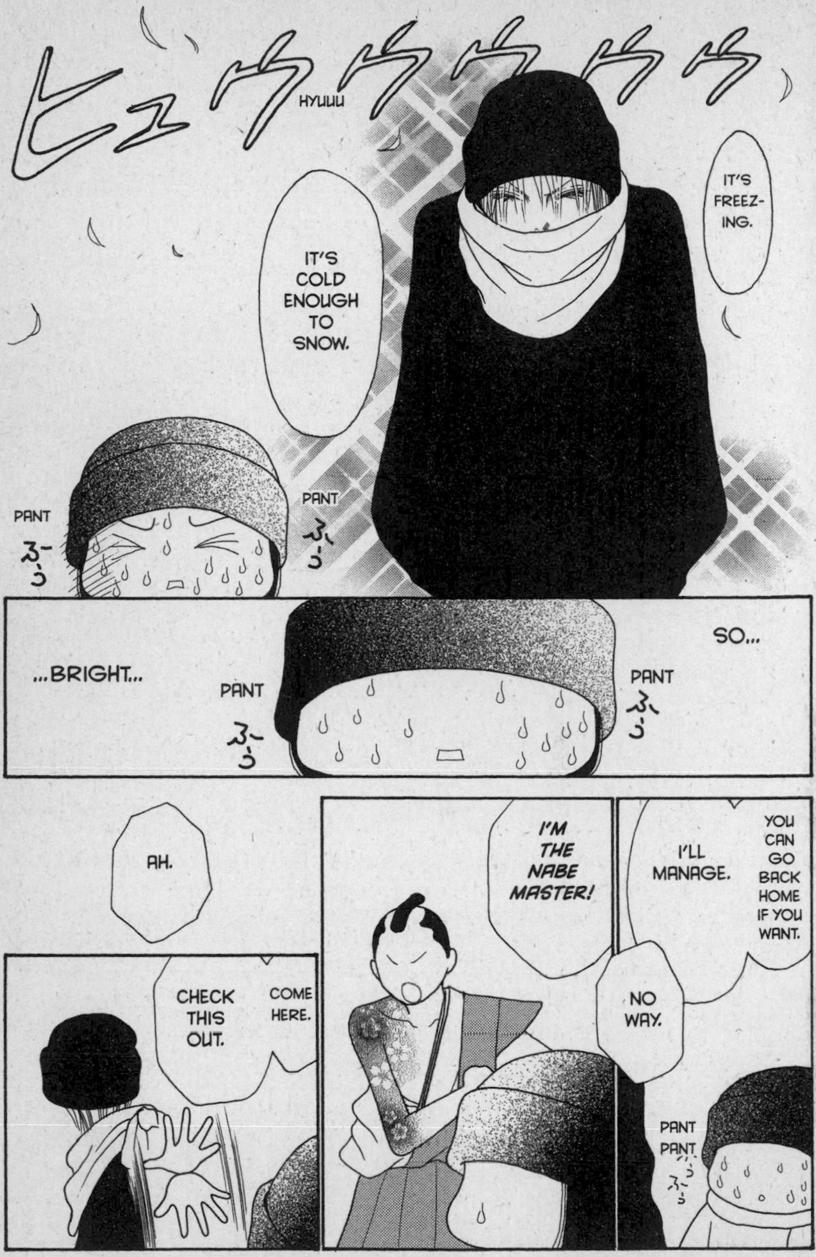
ヒュウウウウ
HYUUU
IT'S FREEZ-ING.
IT'S COLD ENOUGH TO SNOW.
PANT
ふっ
PANT
ふー
SO...
PANT
ふっ
PANT
ふー
...BRIGHT...
YOU CAN GO BACK HOME IF YOU WANT.
I'LL MANAGE.
NO WAY.
PANT PANT
ふっふっ
I'M THE NABE MASTER!
AH.
COME HERE.
CHECK THIS OUT.

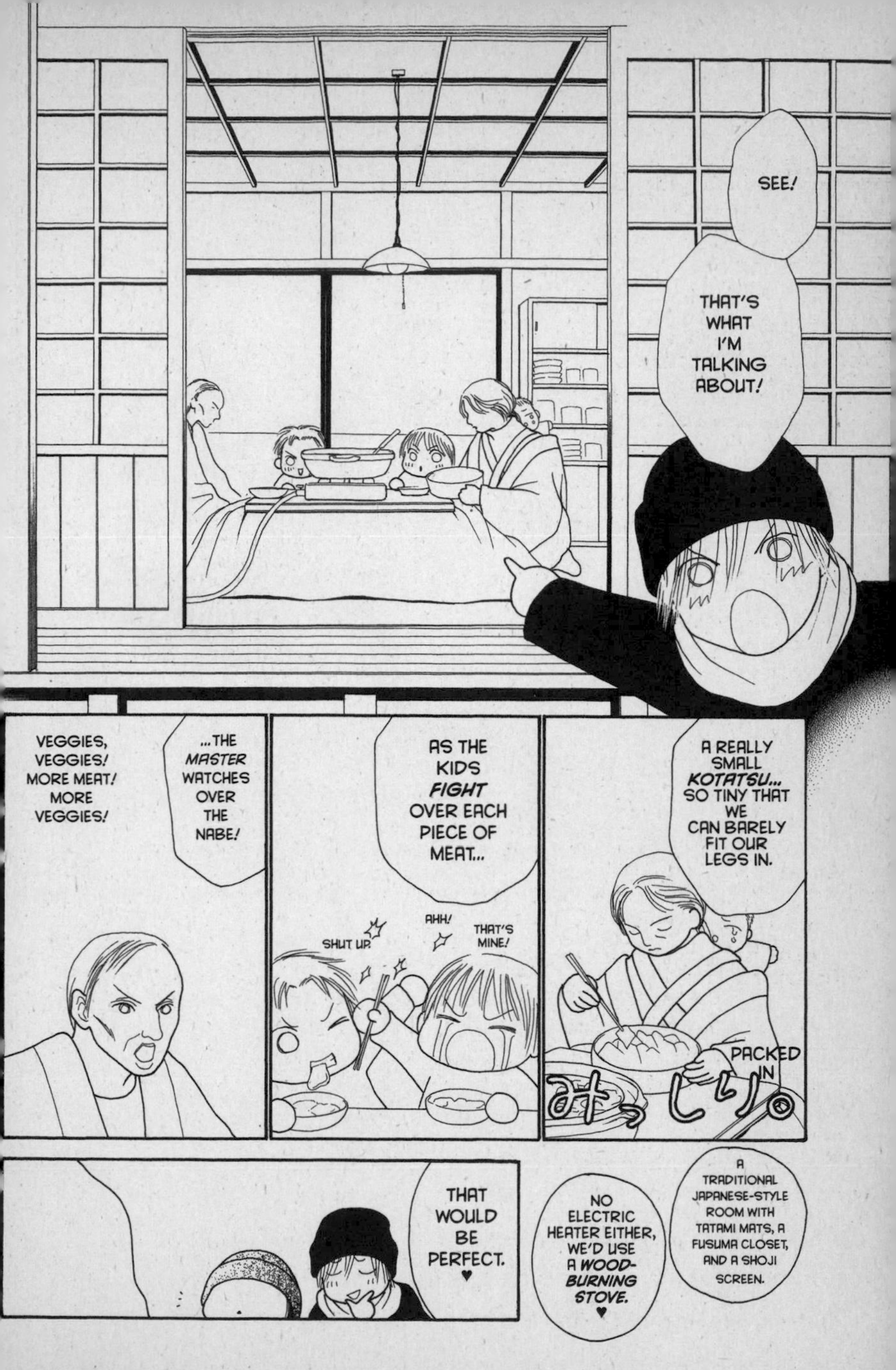
SEE!
THAT'S WHAT I'M TALKING ABOUT!
A REALLY SMALL KOTATSU... SO TINY THAT WE CAN BARELY FIT OUR LEGS IN.
PACKED IN
みっしり。
AS THE KIDS FIGHT OVER EACH PIECE OF MEAT...
AHH!
THAT'S MINE!
SHUT UP.
...THE MASTER WATCHES OVER THE NABE!
VEGGIES, VEGGIES! MORE MEAT! MORE VEGGIES!
A TRADITIONAL JAPANESE-STYLE ROOM WITH TATAMI MATS, A FUSUMA CLOSET, AND A SHOJI SCREEN.
NO ELECTRIC HEATER EITHER, WE'D USE A WOOD-BURNING STOVE. ♥
THAT WOULD BE PERFECT. ♥

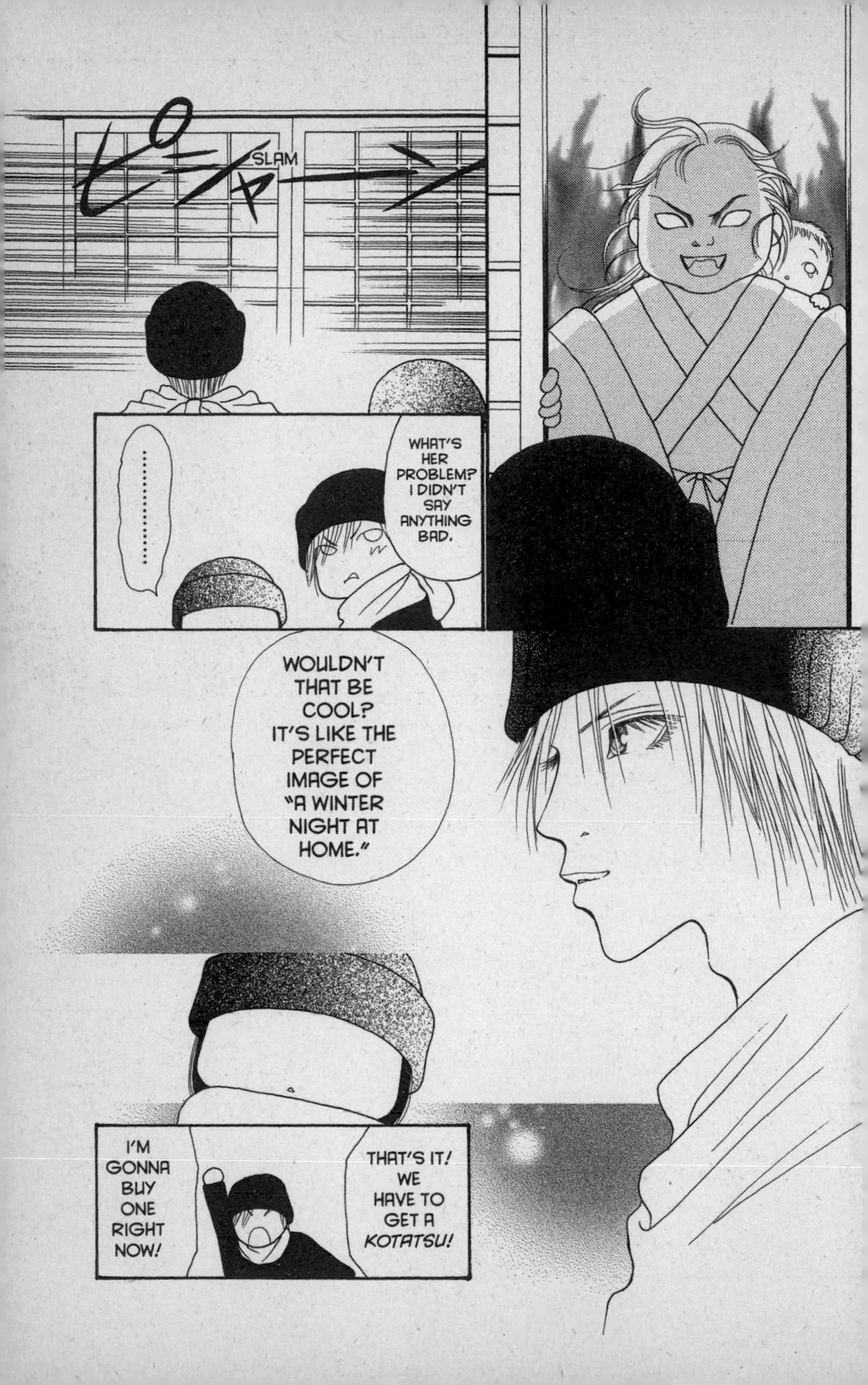
ピシャーン
SLAM
WHAT'S HER PROBLEM? I DIDN'T SAY ANYTHING BAD.
......
WOULDN'T THAT BE COOL? IT'S LIKE THE PERFECT IMAGE OF "A WINTER NIGHT AT HOME."
THAT'S IT! WE HAVE TO GET A *KOTATSU*!
I'M GONNA BUY ONE RIGHT NOW!

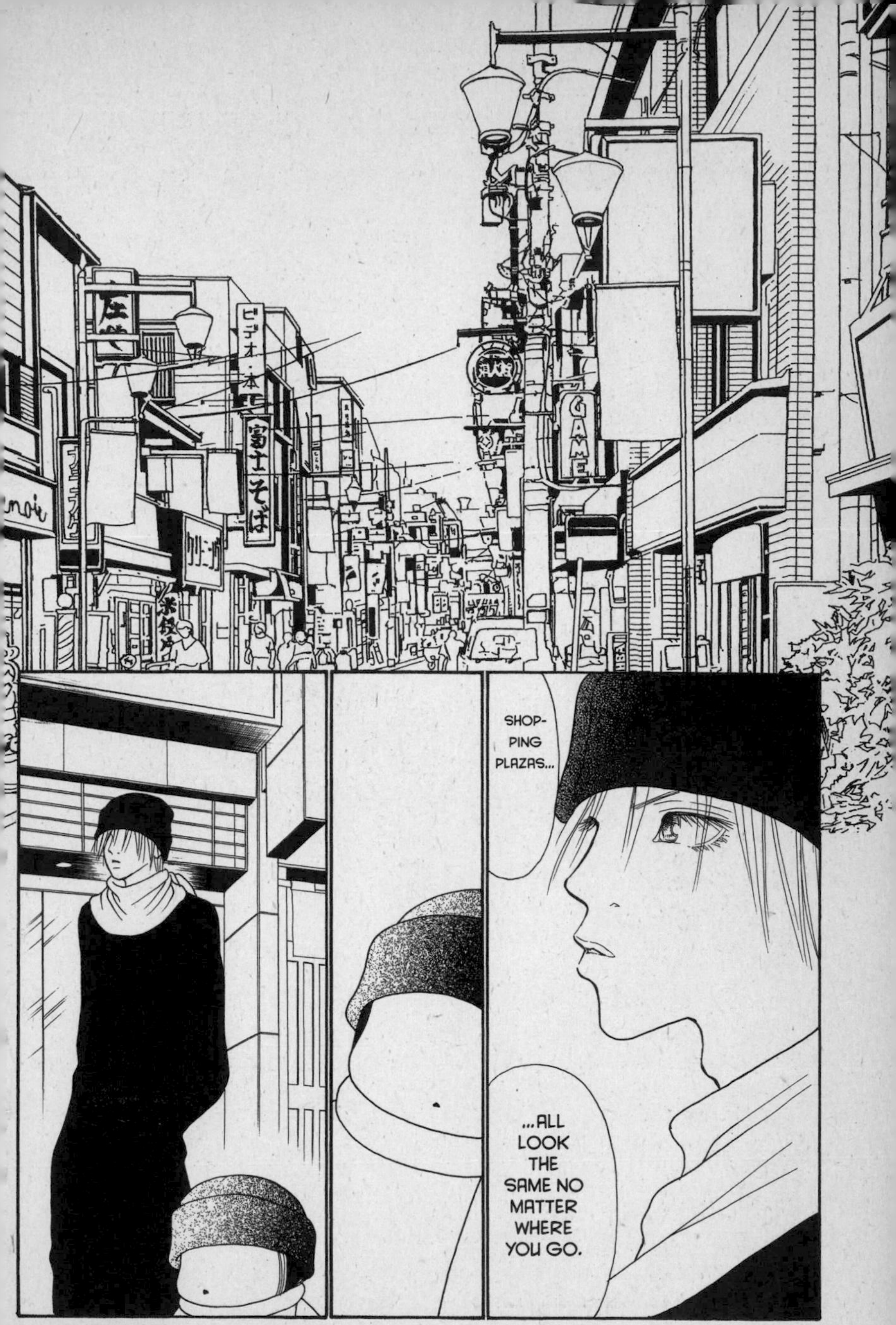
ビデオ・本
富士そば
GAME
SHOP-PING PLAZAS...
...ALL LOOK THE SAME NO MATTER WHERE YOU GO.

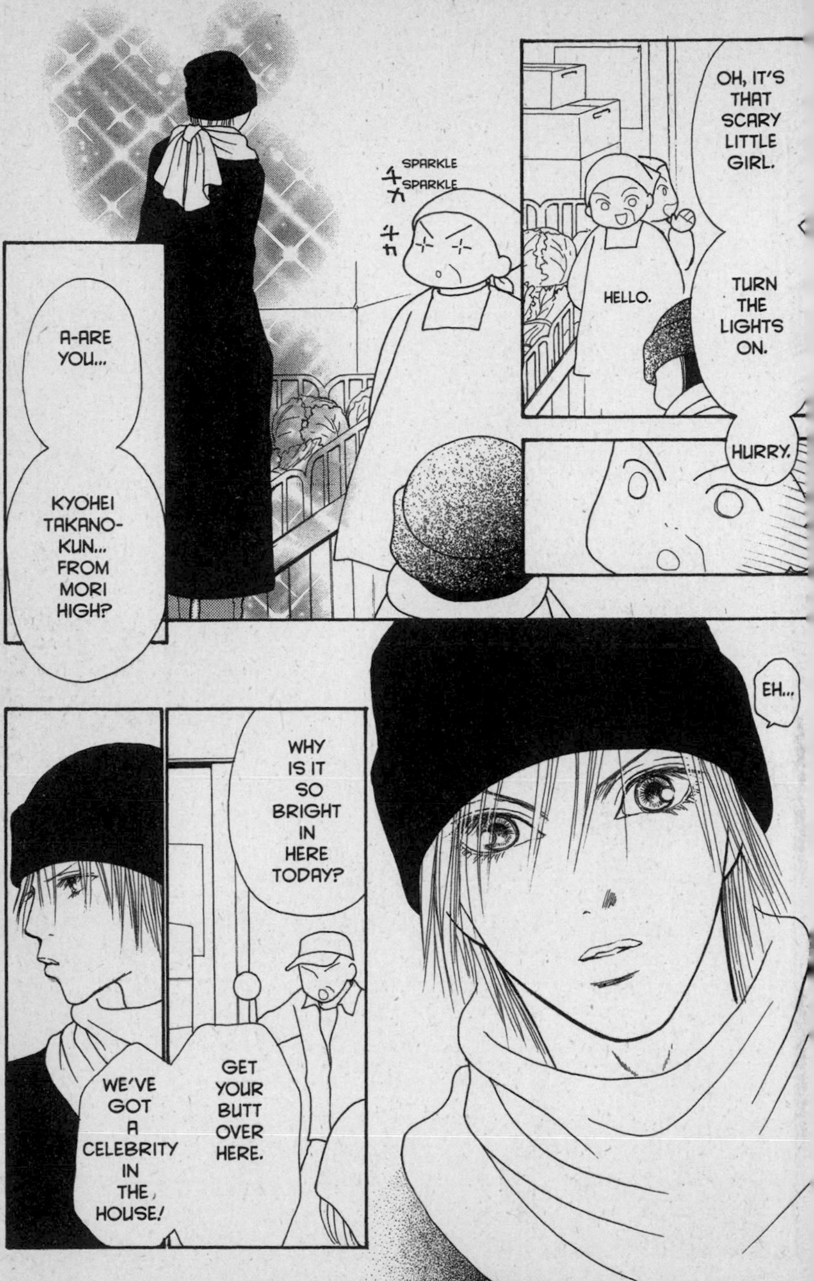
OH, IT'S THAT SCARY LITTLE GIRL.
HELLO.
TURN THE LIGHTS ON.
HURRY.
SPARKLE SPARKLE
A-ARE YOU...
KYOHEI TAKANO-KUN... FROM MORI HIGH?
EH...
WHY IS IT SO BRIGHT IN HERE TODAY?
GET YOUR BUTT OVER HERE.
WE'VE GOT A CELEBRITY IN THE HOUSE!

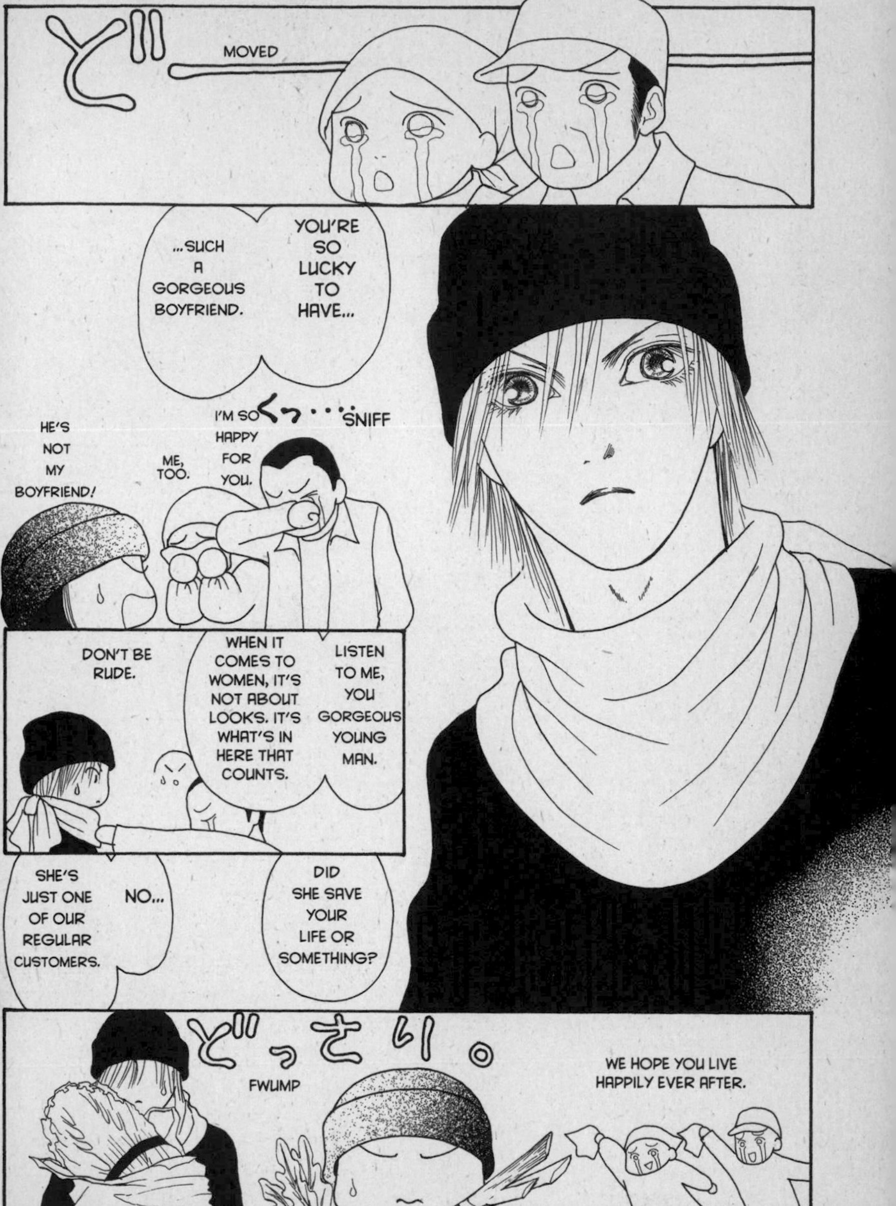
MOVED
YOU'RE SO LUCKY TO HAVE...
...SUCH A GORGEOUS BOYFRIEND.
I'M SO HAPPY FOR YOU.
SNIFF
ME, TOO.
HE'S NOT MY BOYFRIEND!
LISTEN TO ME, YOU GORGEOUS YOUNG MAN.
WHEN IT COMES TO WOMEN, IT'S NOT ABOUT LOOKS. IT'S WHAT'S IN HERE THAT COUNTS.
DON'T BE RUDE.
DID SHE SAVE YOUR LIFE OR SOMETHING?
NO...
SHE'S JUST ONE OF OUR REGULAR CUSTOMERS.
WE HOPE YOU LIVE HAPPILY EVER AFTER.
FWUMP

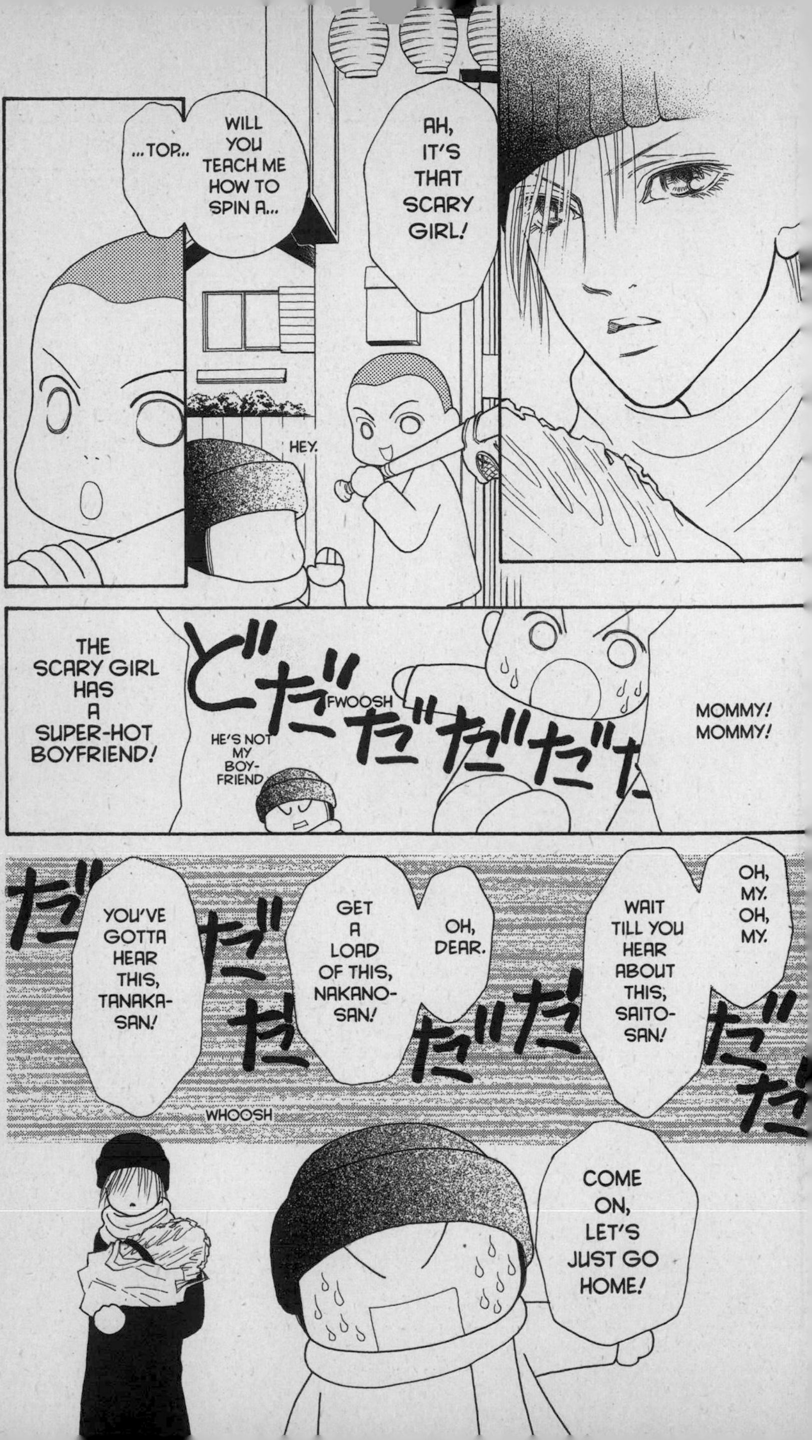
AH, IT'S THAT SCARY GIRL!
HEY.
WILL YOU TEACH ME HOW TO SPIN A...
...TOP...
MOMMY! MOMMY!
どだだだだ
FWOOSH
THE SCARY GIRL HAS A SUPER-HOT BOYFRIEND!
HE'S NOT MY BOY-FRIEND
OH, MY. OH, MY.
WAIT TILL YOU HEAR ABOUT THIS, SAITO-SAN!
OH, DEAR.
GET A LOAD OF THIS, NAKANO-SAN!
YOU'VE GOTTA HEAR THIS, TANAKA-SAN!
WHOOSH
COME ON, LET'S JUST GO HOME!

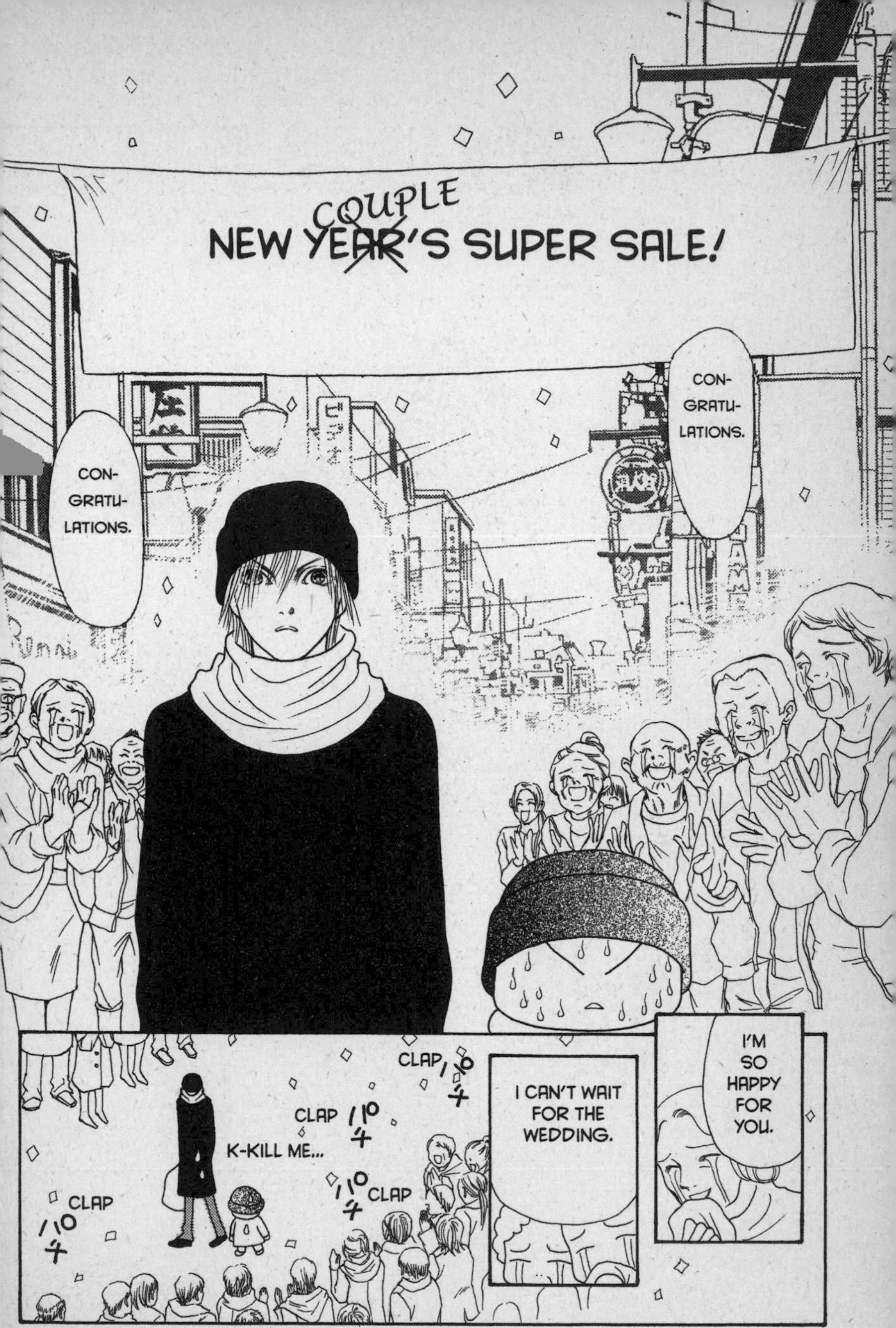
COUPLE
NEW YEAR'S SUPER SALE!
CON-GRATU-LATIONS.
CON-GRATU-LATIONS.
I'M SO HAPPY FOR YOU.
I CAN'T WAIT FOR THE WEDDING.
CLAP
CLAP
K-KILL ME...
CLAP
CLAP

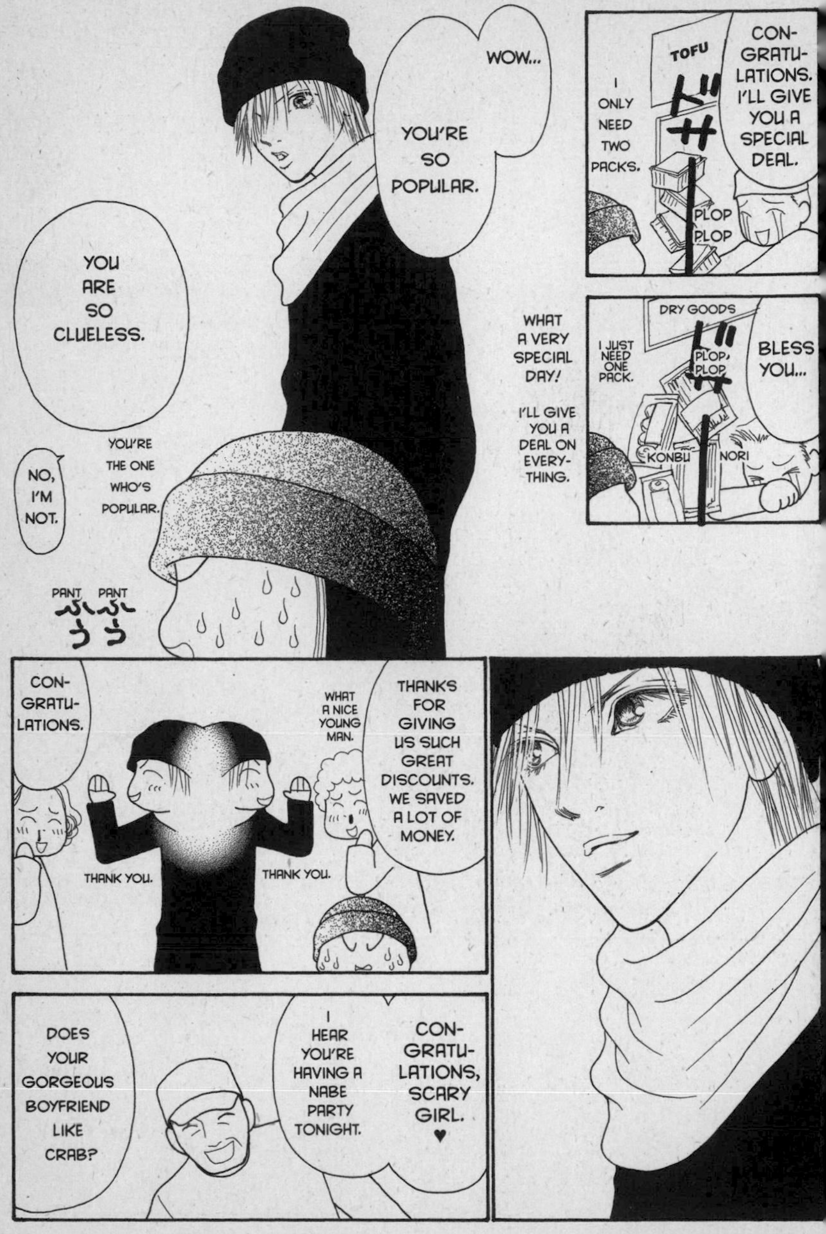
CON-GRATU-LATIONS. I'LL GIVE YOU A SPECIAL DEAL.
TOFU
I ONLY NEED TWO PACKS.
PLOP PLOP
BLESS YOU...
DRY GOODS
PLOP, PLOP
I JUST NEED ONE PACK.
KONBU
NORI
WHAT A VERY SPECIAL DAY!
I'LL GIVE YOU A DEAL ON EVERY-THING.
WOW...
YOU'RE SO POPULAR.
YOU'RE THE ONE WHO'S POPULAR.
YOU ARE SO CLUELESS.
NO, I'M NOT.
PANT PANT
THANKS FOR GIVING US SUCH GREAT DISCOUNTS. WE SAVED A LOT OF MONEY.
WHAT A NICE YOUNG MAN.
THANK YOU.
CON-GRATU-LATIONS.
THANK YOU.
CON-GRATU-LATIONS, SCARY GIRL. ♥
I HEAR YOU'RE HAVING A NABE PARTY TONIGHT.
DOES YOUR GORGEOUS BOYFRIEND LIKE CRAB?

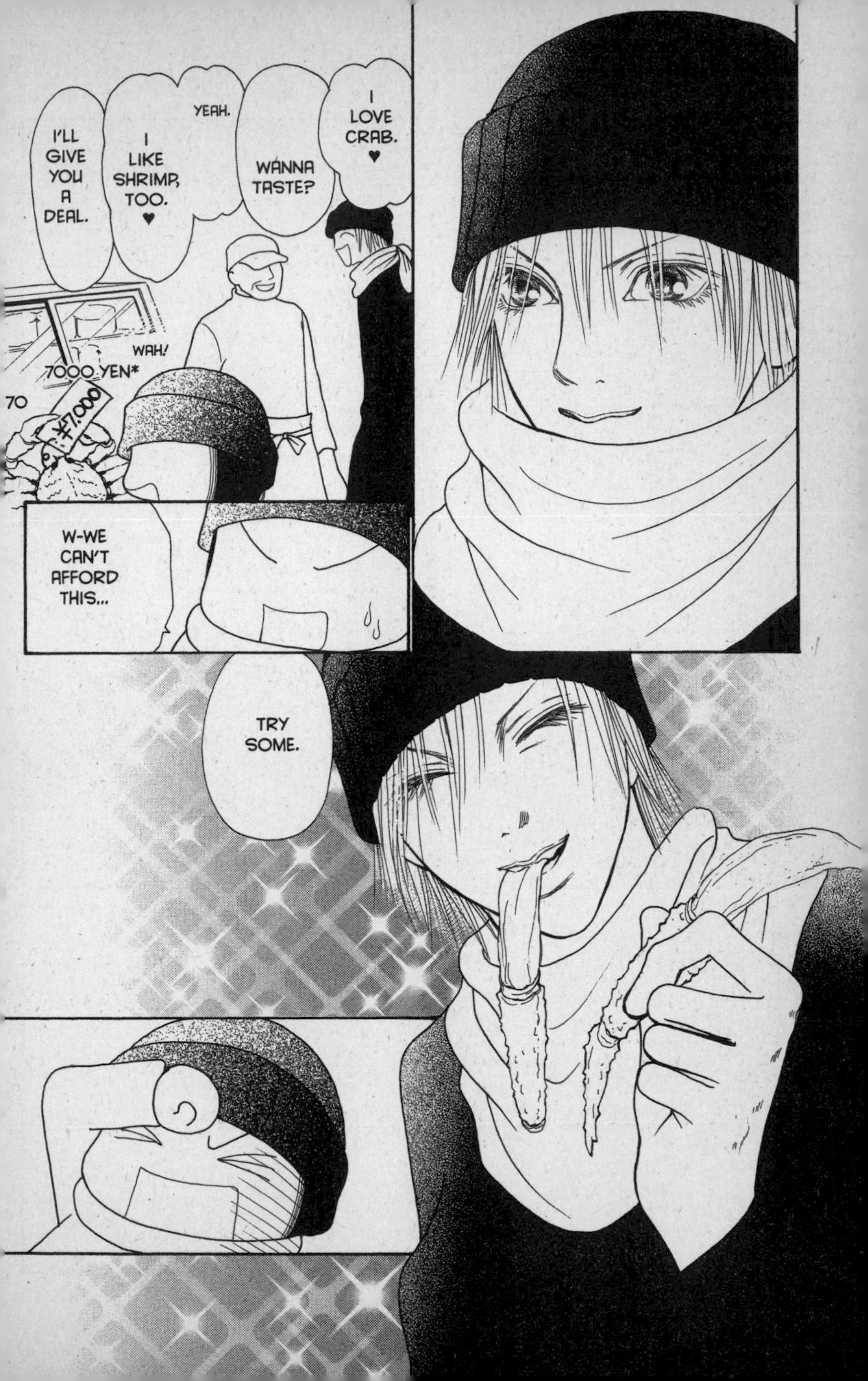
I LOVE CRAB. ♥
WANNA TASTE?
YEAH.
I LIKE SHRIMP, TOO. ♥
I'LL GIVE YOU A DEAL.
WAH!
7000 YEN*
¥7,000
W-WE CAN'T AFFORD THIS...
TRY SOME.

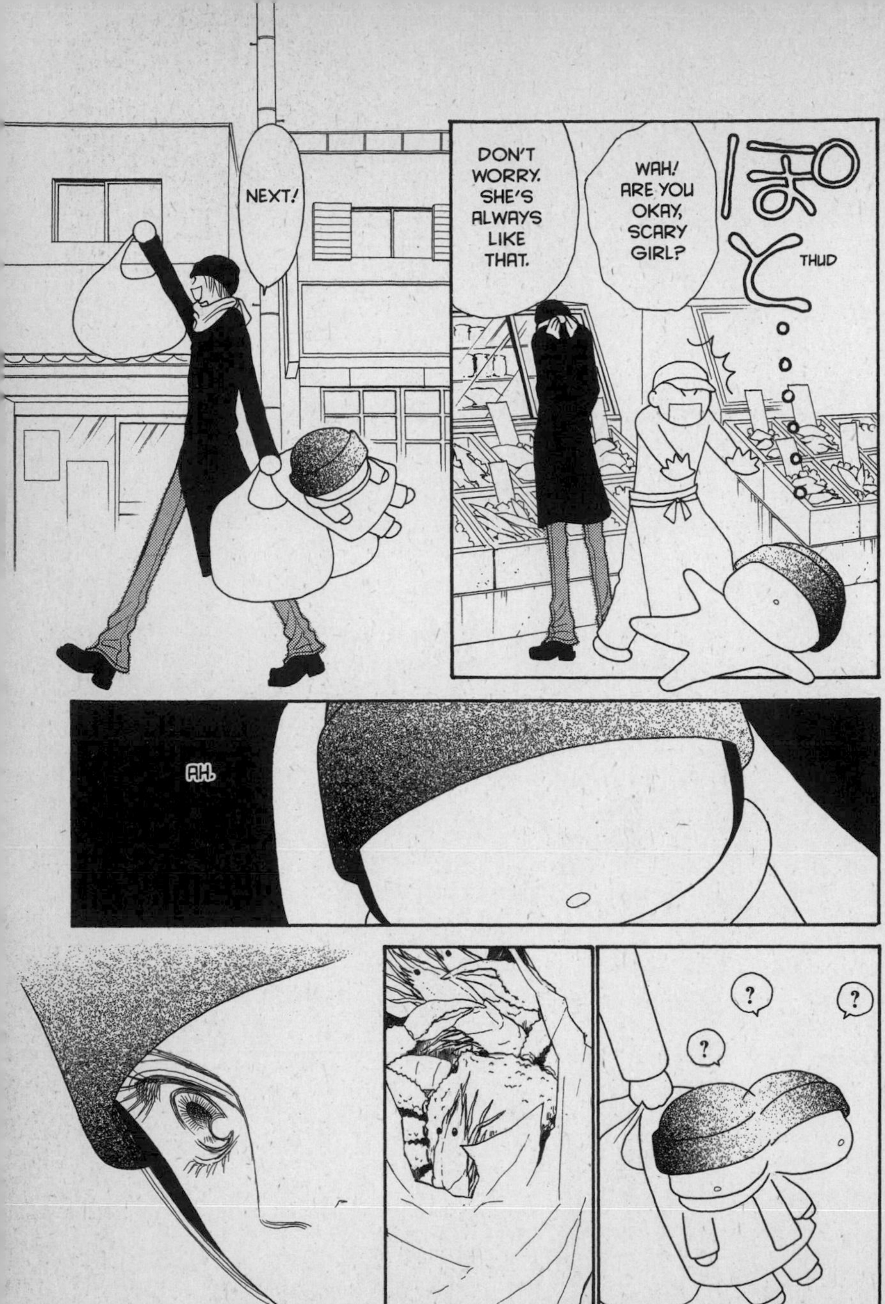
ぽと
THUD
WAH! ARE YOU OKAY, SCARY GIRL?
DON'T WORRY. SHE'S ALWAYS LIKE THAT.
NEXT!
AH.
?
?
?

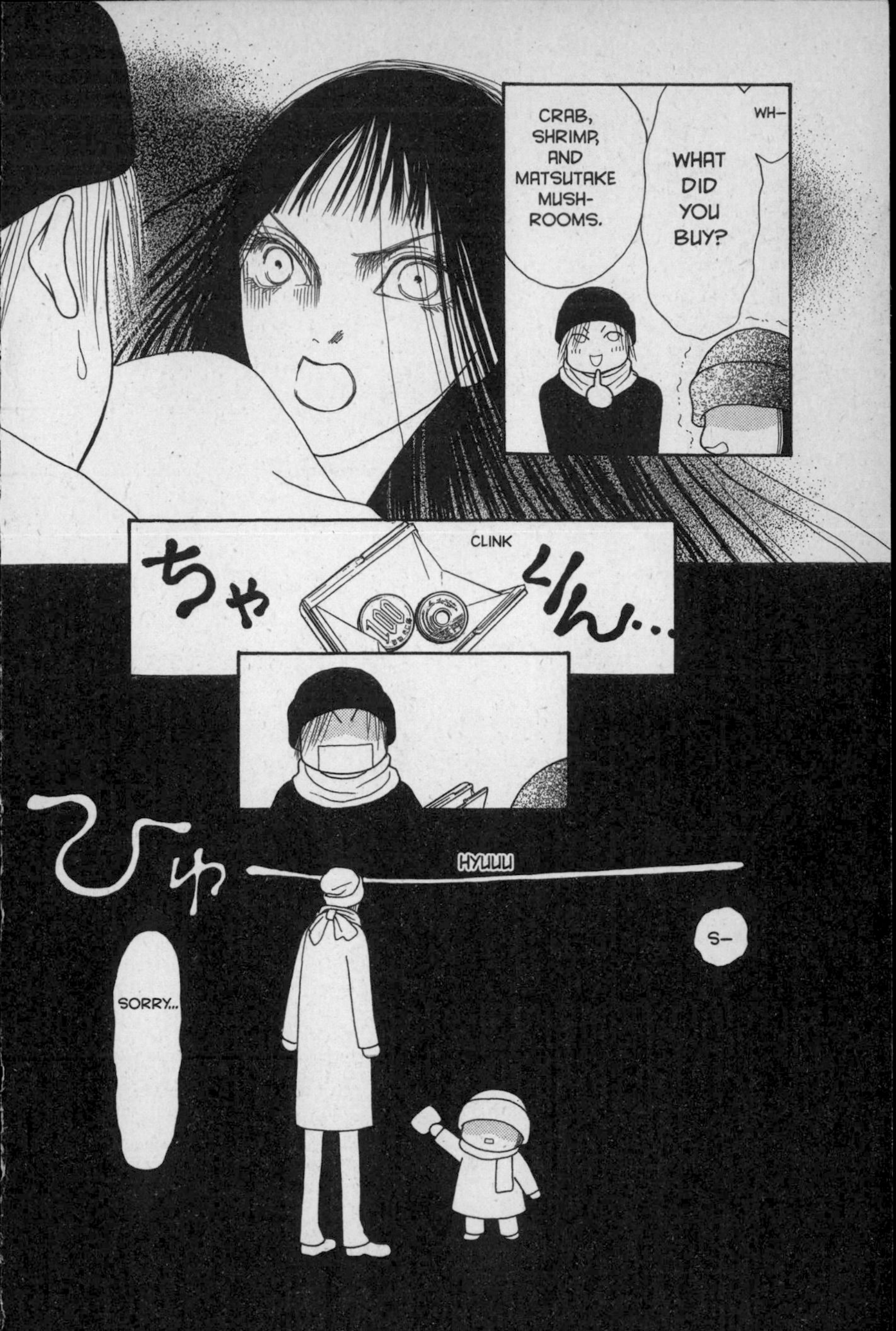

WH-
WHAT DID YOU BUY?
CRAB, SHRIMP, AND MATSUTAKE MUSH-ROOMS.
ちゃりん…
CLINK
ひゅ―
HYUUU
S-
SORRY...

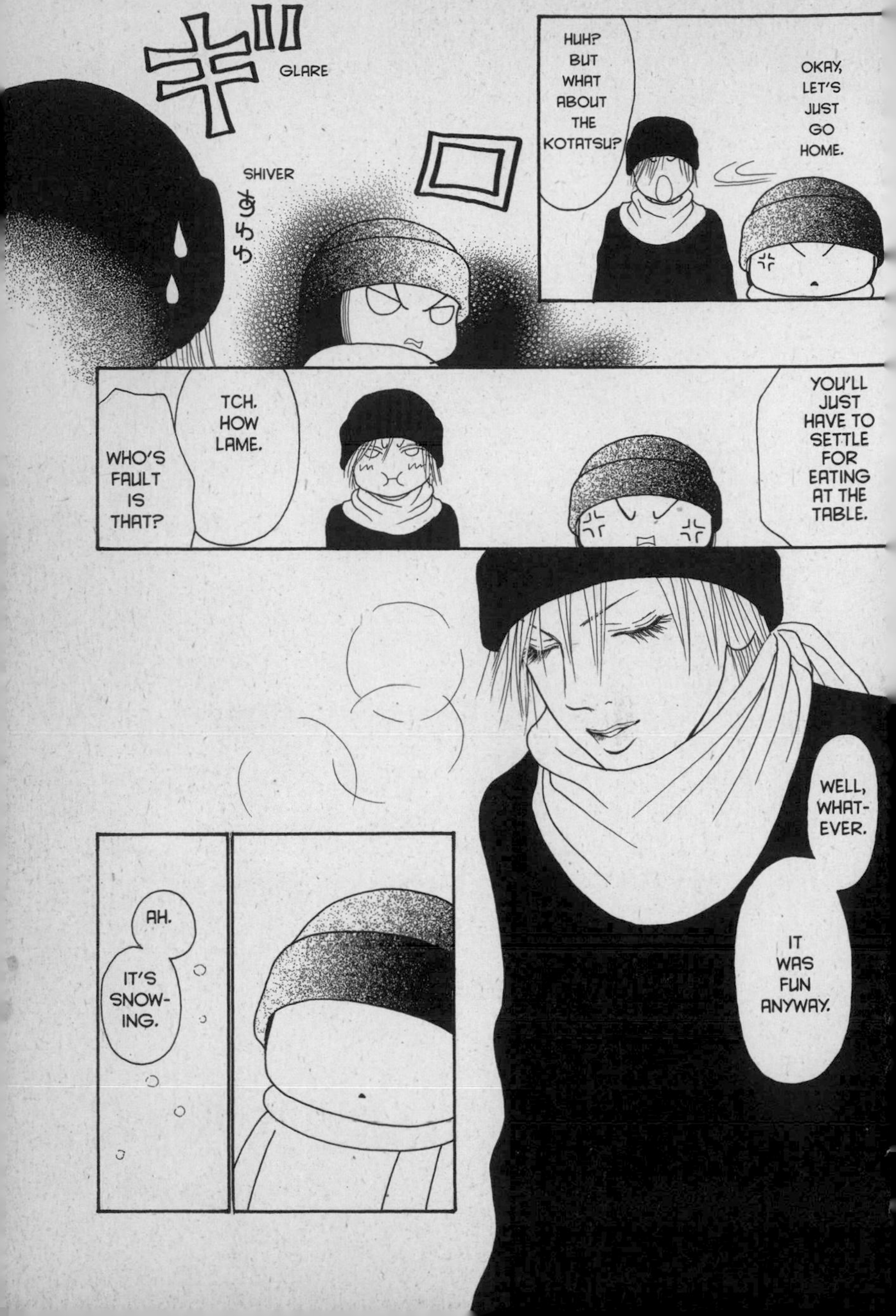
OKAY, LET'S JUST GO HOME.
HUH? BUT WHAT ABOUT THE KOTATSU?
GLARE
SHIVER
YOU'LL JUST HAVE TO SETTLE FOR EATING AT THE TABLE.
TCH. HOW LAME.
WHO'S FAULT IS THAT?
WELL, WHATEVER.
IT WAS FUN ANYWAY.
AH.
IT'S SNOWING.

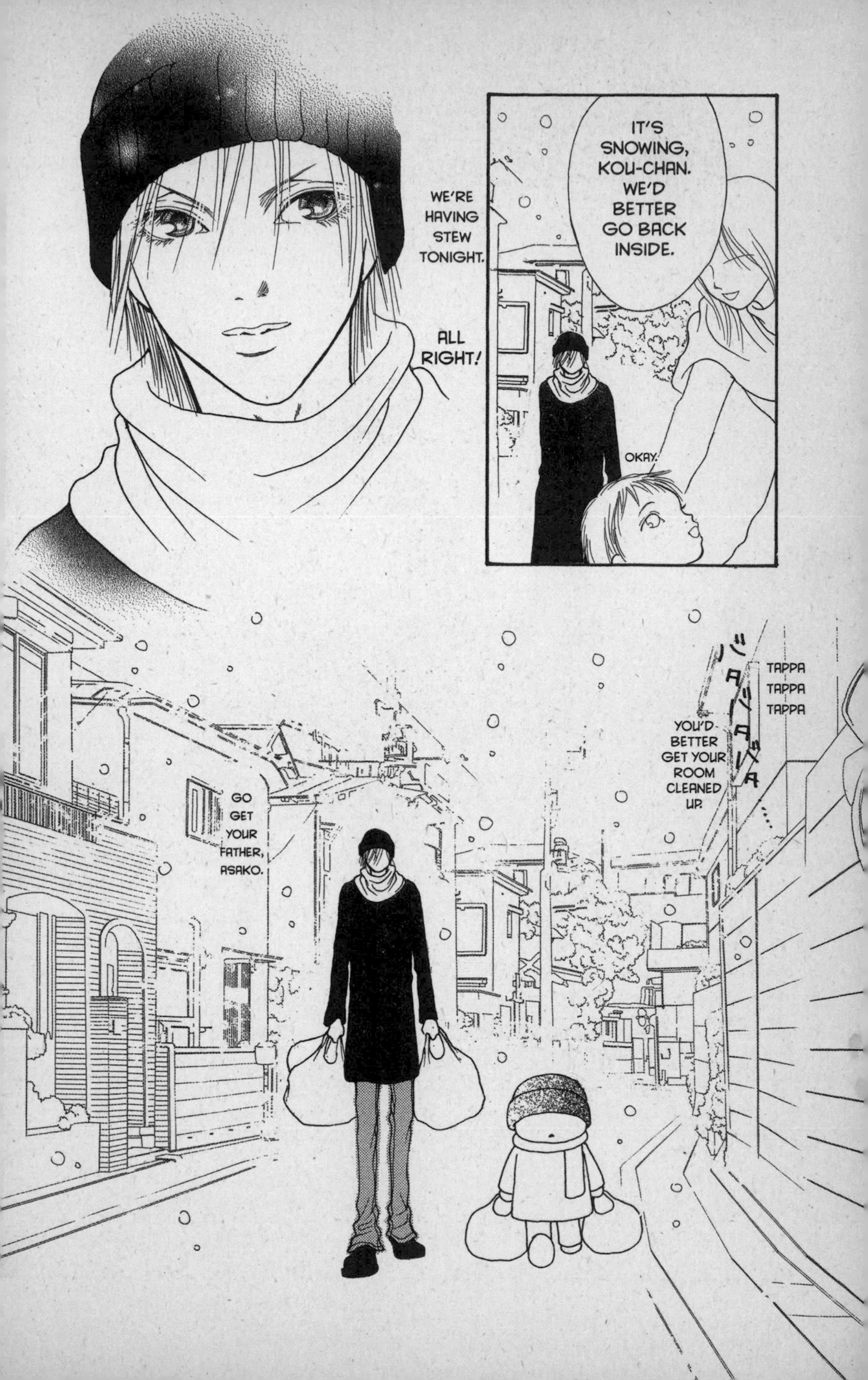
IT'S SNOWING, KOU-CHAN. WE'D BETTER GO BACK INSIDE.
OKAY.
WE'RE HAVING STEW TONIGHT.
ALL RIGHT!
TAPPA TAPPA TAPPA
YOU'D BETTER GET YOUR ROOM CLEANED UP.
GO GET YOUR FATHER, ASAKO.

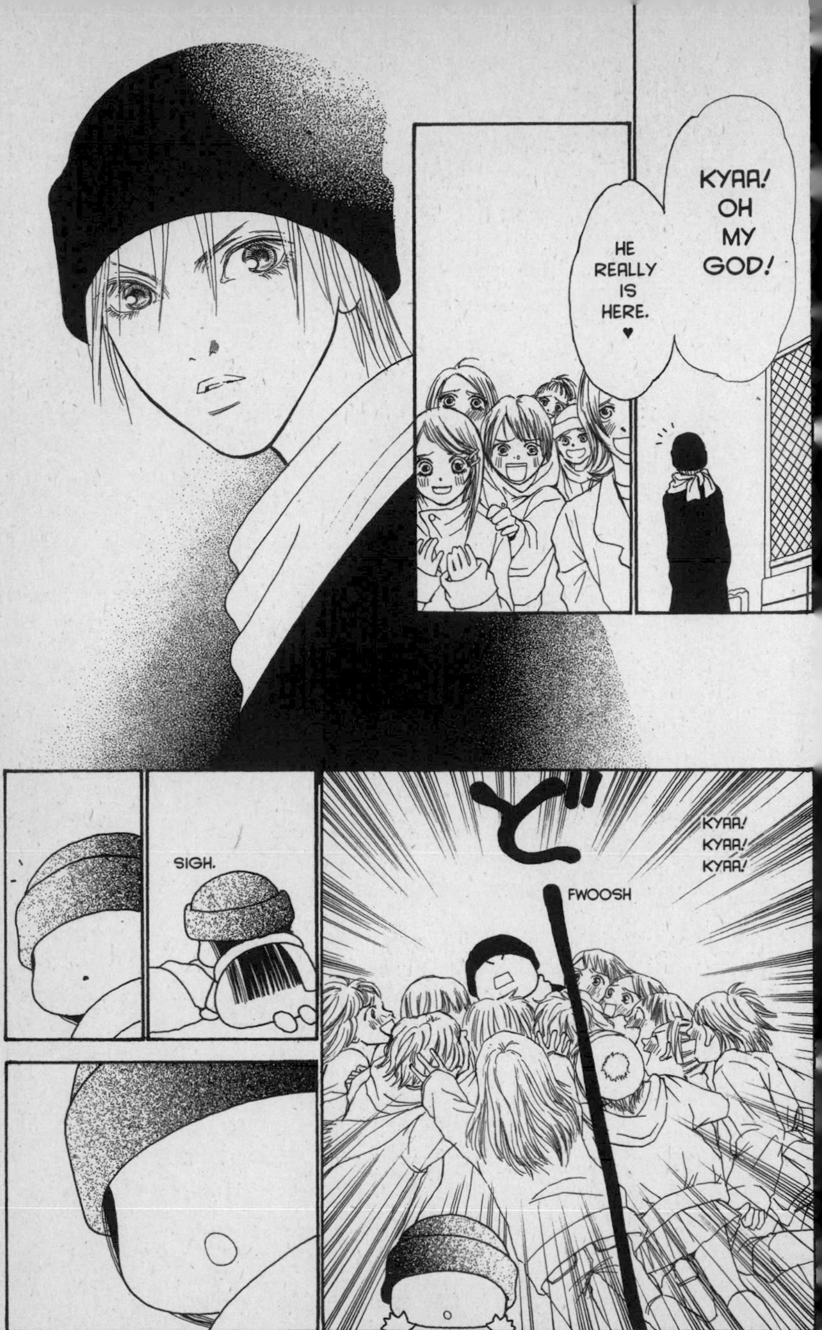
KYAA! OH MY GOD!
HE REALLY IS HERE. ♥
ど
KYAA! KYAA! KYAA!
FWOOSH
SIGH.

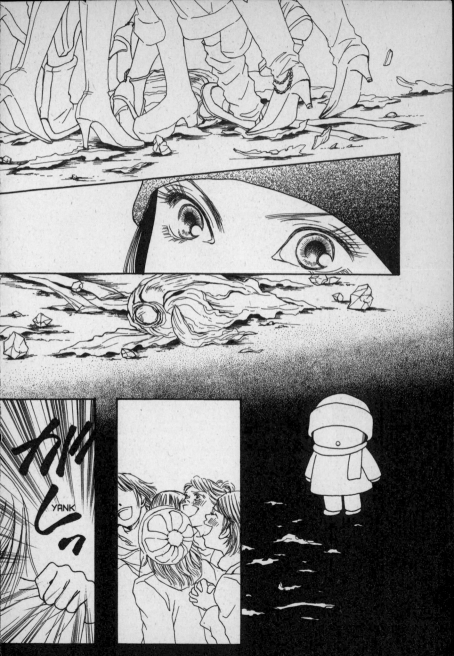

YANK

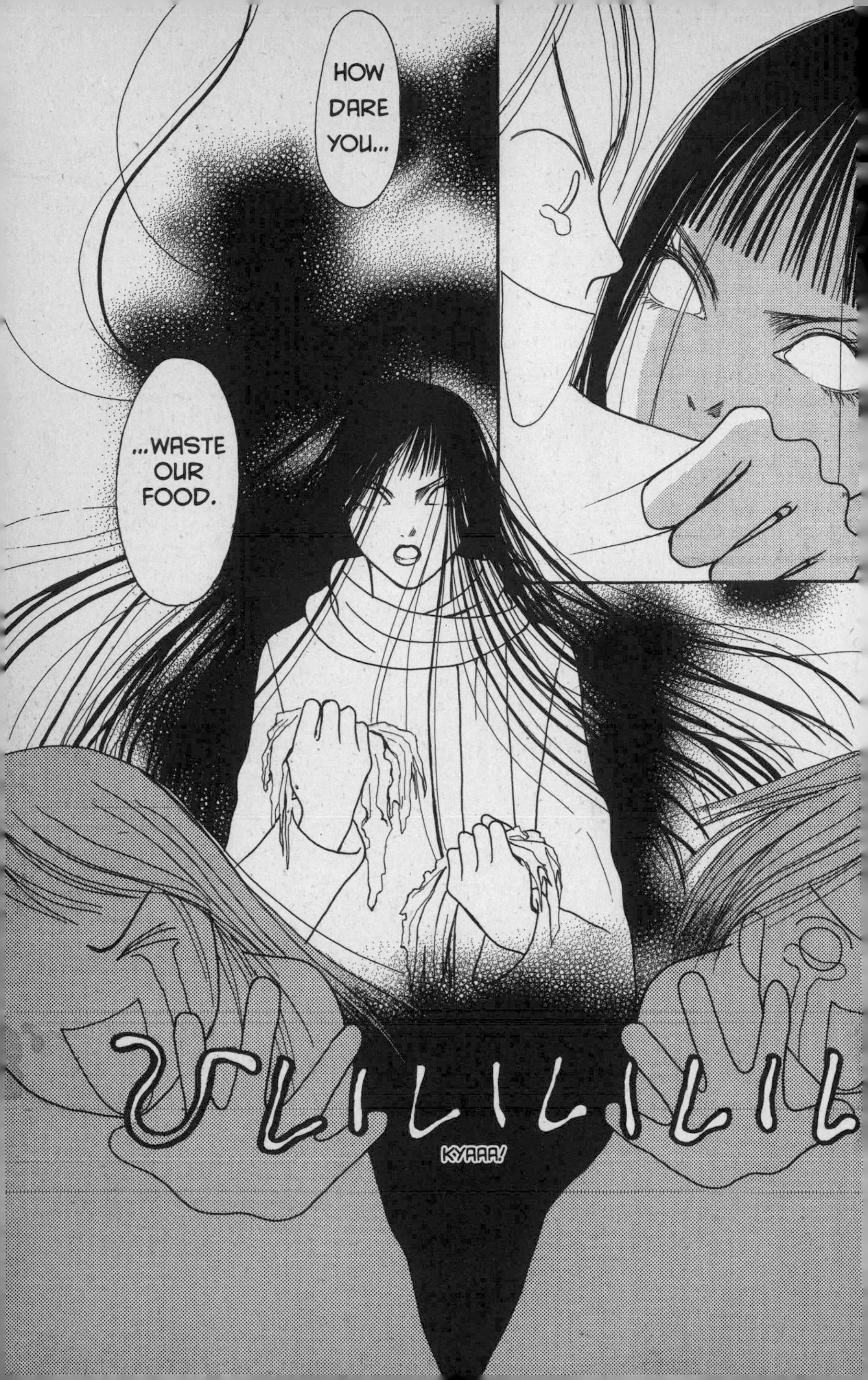
HOW DARE YOU...
...WASTE OUR FOOD.
KYAAA!

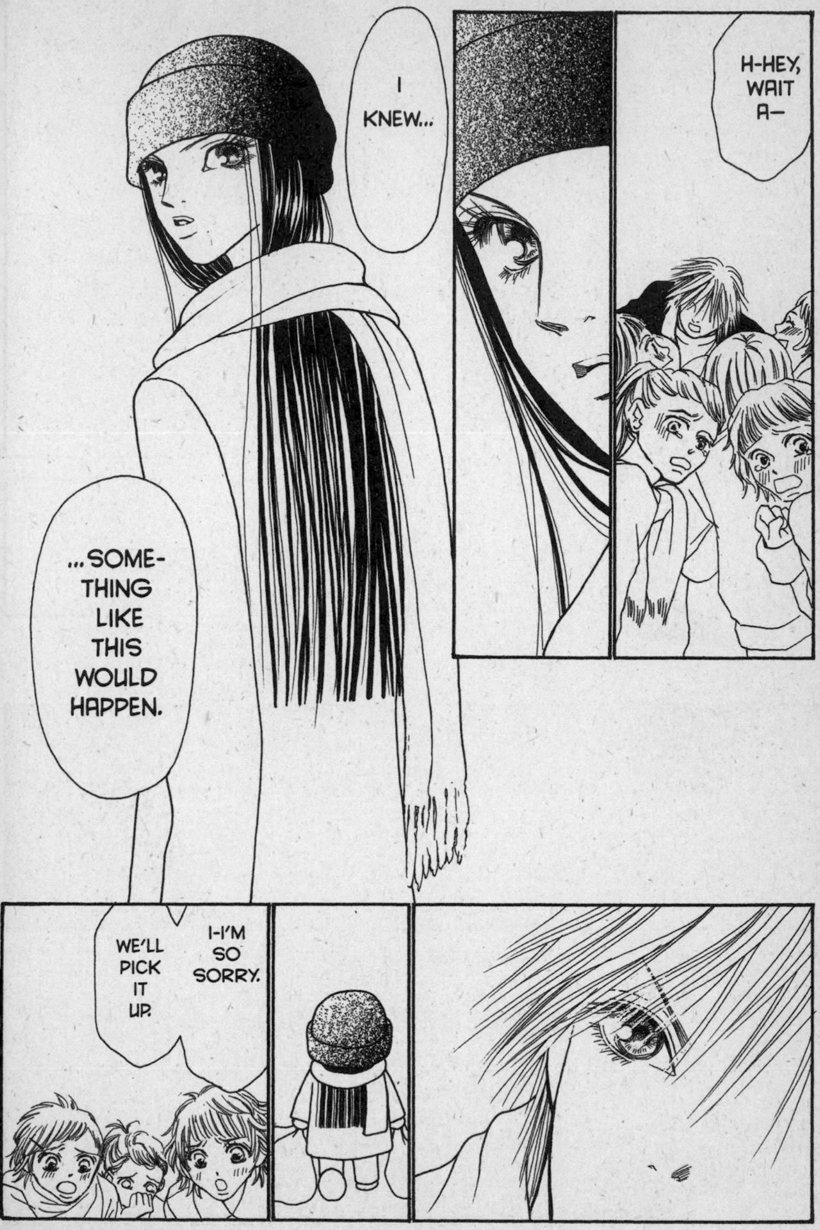
H-HEY, WAIT A—
I KNEW...
...SOME-THING LIKE THIS WOULD HAPPEN.
I-I'M SO SORRY.
WE'LL PICK IT UP.

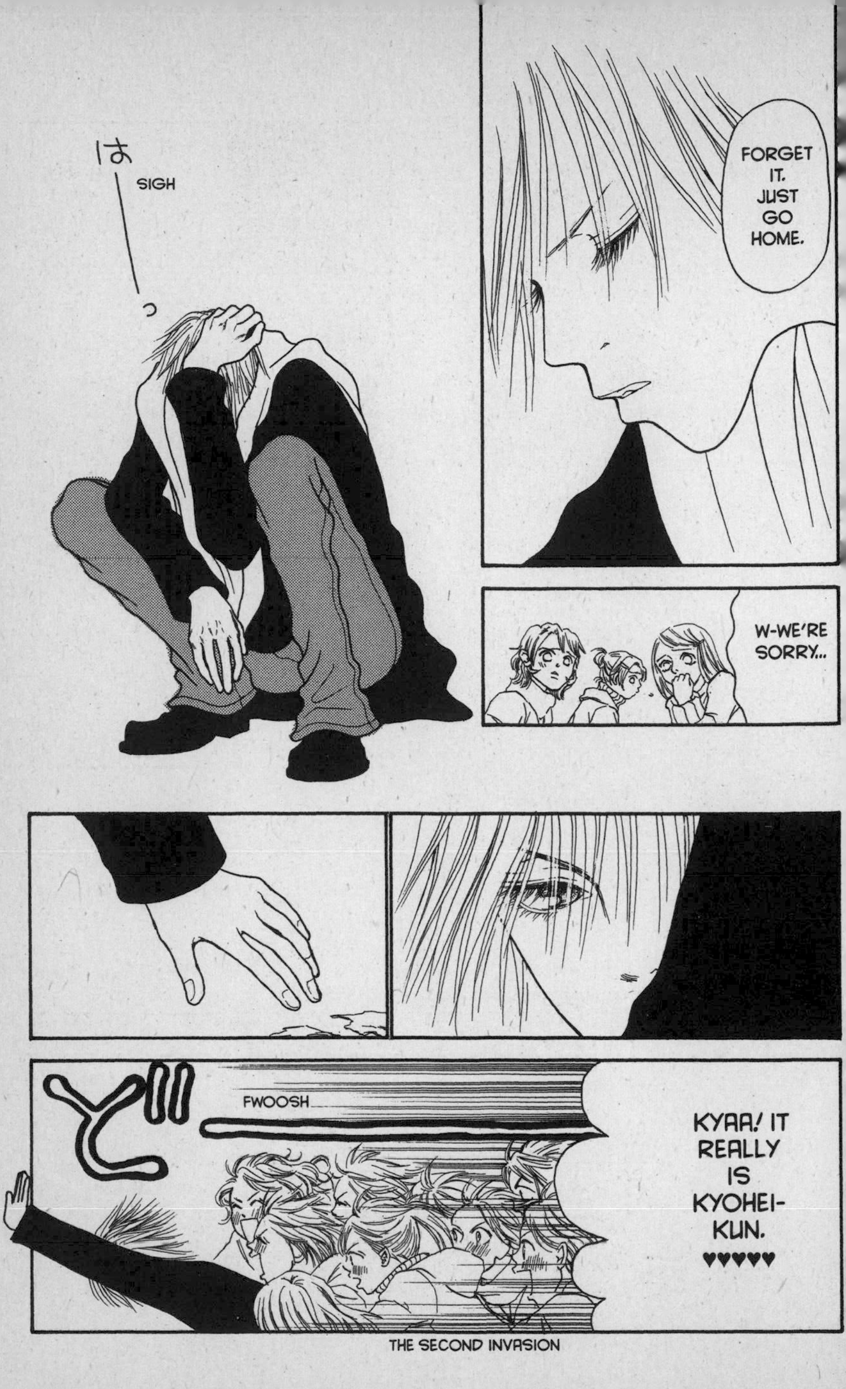
FORGET IT. JUST GO HOME.
W-WE'RE SORRY...
は
SIGH
KYAA! IT REALLY IS KYOHEI-KUN. ♥♥♥♥♥
で
FWOOSH

THE SECOND INVASION

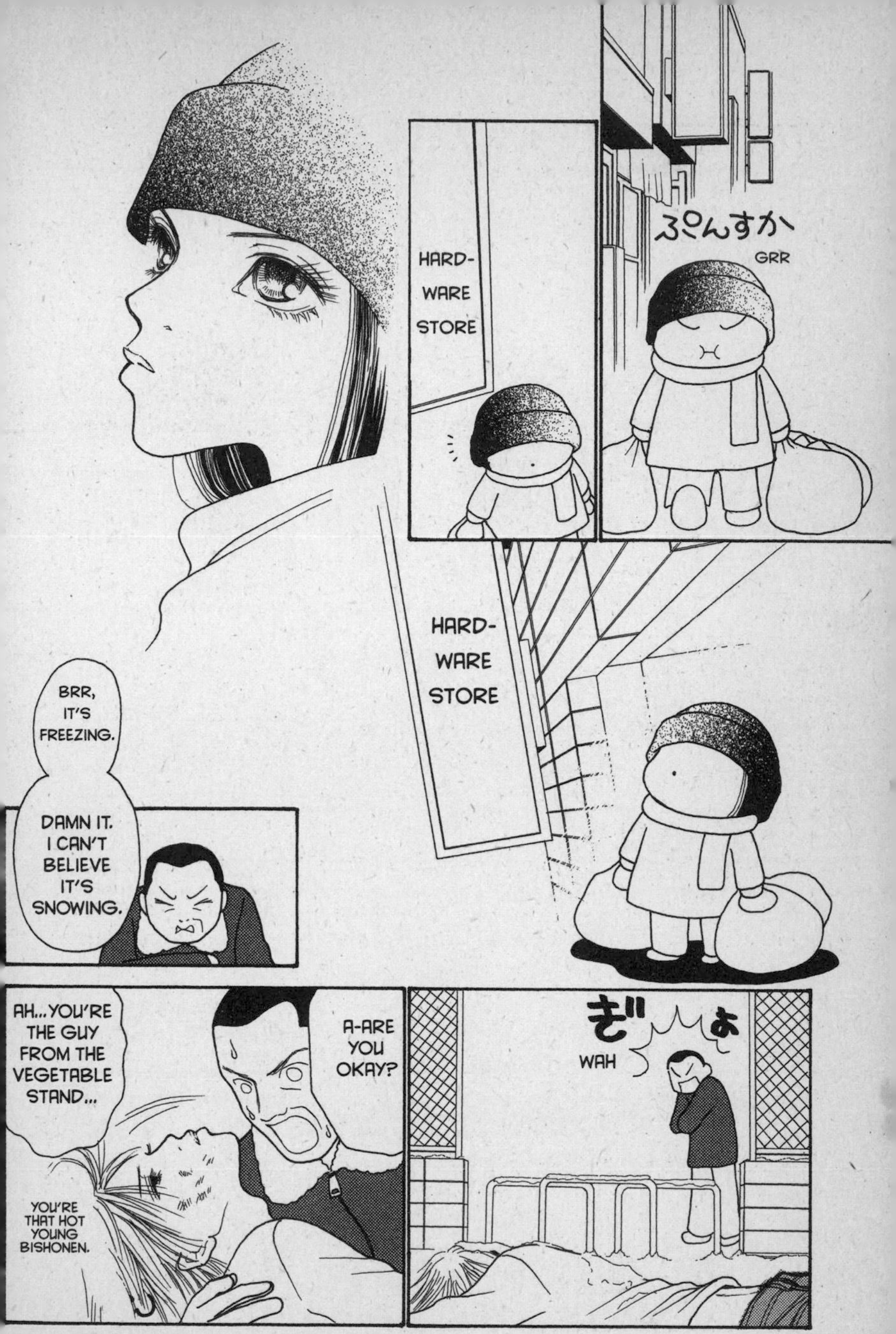
ぷんすか
GRR
HARD-WARE STORE
HARD-WARE STORE
BRR, IT'S FREEZING.
DAMN IT. I CAN'T BELIEVE IT'S SNOWING.
WAH
A-ARE YOU OKAY?
AH...YOU'RE THE GUY FROM THE VEGETABLE STAND...
YOU'RE THAT HOT YOUNG BISHONEN.

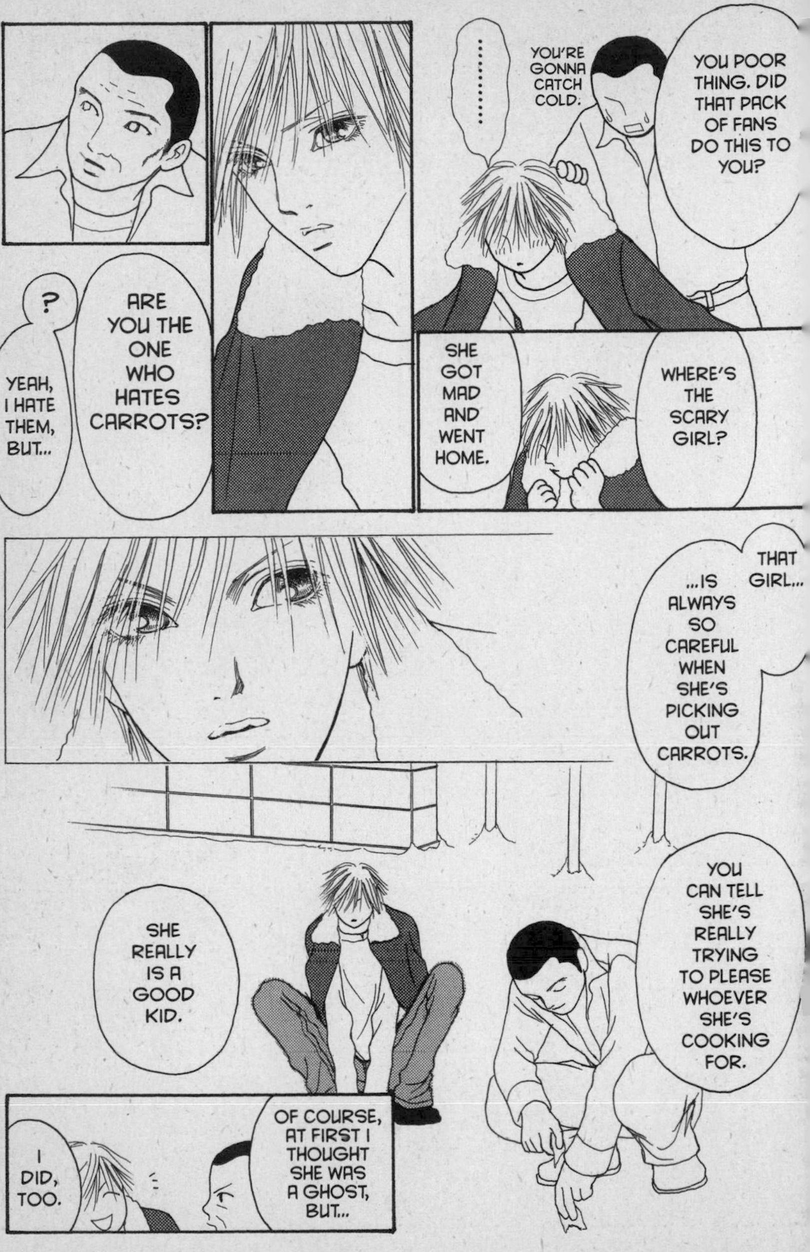
YOU POOR THING. DID THAT PACK OF FANS DO THIS TO YOU?
YOU'RE GONNA CATCH COLD.
......
WHERE'S THE SCARY GIRL?
SHE GOT MAD AND WENT HOME.
ARE YOU THE ONE WHO HATES CARROTS?
?
YEAH, I HATE THEM, BUT...
THAT GIRL...
...IS ALWAYS SO CAREFUL WHEN SHE'S PICKING OUT CARROTS.
YOU CAN TELL SHE'S REALLY TRYING TO PLEASE WHOEVER SHE'S COOKING FOR.
SHE REALLY IS A GOOD KID.
OF COURSE, AT FIRST I THOUGHT SHE WAS A GHOST, BUT...
I DID, TOO.

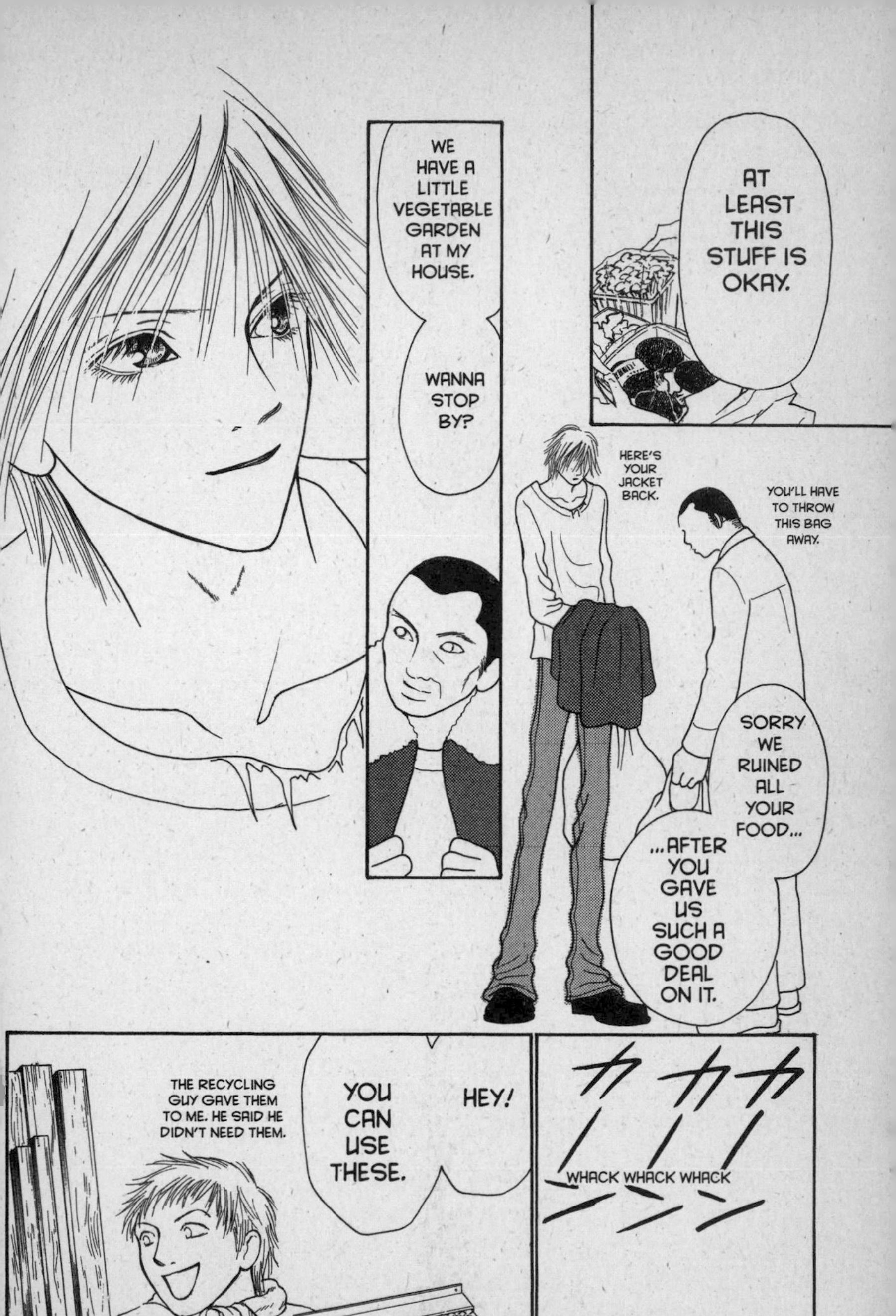
AT LEAST THIS STUFF IS OKAY.
YOU'LL HAVE TO THROW THIS BAG AWAY.
HERE'S YOUR JACKET BACK.
SORRY WE RUINED ALL YOUR FOOD...
...AFTER YOU GAVE US SUCH A GOOD DEAL ON IT.
WE HAVE A LITTLE VEGETABLE GARDEN AT MY HOUSE.
WANNA STOP BY?
WHACK WHACK WHACK
HEY!
YOU CAN USE THESE.
THE RECYCLING GUY GAVE THEM TO ME. HE SAID HE DIDN'T NEED THEM.

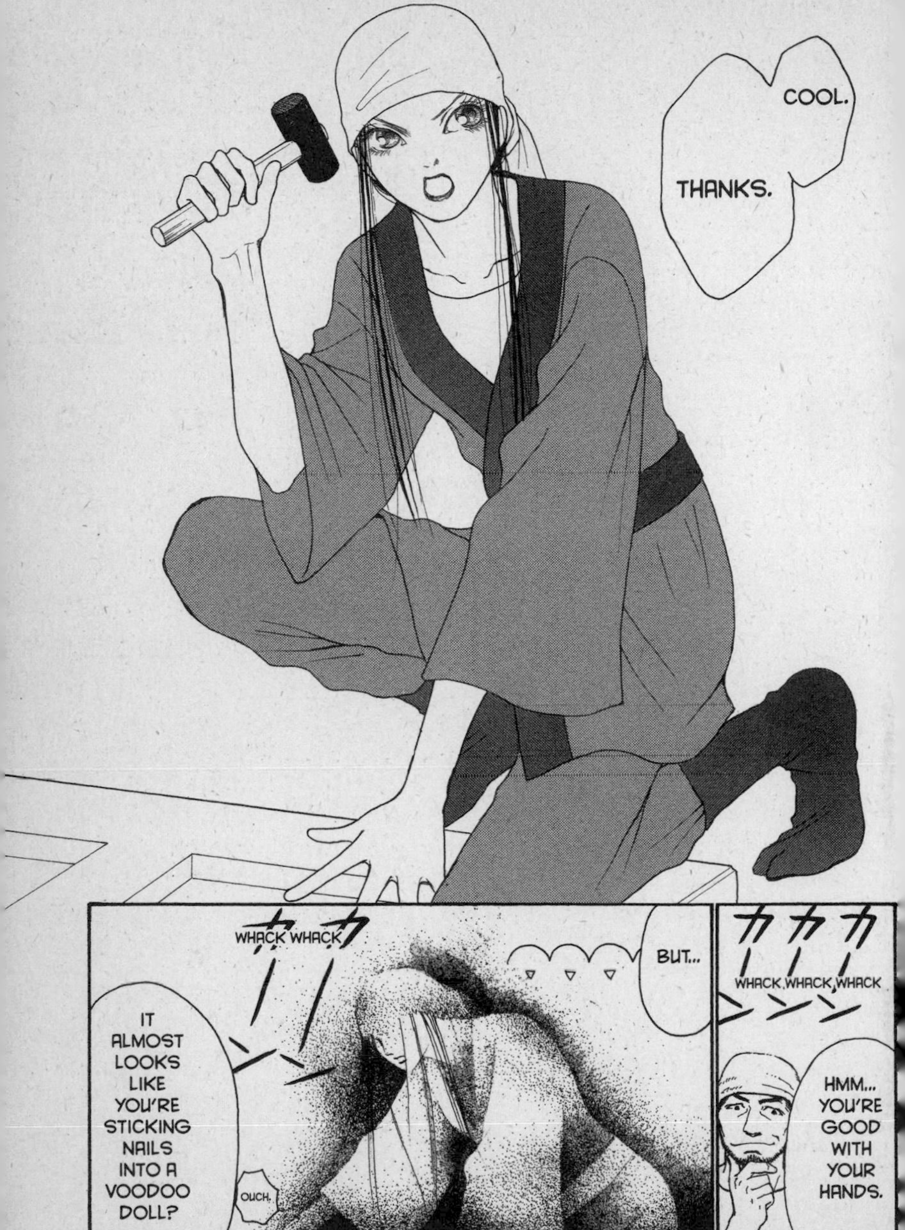
COOL.
THANKS.
WHACK WHACK WHACK
HMM... YOU'RE GOOD WITH YOUR HANDS.
BUT...
WHACK WHACK
IT ALMOST LOOKS LIKE YOU'RE STICKING NAILS INTO A VOODOO DOLL?
OUCH.

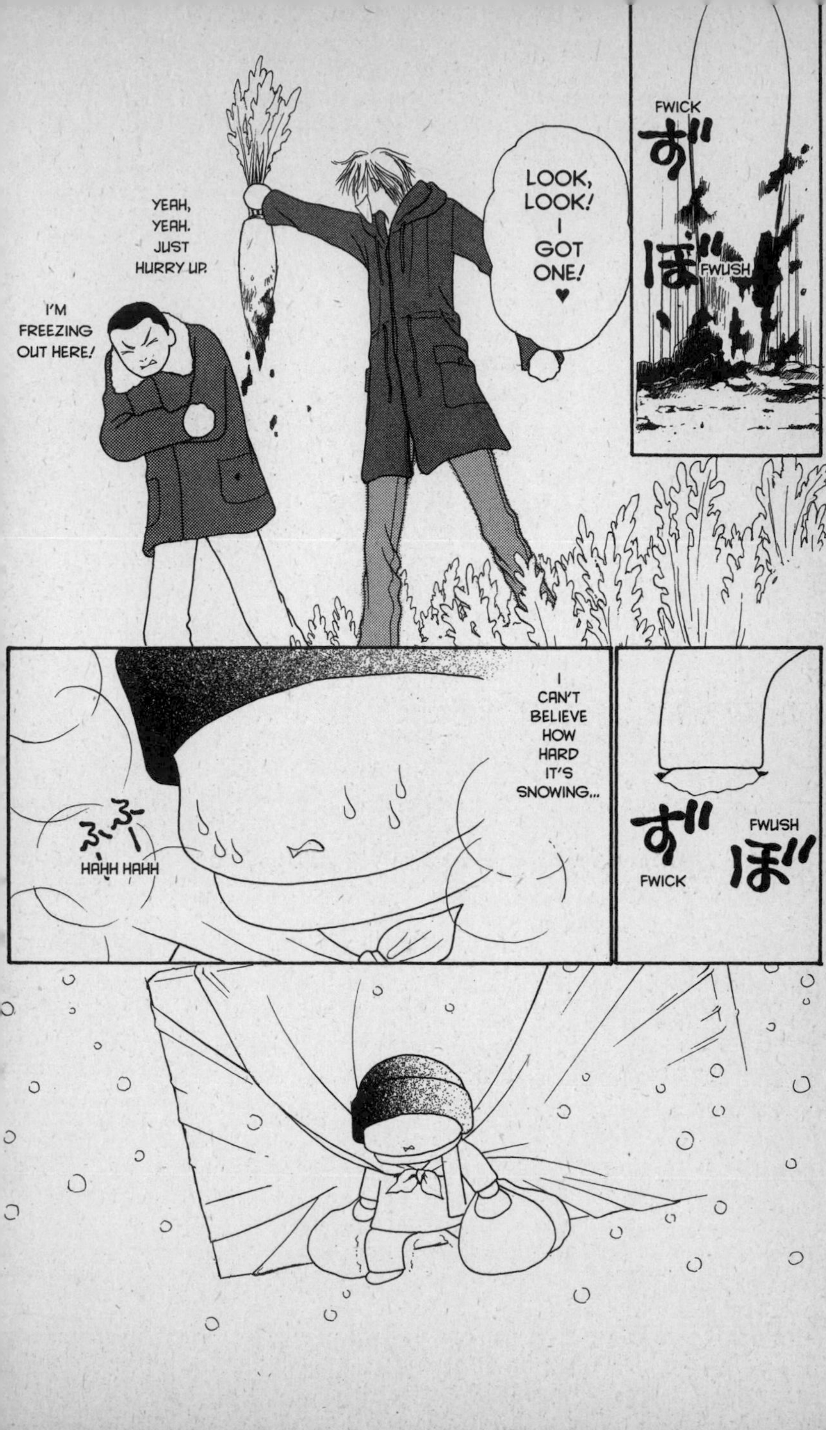
FWICK
ずぼ
FWUSH
LOOK, LOOK! I GOT ONE! ♥
YEAH, YEAH. JUST HURRY UP.
I'M FREEZING OUT HERE!
ずぼ
FWICK
FWUSH
I CAN'T BELIEVE HOW HARD IT'S SNOWING...
ふーふー
HAHH HAHH

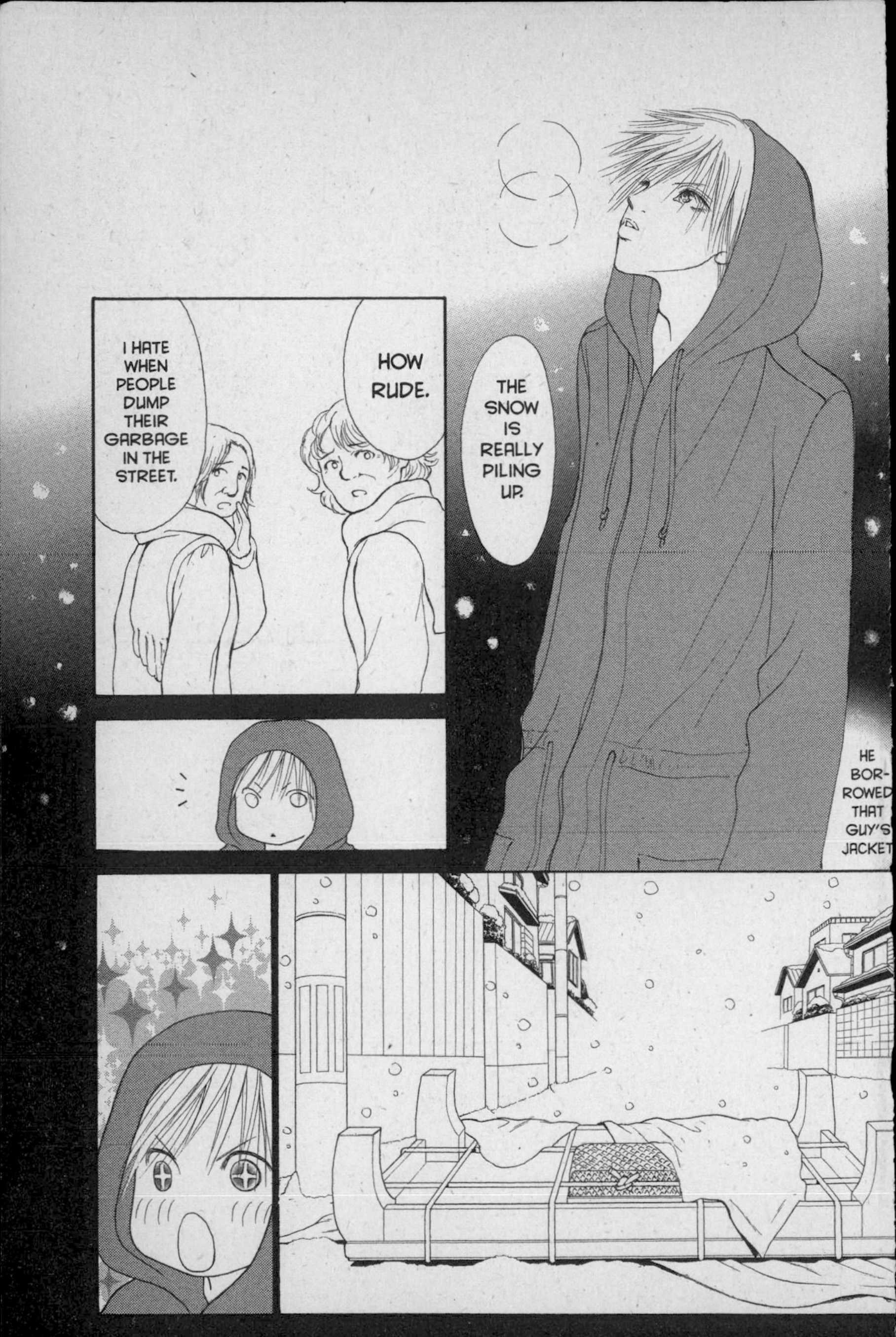
THE SNOW IS REALLY PILING UP.
HE BOR-ROWED THAT GUY'S JACKET
HOW RUDE.
I HATE WHEN PEOPLE DUMP THEIR GARBAGE IN THE STREET.

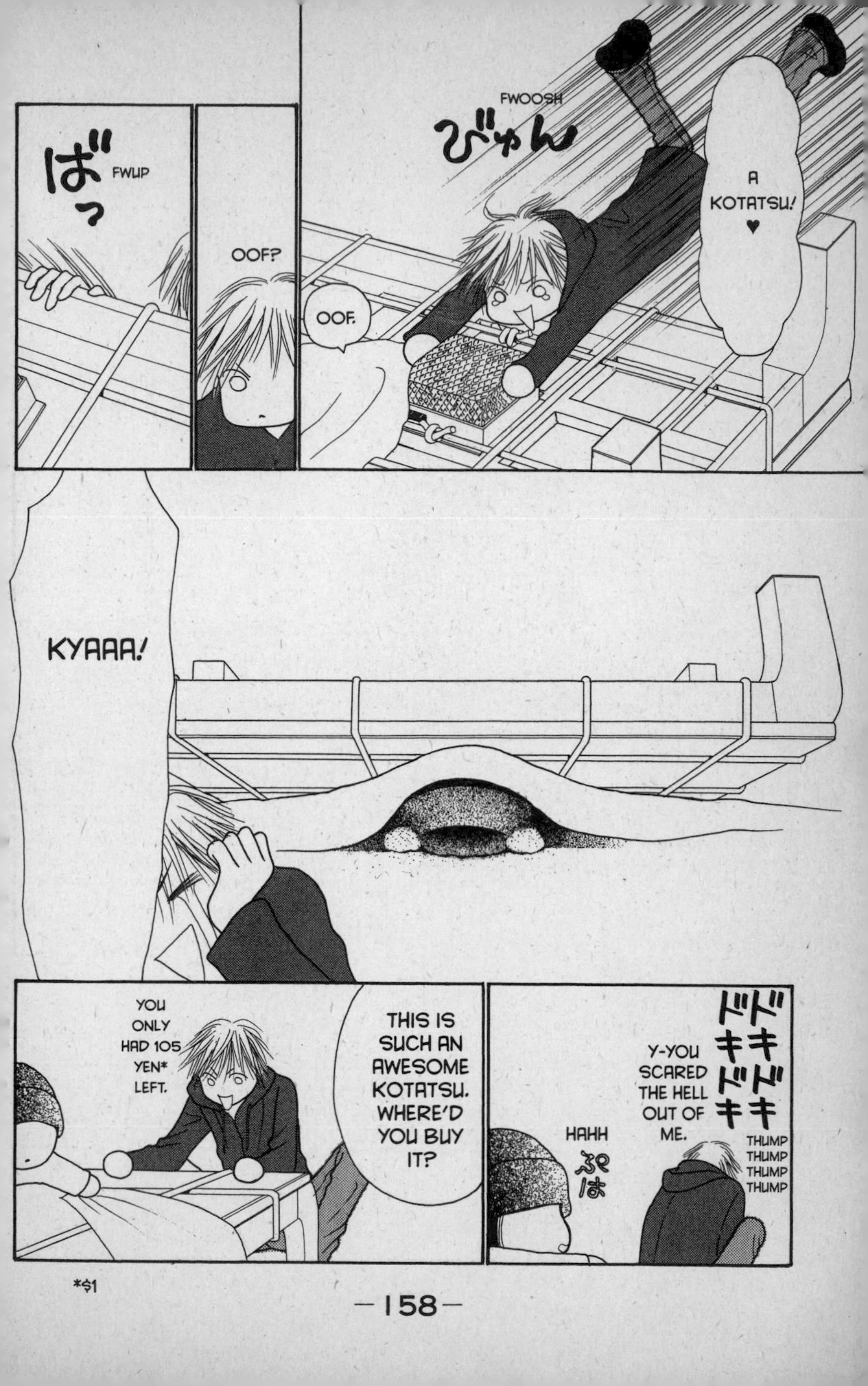
A KOTATSU! ♥
びゅん
FWOOSH
OOF.
OOF?
ばっ
FWUP
KYAAA!
ドキドキドキドキ
THUMP THUMP THUMP THUMP
Y-YOU SCARED THE HELL OUT OF ME.
ぷは
HAHH
THIS IS SUCH AN AWESOME KOTATSU. WHERE'D YOU BUY IT?
YOU ONLY HAD 105 YEN* LEFT.

*$1

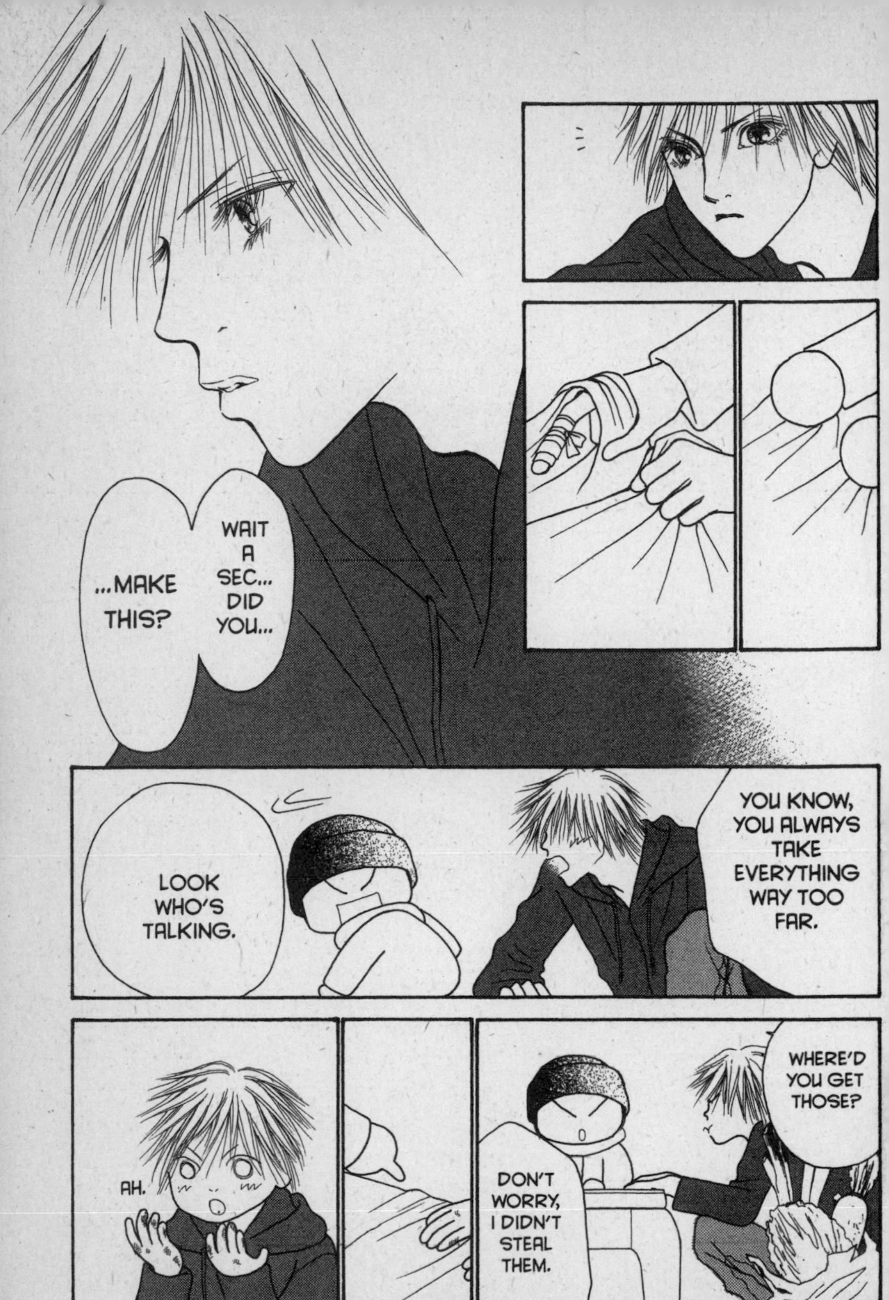
WAIT A SEC... DID YOU...
...MAKE THIS?
YOU KNOW, YOU ALWAYS TAKE EVERYTHING WAY TOO FAR.
LOOK WHO'S TALKING.
WHERE'D YOU GET THOSE?
DON'T WORRY, I DIDN'T STEAL THEM.
AH.

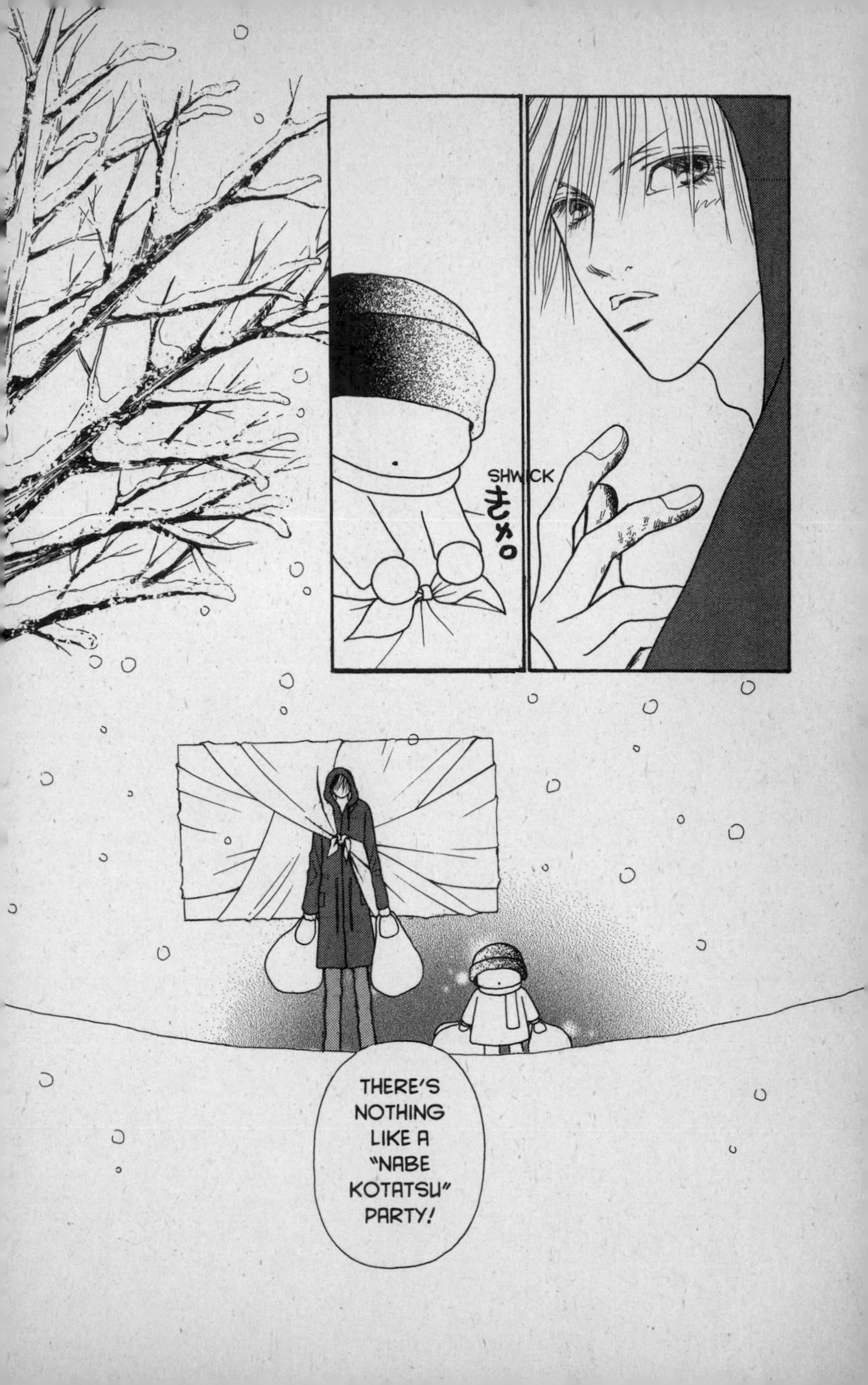
SHWICK
THERE'S NOTHING LIKE A "NABE KOTATSU" PARTY!

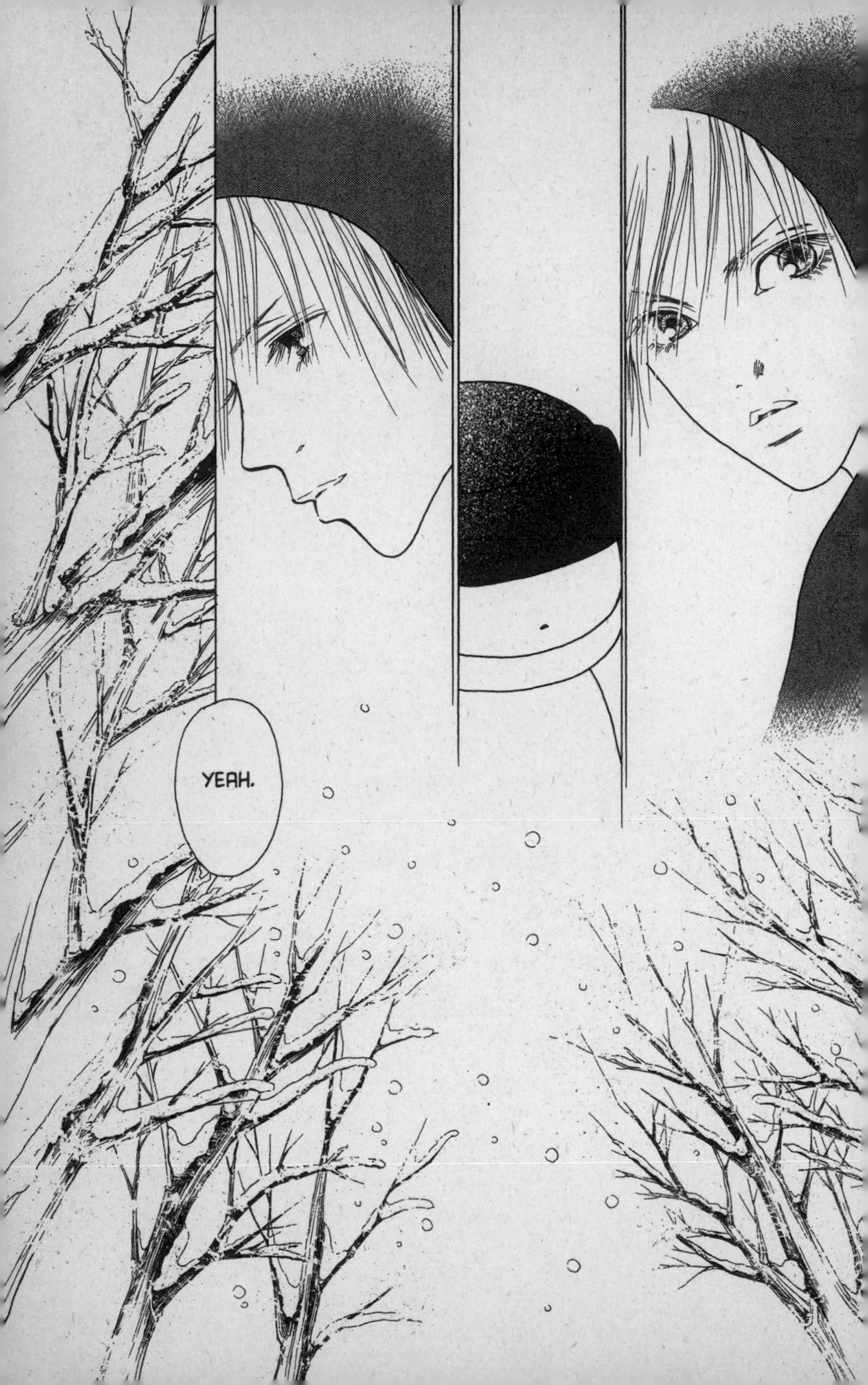
YEAH.

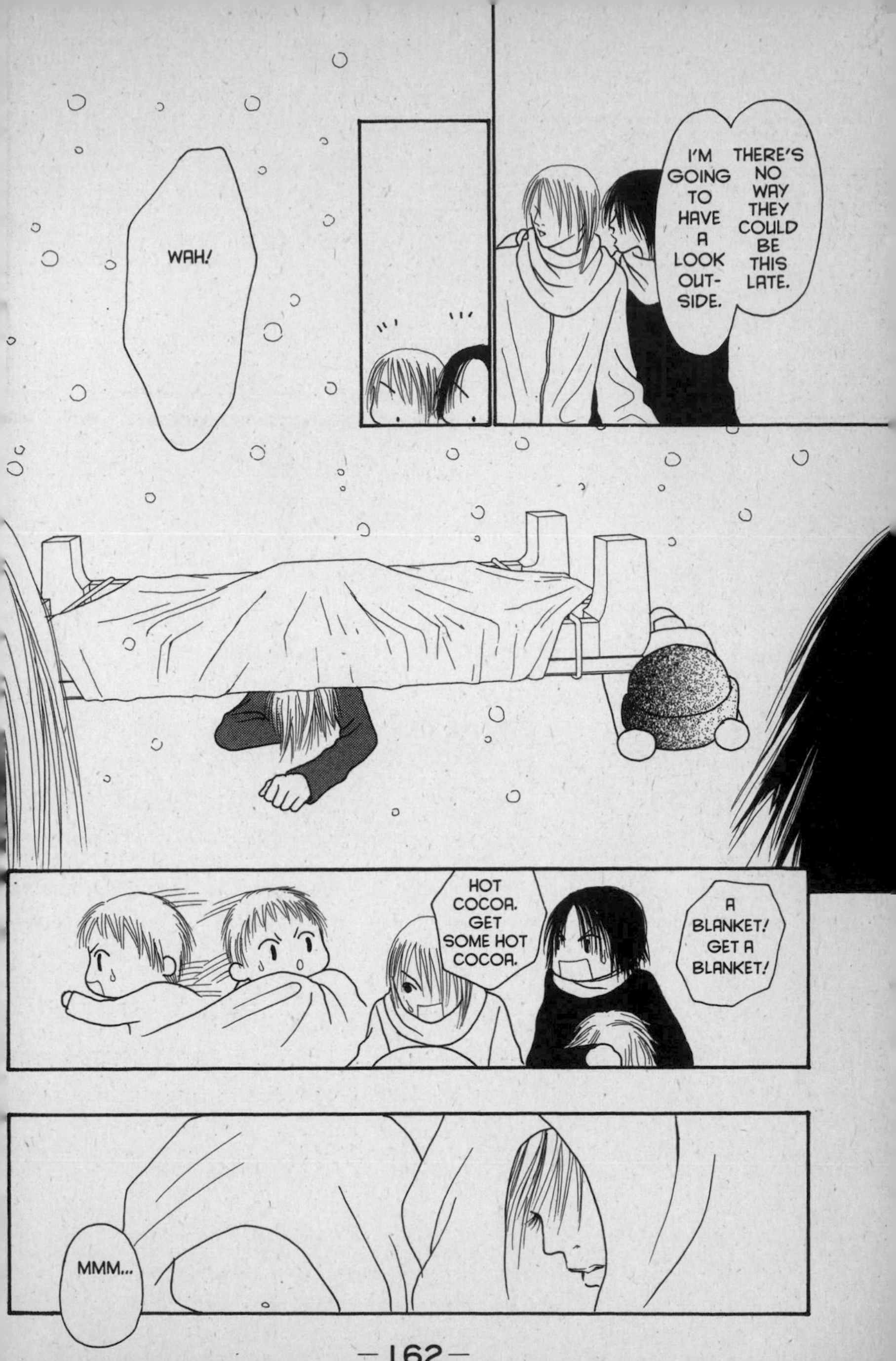
THERE'S NO WAY THEY COULD BE THIS LATE.
I'M GOING TO HAVE A LOOK OUT-SIDE.
WAH!
A BLANKET! GET A BLANKET!
HOT COCOA. GET SOME HOT COCOA.
MMM...

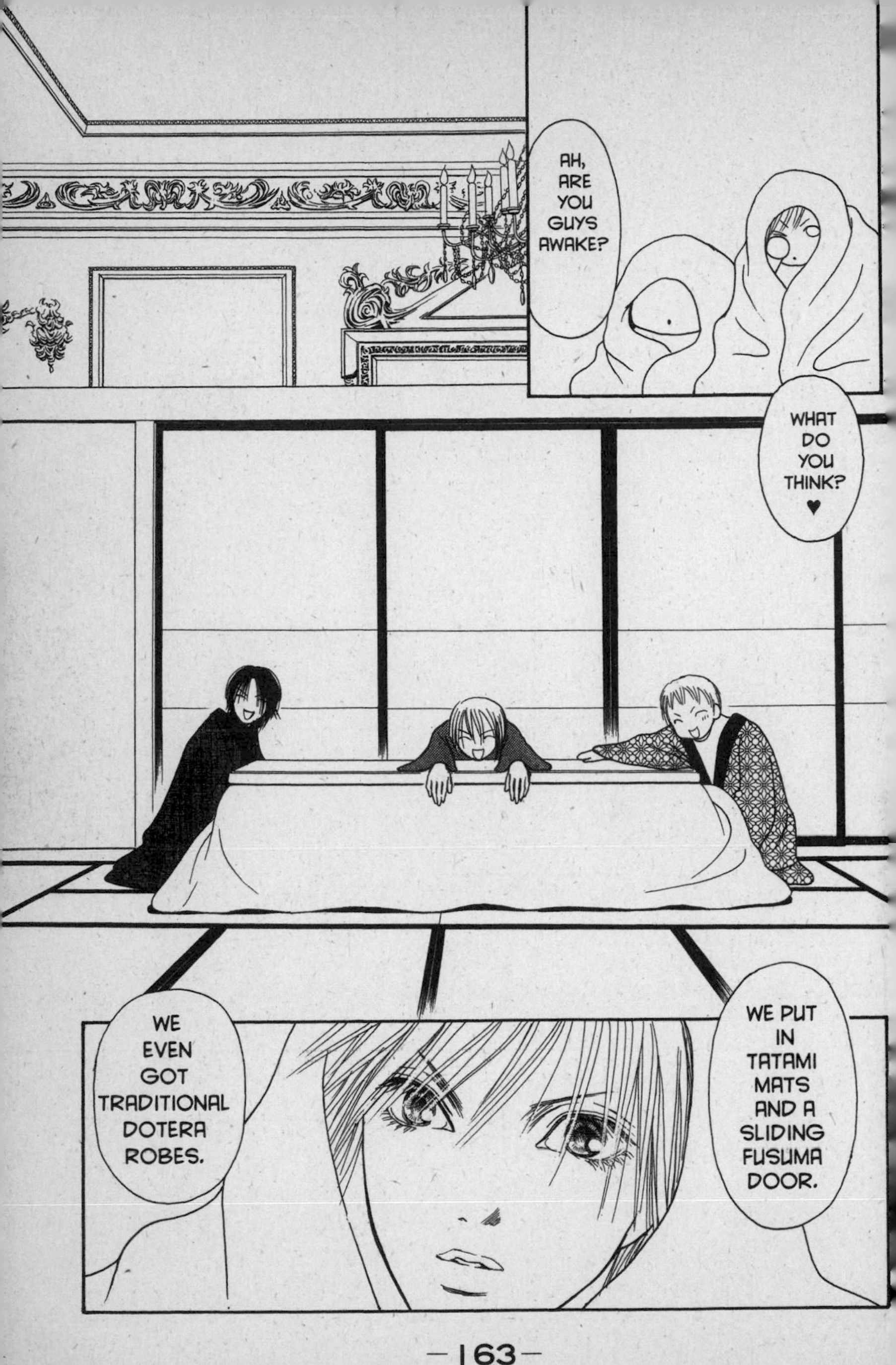
AH, ARE YOU GUYS AWAKE?
WHAT DO YOU THINK? ♥
WE PUT IN TATAMI MATS AND A SLIDING FUSUMA DOOR.
WE EVEN GOT TRADITIONAL DOTERA ROBES.

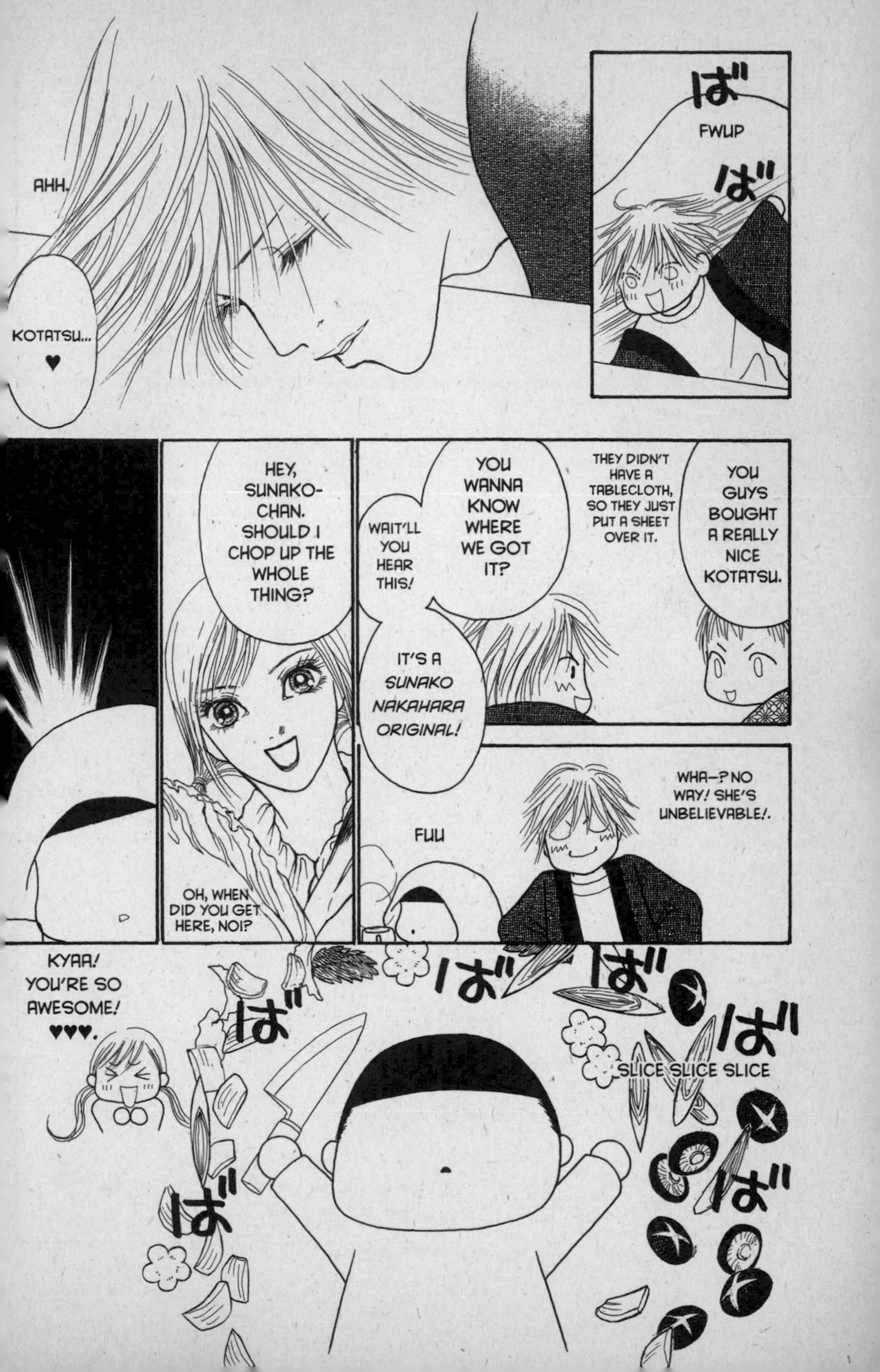
ば
FWUP
ば
AHH.
KOTATSU... ♥
YOU GUYS BOUGHT A REALLY NICE KOTATSU.
THEY DIDN'T HAVE A TABLECLOTH, SO THEY JUST PUT A SHEET OVER IT.
YOU WANNA KNOW WHERE WE GOT IT?
WAIT'LL YOU HEAR THIS!
IT'S A SUNAKO NAKAHARA ORIGINAL!
WHA-? NO WAY! SHE'S UNBELIEVABLE!.
FUU
HEY, SUNAKO-CHAN. SHOULD I CHOP UP THE WHOLE THING?
OH, WHEN DID YOU GET HERE, NOI?
ば
ば
ば
SLICE SLICE SLICE
ば
ば
ば
KYAA! YOU'RE SO AWESOME! ♥♥♥.

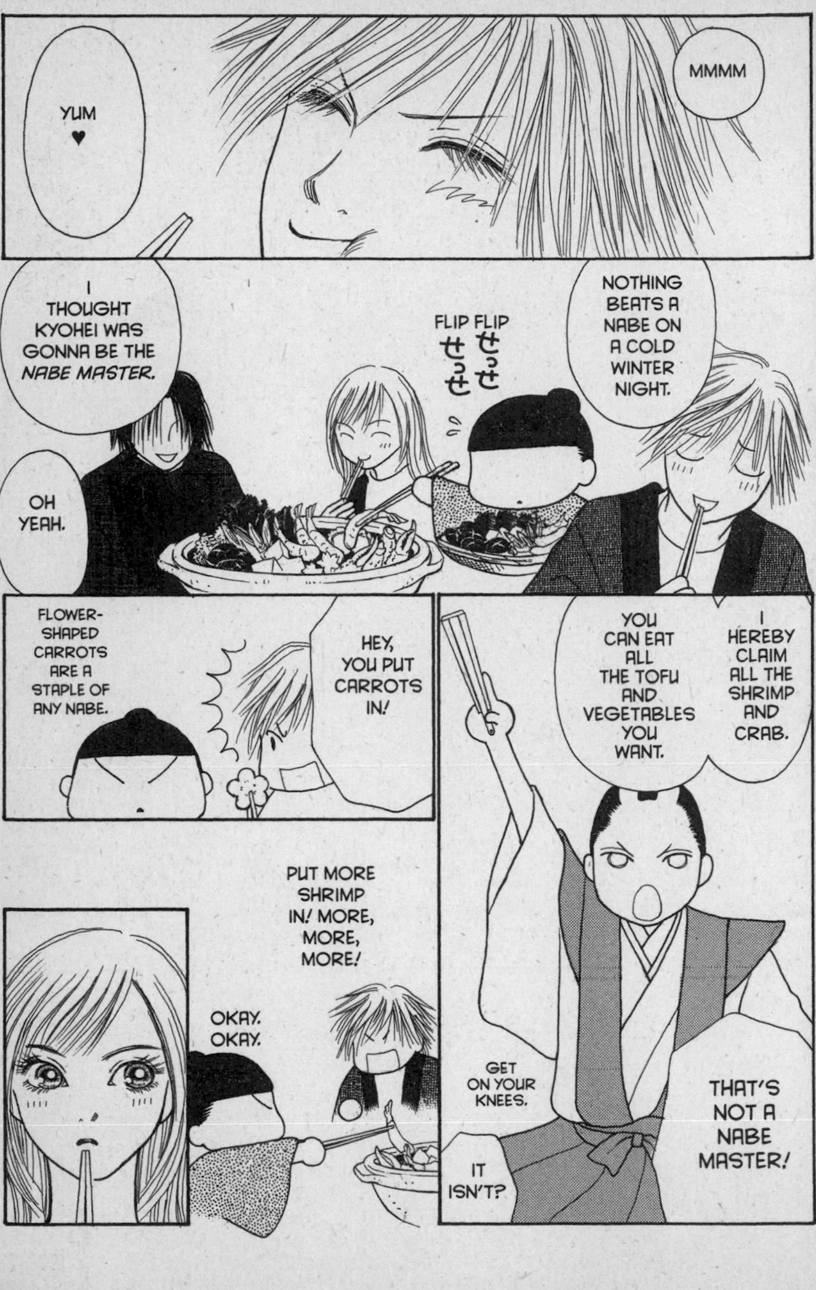
MMMM
YUM ♥
NOTHING BEATS A NABE ON A COLD WINTER NIGHT.
FLIP FLIP
せっせ せっせ
I THOUGHT KYOHEI WAS GONNA BE THE *NABE MASTER.*
OH YEAH.
I HEREBY CLAIM ALL THE SHRIMP AND CRAB.
YOU CAN EAT ALL THE TOFU AND VEGETABLES YOU WANT.
THAT'S NOT A NABE MASTER!
GET ON YOUR KNEES.
IT ISN'T?
HEY, YOU PUT CARROTS IN!
FLOWER-SHAPED CARROTS ARE A STAPLE OF ANY NABE.
PUT MORE SHRIMP IN! MORE, MORE, MORE!
OKAY. OKAY.

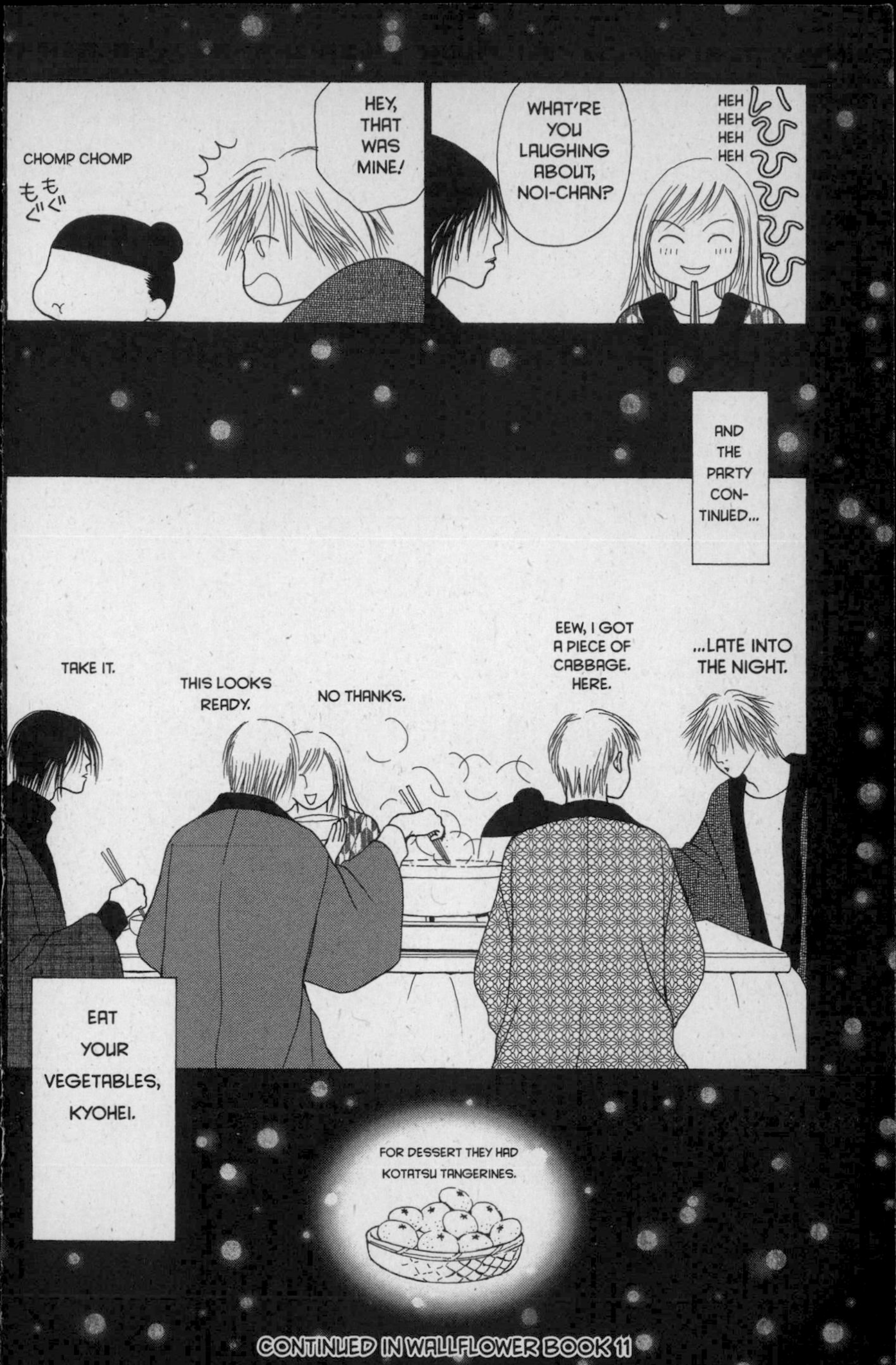
HEH HEH HEH HEH
WHAT'RE YOU LAUGHING ABOUT, NOI-CHAN?
HEY, THAT WAS MINE!
CHOMP CHOMP
AND THE PARTY CONTINUED...
...LATE INTO THE NIGHT.
EEW, I GOT A PIECE OF CABBAGE. HERE.
NO THANKS.
THIS LOOKS READY.
TAKE IT.
EAT YOUR VEGETABLES, KYOHEI.
FOR DESSERT THEY HAD KOTATSU TANGERINES.

CONTINUED IN WALLFLOWER BOOK 11

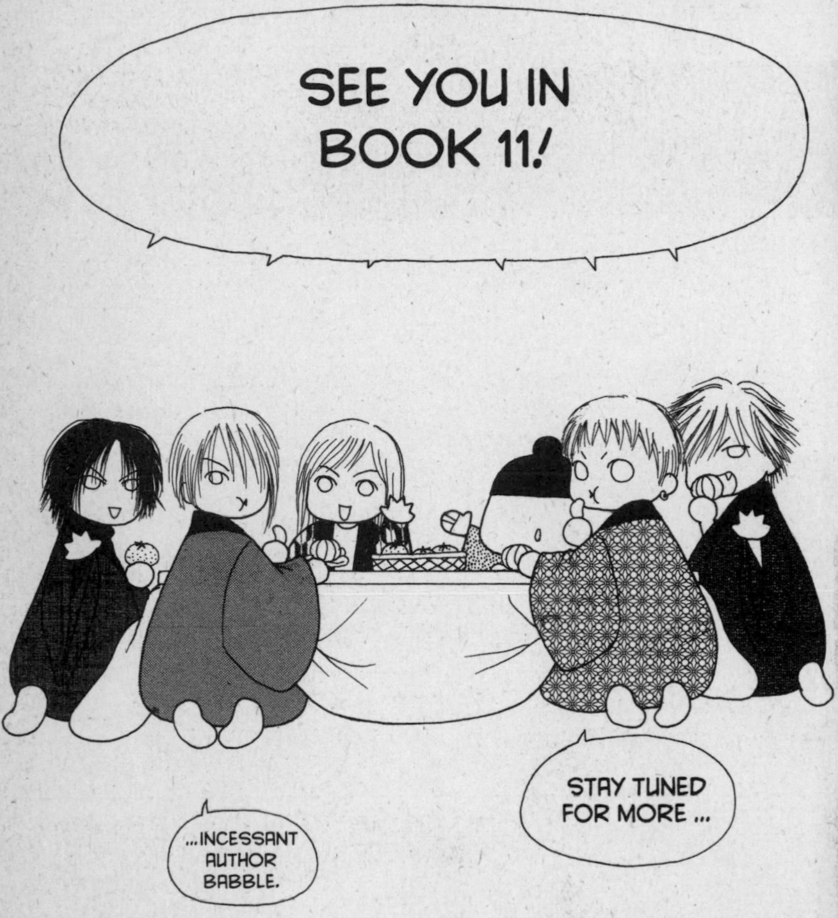
SEE YOU IN BOOK 11!
STAY TUNED FOR MORE ...
...INCESSANT AUTHOR BABBLE.

LET'S CELEBRATE

IT'S BOOK 10. DOUBLE DIGITS! WHOA!

THANKS TO YOU GUYS, I'VE MADE IT THIS FAR. I'M TALKING ABOUT YOU. YEAH, YOU. THE ONE WHO'S READING THIS RIGHT NOW. I CAN'T THANK YOU ENOUGH. I'M SERIOUS.

I HAVE NO IDEA HOW LONG THIS SERIES IS GONNA LAST, BUT I SURE HOPE YOU'LL STICK AROUND. ♥

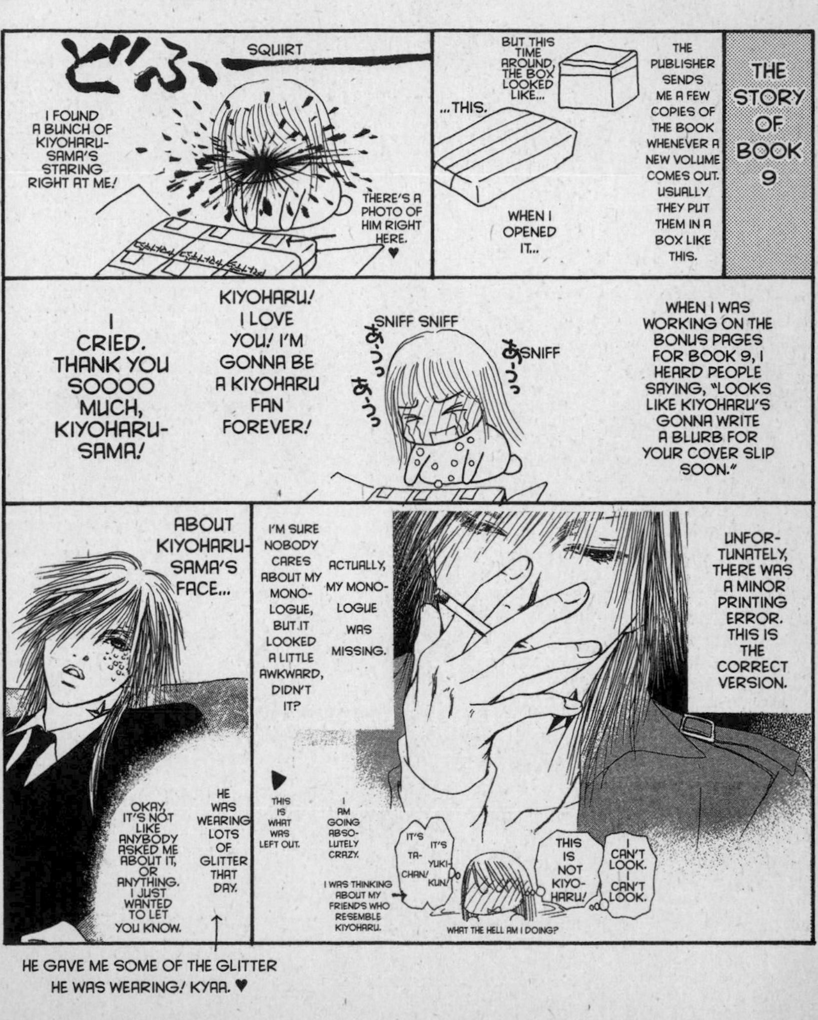
THE STORY OF BOOK 9
THE PUBLISHER SENDS ME A FEW COPIES OF THE BOOK WHENEVER A NEW VOLUME COMES OUT. USUALLY THEY PUT THEM IN A BOX LIKE THIS.
BUT THIS TIME AROUND, THE BOX LOOKED LIKE...
...THIS.
WHEN I OPENED IT...
SQUIRT
I FOUND A BUNCH OF KIYOHARU-SAMA'S STARING RIGHT AT ME!
THERE'S A PHOTO OF HIM RIGHT HERE. ♥
WHEN I WAS WORKING ON THE BONUS PAGES FOR BOOK 9, I HEARD PEOPLE SAYING, "LOOKS LIKE KIYOHARU'S GONNA WRITE A BLURB FOR YOUR COVER SLIP SOON."
SNIFF
SNIFF SNIFF
KIYOHARU! I LOVE YOU! I'M GONNA BE A KIYOHARU FAN FOREVER!
I CRIED. THANK YOU SOOOO MUCH, KIYOHARU-SAMA!
UNFORTUNATELY, THERE WAS A MINOR PRINTING ERROR. THIS IS THE CORRECT VERSION.
ACTUALLY, MY MONOLOGUE WAS MISSING.
I'M SURE NOBODY CARES ABOUT MY MONOLOGUE, BUT IT LOOKED A LITTLE AWKWARD, DIDN'T IT?
I CAN'T LOOK. I CAN'T LOOK.
THIS IS NOT KIYOHARU!
IT'S YUKI-KUN!
IT'S TA-CHAN!
I AM GOING ABSOLUTELY CRAZY.
THIS IS WHAT WAS LEFT OUT.
I WAS THINKING ABOUT MY FRIENDS WHO RESEMBLE KIYOHARU.
WHAT THE HELL AM I DOING?
ABOUT KIYOHARU-SAMA'S FACE...
HE WAS WEARING LOTS OF GLITTER THAT DAY.
OKAY, IT'S NOT LIKE ANYBODY ASKED ME ABOUT IT, OR ANYTHING. I JUST WANTED TO LET YOU KNOW.

HE GAVE ME SOME OF THE GLITTER HE WAS WEARING! KYAA. ♥

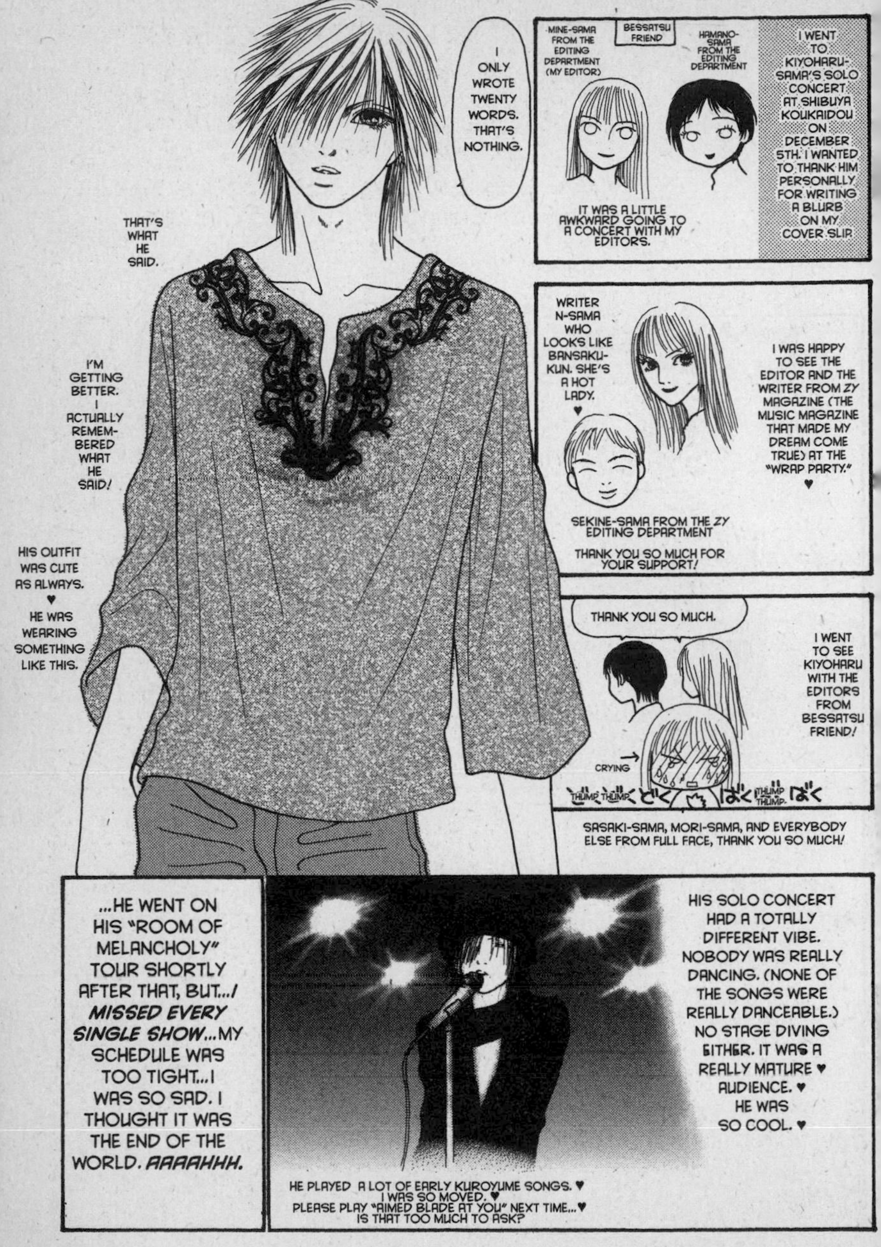
I WENT TO KIYOHARU-SAMA'S SOLO CONCERT AT SHIBUYA KOUKAIDOU ON DECEMBER 5TH. I WANTED TO THANK HIM PERSONALLY FOR WRITING A BLURB ON MY COVER SLIP.
HAMANO-SAMA FROM THE EDITING DEPARTMENT
BESSATSU FRIEND
MINE-SAMA FROM THE EDITING DEPARTMENT (MY EDITOR)
IT WAS A LITTLE AWKWARD GOING TO A CONCERT WITH MY EDITORS.
I WAS HAPPY TO SEE THE EDITOR AND THE WRITER FROM ZY MAGAZINE (THE MUSIC MAGAZINE THAT MADE MY DREAM COME TRUE) AT THE "WRAP PARTY." ♥
WRITER N-SAMA WHO LOOKS LIKE BANSAKU-KUN. SHE'S A HOT LADY. ♥
SEKINE-SAMA FROM THE ZY EDITING DEPARTMENT
THANK YOU SO MUCH FOR YOUR SUPPORT!
I WENT TO SEE KIYOHARU WITH THE EDITORS FROM BESSATSU FRIEND!
THANK YOU SO MUCH.
CRYING
THUMP THUMP THUMP THUMP
SASAKI-SAMA, MORI-SAMA, AND EVERYBODY ELSE FROM FULL FACE, THANK YOU SO MUCH!
I ONLY WROTE TWENTY WORDS. THAT'S NOTHING.
THAT'S WHAT HE SAID.
I'M GETTING BETTER. I ACTUALLY REMEMBERED WHAT HE SAID!
HIS OUTFIT WAS CUTE AS ALWAYS. ♥
HE WAS WEARING SOMETHING LIKE THIS.
HIS SOLO CONCERT HAD A TOTALLY DIFFERENT VIBE. NOBODY WAS REALLY DANCING. (NONE OF THE SONGS WERE REALLY DANCEABLE.) NO STAGE DIVING EITHER. IT WAS A REALLY MATURE ♥ AUDIENCE. ♥ HE WAS SO COOL. ♥
HE PLAYED A LOT OF EARLY KUROYUME SONGS. ♥ I WAS SO MOVED. ♥ PLEASE PLAY "AIMED BLADE AT YOU" NEXT TIME...♥ IS THAT TOO MUCH TO ASK?
...HE WENT ON HIS "ROOM OF MELANCHOLY" TOUR SHORTLY AFTER THAT, BUT...I MISSED EVERY SINGLE SHOW...MY SCHEDULE WAS TOO TIGHT...I WAS SO SAD. I THOUGHT IT WAS THE END OF THE WORLD. AAAAHHH.

I NEVER HAD A CHANCE TO SEE KUROYUME PERFORM IN THEIR EARLY DAYS. I'VE ONLY SEEN THEM IN VIDEOS. ♪♪♪

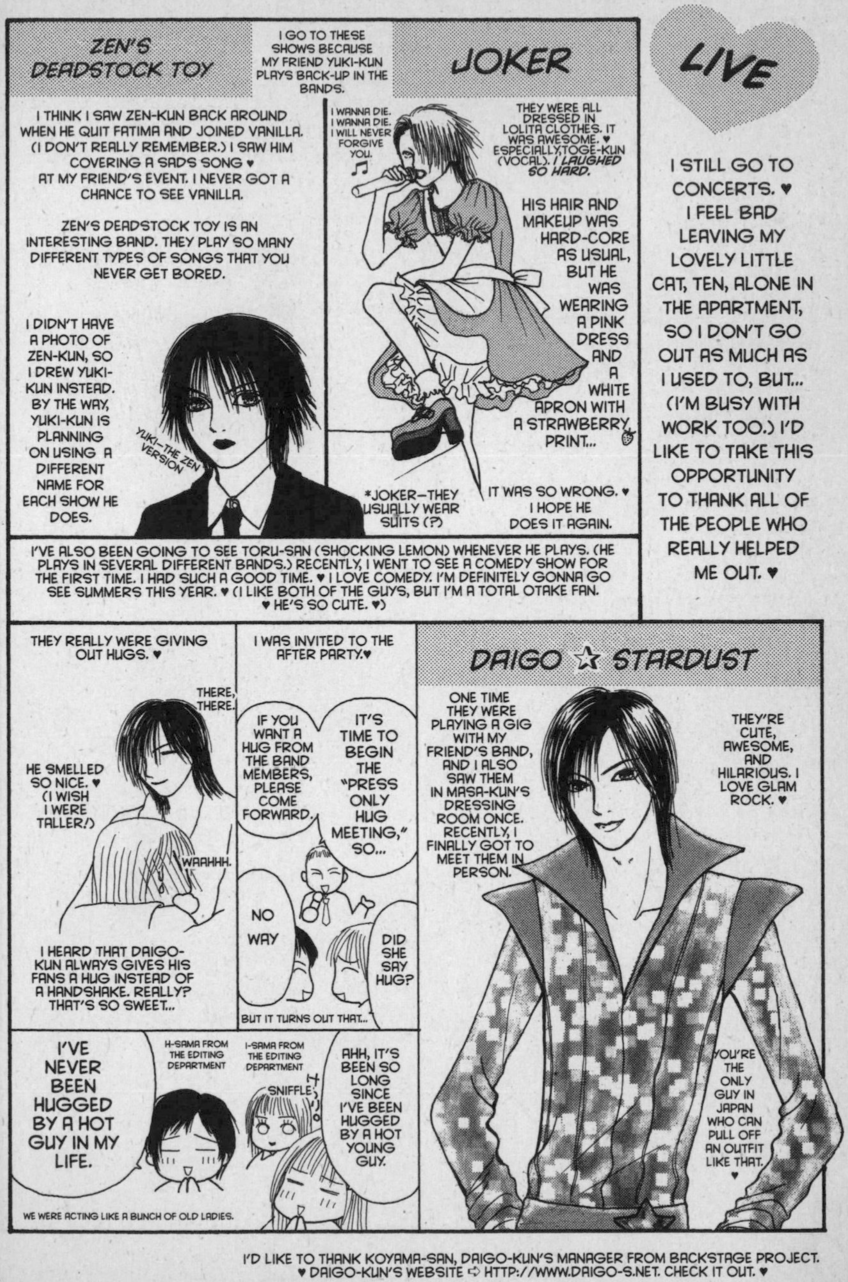
LIVE
I STILL GO TO CONCERTS. ♥ I FEEL BAD LEAVING MY LOVELY LITTLE CAT, TEN, ALONE IN THE APARTMENT, SO I DON'T GO OUT AS MUCH AS I USED TO, BUT... (I'M BUSY WITH WORK TOO.) I'D LIKE TO TAKE THIS OPPORTUNITY TO THANK ALL OF THE PEOPLE WHO REALLY HELPED ME OUT. ♥
I GO TO THESE SHOWS BECAUSE MY FRIEND YUKI-KUN PLAYS BACK-UP IN THE BANDS.
JOKER
THEY WERE ALL DRESSED IN LOLITA CLOTHES. IT WAS AWESOME. ♥ ESPECIALLY, TOGE-KUN (VOCAL). I LAUGHED SO HARD.
I WANNA DIE. I WANNA DIE. I WILL NEVER FORGIVE YOU.
HIS HAIR AND MAKEUP WAS HARD-CORE AS USUAL, BUT HE WAS WEARING A PINK DRESS AND A WHITE APRON WITH A STRAWBERRY PRINT...
IT WAS SO WRONG. ♥ I HOPE HE DOES IT AGAIN.
*JOKER—THEY USUALLY WEAR SUITS (?)
ZEN'S DEADSTOCK TOY
I THINK I SAW ZEN-KUN BACK AROUND WHEN HE QUIT FATIMA AND JOINED VANILLA. (I DON'T REALLY REMEMBER.) I SAW HIM COVERING A SADS SONG ♥ AT MY FRIEND'S EVENT. I NEVER GOT A CHANCE TO SEE VANILLA.
ZEN'S DEADSTOCK TOY IS AN INTERESTING BAND. THEY PLAY SO MANY DIFFERENT TYPES OF SONGS THAT YOU NEVER GET BORED.
YUKI—THE ZEN VERSION
I DIDN'T HAVE A PHOTO OF ZEN-KUN, SO I DREW YUKI-KUN INSTEAD. BY THE WAY, YUKI-KUN IS PLANNING ON USING A DIFFERENT NAME FOR EACH SHOW HE DOES.
I'VE ALSO BEEN GOING TO SEE TORU-SAN (SHOCKING LEMON) WHENEVER HE PLAYS. (HE PLAYS IN SEVERAL DIFFERENT BANDS.) RECENTLY, I WENT TO SEE A COMEDY SHOW FOR THE FIRST TIME. I HAD SUCH A GOOD TIME. ♥ I LOVE COMEDY. I'M DEFINITELY GONNA GO SEE SUMMERS THIS YEAR. ♥ (I LIKE BOTH OF THE GUYS, BUT I'M A TOTAL OTAKE FAN. ♥ HE'S SO CUTE. ♥)
DAIGO ☆ STARDUST
THEY'RE CUTE, AWESOME, AND HILARIOUS. I LOVE GLAM ROCK. ♥
ONE TIME THEY WERE PLAYING A GIG WITH MY FRIEND'S BAND, AND I ALSO SAW THEM IN MASA-KUN'S DRESSING ROOM ONCE. RECENTLY, I FINALLY GOT TO MEET THEM IN PERSON.
YOU'RE THE ONLY GUY IN JAPAN WHO CAN PULL OFF AN OUTFIT LIKE THAT. ♥
I WAS INVITED TO THE AFTER PARTY.♥
IT'S TIME TO BEGIN THE "PRESS ONLY HUG MEETING," SO...
IF YOU WANT A HUG FROM THE BAND MEMBERS, PLEASE COME FORWARD.
DID SHE SAY HUG?
NO WAY
BUT IT TURNS OUT THAT...
THEY REALLY WERE GIVING OUT HUGS. ♥
THERE, THERE.
HE SMELLED SO NICE. ♥ (I WISH I WERE TALLER!)
WAAHHH.
I HEARD THAT DAIGO-KUN ALWAYS GIVES HIS FANS A HUG INSTEAD OF A HANDSHAKE. REALLY? THAT'S SO SWEET...
AHH, IT'S BEEN SO LONG SINCE I'VE BEEN HUGGED BY A HOT YOUNG GUY.
SNIFFLE
I-SAMA FROM THE EDITING DEPARTMENT
H-SAMA FROM THE EDITING DEPARTMENT
I'VE NEVER BEEN HUGGED BY A HOT GUY IN MY LIFE.
WE WERE ACTING LIKE A BUNCH OF OLD LADIES.

I'D LIKE TO THANK KOYAMA-SAN, DAIGO-KUN'S MANAGER FROM BACKSTAGE PROJECT.
♥ DAIGO-KUN'S WEBSITE ⇨ HTTP://WWW.DAIGO-S.NET. CHECK IT OUT. ♥

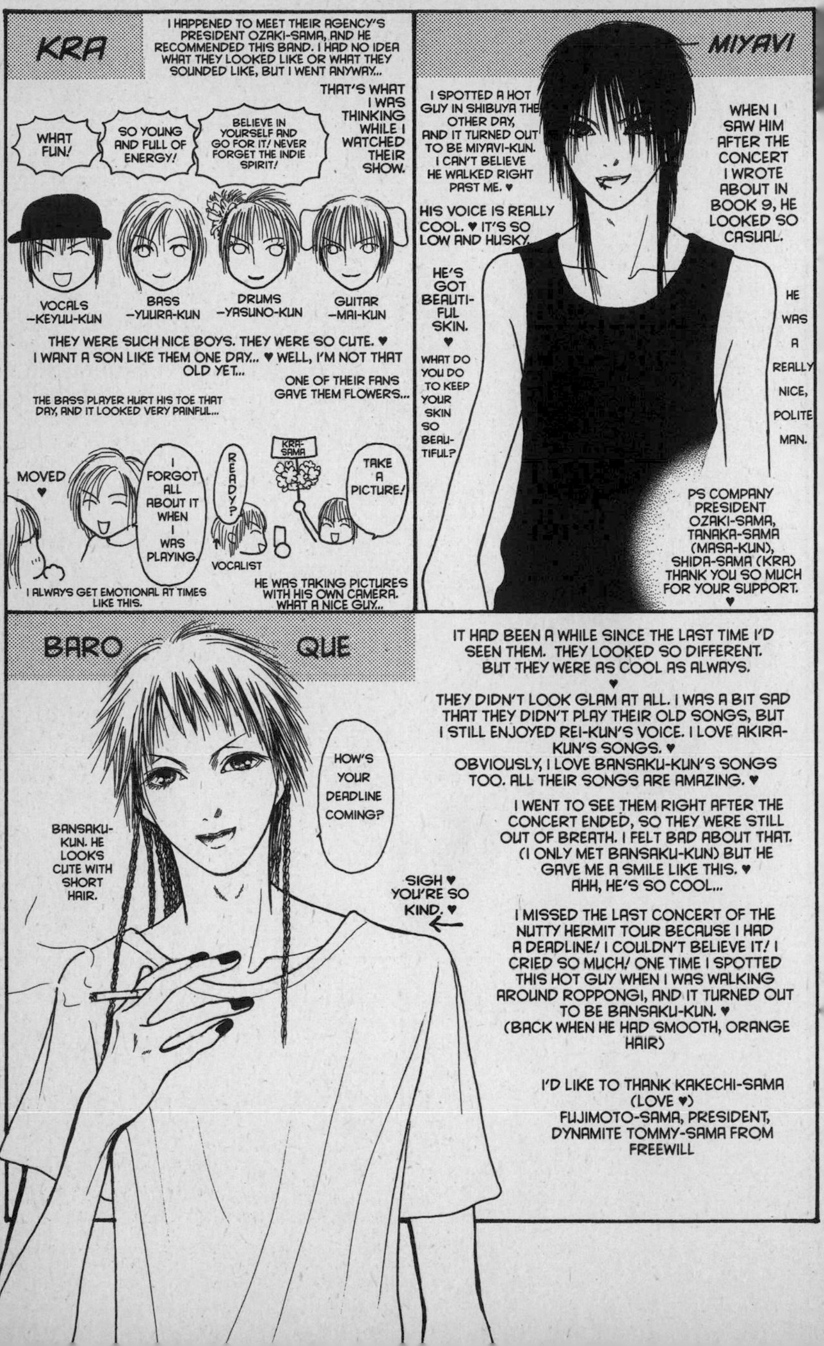
MIYAVI
I SPOTTED A HOT GUY IN SHIBUYA THE OTHER DAY, AND IT TURNED OUT TO BE MIYAVI-KUN. I CAN'T BELIEVE HE WALKED RIGHT PAST ME. ♥
WHEN I SAW HIM AFTER THE CONCERT I WROTE ABOUT IN BOOK 9, HE LOOKED SO CASUAL.
HIS VOICE IS REALLY COOL. ♥ IT'S SO LOW AND HUSKY.
HE WAS A REALLY NICE, POLITE MAN.
HE'S GOT BEAUTIFUL SKIN. ♥
WHAT DO YOU DO TO KEEP YOUR SKIN SO BEAUTIFUL?
PS COMPANY PRESIDENT OZAKI-SAMA, TANAKA-SAMA (MASA-KUN), SHIDA-SAMA (KRA) THANK YOU SO MUCH FOR YOUR SUPPORT. ♥
KRA
I HAPPENED TO MEET THEIR AGENCY'S PRESIDENT OZAKI-SAMA, AND HE RECOMMENDED THIS BAND. I HAD NO IDEA WHAT THEY LOOKED LIKE OR WHAT THEY SOUNDED LIKE, BUT I WENT ANYWAY...
THAT'S WHAT I WAS THINKING WHILE I WATCHED THEIR SHOW.
BELIEVE IN YOURSELF AND GO FOR IT! NEVER FORGET THE INDIE SPIRIT!
SO YOUNG AND FULL OF ENERGY!
WHAT FUN!
GUITAR —MAI-KUN
DRUMS —YASUNO-KUN
BASS —YUURA-KUN
VOCALS —KEYUU-KUN
THEY WERE SUCH NICE BOYS. THEY WERE SO CUTE. ♥ I WANT A SON LIKE THEM ONE DAY... ♥ WELL, I'M NOT THAT OLD YET...
ONE OF THEIR FANS GAVE THEM FLOWERS...
THE BASS PLAYER HURT HIS TOE THAT DAY, AND IT LOOKED VERY PAINFUL...
TAKE A PICTURE!
KRA-SAMA
READY?
VOCALIST
HE WAS TAKING PICTURES WITH HIS OWN CAMERA. WHAT A NICE GUY...
I FORGOT ALL ABOUT IT WHEN I WAS PLAYING.
MOVED ♥
I ALWAYS GET EMOTIONAL AT TIMES LIKE THIS.
BARO QUE
IT HAD BEEN A WHILE SINCE THE LAST TIME I'D SEEN THEM. THEY LOOKED SO DIFFERENT. BUT THEY WERE AS COOL AS ALWAYS. ♥
THEY DIDN'T LOOK GLAM AT ALL. I WAS A BIT SAD THAT THEY DIDN'T PLAY THEIR OLD SONGS, BUT I STILL ENJOYED REI-KUN'S VOICE. I LOVE AKIRA-KUN'S SONGS. ♥
OBVIOUSLY, I LOVE BANSAKU-KUN'S SONGS TOO. ALL THEIR SONGS ARE AMAZING. ♥
I WENT TO SEE THEM RIGHT AFTER THE CONCERT ENDED, SO THEY WERE STILL OUT OF BREATH. I FELT BAD ABOUT THAT. (I ONLY MET BANSAKU-KUN) BUT HE GAVE ME A SMILE LIKE THIS. ♥ AHH, HE'S SO COOL...
I MISSED THE LAST CONCERT OF THE NUTTY HERMIT TOUR BECAUSE I HAD A DEADLINE! I COULDN'T BELIEVE IT! I CRIED SO MUCH! ONE TIME I SPOTTED THIS HOT GUY WHEN I WAS WALKING AROUND ROPPONGI, AND IT TURNED OUT TO BE BANSAKU-KUN. ♥ (BACK WHEN HE HAD SMOOTH, ORANGE HAIR)
I'D LIKE TO THANK KAKECHI-SAMA (LOVE ♥) FUJIMOTO-SAMA, PRESIDENT, DYNAMITE TOMMY-SAMA FROM FREEWILL
SIGH ♥ YOU'RE SO KIND. ♥
HOW'S YOUR DEADLINE COMING?
BANSAKU-KUN. HE LOOKS CUTE WITH SHORT HAIR.

OH NO. THAT DOESN'T LOOK LIKE THEM AT ALL. SORRY.

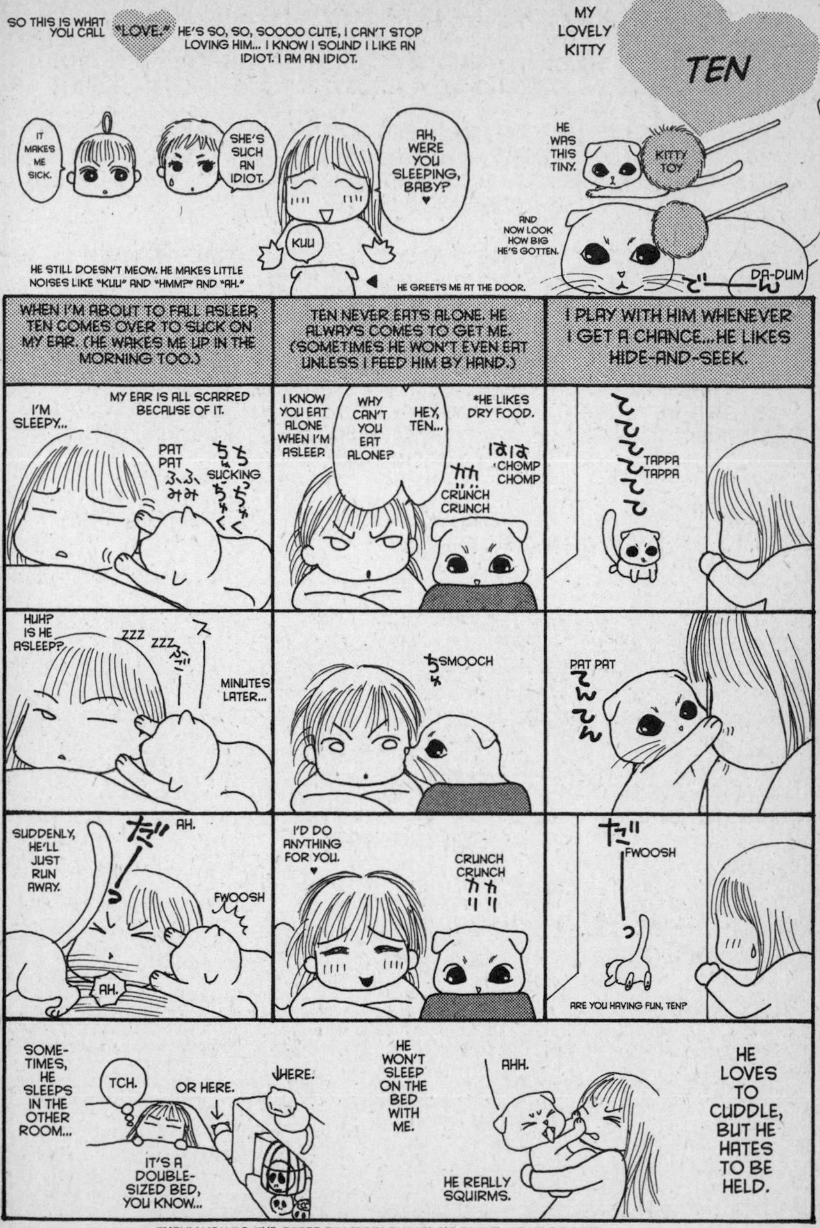
MY LOVELY KITTY
TEN
HE WAS THIS TINY.
KITTY TOY
AND NOW LOOK HOW BIG HE'S GOTTEN.
DA-DUM
でーん
SO THIS IS WHAT YOU CALL "LOVE." HE'S SO, SO, SOOOO CUTE, I CAN'T STOP LOVING HIM... I KNOW I SOUND I LIKE AN IDIOT. I AM AN IDIOT.
AH, WERE YOU SLEEPING, BABY? ♥
KUU
HE GREETS ME AT THE DOOR.
SHE'S SUCH AN IDIOT.
IT MAKES ME SICK.
HE STILL DOESN'T MEOW. HE MAKES LITTLE NOISES LIKE "KUU" AND "HMM?" AND "AH."
I PLAY WITH HIM WHENEVER I GET A CHANCE...HE LIKES HIDE-AND-SEEK.
てててててて
TAPPA TAPPA
PAT PAT
てんてん
たっ
FWOOSH
ARE YOU HAVING FUN, TEN?
TEN NEVER EATS ALONE. HE ALWAYS COMES TO GET ME. (SOMETIMES HE WON'T EVEN EAT UNLESS I FEED HIM BY HAND.)
*HE LIKES DRY FOOD.
HEY, TEN...
WHY CAN'T YOU EAT ALONE?
I KNOW YOU EAT ALONE WHEN I'M ASLEEP.
はは
CHOMP CHOMP
カカ
CRUNCH CRUNCH
ちゅ
SMOOCH
CRUNCH CRUNCH
カカリ
I'D DO ANYTHING FOR YOU. ♥
WHEN I'M ABOUT TO FALL ASLEEP, TEN COMES OVER TO SUCK ON MY EAR. (HE WAKES ME UP IN THE MORNING TOO.)
MY EAR IS ALL SCARRED BECAUSE OF IT.
I'M SLEEPY...
ちちゅちゅく
SUCKING
PAT PAT
ふふみみ
ス
ふご
ZZZ ZZZ
MINUTES LATER...
HUH? IS HE ASLEEP?
だっ
AH.
FWOOSH
SUDDENLY, HE'LL JUST RUN AWAY.
AH.
HE LOVES TO CUDDLE, BUT HE HATES TO BE HELD.
AHH.
HE REALLY SQUIRMS.
HE WON'T SLEEP ON THE BED WITH ME.
↓HERE.
OR HERE.
TCH.
SOMETIMES, HE SLEEPS IN THE OTHER ROOM...
IT'S A DOUBLE-SIZED BED, YOU KNOW...

I STILL SUCK AT DRAWING TEN, EVEN THOUGH I LOVE HIM SO MUCH...

THANK YOU TO THE STAFF AT KASAI ANIMAL HOSPITAL. I'D ALSO LIKE TO THANK SAITO-SAMA (SHE'S A FELINE MASTER) AND ALL MY FRIENDS WHO OWN CATS. ♥

THANK YOU SO MUCH FOR READING ALL THIS. ♥
DOES ANYBODY REALLY READ THE WHOLE THING?

I WANT TO THANK YOU ALL FOR BUYING KODANSHA COMICS AND
SENDING ME YOUR LETTERS. ♥

RECENTLY, MANY PEOPLE HAVE BEEN SENDING ME PHOTOS OF THEIR PETS.
THEY'RE SO CUTE. I GUESS I'M NOT THE ONLY ONE WHO LOVES MY PET. ♥
I'M ALWAYS GLAD WHEN YOU GUYS WRITE ABOUT MY PRECIOUS TEN. ♥ HEH,
HEH, HEH. THANK YOU SO MUCH. (BLUSH)

I LIKE IT WHEN PEOPLE WRITE IN ABOUT THE BONUS PAGES SAYING, "I
REALLY GOT INTO THAT BAND YOU MENTIONED" OR " I LOVE THAT BAND,
TOO. ♥" SO I WROTE ABOUT BANDS AGAIN THIS TIME. SORRY TO ALL YOU
GUYS WHO AREN'T INTO MUSIC. (笑)

THANKS TO EVERYONE WHO SENT IN INFO ABOUT THE BANDS AND
CELEBRITIES YOU LIKE. AND THOSE WHO SENT ME MINI DISCS. ♥ I'VE BEEN
LISTENING TO THEM A LOT. ACTUALLY, I LIKED ONE SONG SO MUCH THAT I
EVEN BOUGHT THE CD.

THANK YOU SO MUCH FOR SENDING ME CLIPPINGS. ♥ I TREASURE THEM. ♥
IT DOESN'T MATTER IF I ALREADY HAVE THEM OR NOT. ♥

THANKS FOR SENDING ME ALL THE SKULL AND *THE NIGHTMARE BEFORE
CHRISTMAS* STUFF. ♥ I KEEP IT ALL IN MY ROOM. I LIKE TO ATTACH SOME OF
THE THINGS TO MY CELL PHONE, TOO. ♥

THANK YOU FOR SENDING ME YOUR HANDMADE GIFTS. ♥ I TREASURE
THEM, TOO. ♥

I KNOW I'VE SAID THIS MANY TIMES BEFORE, BUT DON'T FEEL LIKE YOU
HAVE TO SEND ME GIFTS OR ANYTHING. I'M REALLY HAPPY JUST TO GET
YOUR LETTERS. ♥

OKAY,
SEE YOU IN BOOK 11. BYE.
♥ I HOPE TO SEE YOU AGAIN. ♥

SPECIAL THANKS
HANA-CHAN, YOSHII,
NAKAZAWA-SAN,
YUKIO IKEDA-SAMA

MINE-SAMA,
SHIOZAWA-SAMA,
INO-SAMA,
EVERYBODY FROM THE
EDITING DEPARTMENT

EVERYBODY WHO'S READING THIS SENTENCE RIGHT NOW. ♥

About the Creator

Tomoko Hayakawa was born on March 4.

Since her debut as a manga creator, Tomoko Hayakawa has worked on many shojo titles with the theme of romantic love—only to realize that she could write about other subjects as well. She decided to pack her newest story with the things she likes most, which led to her current, enormously popular series, *The Wallflower*.

Her favorite things are: Tim Burton's *The Nightmare Before Christmas*, Jean-Paul Gaultier, and samurai dramas on TV. Her hobbies are collecting items with skull designs and watching *bishonen* (beautiful boys). Her dream is to build a mansion like the one the Addams family lives in. Her favorite pastime is to lie around at home with her cat, Ten (whose full name is Tennosuke).

Her zodiac sign is Pisces, and her blood group is AB.

Translation Notes

Japanese is a tricky language for most Westerners, and translation is often more an art than a science. For your edification and reading pleasure, here are notes on some of the places where we could have gone in a different direction in our translation or where a Japanese cultural reference is used.

Tama ire, page 65

Kyohei and Sunako are playing *tame ire,* a game in which you throw as many balls as possible into a basket. You're supposed to throw the balls individually, but Sunako and Kyohei are trying to score extra points by dunking them all at the same time.

WHOA! HEY GUYS! THIS IS "TAMA IRE," NOT BASKET-BALL!
PLEASE DON'T IMITATE THEM.
PLOING
PLOING

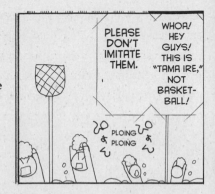

Standing in front of the ocean, page 73

It's supposed to look as if Kyohei is standing in front of the ocean as he screams "Uwahhh." This is probably a play on the concept of "*umi ni mukate sakebu*" or "screaming at the sea." This idea of "screaming at the sea" is commonly seen in Japanese drama. It's often what characters do to express sorrow and frustration.

FWAPPA
FWAPPA
FWAPPA

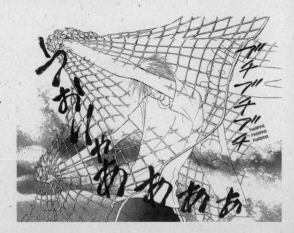

***Tobibako*, page 73**

A *tobibako* is sort of a cross between a hurdle and a box. It looks like a wooden box, but its height is adjustable. They're commonly used in track-and-field events at Japanese schools, at which players must jump over boxes of increasing height.

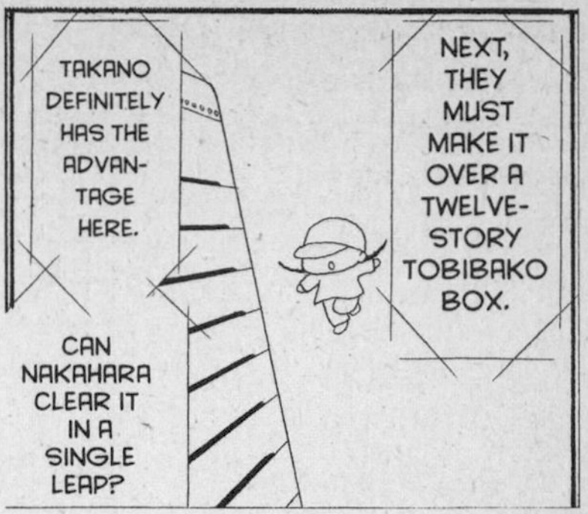
NEXT, THEY MUST MAKE IT OVER A TWELVE-STORY TOBIBAKO BOX.
TAKANO DEFINITELY HAS THE ADVANTAGE HERE.
CAN NAKAHARA CLEAR IT IN A SINGLE LEAP?

***Hikaru Genji*, page 102**

Hikaru Genji is the main character in the classical Japanese literary work *The Tale of Genji*. Genji was a real ladies' man, sort of a Japanese version of Don Juan. Genji ends up taking a young girl named Lady Murasaki and raising her to be his mistress.

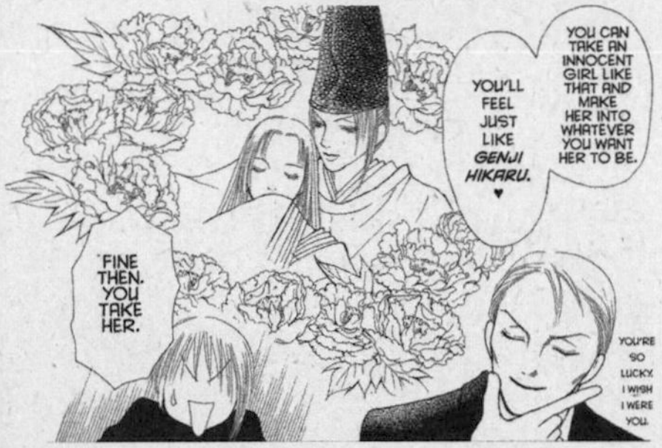
YOU CAN TAKE AN INNOCENT GIRL LIKE THAT AND MAKE HER INTO WHATEVER YOU WANT HER TO BE.
YOU'LL FEEL JUST LIKE *GENJI HIKARU*. ♥
YOU'RE SO LUCKY. I WISH I WERE YOU.
FINE THEN. YOU TAKE HER.

***Nabe* and *kotatsu*, page 130**

A *nabe* is literally a large pot, but the term is used generically to describe any kind of soup, stew, or boiled dish made in a hot pot. Generally, the hot pot sits in the middle of the table and each diner serves herself. A *kotatsu* is a sort of table with a heater underneath it. It's a common fixture in most Japanese households. The idea of having a *nabe* while sitting at the *kotatsu* is the very image of "winter" to Japanese people.

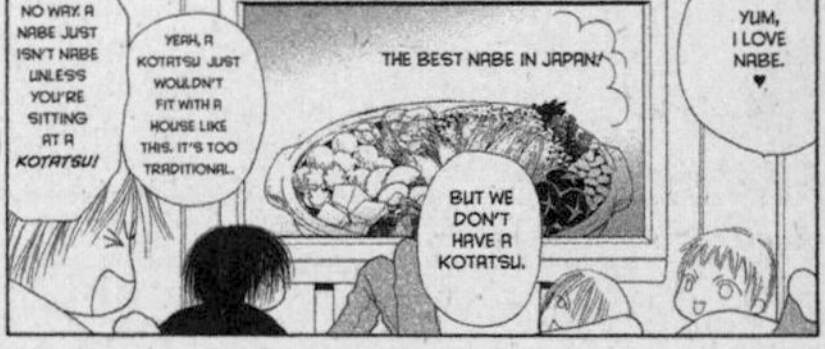
YUM, I LOVE NABE. ♥
THE BEST NABE IN JAPAN!
BUT WE DON'T HAVE A KOTATSU.
YEAH, A KOTATSU JUST WOULDN'T FIT WITH A HOUSE LIKE THIS. IT'S TOO TRADITIONAL.
NO WAY. A NABE JUST ISN'T NABE UNLESS YOU'RE SITTING AT A *KOTATSU*!

Fusuma, page 134

A *fusuma* is a traditional type of sliding door often used to separate two rooms.

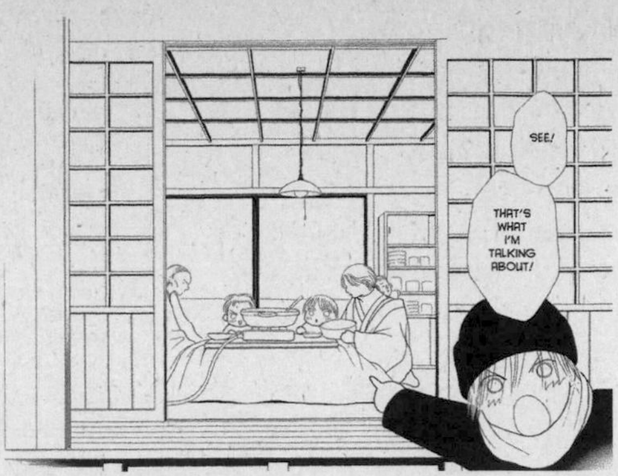
SEE!
THAT'S WHAT I'M TALKING ABOUT!

Matsutake mushrooms, page 144

Matsutake mushrooms are a very expensive delicacy.

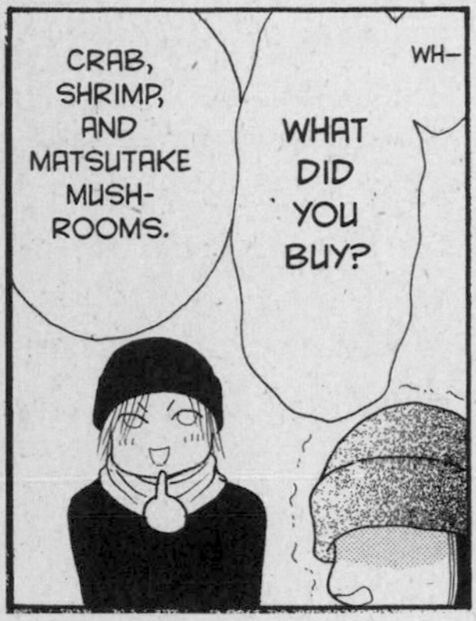
WH—
WHAT DID YOU BUY?
CRAB, SHRIMP, AND MATSUTAKE MUSH-ROOMS.

Dotera, page 163

A *dotera* is a traditional winter jacket that resembles a robe. It's usually worn over a kimono

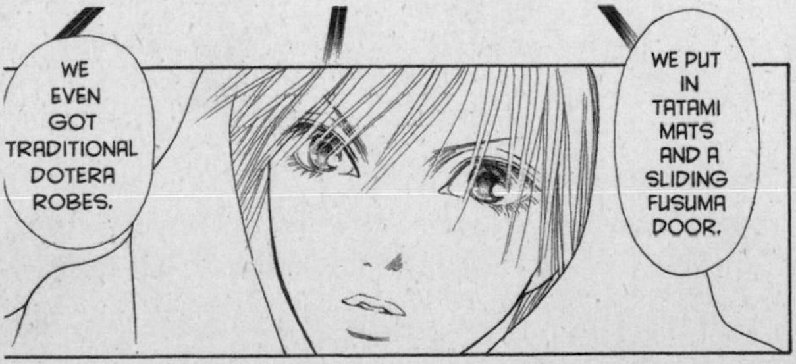
WE PUT IN TATAMI MATS AND A SLIDING FUSUMA DOOR.
WE EVEN GOT TRADITIONAL DOTERA ROBES.

Tangerines, page 166

Eating tangerines while sitting at the *kotatsu* is another winter tradition.

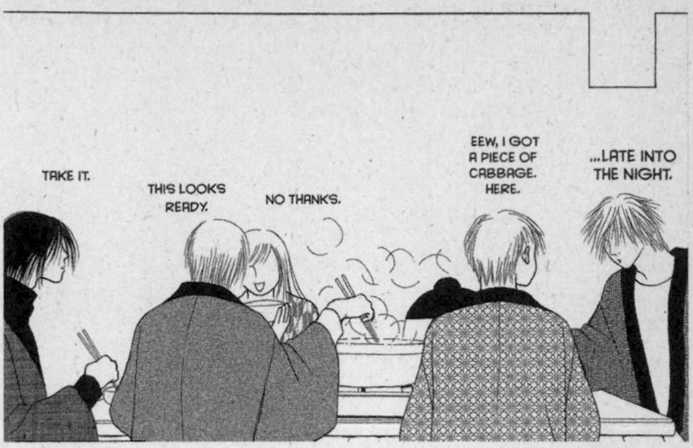
...LATE INTO THE NIGHT.
EEW, I GOT A PIECE OF CABBAGE. HERE.
NO THANKS.
THIS LOOKS READY.
TAKE IT.

Blurb on the cover slip, page 168

Kiyoharu's blurb was actually printed on something called the *obi*. An *obi* is a small cover slip that fits over the actual cover of the book. It's used for advertising.

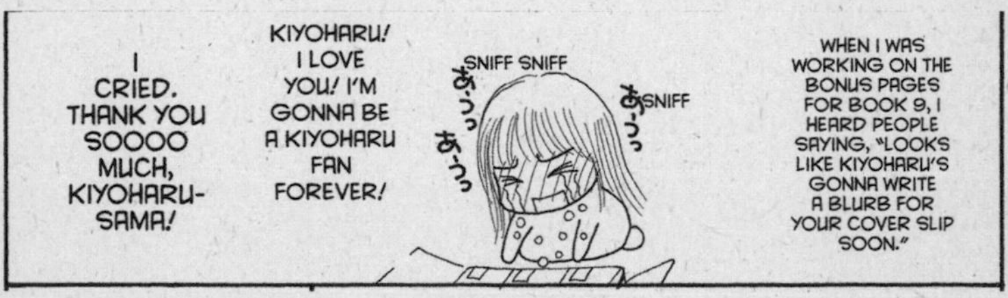
WHEN I WAS WORKING ON THE BONUS PAGES FOR BOOK 9, I HEARD PEOPLE SAYING, "LOOKS LIKE KIYOHARU'S GONNA WRITE A BLURB FOR YOUR COVER SLIP SOON."
SNIFF
SNIFF SNIFF
KIYOHARU! I LOVE YOU! I'M GONNA BE A KIYOHARU FAN FOREVER!
I CRIED. THANK YOU SOOOO MUCH, KIYOHARU-SAMA!

Preview of volume II

We're pleased to present you a preview from volume II. This volume is available in English now!

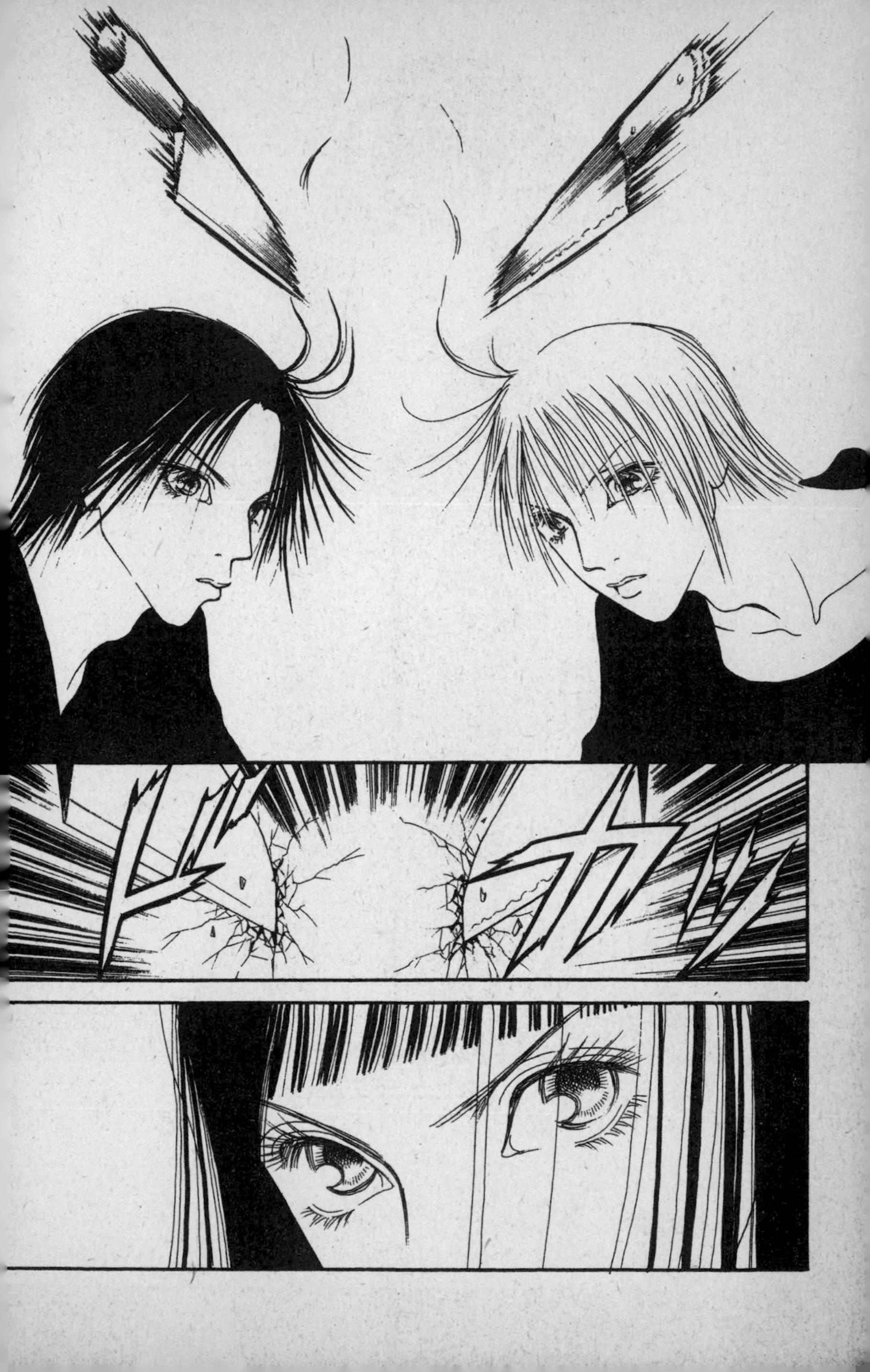
ドカッ

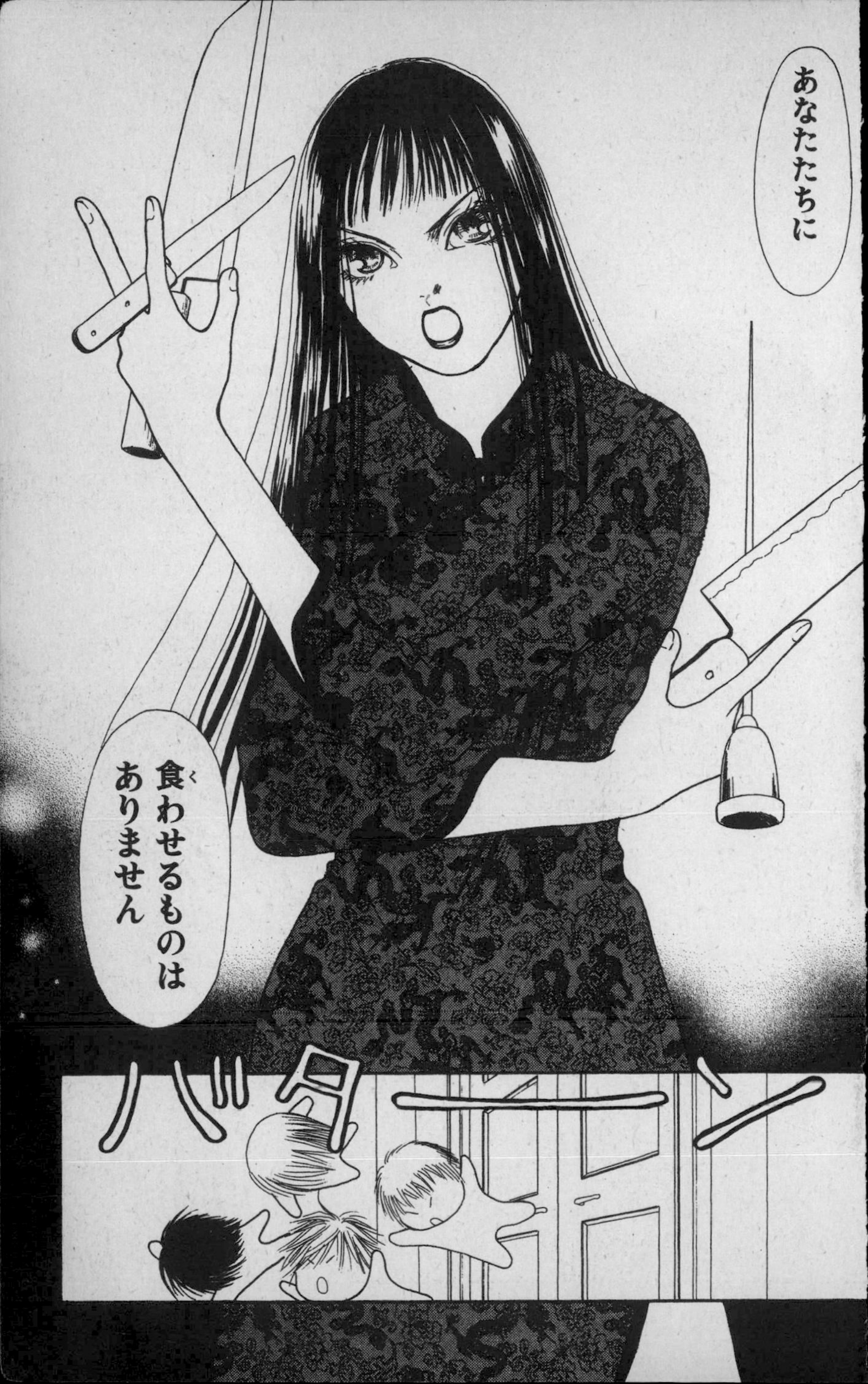
あなたたちに
食わせるものはありません
バッターン

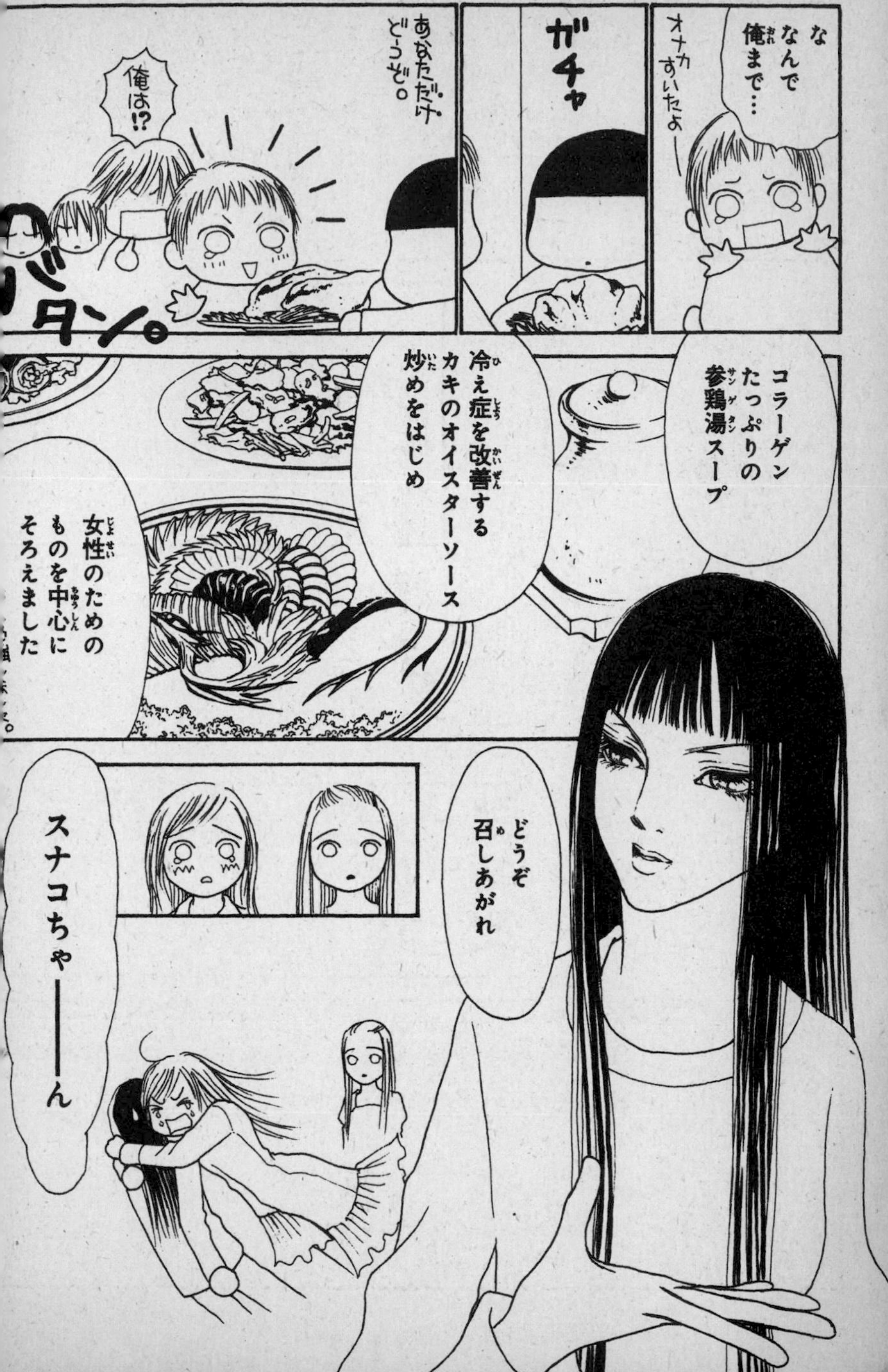
なんで俺まで…
オナカすいたよー
ガチャ
あなただけどうぞ。
俺は!?
バタン。
コラーゲンたっぷりの参鶏湯スープ
冷え症を改善するカキのオイスターソース炒めをはじめ
女性のためのものを中心にそろえました
どうぞ召しあがれ
スナコちゃーーーん

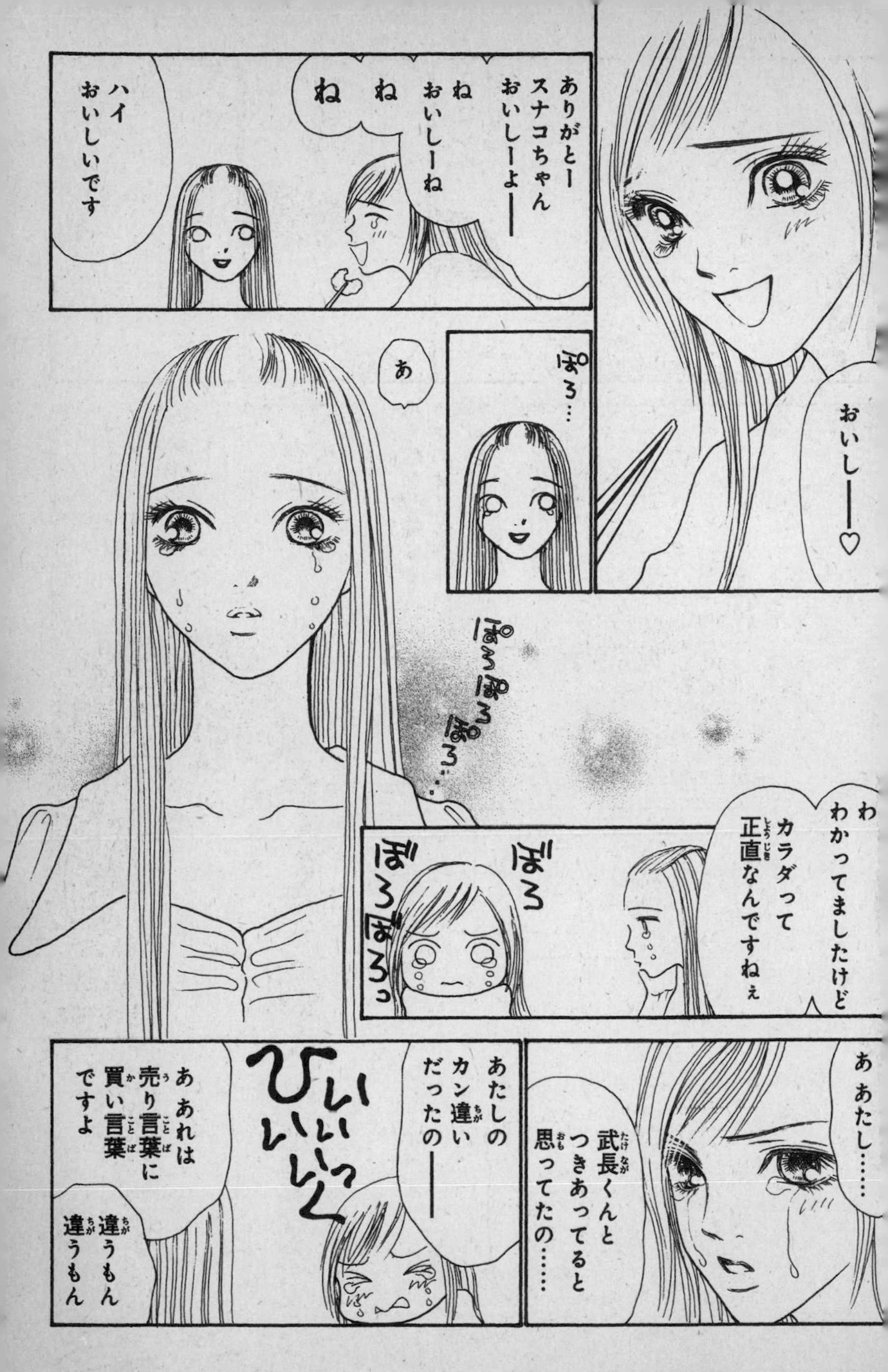
おいしーーー♡
ありがとースナコちゃんおいしーよーー
ねおいしーね
ね
ね
ハイおいしいです
ぽろ…
あ
ぽろぽろぽろ…
わわかってましたけどカラダって正直なんですねぇ
ぼろ
ぼろぼろっ
ああたし……
武長くんとつきあってると思ってたの……
あたしのカン違いだったのーー
ひぃぃぃっく
ああれは売り言葉に買い言葉ですよ
違うもん違うもん

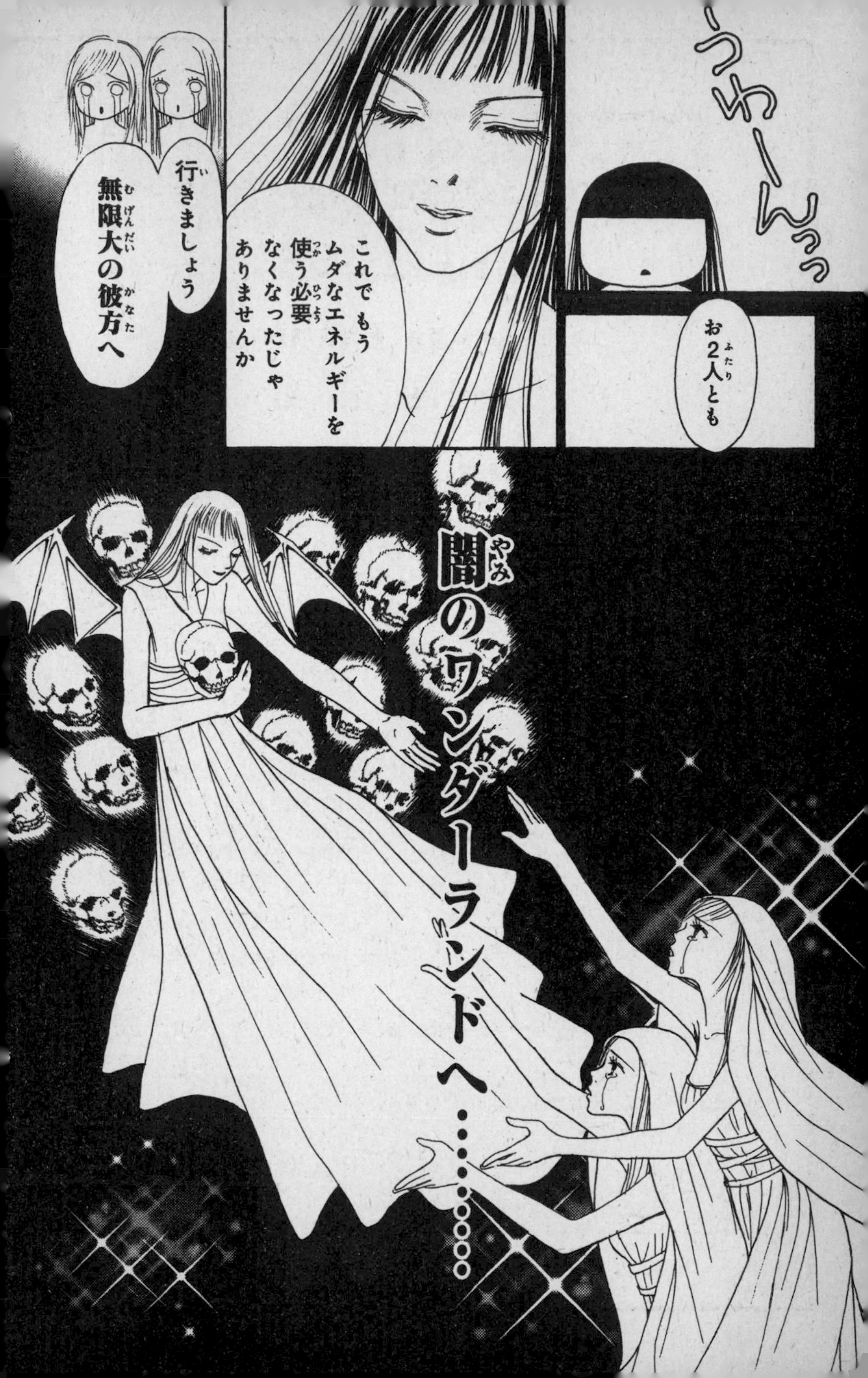
うわーんっっ
お2人とも
これでもう ムダなエネルギーを使う必要なくなったじゃありませんか
行きましょう 無限大の彼方へ
闇のワンダーランドへ……

FREE COLLARS KINGDOM

フリーカラーズキングダム

TAKUYA FUJIMI

THOSE FEISTY FELINES!

It's hard to resist Cyan: He's an adorable catboy, whose cute ears and tail have made him a beloved pet. But then his family abandons him, leaving the innocent Cyan to fend for himself.

Just when Cyan thinks he's all alone in the world, he meets the Free Collars, a cool gang of stray cats who believe that no feline should allow a human to imprison his Wild Spirit. They invite Cyan to join them, and the reluctant housecat has to decide fast, because a rival gang of cats is threatening the Free Collars' territory! Can Cyan learn to free his Wild Spirit—and help his new friends save their home?

1
FREE COLLARS KINGDOM
TAKUYA FUJIMA

Special extras in each volume! Read them all!

VISIT WWW.DELREYMANGA.COM TO:
- Read sample pages
- View release date calendars for upcoming volumes
- Sign up for Del Rey's free manga e-newsletter
- Find out the latest about new Del Rey Manga series

RATING OT AGES 16+

DEL REY MANGA デルレイ

The Otaku's Choice

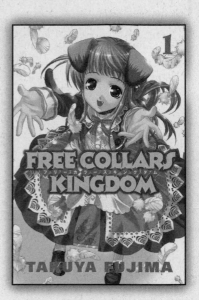

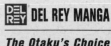

TOMARE!

[STOP!]

You're going the wrong way!

Manga is a completely different type of reading experience.

To start at the beginning, go to the end!

That's right! Authentic manga is read the traditional Japanese way—from right to left. Exactly the opposite of how American books are read. It's easy to follow: Just go to the other end of the book, and read each page—and each panel—from right side to left side, starting at the top right. Now you're experiencing manga as it was meant to be!